With technical assistance from The American Dietetic Association

Live
Longer &
Better

A Lifestyle Guide with
Recipes and Much More

Mindy G. Hermann, R.D.
Elizabeth M. Ward, R.D.

PUBLICATIONS INTERNATIONAL, LTD.

LIVE LONGER & BETTER

Louis Weber, C.E.O.
Publications International, Ltd.
7373 North Cicero Avenue
Lincolnwood, Illinois 60646

Permission is never granted for commercial purposes.

Manufactured in U.S.A.

8 7 6 5 4 3 2 1

ISBN 0-7853-0806-7

Library of Congress Catalog Number: 94-66747

CONTRIBUTING WRITERS:

Mindy G. Hermann, R.D., is a nutrition educator, writer, and registered dietitian. She has authored an American Dietetic Association sponsored magazine supplement on children's nutrition and her articles have appeared in *American Health, Health, Longevity, Woman's Day, Self,* and *New York Magazine*. Ms. Hermann frequently appears on national and local television, including *The Today Show, Good Morning America,* and CNN. She has also served at Memorial Sloan-Kettering Cancer Center providing nutrition support for oncology.

Elizabeth M. Ward, R.D., a registered dietitian, is a nutrition writer and consultant who serves as nutrition counselor at Harvard Community Health Plan. She contributes regularly to such publications as *Cooking Light, Fast and Healthy, Fitness,* and *Environmental Nutrition*. She is frequently interviewed about nutrition and health by national publications such as *The New York Times* and *U.S. News & World Report* and has appeared numerous times on CNN.

ACKNOWLEDGMENTS:

This publication was reviewed by **The American Dietetic Association (ADA).** The ADA, with more than 63,500 members, is the largest group of food and nutrition professionals in the world. The ADA's goal is to promote nutrition, health and well-being for Americans.

Nutritional analysis of recipes provided by Linda Yoakam, M.S., R.D.

Some recipes developed by: Spectrum Communication Services, Inc.

The publishers would like to thank the following organizations for the use of their recipes in this publication: Almond Board of California; American Celery Council; American Lamb Council; California Apricot Advisory Board; California Cling Peach Advisory Board; California Tree Fruit Agreement; Canned Fruit Information Council; Chilean Winter Fruit Association; Florida Department of Citrus; Minnesota Cultivated Wild Rice Council; National Broiler Council; National Dairy Board; National Fisheries Institute; National Live Stock & Meat Board; National Pasta Association; National Pork Producers Council; National Turkey Federation; Pacific Coast Canned Pear Service; The Sugar Association, Inc.; Walnut Marketing Board; Washington Apple Commission; Western New York Apple Growers; and Wisconsin Milk Marketing Board.

PHOTO CREDITS:

Recipe photography by: New View Studios, Rosemont, IL; Photo/Kevin Smith, Chicago and Peter Walters Photography, Chicago.

Front cover: **T.J. Florian/Rainbow** (bottom left).

Back cover: **Bill Losh/FPG International** (top left).

FPG International: 33 (bottom); Age Fotostock: 11 (top); Jose Luis Banus-March: 18, 31 (bottom), 103 (top); Blumebild: 133; Gary Buss: 107, 108; Ron Chapple: Table of contents (center), 75, 88, 96, 111 (top), 128, 142; Ralph Cowan: 103 (bottom); Eugen Gebhardt: 93; George B. Gibbons III: 69; Jeri Gleiter: 16; John Gorman: 20; Steven Gottlieb: 137; Peter Gridley: 86; Rodri Guiterrez: 35 (top); Dennis Hallinan: 132 (top); R. Hamilton Smith: 22 (top), 91; Steve Joester: 99; Peter Johansky: 42, 81, 95 (top); Richard Johnston: 11 (bottom); Steven W. Jones: 15; Michael A. Keller: 24, 28, 31 (top), 56, 60, 80 (top); Michael Krasowitz: 62 (top), 82, 131; L.O.L., Inc.: 130; Richard Laird: 72 (top), 139; Bill Losh: 7, 61, 106; Dick Luria: 8, 27, 37, 51; Scott Markewitz Photography: 6; Alan McGee: 12; Art Montes De Oca: 70; Richard Nowitz: 90; Diane Padys: 43, 53, 78 (top left); Barbara Peacock: 41; Bob Peterson: 135; J. Pickerell: 140; Ralph B. Pleasant: 5; Ken Reid: 65; Sandy Roessler: 35 (bottom); Victor Scocozza: 33 (top); Stan Sholik: 138; J. Sieue: 47; Stephen Simpson: 132 (bottom); Frederic Stein: 38 (bottom); Telegraph Colour Library: 59; Art Tilley: 78 (bottom); Mike Wilson: 84; J. Zalon: 71; **Oregon Dept. of Transportation/Travel Information Section:** 72 (bottom); **Photri:** Table of contents (top), 22 (bottom), 26, 45, 49 (top), 52, 54, 55, 62 (bottom), 67, 74, 77, 79, 85, 87, 100, 104, 105, 129, 136; Bryan Alexander: 19; Bachmann: 63; Robert J. Bennett: 25; Ellsworth: 83; T. Firak: 30, 44, 101; B. Howe: 57; Dennis MacDonald: 95 (bottom); POTOPIC: 9; Skjold: 49 (bottom); Frederick Stork: 32; Wallis/Berchery: 80 (bottom); **Rainbow:** Tom Broker: 66; Larry Brownstein: 144; T.J. Florian: 73, 78 (top right); Tom McCarthy: 58; Coco McCoy: 141; Dan McCoy: 10, 13, 38 (top), 98; **Texas Division of Tourism:** 14; **U.S.D.A.:** 102.

CONTENTS

INTRODUCTION

Americans are living longer than ever before. The average life expectancy in the United States has increased by nearly 30 years since the beginning of the 20th century. To be sure, better medical care accounts for much of the gain, but healthy lifestyle choices also play a formidable role. After decades of research, the verdict is in: Lifestyle and life span are inextricably linked.

We're all getting older, and as we age, we become more vulnerable to disease, particularly the debilitating ones such as heart disease, cancer, and osteoporosis. A healthy lifestyle is your weapon against time; healthy habits stop some diseases in their tracks. Take lung disease, for instance: Quit smoking, and your risk plummets. What you eat and drink and how much you exercise can play a broad role in preventing a number of ailments. For example, a low-fat diet not only aids in decreasing blood cholesterol levels and body weight, but it may enhance your defenses against certain types of cancer, too.

Longevity aside, the question of quality remains. You want to feel your best. There is little doubt about the connection between your health habits and your mood and energy level. When you are under stress or sleep-deprived, you are not up to par, and when your diet is not what it could be, your stamina suffers.

Have you heard the joke about the older gentleman? He said that if he knew he was going to live so long, he would have taken better care of himself. A remark like that underscores the importance of the choices you make. A healthy lifestyle not only improves your odds for a longer life, it can help you live better every day.

THE FOOD–FITNESS CONNECTION

For years, health experts have known that the elements in food, including protein, vitamins, and minerals, promote normal growth and development and prevent nutrient deficiencies. More than 40 nutrients have been identified as crucial to good health.

Nutrition is now at an exciting crossroad. While preventing nutrient deficiencies is still important, there is a new focus on using food to optimize our physical potential and to head off debilitating chronic

disease. For example, witness the explosion of research on the antioxidant vitamins—C, E, and beta-carotene; they may be useful in preventing and treating heart disease, cancer, and cataracts. Scores of scientists are also scrutinizing common foods, such as broccoli, garlic, and tea, for chemicals believed to prevent illness. These findings are promising, but they are preliminary. It may take years before health professionals have enough results to justify making single-nutrient recommendations.

GET A MOVE ON

Exercise is gaining ground as a major player in good health, particularly in fighting heart disease, our number one killer. As rigid diet plans take a back seat to more flexible, and enjoyable, low-fat eating habits, exercise has become even more central to a sensible and long-lasting weight-control regimen.

Some of the most recent breakthroughs in the exercise field hold promise for all of us. As it turns out, it is never too late to reap the benefits of a more active lifestyle. Researchers say that no matter how old you are, you can become stronger and more agile with regular workouts. What's more, say the nation's top

exercise experts, you don't have to spend hours huffing and puffing to get in shape. Just a few minutes daily may do the trick.

STRESSED FOR SUCCESS

Stress has a direct and indirect bearing on health. Prolonged periods of stress may lead to insomnia, poor diet, too many cigarettes, and too much alcohol, all of which affect your well-being.

Stress management techniques such as meditation are getting rave reviews by some in the medical community. Meditation and deep breathing exercises are often prescribed to lower blood pressure and to manage chronic pain. Ask your doctor about biofeedback and other meditative techniques.

Regular exercise may be the best medicine for stress, allowing one to turn negative energy into a healthy workout. The stress and tension go, and the muscle- and bone-building benefits stay.

TAKE CHARGE

There is a gap between knowing what to do to get and preserve good health and putting that know-how into practice. The constant barrage of health advice and a hectic lifestyle often end up cancelling each other out. You may look for a quick fix for your problems, or you may do nothing at all.

Deep down, you know it: There is no magic bullet for good health. It takes some time and thought. What with juggling family, friends, work, volunteer activities, and perhaps night school, there are precious few minutes to devote to yourself. But before you back away, consider this: A few minutes of your time each day can yield big rewards. You don't necessarily need a lifestyle overhaul to influence your overall health. Taking small steps now toward better health will pay off later.

HOW TO GET THE MOST OUT OF THIS BOOK

This book presents you with the facts of life—a healthier life. You'll learn about nutrients, how they work in your body, and where to find them. Peruse the practical tips for eating, exercising, and reducing your disease risk based on the latest scientific breakthroughs and advice from the nation's leading health organizations. Turn to chapter 3 "Guidlines for Healthy Eating" for an in-depth discussion of the latest nutritional recommendations.

An entire chapter is devoted to what foods to eat to prevent a multitude of ailments, including anemia, cancer, heart disease, and osteoporosis, as well as how to treat disorders like lactose intolerance and heartburn. We've included a list of 101 healthy foods, their nutritional profile, and how to use them in delicious and nutritious recipes.

WHAT THIS BOOK IS NOT

Although extensive, the information presented here is not meant to replace a doctor's or registered dietitian's advice. Yearly visits with your doctor and periodic nutrition check-ups with a registered dietitian are still the best ways to keep a close watch on your health and well-being. You can accomplish a lot on your own, but you still need the assistance of a professional periodically.

FOR THE BEST OF YOUR LIFE

The best way to improve your health depends on your own unique medical history and life situation. Be aware of the areas in your life that need work. Too much stress? Get to the bottom of it. Not enough exercise? Try to work in a few minutes daily. Does heart disease run in your family? Get your blood cholesterol level tested. And use this book again and again as your guide to a longer, and better, life.

NUTRIENTS IN FOOD

CALORIES

Although not a nutrient itself, the calorie is a critical part of any nutritional discussion. A calorie is a measure of energy. It is used to represent how much energy is stored in the food you eat and, hence, how much energy you will have available to expend.

Carbohydrate, protein, fat, and alcohol provide calories in different amounts. Every gram of carbohydrate or protein provides four calories; fat has nine calories per gram; and alcohol provides seven calories per gram. Vitamins, minerals, and water are calorie-free, and so is cholesterol.

Food calories have one of two fates: They may be used to satisfy immediate energy needs, many of which you take for granted, including breathing, pumping your blood, and blinking your eyes; or, if they are not needed right away, they can be put away for future use. Extra calories are converted to and stored as fat tissue.

Your body's trillions of cells are constantly busy using food energy. During digestion, your body converts food energy to glucose, a form that can be readily used by the body. The bloodstream transports the glucose around the body to every cell.

CALORIE NEEDS VARY

Calorie needs are highest when we're young, level off in early adulthood, and then begin a slow decline.

Pound for pound, growing and developing children need several times the amount of calories required by an adult.

Infants and teenagers need more calories, because they are growing at a tremendous rate. In fact, on a pound-per-pound basis, an infant requires nearly four times more calories than a 51-year-old person. Pregnant women, who are supporting a new life, have higher calorie needs, too—and mom will need even more calories if she breast-feeds her baby.

METABOLIC RATE IS THE KEY

Part of the reason your calorie needs change so much throughout life is that your basal metabolic rate (BMR) fluctuates. BMR is the rate at which you burn calories to fuel your automatic bodily processes, such as digestion, breathing, and transporting blood. It is, in effect, your idling speed.

Your BMR accounts for about 60 percent of your calorie requirement. Over half of your energy intake goes to running these automatic functions. However, because these functions are automatic doesn't mean that they are completely out of your hands. While many factors that determine your BMR are beyond your control, you can have an effect in other ways.

THE AGING METABOLISM

You might have noticed a few pounds creeping on over the years, even though

PREGNANCY AND BREAST-FEEDING

Pregnant women are eating for two, but not two adults. A full-term pregnancy requires about 60,000 calories, which appears to be a monumental amount of pickles and ice cream. But, alas, it amounts to a mere 300 calories per day extra, beginning with the second trimester.

Breast-feeding moms need 500 extra calories per day to cover the increased energy demands of milk production. Some of the calorie needs of breast-feeding can be met by the four to seven pounds (or more) worth of fat gained in pregnancy—mom's calorie bank account. The National Academy of Science recommends that breast-feeding women eat at least 1,800 calories per day and limit weight loss to 4.5 pounds in the first month after giving birth.

Heredity plays a major role in determining your body shape and calorie-burning capacity.

you haven't changed your eating habits much. Maybe you don't move around as much as you used to, but more likely, your metabolism is slowing down with each passing year, and the calories you take in are not being used up; you're storing the surplus.

Beginning in your mid-twenties, your calorie needs decrease by about two percent every ten years or so. For example, if you maintained your weight on about 2,000 calories per day at age 25, chances are you'll need only about 1,960 daily by age 35. That may not seem like much of a drop, but consider this: If you don't eat less or burn more energy (that is, exercise more), you may wind up with an extra 14,600 calories over a year's time. That amounts to a gain of about four pounds of body fat.

Why does your metabolism slow so much? Because you lose muscle as you age, unless you exercise regularly to preserve what you have. When you gain weight in your later years, it is most likely fat, and not the muscle and bone you gained during adolescence. Fat tissue takes very few calories to maintain; after all; it is merely storage. Muscle tissue, on the other hand, is the workhorse of the body and demands a lot of energy to maintain.

BODY SIZE AND COMPOSITION RULE

Common sense says that bigger bodies need more calories. Obviously, it takes more energy for a 250-pound man to sprint 100 yards than it does for a

150-pound man to do the same. But the composition of your body influences calorie needs, too. Even at rest, muscle tissue burns more calories than fat. The more muscle you have, the more calories you require. So, leaner people tend to have higher BMRs. Men, who have proportionally more muscle than women, typically need about ten percent more calories than women the same age and weight. Up until age ten, boys and girls have similar calorie needs, but the onset of puberty, when boys begin to develop muscle rapidly, changes all that.

ALL IN THE FAMILY

Take a look at your parents and siblings. Are they tall and thin? Or do they struggle to control their weight even on a low-calorie diet? To a certain extent, genetics determines your calorie-burning capacity. For instance, if you're a man and your father is lean, you will most likely be lean, too, barring any drastic changes in your activity level, food intake, or health.

"ENERGY IN" AFFECTS "ENERGY OUT"

Very-low-calorie diets and fasting or starvation decrease metabolic rate. When your body is confronted with a prolonged, severe calorie reduction, it acts as if it is being starved and tries to use to the fullest every calorie you eat, making what fuel it does get last. The body drops its BMR to conserve energy for survival.

THE ACTIVITY QUOTIENT

Most people want to increase their BMR. You can't control the predetermined factors that influence metabolism, such as your age or your sex, but you can change your body composition with regular activity. Movement burns calories, so it comes as no surprise that calorie needs are based, in part, on activity level. But exercise has an added bonus. It may speed up your metabolism even after you've stopped exercising. A workout in the morning can raise your metabolic rate for the rest of the day. Exercise also builds muscle, and since muscle burns more calories than fat, the activity can cause a lasting increase in your BMR.

TEMPERATURE

Cold weather increases calorie requirements by about five percent, some of which can be attributed to hauling around heavier winter wear. Likewise, hot climates increase calorie needs. Yet, the Food and Nutrition Board of the National Academy of Sciences makes no allowances for climate in their calorie recommendations.

Eating BURNS CALORIES

Not exactly what you expected to hear, is it? Eating does require calories, but not enough to counteract that piece of chocolate cake and ice cream. Digestion and absorption account for about ten percent of the calories you need for life. After you eat, your metabolic rate increases steadily for about an hour while your body deals with the new shipment of nutrients; then, it gradually returns to its usual level.

All CALORIES ARE NOT CREATED EQUAL

If you're cutting calories, try trimming some fat from your diet. Fat contains more than double the calories of carbohydrate or protein, so a high-fat diet is usually a high-calorie diet, too, but there's more.

Fat calories make you fat. Why? Because your body handles fat calories differently from the way it handles protein or carbohydrate. You already know that it takes

When an athlete is performing, he or she burns many calories very quickly.

calories to break down and absorb nutrients. It seems that it's easier for your body to convert the fat that you eat into body fat than it is to convert the carbohydrates into body fat. It takes about 3 calories to change 100 fat calories into body fat. However, it takes 25 calories to change 100 carbohydrate calories into body fat. So a low-fat diet is better for weight control because (1) it may contain fewer calories, and (2) it discourages the accumulation of body fat.

Walking THE ENERGY BALANCE TIGHTROPE

There's little mystery to weight control: Fulfill your calorie requirement, and maintain your weight; consume more calories than you need, and gain weight; eat fewer calories, and you may drop a few pounds.

The key to losing weight is creating a calorie deficit by burning more calories than you eat. The safest, and most palatable way to achieve this end is by eating slightly less, especially less fat, while exercising more. That way, you won't feel deprived, and you insure a more healthful diet.

How low can you go? Very-low-calorie diets compromise nutrition. Even the most savvy of dieters would find it difficult to get the nutrients needed on fewer than 1,200 calories a day. It makes sense to discuss your diet with a registered dietitian. That way, you'll get the most nutrition for your limited calorie budget.

FIGURING YOUR CALORIE ALLOTMENT

Select your activity level (*low* if you're relatively sedentary and don't exercise; *moderate* if you get some regular exercise; *high* if you exercise regularly), and find on the charts how many calories you need per day.

WOMEN

Age	Low Activity	Moderate Activity	High Activity
19–24	1,800	2,200	2,600
25–50	1,800	2,200	2,600
51+	1,700	2,000	2,400

MEN

Age	Low Activity	Moderate Activity	High Activity
19–24	2,300	3,000	3,700
25–50	2,300	3,000	3,800
51+	2,000	2,600	3,200

Reprinted with permission from *Recommended Dietary Allowances*, 10th edition. © 1989 by the National Academy of Sciences. Courtesy of the National Academy Press, Washington, D.C.

CARBOHYDRATES

Would you like to be able to eat more bread, pasta, rice, and cereal? Go ahead, say health experts. Why are these foods the darling of nutritionists? Because they are jam-packed with carbohydrate, the body's preferred energy source. The body can easily convert carbohydrates to glucose, the fuel your cells need for life. There's more: Most high-carbohydrate foods also happen to be low in fat and loaded with nutrients.

Despite all of its admirable work, carbohydrate still suffers from an image problem. It has been wrongly accused of being fattening, and it is largely avoided by people bent on weight control. Yet, at only four calories per gram, carbohydrates are one of the least caloric

Complex carbohydrates are our bodies preferred energy source. Breads and pastas are the best sources of this fuel.

nutrients around. According to health professionals, carbohydrates are the basis of a healthy diet, even one that promotes weight loss, but we don't eat enough carbohydrate. American adults consume about 45 percent of their calories as carbohydrate; about half of that is in the form of simple sugars. Experts say we should get 50 to 60 percent of our calories from carbohydrate, and most of that should be the complex variety.

THE LONG AND THE SHORT OF CARBOHYDRATES

You've heard the words plenty of times, but what exactly is a *complex carbohydrate*? On the molecular level, all carbohydrates are made of three elements (carbon, hydrogen, and oxygen) arranged in rings. These rings can stand alone or form small groups (simple carbohydrates), or they can be strung in long chains (complex carbohydrates). During digestion, carbohydrates are broken down to their simplest units, monosaccharides (literally meaning *single sugars*), which are the single rings. One such monosaccharide is glucose, the fuel that circulates for the cells to use.

SHORT AND SWEET

Simple carbohydrates, or simple *sugars* as they're often called, are just that, carbohydrates in their simplest form—

THE FOUNDATION OF A HEALTHY DIET

To get the complex carbohydrate you need, eat more bread, grains, pasta, and cereal—at least six servings daily. Children, teenagers, physically active women, and most men need 9 to 11 servings daily. The following equal one serving: 1 slice of bread, half a bagel, or English muffin; 1 ounce of ready-to-eat cereal or half a cup of cooked cereal; or half a cup of any type of cooked rice or pasta.

Vegetables, especially potatoes and peas, also provide complex carbohydrate, but most do not supply as much as breads and grains. You need at least three to five servings of vegetables a day.

While fruit and low-fat dairy products contain primarily simple sugars, they are healthy foods that play a role in a high-carbohydrate diet. The following sample menu gives you an idea of how to build a high-carbohydrate day.

Breakfast:
1 ounce of ready-to-eat cereal
　　with ¾ cup skim
　　or 1% milk
2 slices of whole-wheat toast

with 2 teaspoons
　　of jelly or jam
1 medium banana

Snack:
5–10 graham cracker squares
8 ounces of orange juice

Lunch:
2 ounces of turkey, chicken, or
　　lean meat on 2 slices of
　　whole-grain bread with low-
　　fat mayonnaise or mustard
　　and lettuce and tomato
Small side salad with 1
　　tablespoon of low-fat
　　dressing
1 medium apple
8 ounces of skim or 1% milk

Snack:
8 ounces of nonfat yogurt

Dinner:
4 ounces of cooked meat—
　　chicken or seafood
1 cup of cooked pasta with
　　½ cup of tomato sauce, or
　　1 cup of cooked rice
1 cup of lightly steamed
　　carrots or broccoli
1 cup of fruit salad topped with
　　½ cup low-fat frozen yogurt

Snack:
3 cups low-fat popcorn or 4
　　graham cracker squares

carbohydrates made up of only one or two molecular rings. Simple sugars, which are intensely sweet, go by many aliases, including sucrose, fructose, maltose, and dextrose, which is helpful to know when you're reading food labels for sugar content. Sugars are present in fruit, table sugar, corn syrup, honey, molasses, pastries, breakfast cereals, and frozen desserts, including frozen yogurt and ice cream. Sugar may also be found in less obvious places. Some brands of ketchup, barbecue sauce, and spaghetti sauce contain added sugar. Dairy products are the only animal foods that provide a significant amount of naturally occurring carbohydrate in our diet. The carbohydrate in milk products is called *lactose*.

GETTING MORE COMPLEX

There's nothing complicated about complex carbohydrates. They are simply longer chains of sugars, much less sweet to the taste. Starch is the best-known complex carbohydrate. Complex carbohydrates are found exclusively in plant foods, including bread, grains, rice, cereal, vegetables, beans, and pasta.

WHERE DO YOU GET YOUR ENERGY?

From carbohydrate, of course. After your body breaks the carbohydrate down to the simple form called *glucose*, the cells take what they need. Remaining glucose is converted to a temporary storage form called *glycogen*. Depending on the intensity and duration of exercise, most of the fuel for your daily walk or run is supplied by this glycogen.

The body can easily convert the complex carbohydrates from grains to glucose—the form of fuel that cells use.

Making complex carbohydrates the focus of the meal guarantees that you get enough energy without too much fat.

Glycogen is mobilized to keep blood glucose levels within normal range especially between meals. The liver stores about a third of the body's glycogen and the muscles harbor the rest. For the most part, liver glycogen regulates blood glucose levels at rest and somewhat during exercise. Muscle glycogen provides working muscles with energy during exercise.

Glycogen stores have their limits. A 154-pound man can store between 1,500 to 2,600 calories as glycogen, depending on the amount of exercise he does. The more you exercise, the more muscle you build and the greater your capacity to store muscle glycogen, which is good news for marathoners who run for hours without eating. After you fill up your glycogen stores and satisfy any immediate calorie needs, your body converts extra carbohydrate to fat and deposits it in your fat tissue for long-term storage.

WHEN MORE IS LESS

It may seem strange that you can eat more carbohydrate and end up with fewer calories, especially when starch has been sworn off by every dieter at one time or another. Poor starch. People blame it for weight gain, but it is innocent. The blame should be put on the high-fat dressings, such as butter and Alfredo sauce, added to starchy foods that drive up the calorie count of blameless pasta and potatoes.

Contrary to public opinion, carbohydrates are a dieter's delight. You don't really have to give up high-fat foods to lose weight either, but you must eat smaller portions. For example, substitute a half cup of cooked pasta and a quarter cup of tomato sauce for three ounces of lean ground beef, and you'll save about 110 calories and 13 grams of fat; you'll probably feel more satisfied, as well.

Many fad diets are too low in carbohydrate, and that can be dangerous. When your body is deprived of its primary energy source, it is forced to run on fat and protein. Not only does this keep protein from being used for its other, more vital purposes, but also, breaking down protein for energy generates harmful waste products. Carbohydrates burn clean. Don't eat less than 100 grams of carbohydrate daily, the amount found in two slices of bread, six ounces of orange juice, one medium baked potato, and a half-cup of cooked carrots.

COMPLEX CARBOHYDRATES BENEFIT HEALTH

Simple and complex carbohydrates have the same potential to provide energy. Regardless of complexity, all carbohydrates contain four calories per gram. Yet health professionals favor complex carbohydrates. Why? Because they are almost always found in low-fat, cholesterol-free foods considered good sources of vitamins, minerals, and fiber. On the other hand, most high-sugar foods, with the exception of fruit, contain little more than calories.

Consider this: At 110 calories, one medium baked potato with the skin dishes up hearty amounts of B vitamins, vitamin C, potassium, and fiber. Potatoes are virtually sodium- and fat-free, too. But 12 ounces of a sugary sweet beverage, such as cola with its nearly ten teaspoons of added sugar and 150 calories, provide calories only.

Another advantage to complex carbohydrates: They provide a more lasting energy source than their simpler counterparts, because it takes your body longer to digest them. Simple sugars are taken up quickly by the bloodstream, causing what some have labeled a *sugar high*. The energy boost provided by sugar is fleeting and may lead to a sugar crash as the body tries to normalize the elevated glucose level. Complex carbohydrate, on the other hand, allows your body to sustain a relatively constant energy level over an extended period.

Runners count on the energy that complex carbohydrates provide. The more complex, the more lasting the energy.

SUGAR—IT'S NOT AS BAD AS YOU THINK

It's time to clear the air. Sugar is not the nutritional villain it's made out to be. Sugary foods are problematic only when they crowd out other more nutritious foods. For instance, drinking soda instead of low-fat milk and eating cookies instead of a banana are not the wisest food choices, especially if you make them on a daily basis. But if your diet is otherwise nutritious, then you have room for a bit of sugar.

There is a caveat: Many sugary favorites, such as ice cream, chocolate, cake, and cookies are also the ones laden with fat and calories. Eating too many calories, no matter what the source, can result in weight gain if not balanced by activity. Yet, research shows that people who consume more sugar are not always heavier.

Be aware, too, that the sugar we add to foods either in the manufacturing process or in the kitchen—corn syrup, fructose, sucrose, maple syrup, to name a few—are nearly devoid of nutrients, with the exception of black strap molasses, which is rich in calcium and potassium. Forget about honey being more nutritious; it provides only trace amounts of nutrients too small to consider beneficial to health.

If you get an urge for something sweet, feast on fruit. Fruit is full of fructose, a simple sugar, but fruit offers nutrients that candy can't. Fruit is packed with vitamins, minerals, and fiber, making it nutrient-dense. In other words, fruit offers good nutrition at a low-calorie cost. You can satisfy the adult Recommended Dietary Allowance (RDA) for vitamin C for a mere 65 calories simply by eating one medium-sized orange.

SUGAR—THE CULPRIT IN DISEASE?

Sugar is the scapegoat for any number of ailments, but this demonization is hardly warranted. Here are some of the most common charges leveled against sugar.

TOOTH DECAY: The only disease we can pin on sugar is tooth decay, and even that role is becoming less important. Sugar does provide food for enamel-eroding bacteria, but they aren't picky. Bacteria eat complex carbohydrates, including starch, too.

As it turns out, dentists are concerned more with how long the carbohydrate sticks to your teeth than with what type of carbohydrate it is. Caramels or jelly beans are often called cavity causers, but there are worse foods. Take a granola bar, for example, a mixture of simple and complex carbohydrates. Pieces of the granola bar or bits of potato chips may stick between teeth for hours, supplying a steady flow of nutrients on which bacteria feed. Put simply, the longer any form of carbohydrate clings to your teeth, the greater the risk for cavities. Brush your teeth immediately after meals and snacks to avoid tooth decay. (For more on dental disease, see pages 61–62.)

HYPERACTIVITY: Research has debunked the myth that sugar causes hyperactivity. However,

Not all sugar is to be avoided. The simple carbohydrates in fruit are paired with lots of essential vitamins and minerals.

THE SWEET LIFE

Simple sugars are found in the most unexpected places. Many of your favorite foods contain more sugars than you know. Some sugar is added to foods such as salad dressing and soft drinks during manufacturing; others are naturally occurring. Although not a dietary taboo, added sugar can crowd out some nutritious alternatives. It often contributes calories without much in the way of nutrients. Here are some sugary facts.

Food	Amount of sugar (teaspoons)
Beverages	
Soft drinks, 12 ounces	10
Flavored instant coffee, prepared from powdered mix, 6 ounces	1–2
Lemonade, prepared from powdered mix, 8 ounces	4–5.5
Candy	
Milk chocolate, 1.55 ounces	4
Gum drops, 10 small	4
Licorice, 2.5 ounces	8
Snacks	
Caramel popcorn, 1 cup	3
Frozen yogurt, vanilla, 1 cup	4
Sauces and Condiments	
Barbecue sauce, 2 tablespoons	2
Russian salad dressing, 2 tablespoons	0.5
Spaghetti sauce, 4 ounces	2–3
Sweeteners	
Honey, 1 tablespoon	4
Molasses, 1 tablespoon	3
Vegetables	
Canned beans with pork, 1 cup	5
Cauliflower, frozen with cheese sauce, 1 cup	2.5

many parents and pediatricians refuse to give up the notion that sugar is responsible for impulsive and inappropriate behavior. In blaming sugar for bad conduct, adults often fail to account for the impact of the environment on youngsters' rambunctious play. Children often consume sweets at holiday get-togethers and birthday parties, when they are more likely to become excited anyway.

DIABETES: Sugar does not cause diabetes. Diabetes is a genetic disorder of faulty insulin production or use and carbohydrate metabolism. Diabetes may lay dormant for years, only to be triggered by advancing age, illness, or obesity, but never just by eating sugary foods. Diabetics should follow a low-sugar diet to control their disease, but a low-sugar diet is not a preventive measure.

CHOLESTEROL

Cholesterol is perhaps the most baffling of all health topics, because it is so often confused with fat. True, both are major players in heart disease, and both are often linked in conversation, but that's where the similarity ends.

WHAT EXACTLY IS IT?

Cholesterol is a waxy, fat-like substance. It's made mainly in the liver, but all cells are capable of producing cholesterol. The body needs cholesterol to make bile acids, which aid in the digestion and absorption of fat, and to make hormones, which orchestrate the workings of your organs and tissues. Cholesterol is an essential part of cell membranes, too, and it contributes to strong bones as the raw material for vitamin D, which directs the absorption and distribution of calcium.

CHOLESTEROL AND FAT—SEPARATE IDENTITIES

Fat is fat and cholesterol is cholesterol and never the twain shall meet. At least not from a chemical standpoint. Cholesterol and fat are often found in the same foods, which is one of the reasons for the confusion, but there are several very important distinctions:

You'll never find cholesterol in fruits, vegetables, and grain. Cholesterol is found only in animal products.

- Cholesterol is found only in animal foods. Fruits, vegetables, grains, and other plant products do not contain cholesterol, no matter how high they are in fat. For example, margarine, corn oil, and coconut oil are 100 percent fat, but they contain no cholesterol.

- Cholesterol has no calories. So, it cannot contribute energy or be blamed for weight gain. By contrast, fat is packed with calories—nine calories per gram.

- Cholesterol is not stored in the body for future use. Too much fat, or any other form of calories for that matter, will be converted to body fat for storage. Too much cholesterol, if not excreted, may wind up lining your blood vessels, contributing to blockages and possibly a heart attack or stroke.

- Your body makes all the cholesterol it needs. There is no minimum cholesterol requirement, but you must consume some fat, albeit it a small amount. One thing that fat and cholesterol have in common: Health experts counsel moderation and recommend upper limits on the consumption of both.

THE GOOD, THE BAD, AND THE CONFUSION OF IT ALL

Talk of *good* and *bad* cholesterol can tie you up in knots, but references to good and bad cholesterol pertain to how your body packages and transports cholesterol and has nothing to do with dietary cholesterol. As far as food goes, there is no good or bad cholesterol.

Cholesterol is ferried around your body in packages called lipoproteins. High-density lipoprotein (HDL) cholesterol is favorable, because it removes cholesterol from cells and brings it back to the liver for excretion. In addition, HDL cholesterol packs considerably less cholesterol than low-density lipoprotein (LDL) cholesterol. LDL cholesterol consists of mostly cholesterol and is harmful, because it carries cholesterol away from the liver to the cells, dumping it along artery walls as it makes its way through the body. LDL cholesterol deposits in the blood vessels promote plaque buildup, increasing the risk of heart disease.

WHAT'S YOUR DIETARY CHOLESTEROL REQUIREMENT?

Zero, unless you're a baby. Infants and small children need dietary cholesterol to support their rapid growth

Only babies actually need cholesterol in their diets. Adults and children over two make all the cholesterol they need.

and development. In fact, pediatricians strongly advise parents against restricting fat and cholesterol intake until after two years of age.

There is no cholesterol RDA for adults because we're animals, and we make all the cholesterol we need, about 800 to 1,000 milligrams (mg) daily. Animals alone produce cholesterol. That's why you'll never find cholesterol in plant foods, such as peanut butter, vegetable oil, and margarine—*no matter what the fat content.* Cholesterol is present in varying amounts in meat, poultry, seafood, eggs, and dairy products.

Put a Lid on It

Excessive cholesterol consumption has been blamed for raising blood cholesterol levels and contributing to heart disease, but that's only partially correct. Studies show that while too much cholesterol may increase blood cholesterol levels, saturated fat is by far the biggest dietary culprit.

Saturated fat increases LDL cholesterol production. For most people, the more cholesterol they eat, the less their body makes and vice versa. Only about 20 percent of the population are cholesterol sensitive, that is, affected by their cholesterol intake. Mostly, it's the saturated fat intake that affects the damaging LDL cholesterol levels.

The Surgeon General's office and the American Heart Association recommend capping cholesterol intake at 300 mg daily, about the amount found in one fast food double bacon cheeseburger, 16 ounces of whole milk, and one cup of vanilla ice cream.

Cholesterol-containing foods, such as poultry, cheese, and eggs, are nutritious. It may be heartening to know that you don't need to cut out cholesterol completely, but you should honor the recommended upper limit. All you need to do is remember the golden rule of good nutrition: Make it low in fat.

As fat goes, so too goes cholesterol. With only a few exceptions, lower-fat animal foods contain little cholesterol. Here are some examples of substitutions that can cut your cholesterol intake:

- Eight ounces of whole milk contains 33 mg of cholesterol; the same amount of 1% milk has 4 mg—a difference of 29 mg.

- A half cup of premium vanilla ice cream has 45 mg of cholesterol, while a half cup of vanilla frozen yogurt has about 2 mg, for a savings of 43 mg.

- Three and a half ounces of cooked white chicken meat (with skin) has 84 mg of cholesterol; the same amount of bluefin tuna has 56 mg. You save 28 mg.

- One tablespoon of butter contains 33 mg of cholesterol; one tablespoon of margarine has 0 mg. (Butter and margarine are both all fat, though, so go easy.)

- Two tablespoons of light cream in your coffee adds 20 mg of cholesterol; the same amount of low-fat milk contributes slightly more than 1 mg. That's about 19 mg of cholesterol saved every time you have a cup of coffee.

- One cup of homemade egg custard contains about 240 mg of cholesterol, but 1 cup of pudding prepared from mix with low-fat milk has about 20 mg—a difference of 220 mg.

DOUBLE-WHAMMY FOODS

Some foods are rich sources of saturated fat *and* cholesterol; they pack a powerful one-two punch for heart disease. If you're taking steps toward a more heart-healthy diet, make it a rule to consume these foods in moderation only. The major offenders include:

- Cream
- Ice cream
- Hot dogs
- Lamb
- Whole and 2% milk
- Steak
- Quiche
- Salami
- Poultry skin

- Cream cheese
- Butter
- Pork
- Beef
- Whole-milk cheese
- Hollandaise sauce
- Liverwurst
- Duck
- Sour cream

FAT

If you've heard it once, you've heard it a thousand times: *Eat a diet low in fat.* According to health experts, a high-fat diet is at the root of many debilitating diseases, including our number one killer, heart disease. Cutting back on your fat intake makes room for other vital nutrients, such as complex carbohydrate, and usually results in a lower cholesterol intake, too.

Realizing that you should decrease fat consumption and actually putting your know-how to work may be worlds apart. To figure out how to live a healthier lifestyle, you must first understand the basic facts about fat.

WHY EAT FAT AT ALL?

Dietary fat is the sole provider of linoleic acid, a fatty acid crucial to the proper functioning of every body tissue. Nutritionists have designated linoleic acid as essential, because your body cannot make it. You must consume linoleic acid for good health. Linoleic acid supplies the raw material for a number of structures including cell membranes. It also plays a key role in metabolizing and transporting cholesterol, in regulating blood pressure, and in the production of prostaglandins (hormone-like chemicals that regulate certain bodily functions).

FAT TASTES GOOD

Many fats, such as peanut oil, have distinct flavors. What would a chocolate confection be without cocoa butter? Cheese without butterfat? Italian food without olive oil? Not nearly as tasty. Fat also adds appeal to foods by providing texture. Make the mistake of forgetting the fat in a cookie or muffin recipe and your results will resemble, and perhaps taste like, hockey pucks.

FAT PHOBIA

Despite all the reasons to like it, there's little doubt these days that fat is not your friend. Some people even try to avoid it entirely, but that's virtually impossible and not even necessary. Fat is found in nearly every animal and plant food, even if only in trace amounts. Furthermore, a no-fat diet is unhealthy. Aside from supplying linoleic acid, fat provides energy, dissolves and transports vitamins A, D, E, and K, and helps us feel full when we eat.

Fat packs more calories than other nutrients. It is easily converted into body fat and is linked to many health problems.

WHEN FAT SPELLS TROUBLE

When is fat a dietary thorn in your side? When you eat too much; for many Americans, that's most of the time. We need about as much fat for good health as will fit into a tablespoon—about 11 grams—but we eat much more.

Fat is linked to much of what ails us. A fat-laden diet contributes directly and indirectly to a host of health problems, especially heart disease. Too much fat may increase your blood cholesterol level, boosting heart disease risk.

At nine calories per gram, fat contains more than twice the calories of carbohydrate and protein. What's more, your body has a relatively easy time of converting food fat into body fat, making a low-fat diet central to weight control. Eat too many fat calories, and chances are you'll become overweight, which can lead to many health problems and degenerative diseases, including high blood pressure and diabetes.

The link between fat and cancer is not so clear, however. Some studies have found a connection between a high-fat intake and breast and colon cancer, but that's debatable. It's difficult to determine which is to blame, the fat alone or the excess calories that a high-fat diet provides.

Nevertheless, some experts recommend limiting fat to 20 percent or less of your total calorie intake to hedge against cancer. While that suggestion is not yet mainstream thinking, it wouldn't hurt to think about dropping fat intake that far for reasons other than cancer protection; at the very least, a low-fat diet makes weight control easier. For now, however, most of us would do well to aim for a more modest fat level—say, 25 to 30 percent of calories from fat (see chapter 3 for specific guidelines).

THERE'S GOOD NEWS AND BAD NEWS

Some of us are eating less fat. Only a few years ago, Americans got an average of about 41 percent of their calories from fat; that's been reduced to nearly 37 percent. We eat less butter and lard, which has lowered our saturated fat and, as an added bonus, cholesterol consumption.

We still have a way to go. Thirty-seven percent of our total calories come from fat—that is still much too high. According to several health organizations, including the Surgeon General's office, The American Heart Association, and The American Dietetic Association, a diet with 30 percent or fewer fat calories is one method of achieving and maintaining a healthy body weight and normalizing blood cholesterol levels.

THE BIG THREE

Food contains three distinct fat types: saturated, monounsaturated, and poly-unsaturated. All can be found in plant and animal foods, and all have the same number of calories. But they differ in their health effects.

SATURATED FAT

There is no question that saturated fat has few redeeming qualities. Excessive consumption raises blood cholesterol values like no other element in the diet, including food cholesterol itself. And, like its counterparts, saturated fat packs calories.

WHERE DOES IT HIDE? Animal foods including lamb, beef, pork, and, yes, even chicken, contain saturated fat. So do full-fat dairy products such as butter, whole milk, cheese, cream, and ice cream.

As a rule, saturated fat is solid at room temperature. You know that fat that surrounds a juicy piece of steak? It's mostly saturated. And butter, which is relatively hard at room temperature, is primarily saturated, too.

There are exceptions, however. Palm oil, palm kernel oil, cocoa butter, and coconut oil are not animal products and are liquid at room temperature, yet they are highly saturated. Tropical oils, as they are sometimes called, can be found in processed cookies, crackers, candy, and baked goods and in some nondairy coffee lighteners and whipped toppings.

HOW MUCH IS TOO MUCH? There is no Recommended Dietary Allowance (RDA) for any type of fat. Health experts suggest keeping the lid on saturated fat intake, however. Saturated fat should account for ten percent or fewer of your daily calories. For a person eating about 2,000 calories a day, that amounts to fewer than 22 grams of saturated

---

According to several major health organizations, consuming fewer than a third of your calories as fat is part of the wellness equation. But a question looms large: How in the world does that suggestion translate into what you should eat for breakfast, lunch, and dinner? To understand food labels and have an easier time comparing the amount of fat you are eating with what you should eat, figure your daily fat budget. The calculations go something like this:

- Let's say you need 2,000 calories daily for weight maintenance. A third or less from fat amounts to 600 or fewer calories.

- To get the number of fat grams you are allowed, divide 600 by 9 calories per gram (the amount found in fat).

- That amounts to about 67 grams of fat allowed per day. Do you have to eat all 67? No way. You could eat much less and stay healthy.

Skip the math and go straight to the fat facts by using the chart below as a quick reference for your daily fat quota.

- Pick a desired calorie level, for weight maintenance or for weight loss (see page 9).

- Decide what percentage of your calories you want to come from fat— that is, how low you want to go—and stick to it.

Calorie intake	20% or fewer fat calories	30% or fewer fat calories
1,200	27 grams	40 grams
1,400	31 grams	47 grams
1,600	35 grams	53 grams
1,800	40 grams	60 grams
2,000	44 grams	66 grams
2,400	53 grams	80 grams
2,800	63 grams	93 grams

CHOOSING THE BEST FAT

Food often contains a mixture of the three fats, saturated, mono-unsaturated, and polyunsaturated. For example, while olive oil is recognized as an excellent source of monounsaturated fat, it contains about 14 percent saturated fat. If you use enough olive oil, you'll take in substantial amounts of saturated fat in the bargain. That's why added fat should be used sparingly.

At times, the decision to cook with one fat over another rests on its intended use: peanut oil for Chinese food, corn oil for frying chicken, or lard for perfect pie crusts. But more and more, health concerns are driving consumers' decisions about fat, both in the kitchen and in the supermarket. Bear in mind that added fats contain about 100 calories and 11 grams of fat per tablespoon. The healthiest ones have the least saturated fat and cholesterol. Here is some useful information about widely used fats.

- Coconut oil is highest in saturated fat. Butter comes in second, whereas beef fat and palm oil vie for third place.

- Canola oil boasts the least saturated fat, and more monounsaturated fat than polyunsaturated.

- Lard is nearly 50 percent monounsaturated fat. The downside is that lard packs about 40 percent saturated fat. And since it's an animal product, it has cholesterol, too.

- Safflower, sunflower, and corn oil consist of polyunsaturated fat.

- Margarine has twice as much saturated fat as safflower oil.

- Butter contains three times as much saturated fat as margarine and 33 times the cholesterol.

Hydrogenating oil improves the products stability and resistance to spoilage, but there is a downside. Hydrogenated fat contains *trans* fatty acids, a form of fat that increases blood cholesterol levels, much like saturated fat. Although the exact method by which these fats raise blood cholesterol levels is unknown, it may be that the body mistakes *trans* fatty acids for saturated fatty acids. Whatever the process, though, hydrogenated and partially hydrogenated fats are definitely not heart healthy.

There is little agreement about how many *trans* fatty acids we eat. Some studies report that Americans consume about 20 grams daily; others say upwards of 38 grams, particularly if you consume a lot of processed foods, margarine, and baked goods made with margarine. Too much of any type of fat is unhealthy, but a little bit of hydrogenated fat probably won't do much harm, as long as your diet is generally low in fat.

To cut back on hydrogenated fat, limit margarine and eat fewer processed foods, such as crackers, cookies, snack foods, and french fries. Cook with vegetable oils instead of margarine, and if you cannot resist, choose the soft tub margarine (it has less hydrogenated fat) over the stick form.

fat daily, but take note: Your body does not require any saturated fat. How much fat is 22 grams? Here's some idea of the amount of saturated fat in some common food items:

- Beef short ribs, cooked, 3.5 ounces—18 grams

- Fast-food double cheeseburger—18 grams

- Cheddar cheese, 2 ounces—12 grams

- Milk chocolate, 1.55-ounce bar—8 grams

- Butter, 1 tablespoon—8 grams

A DIFFERENT NAME, BUT THE SAME GAME

If you read labels, you've probably come across the term *hydrogenated*. Hydrogenation is the process of forcing hydrogen into oil, a liquid at room temperature, to make more solid food products. A prime example is margarine, which, depending on the brand, is made from a variety of hydrogenated and liquid vegetable oils.

Monounsaturated fat, as in olive oil, lowers blood cholesterol when used in place of saturated fat.

Monounsaturated Fat

Once thought to have no effect on blood cholesterol levels, health professionals now say that mono-unsaturated fat is, in fact, heart healthy. Some studies have shown that monounsaturated fat lowers blood cholesterol *when it replaces saturated fat in the diet.* Monounsaturated fat is found predominantly in olives, olive oil, walnuts, walnut oil, canola oil, avocados, peanuts, peanut butter, and other nuts.

HOW MUCH CAN YOU HAVE? Even though health professionals have deemed monounsaturated fat healthy, resist the temptation to go overboard. Too much fat of any kind may lead to obesity and will increase your risk of heart disease. Limit mono-unsaturated fat intake to ten percent or less of your total calorie intake. For example, on a diet of 2,000 calories per day, you're allowed no more than 22 grams of monounsaturated fat. Here are some common sources of monounsaturated fat:

- Avocado, raw, 1 medium California—20 grams
- Macadamia nuts, dry roasted, 1 ounce—16 grams
- Olive oil, 1 tablespoon—10 grams
- Peanut butter, 2 tablespoons—8 grams

Polyunsaturated Fat

Most health professionals agree that polyunsaturated fat lowers blood cholesterol levels, but only when it takes the place of saturated fat in the diet. One form of polyunsaturated fat, omega-6, is found primarily in margarine and vegetable oils, such as corn oil, sunflower oil, and safflower oil.

Polyunsaturated fat is also found in seafood, as omega-3 fatty acids, commonly known as fish oils. Omega-3 fatty acids have been heralded for their possible role in reducing the risk of heart disease. Omega-3 fats may prevent the formation of clots that block the flow of life-giving blood to your heart. While the evidence is mixed, omega-3s appear promising for curtailing arthritis pain by reducing tissue inflammation, and they may help in treating psoriasis, a chronic skin disorder.

THE ESKIMO DIET: Interest in fish oils was piqued in the mid-1980s by the results of several research studies. In one, scientists investigated the diet of Greenland Eskimos, who suffer very little heart disease. At first glance, the Eskimos' diet seemed a

The dietary emphasis on fish oils may be the reason some Eskimo peoples experience very little heart disease.

prescription for illness: Nearly 45 percent of their calories came from fat. However, the majority of fat was the omega-3 type, leading researchers to deem fish oils protective against heart disease.

MORE SURF, LESS TURF: Despite the potential benefit, no recommendation for fish-oil consumption exists. Health professionals do recommend that we eat more fish, however, because fish tends to be much lower in fat, saturated fat, and cholesterol than the meat and poultry we eat instead.

Americans eat an average of 15 pounds of fish annually. By contrast, Greenland Eskimos eat nearly a pound of seafood a day—about 320 pounds annually, but you don't need to eat heaps of fish to benefit from omega-3s. Research suggests that as little as one to two fish dishes weekly may improve your chances of avoiding heart disease.

Nearly all seafood has some omega-3 fat, but cold-water fish has the most. Herring, sea bass, sardines, salmon, trout, bluefish, smelt, and bluefin tuna are among the richest sources. Even canned tuna, one of

Bluefish, along with herring, sea bass, sardines, salmon, trout, smelt, and bluefin tuna, are excellent sources of omega-3 fatty acids—a substance that may ward off heart disease.

America's most popular fish choices, has more omega-3 fat than chicken or turkey. Surprisingly, lobster, orange roughy, and surimi (imitation crab meat made from pollack) have next to zero.

SKIP THE FISH? If you dislike seafood, you may be tempted to take fish-oil pills to get the benefits without the taste. Think again. Taking fish-oil supplements can be a recipe for disaster. First of all, there is no official word on how much omega-3 fat we should eat daily, and because supplements are more concentrated in omega-3s than fish, it's easy to overdose, which could result in excess bleeding and interfere with wound healing. Furthermore, fish-oil supplements are made from fish livers, which are prone to accumulating toxic chemicals from the environment, particularly pesticides and heavy metals. Because fish-oil pills are made of fat, your daily dose may be highly caloric and could contribute to weight gain. Lastly, the effectiveness of fish-oil pills is entirely unproved. Taking them is considered unsafe.

PUSHING THE LIMIT: You should limit polyun-saturated fat intake to ten percent of your total calories, which amounts to fewer than 22 grams daily on a 2,000-calorie diet. Here are some common sources of polyunsaturated fat:

- Safflower oil, 1 tablespoon—10 grams
- Sunflower oil, 1 tablespoon—10 grams
- Corn oil, 1 tablespoon—8 grams
- Mackerel, cooked, 6 ounces—7 grams
- Salmon, Atlantic, cooked, 6 ounces—6 grams

CHART A LOW-FAT COURSE

Does a low-fat diet lack taste? Before you answer, consider this: A low-fat diet can include your favorite foods. Surprised? We thought so. Live by a few simple rules, and you can cut fat without drastically changing your eating habits.

- Limit red meat, including beef, lamb, and pork, to three servings a week. Eat no more than four ounces (a piece slightly bigger than a deck of cards) per meal.

- Consume more seafood and skinless poultry, but keep portions to three to four ounces.

- Eat a meatless dinner once or twice a week.

- Try cutting fat by half during preparation and at the table. For example, use less oil in a stir-fry dish or half as much fat in your favorite quick bread or muffin recipe. Use less salad dressing, or substitute a low-fat version.

- Switch to low-fat products. Seek nonfat or low-fat mayonnaise and sour cream to reduce your fat intake further.

- Concentrate on eating the freshest foods possible. For instance, opt for a baked potato instead of french fries (the more processed alternative) to save on fat and calories and to get more nutrients to boot.

- Eat at least five servings of fruits and vegetables daily. You'll feel more satisfied and have less room for high-fat snack foods such as chips and cookies.

- Switch to one-percent or nonfat dairy products, including milk, yogurt, frozen yogurt, and ice milk.

- Substitute two teaspoons of jam, jelly, or preserves for butter, margarine, or cream cheese on your morning bagel or toast.

- Use milk in your coffee or tea instead of cream, half and half, and nondairy creamers. Even whole milk will save lots of fat and calories over cream in the long run.

- Study food labels. Use foods high in saturated fat sparingly.

- Munch on jelly beans, gum drops, or hard candy when your sweet tooth strikes instead of chocolate, which is

LESS FAT MAY MEAN MORE FOOD

Want to know the best part of a low-fat lifestyle? You don't necessarily have to eat less if you make low-fat food choices. Translation: Pick the lower-fat alternative and have another helping. But beware, this is not an all-you-can-eat diet. While it is easier to control your weight on a low-fat diet, too many calories will always result in extra pounds if not balanced by physical activity. Your other option is to eat your favorite foods, only in smaller portions. Won't give up steak? Try eating four ounces instead of eight. Consider these ways to save calories and fat:

Choose:	Instead of:	Save this fat: (*grams*)	And these calories:
8 oz. 1% milk	8 oz. whole milk	6	48
1 c. orange sherbet	1 c. premium ice cream	26	176
1 oz. pretzels	1 oz. potato chips	19	146
1 T. mustard	1 T. mayonnaise	10	85
1 T. low-fat mayonnaise	1 T. mayonnaise	5	50
2 c. air-popped popcorn	2 oz. snack chips	14	176
1 oz. part-skim mozzarella cheese	1 oz. American cheese	4	34
3.5 oz. lean beef, cooked	7 oz. lean beef, cooked	18	268
3.5 oz. chicken, light meat roasted, no skin	fried, with skin	8	73
10 jelly beans (1 oz.)	1.55-oz. chocolate bar	14	122
2 egg whites	1 whole egg	5	41
4 graham cracker squares	2 oz. trail mix	15	42
Angel food cake, ¹⁄₁₂ mix	Carrot cake, ¹⁄₁₂ mix	11	124

A chicken dinner can be just as tasty with much less fat if you remove the skin and grill or broil it instead of frying.

high in fat. (Beware: Even though some candy is low fat, it may be high in calories.)

- Try switching to reduced-fat cheese and low-fat cottage cheese.

- Reach for the tub instead of the stick. Tub margarine has more polyunsaturated and less saturated fat than margarine. But remember to use added fat sparingly.

- Trim the fat from meat and the skin from chicken before cooking. That way you won't be tempted to eat it after it's cooked, and the seasonings that you use will go directly into the meat instead of the fat and skin.

- Cook meat and poultry on a rack so that the fat drains off.

- Save fried foods for infrequent special treats. Frying boosts fat and calorie levels.

- Above all, remember this: A low-fat diet includes the element of balance. Not every food that passes your lips has to be low fat. Mixing high-fat food choices with low-fat ones will make healthy eating more enjoyable.

FIBER

Known to some as *roughage*, fiber is the indigestible part of plants, including fruits, vegetables, and grains. Fiber is indigestible, because your body lacks the enzymes to break it down into an absorbable form. Even though fiber can't provide energy, it is a valuable part of the diet for several other important reasons.

TWO TYPES, BOTH WITH A MISSION

There are two different types of fiber, each with its own role in good health. Insoluble fiber, found primarily in wheat bran, whole grains, and vegetables, is needed for the proper functioning of the digestive system. Soluble fiber, mostly found in oat bran, oatmeal, fruit, and beans, is beneficial for lowering blood cholesterol levels and normalizing blood glucose concentrations. But don't bother too much with the distinction. A fiber-filled diet will usually provide a hearty amount of soluble and insoluble fiber.

FILLING UP WITH FIBER

Waist watchers, take note. Fiber contributes to feelings of fullness without unwanted calories, making a high-fiber diet all the more important for

Fresh fruits, such as apples, are excellent sources of fiber that just happen to be delicious and full of vitamins and minerals.

dieters. Eating foods rich in fiber usually translates into fewer calories overall, which may seem a bit confusing to dieters, who are, more often than not, told that they need to eat less.

You may actually eat fewer calories by consuming more high-fiber foods, such as fruits, vegetables, beans, whole grains, breads, and cereals. For example, dishes such as vegetable stir fry served with rice, rice and beans, and black bean soup all contain more fiber than a hamburger and french fries. Because the vegetable dishes are so filling, you may eat smaller portions, getting fewer calories and less fat in the bargain. Remember, fiber has no calories.

FIBER TAKES ACTION

Is your digestive system out of order? Send fiber to the rescue. Fiber heads off constipation, hemorrhoids, and diverticulosis, a disease in which tiny pouches form in the large intestine and can become infected.

Here's how it works: Fiber softens and adds bulk to the stool; the increased size stimulates your intestines to pass it more quickly through your digestive system, reducing the potential for the discomfort and aggravation constipation causes. When your risk of constipation is curtailed, your chance of developing hemorrhoids, often caused by straining to move your bowels, diminishes. In general, your whole digestive tract runs smoother when you get enough fiber.

The fiber in grain is mostly in the bran, which is the outer casing of the kernel. Only whole-grain products retain this fiber.

FIBER AND FLUID—THE DYNAMIC DUO

Fiber has the amazing ability to absorb many times its weight in water. In fact, that's how it increases the bulk and softness of your stool—by absorbing fluid.

FILLING UP ON FIBER

Fiber is not all bran and brown rice. Many of your favorite foods are probably high in fiber. Use this chart to keep tabs on your fiber intake.

Less than two grams of fiber:

1 slice whole-wheat bread (Check the label.)
1 ½ cups grapes
1 medium carrot, raw
2 cups watermelon
1 medium tomato
⅙ medium head iceberg lettuce
1 medium banana

About two to four grams of fiber:

5 spears asparagus, raw
1 medium potato
⅓ medium avocado
8 medium strawberries
1 medium nectarine
2 medium celery stalks
1 cup blueberries
¾ cup cooked, plain oatmeal
1 cup carrots, cooked
½ cup corn, cooked
½ cup winter squash, cooked
1 medium sweet potato

About four to six grams fiber:

1 medium apple
1 medium stalk broccoli, raw
¼ cup wheat germ
1 medium orange
½ medium grapefruit
2 medium kiwi
cereal (Check the label.)
1 medium pear
⅔ cup raisins
10 prunes

About six to eight grams fiber:

1 cup cooked kidney beans
1 cup cooked lentils
1 cup cooked garbanzo beans
1 cup cooked navy beans
5 figs

So, to realize fiber's potential benefits, you must make sure its partner is there to help. Drink at least eight glasses of fluid daily, preferably water, milk, seltzer, or juice, to keep your system running smoothly and to insure that your fiber intake pays off. Caffeinated beverages, including coffee, tea, and cola, and alcoholic beverages increase water loss, so try to moderate your consumption.

FIBER'S KEY ROLE AS ANTI-CANCER AGENT

In some countries, people eat far more fiber and much less fat than we do. And perhaps as a result, they have much lower rates of colon cancer, the second most deadly cancer in the United States. Although health professionals concede that many factors play a role in the development of colon cancer, large population studies suggest that a high-fiber, low-fat diet may work to decrease risk.

How exactly fiber protects against cancer is still unclear, but researchers think that because fiber speeds up food's movement though the body, it lessens the chances for carcinogens (cancer-causing agents) to attack the lining of the digestive tract. Because fiber increases stool size, it may also inhibit tumor development by watering down the concentration of carcinogens in the stool.

LENDING A HAND TO FIGHT HEART DISEASE

Fiber may also help ward off heart disease in two ways. First, it may lower the levels of cholesterol in the blood. Second, a diet high in fiber can crowd out other foods that are high in fat and cholesterol that you might choose instead.

Soluble fiber lowers blood cholesterol levels, perhaps by binding with cholesterol in the digestive tract and speeding its elimination from the body before it is absorbed. But there is a catch: Devouring a bowl of oatmeal or oat bran cereal for breakfast is not enough to reduce your blood cholesterol. Adding soluble fiber works only when you eat a low-fat, low-cholesterol diet, too.

High-fiber intakes usually muscle out a good deal of fat from the diet. It would be difficult to include a lot of fatty foods in a diet that satisfied the suggested fiber quota. In this sense, fiber is a weapon in the battle against heart disease. A low-fat diet makes it

Legumes—dried peas and beans—are excellent sources of both soluble and insoluble fiber.

easier to keep blood cholesterol at desirable levels while making it easier to maintain a healthy body weight. For example, opting for cereal topped with fruit instead of a fat-laden muffin and halving meat portions while filling your plate with potatoes, vegetables, and whole-wheat bread boost fiber while slashing fat intake.

FIBER FOR BETTER BLOOD SUGAR CONTROL

Fiber may help people with diabetes keep blood glucose, the energy source for cells, closer to normal levels by slowing the absorption of nutrients into the bloodstream. Eating high-fiber foods along with a meal containing protein, carbohydrate, and fat may keep blood glucose levels on a more even keel. Soluble fiber appears to have the greatest affect on after-meal blood glucose levels. If they are left unchecked in diabetes, glucose levels can get out of control and be dangerous.

FITTING IN FIBER

Chances are, you're short on fiber. A steady diet of highly refined foods, eating on the run, and too few fruits and vegetables leave little room for fiber in the typical American diet. According to The American Dietetic Association, adults require between 20 and 35 grams of dietary fiber daily, but the average consumption is about 11 grams, according to a national survey.

Increase your fiber intake properly. A sudden shift to high fiber can wreak havoc on your digestive system. Start slowly to avoid the bloating, gas, and diarrhea that can accompany an abrupt fiber increase. Remember to increase fluid intake, too. Fluid enhances the action of fiber, helping to decrease digestive tract distress.

Here are some hints on high fiber:

- Start your morning with cereal. Choose a brand that offers five or more grams per serving. Top your cereal with dried fruit, such as raisins, or sliced fruit to boost fiber content. For example, a meal of high-fiber cereal topped with fruit and two slices of whole-wheat toast adds up to nearly ten grams or more of fiber, or about a third of the daily requirement.

- Choose whole-wheat bread and grains, such as brown rice and whole-wheat noodles, to satisfy your daily need for 6 to 11 servings of grain products. (See page 102 for more specific guidelines.) Whole grains contain the entire fiber-filled wheat kernel, making them richer in fiber than more refined grains that have been stripped of their fiber content.

- Snack on fresh or dried fruit or sliced fresh vegetables.

- Substitute a green or bean salad or bean soup at lunch for snack chips.

- Include at least one meatless dinner weekly, such as vegetarian chili, vegetable stir fry with tofu, or rice and beans.

- Be prepared when the munchies strike at work. Keep fruit and high-fiber crackers and cookies, such as graham crackers and fig bars, handy to avoid the temptation of the no-fiber choices in the vending machines.

- Eat your fruit and vegetables instead of drinking their juice. Juicing takes the fiber out. One medium apple has three times the fiber of eight ounces of apple juice.

- Strive for at least five servings of fruit and vegetables a day. What's a serving? One cup of raw leafy vegetables, such as spinach; a half-cup of cooked vegetables or chopped fruit, such as green beans or pineapple; or one medium-sized piece of fruit, like a pear or an orange.

- Keep frozen vegetables on hand; their fiber content is just as high as fresh vegetables, and you don't have to worry about using them right away.

MINERALS

Minerals are the movers, shakers, and stabilizers of the body. Some, such as calcium, seem like nothing more than immovable structural components, but many minerals call the shots by directing and regulating a multitude of body processes. Minerals may form partnerships to get work done: Sodium and potassium toil together to regulate fluid balance, while calcium and phosphorus specialize in keeping bones strong. Despite their invaluable function, some minerals are needed in amounts hardly visible to the naked eye.

CALCIUM

Calcium is the most abundant body mineral. The skeleton—bones and teeth—packs nearly 99 percent of your calcium. A mere 2.5 pounds of calcium lends structure, shape, and strength to the large adult body.

NOT FOR BONES ONLY: The remaining calcium is found in the bloodstream and soft tissues. Although infinitesimal, this calcium level is critical for normal cell function. Without constant cellular contact with calcium, normal nerve transmission, muscle contraction, and heartbeat would fail. Calcium helps control blood pressure and blood clotting, too. Some preliminary research suggests a possible link between calcium intake and the prevention of colon cancer.

OF PRIME IMPORTANCE: Circulating calcium is so important that its level is maintained at the expense of skeletal stores. It works like this: Bones and teeth serve as your calcium bank account. Ongoing deposits and withdrawals—about 23 ounces a day—are facilitated in part by vitamin D. When blood calcium levels drop below normal levels, bones are forced to contribute calcium to the blood stream. When blood

Children, whose skeletons are still forming, need a lot of calcium to strengthen their new bone tissue and teeth.

calcium levels get too high, the body deposits calcium into its reserve fund—your bones and teeth.

BEYOND CHILDHOOD: When we're young, bones thicken and lengthen rapidly, and calcium needs are high. You may have been led to believe that once you stopped getting taller, your bones shut down for business. Nothing could be further from the truth.

You can't always judge a book by its cover. Bones may seem solid and static from the outside, but on the inside, they are bustling with activity. Bone tissue contains a busy network of blood vessels that carry nutrients to and wastes away from bone cells. Bones are in a state of perpetual makeover: As bone tissue donates and receives calcium and other minerals, it is constantly breaking down and being built up again. This process, known as *remodeling*, allows the bloodstream to get what it needs out of its reserve fund. Bones benefit as the recipients of calcium and other minerals that make them strong.

FEED YOUR BONES NOW OR PAY LATER: During adolescence, bone development is at its height. No one, with the exception of pregnant and breast-feeding women, needs more calcium than teenagers. The need for calcium does not cease with adulthood, however, and many adults do not achieve their calcium quota.

If you fail to consume adequate calcium, you risk overdrawing your calcium account; your bones continue to donate calcium to the bloodstream, regardless of what you eat. The worst part is that you won't even know that you've made too many calcium withdrawals until it's too late. It's only later in life that you may discover you have osteoporosis, a bone disease marked by fragile and brittle bones, which are

---

MINERALS

Health experts categorize minerals as major or minor based on the amount found in the body. In no way does a mineral's classification confer importance, however.

Major Minerals	Minor Minerals
Calcium	Iron
Phosphorus	Iodine
Magnesium	Fluoride
Sodium	Zinc
Potassium	Selenium
	Copper
	Manganese

highly susceptible to fracture. A habitually inadequate calcium intake, along with other risky lifestyle habits, could come back to haunt you in old age.

RECOMMENDED DIETARY ALLOWANCES:
Calcium needs vary with age and stage of life. The RDA for pregnant and breast-feeding women and young adults under 25 is 1,200 milligrams (mg) daily. After 25, men and women need 800 mg daily, according to the Food and Nutrition Board of the National Academy of Sciences. Some experts differ with the calcium RDAs. The National Institutes of Health Consensus Panel on Osteoporosis recommends 1,000 mg daily for men and premenopausal women, and 1,500 mg daily for postmenopausal women.

STRAIGHT TO THE SOURCE: Dairy foods supply the most calcium by far. Not only do they boast high calcium levels, but they contain lactose (milk sugar), protein, and vitamin D, all of which promote calcium absorption and deposition in the bones. Dairy products supply more than half the calcium found in the American diet.

Plant foods contain calcium, too. Some dark green, leafy vegetables such as kale, broccoli, and bok choy are considered good sources. Some plant foods, including spinach, navy beans, pinto beans, and red beans, are not such good sources, because they contain oxalates which interfere with calcium absorption. Some plant foods also contain phytates that can block your body from absorbing calcium. Here are some good calcium sources:

- Yogurt, nonfat, vanilla, 8 ounces—389 mg

- Milk, all types, 8 ounces—about 300 mg

- Frozen yogurt, chocolate, soft-serve, 1 cup—212 mg

In addition to dairy products, calcium can be found in the cruciferous vegetables and other dark, leafy vegetables.

- Cheese, cheddar, 1 ounce—204 mg

- Cottage cheese, nonfat, 1 cup—138 mg

Phosphorus

Most likely, phosphorus does not come to mind when you contemplate what keeps your teeth and bones strong. This mineral is second only to calcium as a bone component. Like calcium, nearly all body phosphorus is found in the skeleton. The small amount not in bones is divided among muscle and nerve tissue, skin, and other organs.

As a part of each and every cell's genetic material, phosphorus is critical for proper growth and renewal. Phosphorus is particularly important as a component of cell membranes, which guard against cell destruction, and phosphorus plays a major role in energy release.

RECOMMENDED DIETARY ALLOWANCES:
Phosphorus needs are highest for pregnant and lactating women, teenagers, and young adults, who all require 1,200 mg daily. Men and women over the age of 24 need 800 mg daily. According to the National Academy of Sciences, phosphorous deficiency is very rare in healthy people.

THE FORMATIVE YEARS

Nearly half of all bone is formed during the teen years. That's why it is crucial for teens and young adults to meet their calcium needs. Several studies show that girls and young women fall short of their calcium requirement. Why? For one, girls may go on diets at young ages, resulting in nutrient deficiencies. Teenagers, especially girls, often shortchange themselves of calcium by choosing soft drinks over milk. The avoidance of milk, yogurt, and cheese may be fueled by the perception of dairy products as high in calories, fat, and cholesterol, which is largely untrue: There are many delicious and nutritious nonfat and low-fat dairy foods on the market today.

CALCIUM-PACKING TIPS

Don't like the taste of milk straight up? Here's how to pack calcium into your diet.

- Drink low-fat chocolate milk or hot cocoa, or try disguising milk in a fruity frappe. Blend fruit with eight ounces of milk and two ice cubes in a blender or food processor.

- Add a slice of low-fat cheese to your lunchtime sandwich.

- Snack on low-fat or nonfat fruited yogurt instead of cookies or candy.

- Rely on frozen yogurt or ice milk to satisfy your sweet tooth.

- Have cereal with low-fat milk or yogurt for breakfast instead of a muffin or pastry.

- Enjoy pudding prepared with skim or low-fat milk for dessert.

- Include more green, leafy vegetables, including broccoli, collard greens, and mustard greens.

- Eat more canned salmon and sardines with bones.

- Buy tofu processed with calcium sulfate and mix with stir-fried vegetables and rice for a high-calcium meal.

- Add blackstrap molasses to hot cereal.

- Sip calcium-fortified beverages, such as fortified orange juice, instead of soft drinks.

EVER PRESENT: Not only is phosphorus everywhere in the body, but it is present in a multitude of foods. Milk, meat, poultry, and fish rank as the best phosphorus sources. In fact, we get most of our phosphorus from these high-protein foods. Baked goods often contain phosphorus-rich additives. Here are some good phosphorus sources:

- Yogurt, low-fat, fruit-flavored, 8 ounces—247 mg

- Tofu, firm, ½ cup—239 mg

- Steak tenderloin, lean, 3.5 ounces—238 mg

- Milk, 1% fat, 8 ounces—235 mg

- Salmon, Atlantic, cooked, 3 ounces—218 mg

- White beans, boiled, 1 cup—202 mg

- Eggs, 2—178 mg

- Whole-wheat bread, 2 slices—130 mg

Magnesium

Magnesium is often overlooked as contributing to bone strength. Upwards of 60 percent of body magnesium is found in bone tissue. The remainder is distributed evenly for use amongst every cell in your body.

Magnesium is needed for numerous tasks, including muscle contraction, protein synthesis, cell reproduction, energy metabolism, and nutrient transport. Deficiencies can be caused by prolonged illness, alcoholism, and poor diet. A low magnesium level could result in a fatally abnormal heartbeat.

RECOMMENDED DIETARY ALLOWANCES: Adult men over the age of 24 need 350 mg of magnesium daily, whereas women require 280 mg. Pregnant women need 320 mg daily. Lactating women require 340 to 355 mg daily.

AU NATURAL: Unprocessed foods, particularly whole grains, contain high levels of magnesium. Processing strips grains of their magnesium-rich wheat germ and outer hull. Legumes and nuts are fine magnesium sources. Bananas are magnesium-rich, but other fruits are not.

- Tuna fish, light, 3 ounces—81 mg

- Cashews, dry-roasted, 1 ounce—74 mg

- Wheat germ, ¼ cup—70 mg

- Black beans, cooked, ½ cup—60 mg

- Banana, medium—33 mg

The mineral needs of pregnant women are considerably higher than other women. Calcium and phosphorus, both abundant in milk, are crucial to the fetus' bone development.

The majority of our diet's sodium doesn't come from the salt we add to our food, but is hidden in prepared and fast food.

Sodium

Ask nearly anyone and chances are they'll say sodium is bad for you; it makes you retain fluid; or it causes high blood pressure. But for all the negative press sodium receives, it is really quite valuable. Sodium helps the body strike the perfect fluid balance, participates in muscle contraction, and helps nutrients and wastes get in and out of cells.

SHAKE IT OFF: Here's one for you: Where do Americans get most of their sodium? If you said processed foods, go to the head of the class. Nearly 75 percent of our sodium is found in the likes of fast-food french fries, burgers, store-bought cookies and crackers, snack chips, pizza, and frozen dinners. About 15 percent is added at the table and in food preparation, and a mere 10 percent of the sodium we eat is present naturally in foods.

RECOMMENDED INTAKE: There is no sodium RDA. But there are suggested minimum and maximum consumption levels. According to the Food and Nutrition Board, adults need a mere 500 mg of sodium daily for top efficiency.

IS THAT ALL THERE IS? Health professionals have established your minimum sodium requirement at 500 mg per day, but few people could keep to a diet with such a low sodium level. What's more, you'd be hard pressed to limit yourself to that little, since many common foods contain naturally occurring sodium. The National Academy of Sciences also suggests a

maximum sodium intake of no more than 2,400 mg of sodium daily, which is a more realistic and helpful recommendation.

WE EAT TOO MUCH: Our diet is jam-packed with sodium, courtesy of processed foods. Research suggests that many people eat far more than 2,400 mg daily. Is this a problem? If you are one of the 25 percent of American adults who suffer from high blood pressure, the answer is yes. A high-sodium diet can aggravate high blood pressure. Worst of all, too much sodium can work against the medication you may be taking to normalize blood pressure. (For more about sodium and high blood pressure, see pages 83–84.)

SODIUM SOURCES: Sodium is present in nearly every food. It is added to hundreds of processed foods, in the form of salt, soy sauce, monosodium glutamate (MSG), sodium benzoate, sodium caseinate, sodium citrate, sodium nitrate, sodium saccharin, baking powder, and baking soda. Sometimes you can't even taste it. Here are some leading sources:

- Salt, 1 teaspoon—2,300 mg
- Chicken noodle soup, 1 can—880–990 mg
- Chocolate pudding, from instant mix, 1 cup—952 mg
- Double fast-food hamburger with lettuce and tomato—825 mg
- Canadian bacon, grilled, 2 ounces—719 mg

IS SODIUM TO BLAME FOR HIGH BLOOD PRESSURE?

Whether a high-sodium intake causes high blood pressure is debatable. An estimated ten percent of the population is so-called *sodium sensitive*. That means that a high-sodium diet increases their blood pressure more readily. The Food and Nutrition Board's sodium recommendations are conservative for two reasons: (1) It's difficult to tell who is sodium sensitive, because there is no test for it; and (2) almost everyone's blood pressure goes up to some degree with a high-sodium diet. Furthermore, high blood pressure is often symptom-free, so your blood pressure could get too high and you would be unaware that your sodium intake is dangerously exacerbating the problem. You may want to limit your sodium intake to the recommended 2,400 mg per day as a precautionary measure. Out-of-control blood pressure is very serious. It is a major risk factor for heart disease and increases your chance for stroke (see pages 83–84).

- Hot dog, 2 ounces—585 mg
- Cottage cheese, 1% milk fat, ½ cup—459 mg
- Peas, canned, 1 cup—372 mg

POTASSIUM

Potassium plays a role in normal muscle activity, the transmission of nervous impulses, fluid balance, and the regulation of blood pressure. If too much sodium is the dietary devil in blood pressure control, then potassium is positively angelic. Current research suggests that adding more potassium to the diet may help to bring down blood pressure and keep it within a healthy range.

RECOMMENDED INTAKE: The Food and Nutrition Board of the National Academy of Sciences suggests that adults consume at least 1,600 to 2,000 mg of potassium daily. Some researchers recommend a minimum of 3,500 mg daily to keep blood pressure in line.

Because potassium is so widespread in foods, deficiencies are rare, but if you're taking medication to control high blood pressure, you may need added potassium. Some medications, including diuretics, cause potassium loss. At the very least, you should make an effort to consume more potassium-filled foods. Ask your doctor, dietitian, or pharmacist if you need added potassium.

POTASSIUM LURKS WHERE YOU LEAST EXPECT: Say potassium and people go for bananas, but this healthy fruit is hardly the sole source of potassium. For instance, one cup of plain low-fat yogurt contains more potassium than a medium banana. Bran cereals, meat, fish, and poultry are good potassium sources, too.

Potassium is present in nearly all foods, but processing causes potassium loss. That is why the freshest foods contain the most potassium. Here are some good potassium sources:

- Raisins, seeded, ⅔ cup—825 mg
- Cantaloupe, diced, 1 cup—494 mg
- Broccoli, cooked, 1 cup—456 mg
- Grapefruit, ½ medium—400 mg

OUT WITH THE SODIUM, IN WITH THE POTASSIUM

A low-sodium, high-potassium diet may keep your blood pressure in line. In general, sodium is found where potassium is lacking: in highly processed foods. There's your first clue about getting more of the mineral you need. Here are some more:

- Choose the least-processed breakfast cereals with little, or no added sodium. For example, old-fashioned and one- or five-minute oatmeal have much less sodium than the instant packets of oatmeal. Most ready-to-eat cereals contain sodium, some more than others. Many high-fiber wheat-bran cereals are rich in potassium.
- Rely on fresh or frozen vegetables. Steam lightly to preserve nutrient content, and resist the urge to salt them at the table. Use a different spice—black pepper, perhaps.
- Choose fruit over baked goods and vending machine items for snacks. Fruit is high in potassium.
- Don't overlook dairy as a viable potassium source.
- Consume fast-food meals infrequently. Fast food contains little potassium and loads of sodium.

- Sweet potato, with skin, baked, 1 medium—397 mg
- Strawberries, 1 cup—354 mg
- Milk, any type, 8 ounces—about 233 mg

IRON

Your body contains a minute amount of iron. Men carry around an amount equal in weight to about one teaspoon of water, and women have even less. Yet, every bit is precious. Although it is considered a trace mineral, iron is paramount to life.

Iron is crucial for oxygen transport, energy production, and a healthy immune system. Hemoglobin, a component of red blood cells, uses iron to ferry oxygen to each cell; upwards of 70 percent of your iron is attached to red blood cells. A low-iron diet could result in iron-deficiency anemia and a decreased resistance to infection. The symptoms include fatigue, sluggishness, irritability, and inability to concentrate. (For more about anemia, see pages 49–50.)

Food contains two types of iron, heme and nonheme, so named for the presence, or absence, of the iron-containing portion of hemoglobin, known as heme.

ANIMAL VERSUS VEGETABLE: Animal foods, including meat, poultry, and seafood, contain both types of iron. Plant foods, such as dried beans, grains, and vegetables, contain nonheme iron only.

Your body absorbs heme iron the best. Animal flesh, such as red meat and steak, enhances iron absorption. Furthermore, animal foods are treasure troves of iron. In fact, most of the iron we eat comes from meat, poultry, and seafood, but you may be surprised to know that we get almost as much iron from cereals, breads, and grains fortified with nonheme iron. Some dried fruits and beans are good iron sources, too.

RECOMMENDED DIETARY ALLOWANCES: Until menopause, women need more iron. From age 24 to 51, adult women should consume 15 mg of iron daily; men need 10 mg. After 51, both men and women require 10 mg to satisfy the RDA. Pregnant women require 30 mg of iron daily, whereas lactating women need 15 mg.

POPEYE WAS WRONG: Spinach is not a good source of iron. It may look great on paper, but in reality, the iron from spinach is poorly absorbed. Spinach contains oxalates, substances that render iron unavailable to your body. Also prone to oxalates is the iron in lentils and wheat germ. Vitamin C may counteract some of the oxalates; a glass of orange juice with your lentil soup can boost your iron absorption. Here are some of the best iron sources:

- Oysters, cooked, 3 ounces—11 mg

- Instant oatmeal, cooked, 1 packet—6.3 mg

- Fast-food hamburger, 1 patty, 3 ounces, cooked— 2.4 mg

Red meat, although high in fat, is a great source of many nutrients, including iron.

- Apricots, dried, 5 whole—1.8 mg

- Chickpeas, cooked, ½ cup—1.6 mg

IODINE

Iodine directs your calorie-burning rate as part of the hormone thyroxin, which is produced in the thyroid gland. Thyroxin production falters without iodine. A deficiency results in an enlargement of the thyroid gland known as a goiter, and symptoms include sluggishness and weight gain due to an abnormally low metabolic rate. Goiter is not reversible, but it is preventable with adequate iodine consumption.

The threat of iodine deficiency has largely been eradicated in this country. That's because many salt producers have been adding iodine to table salt during production since 1924. About 50 percent of salt is iodized and will say so on the label. Surprisingly, most of our iodine comes from baked goods and milk. That's because iodine is part of the dough softeners used in commercially prepared breads and is also present in cow's feed.

UNDER THE SEA: Iodine is present naturally in the ocean, so seafood and seaweed are excellent and reliable iodine sources. But not everyone lives near the ocean, nor does everyone eat seafood. Because soil is generally iodine poor, people in landlocked areas may be at risk for iodine deficiency, especially those who have poor access to food from outside of their immediate area.

RECOMMENDED DIETARY ALLOWANCES: Men and women over the age of 24 should get 150 micrograms (µg) per day. Pregnant women

MAKING THE MOST OF IRON

The only drawback to plant iron is that it is not well absorbed by the body, but you can boost iron availability with vitamin C. Consuming a vitamin C–rich food with nonheme iron enhances its absorption rate. For example, pair orange juice with an iron-fortified breakfast cereal. Combining heme iron with nonheme improves nonheme's absorption, too. Meat and vegetables are a good example of this type of teamwork.

Iron is the sensitive type. Coffee, tea, bran, and phytates—iron-binding food substances found mainly in whole-grain products and legumes—decrease nonheme iron absorption. That's why it's a bad idea to wash down iron-rich food or iron supplements with coffee or tea, decaffeinated or not. To help nonheme iron absorption, limit coffee and tea drinking to between meals.

require 175 µg daily, and lactating women require 200 µg per day.

FLUORIDE

If there is one food element that can prevent tooth decay, it's fluoride. Fluoride is found in bones, too, where it lends strength and structure.

DECAY BUSTER: Fluoride is absorbed in the digestive tract and then routed to the teeth, bones, or to the urine for excretion. Fluoride is incorporated into developing tooth enamel, giving teeth added strength to deter decay. Along with regular brushing and flossing, fluoride helps combat the erosive effects of tooth-rotting acid produced by the bacteria in the mouth that feast on carbohydrate. Some research suggests that fluoride may also thwart acid production, in addition to fighting off acid's effects.

DRINK TO STRONG TEETH: Fluoridated water is available in communities in nearly every state. Research shows that communities with fluoridated drinking water have lower rates of tooth decay. Fluoridated water has its greatest effect on developing teeth, up to about age 13, but adults reap the benefits of lifetime exposure to fluoride, too.

RECOMMENDED INTAKE: There is not enough known about fluoride to establish an RDA, but the Food and Nutrition Board of the National Academy of Sciences has set a safe and adequate daily intake for fluoride. They advise adult men and women to consume 1.5 to 4 mg of fluoride daily for good health.

SERVING UP FLUORIDE: Fluoridated water is the most potent source of fluoride. Tea is a rich source, made even richer when prepared with fluoridated water. Fish, especially the type eaten with bones

Lobster, if available in your area, can be a great treat that replenishes your iodine, zinc, and copper supplies.

Fluoridated water is the best source of fluoride. If it is not in your area, be vigilant about consuming other sources.

intact, such as salmon and sardines, is a good source of fluoride, too. Cooking in pans coated with a fluoride-packed nonstick lining increases food fluoride levels, as does preparing foods in fluoridated water.

ZINC

Zinc is part of more than 200 enzymes that direct myriad cell functions, including protein digestion and carbohydrate metabolism. Zinc is versatile: It aids in wound healing; it's part of the hormone insulin, which regulates blood glucose levels; it helps the body make genetic material and proteins; it's involved in normal fetal growth and development; and it is vital for normal sexual reproduction.

Deficiency symptoms include poor appetite and poor growth, rough and dry skin, slow wound healing, and a reduced resistance to disease.

BORDERING ON DEFICIENCY: According to government consumption surveys, the per capita zinc intake is about 12 mg daily, not enough to meet any

Seafood is rich in iodine, zinc, and copper. If you don't live where fresh seafood is available, seek out alternate sources.

adult's RDA. Studies show that many seniors are on the brink of zinc deficiency; they get a mere 7 to 10 mg of zinc a day.

RECOMMENDED DIETARY ALLOWANCES: Adult men over 24 require 15 mg of zinc daily, whereas women need 12 mg. Pregnancy boosts zinc requirements to 15 mg, and lactating women need 16 to 19 mg daily. Too much zinc can upset the body's balance with the mineral copper.

ZOOMING IN ON ZINC: Like iron, most of the zinc in our diets comes from animal products. Meat and seafood harbor the highest zinc levels. Some of the richest zinc foods include:

- Crab, Alaska king, cooked, 3 ounces—6.5 mg
- Lamb, loin, roasted, 3.5 ounces—3.41 mg
- Pork loin, broiled, 3.5 ounces—2.5 mg
- Lobster, cooked, 3 ounces—2.5 mg
- Turkey, skinless, light meat, roasted, 3 ounces—2 mg
- Peas, cooked, 1 cup—1.9 mg

SELENIUM

In 1989, the Food and Nutrition Board of the National Academy of Sciences added an RDA for selenium for the first time. Compared with some other minerals, little is known about selenium's exact role in keeping us healthy. Human needs have been largely determined from animal studies.

Selenium is considered an important antioxidant, and it is part of an enzyme that fights off free radicals, by-products of metabolism lethal to cells (see page 45). Selenium teams up with vitamin E to protect cells from destruction.

Selenium is necessary for the growth of cells. Extremely low intake increases the likelihood of heart abnormalities, perhaps because of free radical damage. Deficiency symptoms may include poor growth, poor appetite, and dizziness.

RECOMMENDED DIETARY ALLOWANCES: Men over the age of 24 need 70 µg of selenium daily; women require 55 µg. Pregnant women need 65 µg, and breast-feeding moms should get 75 µg daily.

SELENIUM SOURCES: High-protein foods, such as seafood, kidney, liver, and meat, are selenium-rich, but the exact selenium content of foods has not been pinned down. Grains are good sources, but their content varies with the amount of selenium in the soil in which they are grown.

COPPER

Copper is a little-known mineral with a big role in good health. This mineral is necessary to produce a number of enzymes that direct metabolism. It plays a role in connective-tissue synthesis, the proper use of iron, and red blood cell formation, to name a few. A copper deficiency may result in anemia, nervous system malfunctions, and heart problems.

RECOMMENDED INTAKE: There is no RDA for copper, but there is a suggested daily intake. Adults should get between 1.5 and 3 mg of copper daily.

COPPER'S CONTRIBUTORS: Copper is found in a variety of foods, primarily in muscle tissue, including meat and seafood. Cooking acidic foods, such as tomato sauce, in copper pans increases copper content. Here are some good copper sources:

- Lobster, cooked, 3 ounces—1.6 mg
- Clams, cooked, 3 ounces—0.6 mg
- Navy beans, cooked, ½ cup—0.27 mg
- Spaghetti, whole-wheat, 1 cup—0.25 mg
- Bread, whole-wheat, 2 slices—0.17 mg

MANGANESE

Manganese is mainly involved with proper sexual reproduction and the regulation of carbohydrate, protein, and fat metabolism. Deficiency results in an inability to reproduce, poor growth, and abnormal bone formation.

RECOMMENDED INTAKE: Manganese does not have an RDA. According to the National Academy of Science's Food and Nutrition Board, adults need between 2 and 5 mg of manganese daily.

MANAGING MANGANESE: Plant foods are rich in manganese. Some sources of this little-known nutrient include:

- Pineapple, 1 cup—2.6 mg
- Brown rice, medium grain, cooked, 1 cup—2.1 mg
- Raspberries, 1 cup—1.3 mg
- Peanuts, dry roasted, 1 ounce—0.58 mg
- Strawberries, 1 cup—0.43 mg

CHROMIUM

In working with insulin, a hormone that controls blood glucose levels, chromium is a gatekeeper of sorts. Insulin is the key to the lock on all cells. Insulin must bind with cells to allow blood glucose to get in, and chromium facilitates this hookup. Because chromium deficiency causes a decline in circulating insulin, resulting in uncontrolled blood glucose levels that mimic diabetes, it is necessary for normal metabolic function. Low chromium levels do not

Peanuts provide varying amounts of several important minerals—among them, manganese, chromium, and molybdenum.

Delicious, low in saturated fat, packed with minerals from calcium to zinc—fish is one dish that you should not skip.

cause diabetes, however. Recent research suggests that tissue stores of chromium decline with age, which may explain why some older people have difficulty keeping blood glucose levels in check.

RECOMMENDED INTAKE: Until there is more information about chromium, the Food and Nutrition Board of the National Academy of Sciences has determined a safe and adequate daily intake for chromium, rather than an RDA. Adults should consume between 50 and 200 µg per day of chromium.

FOOD SOURCES: Calf's liver, brewer's yeast, American cheese, wheat germ, mushrooms, prunes, nuts, and asparagus are all good sources.

MOLYBDENUM

Little is known about molybdenum or symptoms of its deficiency. Experts say that it appears to have a wide range of metabolic functions, including a role in oxygen transfer.

RECOMMENDED INTAKE: There is no RDA for molybdenum, but the Food and Nutrition Board of the National Academy of Sciences suggests that adults consume 75 to 250 µg daily.

FOOD SOURCES: Molybdenum is widespread in foods. Data is lacking on the exact content of molybdenum in foods, but milk, beans, bread, cereals, legumes, grains, pork, fish, and nuts are considered good sources.

PROTEIN

Protein is paramount. Without it, life would be impossible. Protein is needed for such lofty functions as the cultivation of cells; the transportation of fat and cholesterol; the formation of the enzymes and hormones that regulate life; the control of fluid balance; and in a pinch, the supply of energy.

Yes, protein is wonderful. But we give it more dietary emphasis than it deserves. We eat too much protein and, in the process, get more fat and cholesterol than we should. Even though plant and animal foods provide this vital nutrient, all too often, the typical American meal centers around animal protein sources, such as meat, poultry, and fish. Yet, many adults would do just fine with about half as much protein as they do.

IT'S NOT THE PROTEIN YOUR BODY'S AFTER

The idea of a protein requirement is a bit misleading. What your body is really after is the building blocks of protein called *amino acids*. You need 21 different amino acids, but your body makes only 12; the other 9 must come from food. These 9 amino acids that your body cannot make are called the *essential amino acids*. Despite what their name suggests, they are no more important to your life functions than the amino acids that your body can produce.

Eggs are the gold standard of protein. Egg protein contains all the essential amino acids necessary to support life. Other animal foods, such as milk and seafood, provide nearly all of the essential amino acids in sufficient amounts.

Plant foods, including bread, rice, and beans, are a different story. They contain fewer essential amino acids, and unlike animal foods, no single plant food supplies every essential amino acid.

BREAK DOWN, BUILD UP

Like a child playing with blocks, your body takes apart protein chains only to put them back together again. During digestion, the body breaks down protein into amino acids. These amino acids help replenish the body's "amino acid pool," the lumberyard containing the raw materials for building the proteins needed for good health.

Amino acids are used to build proteins such as hair, nails, red blood cells, tendons, ligaments, and antibodies

PROTEIN—HOW MUCH IS ENOUGH?

Protein needs are greatest during infancy, adolescence, pregnancy, and lactation. The National Academy of Sciences has set protein-intake standards, which are included below. Don't worry if you don't get the exact amount listed every day. These values are averages, so if you eat a bit less on one day, try to make it up on the next.

Age (years)	Weight (pounds)	Protein (grams)
Infants		
0–0.5	13	13
0.5–1.0	20	14
Children		
1–3	29	16
4–6	44	24
7–10	62	28
Adolescents		
Male		
11–14	99	45
15–18	145	59
Female		
11–14	101	46
15–18	120	44
Adults		
Male		
19–24	160	58
25–50	174	63
51+	170	63
Female		
19–24	128	46
25–50	138	50
51+	138	50
Pregnant		60
Lactating		
First six months		65
Second six months		62

Note: Adult athletes: Multiply your body weight in pounds by 0.45 to get your protein requirement.

The egg is one of the most complete protein sources. It contains all the amino acids that your body cannot produce itself.

(antidisease agents). Amino acids also play a role in relaying nervous system messages throughout the body. Some lend color to hair, skin, and eyes; others are part of a hormone that regulates your calorie-burning capacity, and still others form enzymes, cell membranes, and genetic material.

Cells contain the genetic blueprints that direct the construction of these thousands of different proteins. Each protein has a unique amino acid sequence. The pattern for connective tissue differs from the one for the hormone, insulin, for example. No amino acid substitutions are allowed: All the required amino acids must be available for protein synthesis to occur; if even one is missing, the process fails, and the protein cannot be made.

DIETERS BEWARE

A calorie shortage will force your body to start converting protein to energy. Protein has as many calories as carbohydrate, but using protein for fuel is not a good move. It takes calories to reorganize protein's chemical structure, which only exacerbates the calorie-shortage problem. To make matters worse, the breakdown of protein for energy generates waste products that must be excreted in the urine, which may strain the kidneys. Above all, sacrificing protein for energy means that its other vital tasks go undone, which may lead to poor health; it's like using good lumber for firewood.

THE PERILS OF LOW-PROTEIN DIETS

When your diet lacks protein, your body turns to its own protein-packed tissues, such as muscles, for amino acids. While protein can be converted to energy, your body cannot make carbohydrate and fat into protein. Faced with a prolonged, severe protein

deficiency, lean tissue, including your organs, begins to weaken as your body starts to dismantle itself for needed spare parts.

DO ATHLETES NEED MORE PROTEIN?

Yes, but not a whole lot. Many athletes try to beef up on high-protein diets, with the idea that more protein makes bigger muscles. That isn't necessarily so. While good nutrition is critical for peak performance, muscle is built through exercise, not by eating excessive protein.

Contrary to popular belief, there is no direct route from your mouth to your muscles. After you digest protein, either the amino acids are used to make body proteins, or they are broken down for energy. Like carbohydrates, if protein and energy needs have been met, the excess is converted to fat and stored in the fat tissue.

Athletes may need a little more protein than their nonactive counterparts, though, according to The

Body builders go on high-protein diets to bulk up, but the relationship of protein to muscles is not that simple.

HIGH–PROTEIN FOODS AND THEIR FAT CONTENT

Part of the problem with finding good protein sources is the fat that often comes with them. In general, vegetable sources of protein are lower in fat than meat sources, and they contain zero cholesterol.

The trick to a low-fat diet is moderation. You don't need to make every food choice a low-fat one, but you do need to balance high-fat foods with low-fat ones. Use this chart to choose more low-fat sources of protein.

Food	Calories	Protein (grams)	Fat (grams)
Barley, pearled, cooked, 1 cup	193	4	1
Beef, extra lean, baked,			
3.5 ounces	268	23	16
Bulgur, cooked, 1 cup	152	6	trace
Cheese, 1 ounce			
American	106	6	9
Part-skim mozzarella	90	6	5
Chicken, roasted, 3.5 ounces			
white meat, no skin	173	31	5
dark meat, no skin	205	27	10
Egg, 1 large	75	6	5
Garbanzo beans, cooked, 1 cup	285	12	3
Kidney beans, boiled, 1 cup	225	16	1
Lentils, boiled, 1 cup	231	18	1
Lobsters, cooked, 3 ounces	83	17	1
Milk, 8 ounces			
whole	150	8	8
skim	86	8	0
Pasta, cooked, 1 cup	197	6	1
Peanut butter, 2 tablespoons	190	9	16
Pork, center loin, broiled,			
3.5 ounces	316	27	22
Rice, cooked, long grain, 1 cup			
white	264	6	1
brown	216	5	2
Salmon, Atlantic, cooked,			
3 ounces	155	22	7
Sea scallops, 3.5 ounces	59	11	1
Shrimp, cooked, 3.5 ounces	84	18	1
Tofu, raw, 1/2 cup	94	10	6
Tortilla, 1	67	2	1
Tuna, white, drained, 3 ounces	116	23	7
Walnuts, black, dried, 1 ounce	182	4	16
Wheat germ, 1/4 cup	104	7	3
Yogurt, low fat, fruited, 8 ounces	225	9	3

American Dietetic Association. For example, a 125-pound woman needs about 45 grams of protein daily. Her athletic counterpart needs about 58 grams, a mere 13 grams more, the amount found in about 12 ounces of milk; two ounces of meat, chicken, or fish; or two tablespoons of peanut butter and eight ounces of yogurt—not the enormous difference you might think.

Athletes eat more food, and by making wise food choices, they will get the extra protein they need. That's one of the reasons that athletes are warned against overdosing on protein supplements, such as high-protein drinks and amino acid pills.

Too much protein may actually hurt performance by causing dehydration. As mentioned previously, the process of breaking down protein makes for waste products that must be excreted through the urine, using valuable fluid for waste removal. The National Research Councils' 1989 Diet and Health report cautions against exceeding double the Recommended Dietary Allowance (RDA) for protein.

Assessing Protein Needs

On a pound-per-pound basis, protein needs vary widely across the age spectrum. Infants in their first six months of life require nearly three times as much protein as a 51-year-old man. Adolescents and pregnant or lactating women need more, too.

Most adults need less than you probably think. According to the Food and Nutrition Board of the National Academy of Sciences, the RDA for adult men between the ages of 25 and 50 is 63 grams of protein; women in the same age group require 50 grams. Most of us eat a lot more than that. According to national surveys, the average adult man consumes between 90 and 110 grams of protein daily, whereas the average woman eats between 65 and 70 grams.

Meat, poultry, and fish lead the list of protein sources in the American diet. Dairy foods come in a distant second, and eggs lag way behind.

Please Pass the Plant Protein

Vegetarians, on the other hand, eat less, although enough, protein. They certainly eat less animal protein than people on a mainstream diet. Many vegetarians

A piece of meat has traditionally been the center of meals, but protein and fat may not be a very healthy focus.

vegetarians were encouraged to combine certain plant foods at every meal to provide the full range of essential amino acids at the same time. Eating two plant proteins that made up for each other's amino acid shortcomings formed a "complementary protein" or one that mimicked animal protein in its amino acid profile. One example is the well-known combination of rice mixed with beans.

We now know that this level of conscientiousness is unnecessary. As long as you eat a mixture of proteins from grains, seeds, nuts, legumes, and vegetables throughout the day, you will, more than likely, get enough protein. The amino acids from the rice you ate at lunch can be combined with the amino acids from the beans you had at dinner.

ARE VEGETARIANS HEALTHIER?

According to the statistics, yes. Vegetarians suffer from less heart disease, high blood pressure, diabetes, and cancer than their meat-eating counterparts. Why? Researchers suspect a link between eating excessive amounts of animal protein and certain cancers, even though they admit the difficulty of pinpointing protein, or the fat found in the same high-protein foods, as the culprit.

The health benefits of vegetarianism may also be a compound of many other factors besides the lack of animal protein, though. Vegetarian diets contain more fiber, which may ward off colon cancer, and usually contain less fat and cholesterol, too. (For more about diet and cancer, see pages 55–58.)

rely strictly on plant foods as their protein mainstay, but the term *vegetarianism* covers a wide range.

The majority of American vegetarians subscribe to lacto-ovo-vegetarianism, which includes dairy products and eggs. On the other end of the spectrum are vegans, who eat no animal products whatsoever.

According to The American Dietetic Association, vegetarians can be well-nourished if they make the right food choices. Vegans must be particularly careful to choose wisely. Plants offer some good sources of protein, including grains, nuts, seeds, and legumes, but animal products offer some nutrients that are difficult, if not impossible, to come by on a strict plant-food diet. For example, vegetarians may not get adequate amounts of vitamin D without dairy products or vitamin B_{12} without a fortified cereal or a supplement.

COMPLEMENTING IS PASSÉ

Plants are deficient in one or more essential amino acids. So, in the past,

---

VEGETARIANISM RUNS THE GAMUT

By definition, a vegetarian consumes no meat, poultry, or seafood. Vegetarian diets consist primarily of plant foods including grains, cereal, rice, pasta, nuts, seeds, fruits, and vegetables.

People choose vegetarianism for a wide variety of reasons, which may include one or more of the following: compassion for animals, preference for plant foods, health concerns, religious affiliation, concern about world hunger, and environmental concerns. Vegetarians differ on why they choose vegetarianism over the mainstream American diet. They also differ in their eating styles.

Lacto-ovo-vegetarianism is the most popular in the United States. Although this type excludes flesh foods (meat, poultry, and seafood), it does include dairy products and eggs.

Lacto-vegetarians exclude meat, poultry, and seafood, but eat dairy products. They do not eat eggs.

Vegans do not eat meat, poultry, fish, eggs, dairy products, or any other animal product, including gelatin and lard.

VITAMINS

If carbohydrate, protein, and fat are the energy stars, then the 13 essential vitamins are the supporting cast. Vitamins do not deliver instant vigor, but most of them play a pivotal role in harvesting food energy. Vitamins are involved with the metabolism, digestion, and absorption of carbohydrate, fat, and protein, the fuels that make your body run. Although the body requires some vitamins in amounts too small to imagine, their importance is paramount. Your body is able to make only a few vitamins to any great extent, so you must rely on a balanced and varied diet to satisfy vitamin needs.

FAT OR WATER?

Vitamins are classified as fat- or water soluble. Fat-soluble vitamins, A, D, E, and K, dissolve and are transported in fat. Once in the body, whatever is not used is stored in the liver and fat tissue.

The water-soluble vitamins, B-complex and vitamin C, dissolve and move around in water. While some tissues store more of the water-soluble vitamins than others, the B vitamins and vitamin C don't hang around your body for more than a few days. That's why it's a good idea to satisfy your requirements for the B vitamins and vitamin C almost daily.

VITAMIN A

A IS FOR ALL-IMPORTANT: "Eat your carrots. They're good for your eyes." How true. Vitamin A is vital for good vision, and that's how most people

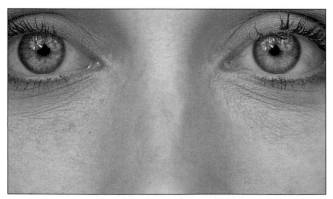

Everyone knows that vitamin A is good for your eyesight, but its other health benefits are not always seen so clearly. Carotinoids, the precursor chemicals that your body converts into vitamin A, may help prevent serious diseases, including certain forms of cancer and possibly even heart disease.

Dark green or deep yellow or orange is usually an indication that the vegetable is a good beta-carotene source.

remember its usefulness. Vitamin A's other roles garner less recognition, but are no less important. For example, vitamin A contributes directly or indirectly to the health of most of your organs. It even has a bearing on your ability to have children. Vitamin A bolsters the immune system and keeps all of your tissues, including your skin, healthy. Deficiencies cause blindness, scaly skin, poor growth, and reproductive failure.

ANIMAL OR VEGETABLE? Animal foods contain vitamin A in its ready-to-use form known as *retinol*. Liver and fish-liver oils are excellent vitamin A sources. Milk provides much of the vitamin A we get from animal foods, but that's because milk is fortified with vitamin A.

Plant foods are excellent sources of vitamin A, too. Fruits and vegetables contain carotenoids, substances that are made into vitamin A by the body.

Beta-carotene is one of the 50 carotenoids found in foods and supplies the largest amount of raw material for vitamin A production, which the body conducts on an as-needed basis. But beta-carotene does more than make itself available for vitamin A production. Unlike vitamin A, beta-carotene is a powerful antioxidant that subdues free radicals, destructive forms of oxygen that are by-products of normal metabolism (see page 45).

Beta-carotene is abundant in most deep orange, yellow, and dark green, leafy fruits and vegetables, including carrots, cantaloupe, acorn squash, sweet potato, and broccoli. You can't always judge a plant by its color: Not every orange, yellow, and dark green plant food is packed with beta-carotene. For example, zucchini is dark green, but contains little beta-carotene.

RECOMMENDED DIETARY ALLOWANCES (RDA):
Adult males 24 and older need 1,000 Retinol
Equivalents (RE) of vitamin A daily; women require
800 RE. Pregnancy does not increase vitamin A
requirements, but breast-feeding women should
consume between 1,200 and 1,300 RE daily. There is
no RDA or any other official recommendation for
beta-carotene consumption.

SATISFYING VITAMIN A NEEDS: Many popular
foods are jam-packed with beta-carotene and retinol,
so meeting your vitamin A needs is rarely
problematic. Here are some good sources:

- Sweet potato, 1 medium, baked—2,488 RE

- Carrot, 1 medium, raw—2,025 RE

- Spinach, cooked, 1 cup—1,474 RE

- Cantaloupe, cubed, 1 cup—516 RE

- Broccoli, cooked, 1 cup—216 RE

- Milk, fortified, 8 ounces—145 RE

VITAMIN SUPPLEMENTATION

Are you a candidate for a vitamin supplement?
Vitamin pills are no substitute for a healthy lifestyle,
which includes weight control, regular exercise, and
quitting smoking. Health experts say that adopting
these healthy habits alone could prevent the majority
of our health problems.

If anything, the American diet is over fortified.
Most processed foods pack hefty amounts of
vitamins and minerals. Yet, some people may need a
supplement at some point in their lives. Are you one
of them? Read on.

- *Dieters:* Even the savviest of dieters will find it
difficult, if not impossible, to get all the nutrients
they need on much less than 1,200 calories a day.
Chronic dieters consuming even lower calorie
levels are at greater risk for dietary deficiencies—
they repeatedly get fewer nutrients than they
require.

- *The elderly:* Older people are at nutritional risk for
a number of reasons, mainly because they eat less.
Studies show that most of the elderly population
take at least one medication, some of which may
interfere with nutrient absorption or cause nutrient
losses. On top of that, some experts feel that the
elderly require more than the RDAs for some
nutrients. Although evidence about the elderly's
nutritional requirements is growing, the matter
remains under investigation.

- *Smokers:* Smokers need more vitamin C,
according to the RDAs. Some researchers say that
smokers need more folate and B_{12}, too, but they
seldom get what they need. Smokers tend to have
poorer nutritional habits than their nonsmoking
counterparts. Smoking decreases sense of taste and
may change it so that smokers end up avoiding certain
healthy foods altogether.

- *Heavy drinkers:* Alcohol robs the body of vital
nutrients. In addition, drinkers are prone to unhealthy
eating habits, which adds insult to injury. The bottom
line is that drinkers come up short for most nutrients,
particularly the B vitamins, folate, thiamin, and
vitamin B_6.

- *Women in their childbearing years:* The U.S.
Public Health Service recommends a daily supplement of 400 µg of folate for all women who can
become pregnant, because the proper folate intake can
cut the risk of birth defects in half. Getting much-
needed folate from foods may be difficult, especially
because Americans rarely get the required amount of
folate-packed fruits and vegetables. While supplements cannot compensate for an unhealthy diet,
women may benefit by taking a multivitamin with
adequate folate to make sure they are getting all the
nutrients they need for the health of their future child.

- *Vegetarians:* Vegans, who avoid all animal products,
should consider vitamin supplements. Animal
products are excellent sources of vitamins B_{12} and D.
In fact, animal products alone provide naturally
occurring B_{12}. A multivitamin that supplies no more
than 100 percent of the RDAs may be useful.

- *People who omit an entire food group:* For
example, if you leave out milk, cheese, and yogurt
from your diet, you are at risk for inadequate amounts
of vitamin D and a lower-than-desirable B vitamin
intake, not to mention the mineral calcium. Consider a
multivitamin with no more than 100 percent of the
RDAs.

VITAMIN D

THE BONE VITAMIN: You know that calcium is necessary for strong teeth and bones. Well, calcium would be out of work if not for vitamin D. Vitamin D regulates blood calcium levels, encourages the incorporation of calcium into the bones, and prevents faulty bone growth. Vitamin D heads off rickets, or soft bones, in the young, and the brittle bone disease, osteoporosis, in older people.

LET THE SUN SHINE: After all the bad press unprotected exposure to sunlight has received, you may be surprised to find out that sunlight sparks vitamin D production. The process begins in the skin, where an immature form of vitamin D lurks. Strong ultraviolet rays activate the conversion process, which is finished off in the liver and kidneys. Healthy people who get 10 to 15 minutes of sun every summer day typically make enough to last the year, but remember not to overdo it.

SO WHY THE RECOMMENDED DIETARY ALLOWANCE? If we make vitamin D, then why has the Food and Nutrition Board of the National Academy of Sciences established a dietary goal? Because many of us do not get enough sun to produce the vitamin D we need.

The elderly head the list of people at risk for vitamin D deficiency. Seniors may have limited exposure to sunlight. Their bodies produce only about half as much vitamin D as younger people, because their aging skin has lost some of its ability to initiate the conversion process.

Sunscreens that block damaging rays also stifle vitamin D production. So does having dark skin. Production is also hampered by excessive tanning and air pollution.

RECOMMENDED DIETARY ALLOWANCES: Adults over 24 need 100 International Units (IU) of vitamin D daily. Pregnant and lactating women require 400 IU of vitamin D daily.

HURRAH FOR FORTIFICATION: Unlike several of its peers, vitamin D is not widely distributed in foods. It's present naturally in eggs, liver, and sardines, but the predominant source of vitamin D in the American diet is milk. Milk, which also boasts hefty amounts of naturally occurring calcium, is fortified with vitamin D.

- Milk, fortified, 8 ounces—100 IU
- Margarine, 1 tablespoon—60 IU
- Fortified breakfast cereal, per serving—40–50 IU
- Egg, 1 large—25 IU

THE RECOMMENDED DIETARY ALLOWANCES: SEPARATING FACT FROM FICTION

The Recommended Dietary Allowances (RDAs) are goals for nutrient intakes determined by the Food and Nutrition Board of the National Academy of Sciences. The first RDA edition appeared in 1943. RDAs are revised periodically to reflect the latest scientific findings about nutrient needs.

The RDAs define the nutrient needs of nearly all healthy Americans. The standards are designed with age, sex, and stage of life in mind. RDAs delineate between men and women, encompass ten age categories, and provide goals for pregnancy and lactation. However, people who have special nutritional needs as a result of disease are not included.

Only when the research is conclusive does the Board issue an RDA. The Board is very cautious; while there are more than 40 recognized essential nutrients, the Board has set standards for only 19, 11 of them vitamins. That shows how much more there is to learn. The committee also designates safe and adequate intakes for 7 other nutrients, including fluoride, and has established minimum daily requirements for the minerals sodium, potassium, and chloride.

RDAs are average intake goals as opposed to minimum daily requirements. In other words, they are set high enough to enable your body to go for a few days without some nutrients, particularly the water-soluble vitamins, which are stored only briefly in body tissues. For example, consuming only half the RDA for vitamin C on Tuesday will not render you unhealthy if you make up for it on Wednesday and Thursday by getting a bit more than the RDA.

RDAs are considered by many to be the last word in nutrient requirements. Yet, they do not account for individual differences. They are general requirements for nutrient intake and serve as general goals rather than personal standards. For that reason, each recommendation includes a generous safety margin. Many people could actually stay quite healthy on far less than the designated amounts.

Some exposure to sunlight sparks vitamin D production. Be careful not to overexpose yourself; the sun can damage skin.

VITAMIN E

THE BODY GUARD: That's a not-so-technical, but accurate, term for vitamin E's mission. In short, vitamin E takes the hit for cells and for vitamin A, which would otherwise be destroyed by free radicals, by-products of normal metabolism and of exposure to pollutants, such as cigarette smoke and smog (see page 45).

Luckily, the body possesses an elaborate system to cope with free radicals. Cells have natural enzymes that squelch free radicals and destroy harmful products. Vitamin E is part of this system, which is also supported by vitamin C, the mineral selenium, and beta-carotene.

RECOMMENDED DIETARY ALLOWANCES: Adult men over the age of 24 need 10 milligrams (mg) of vitamin E daily; women need 8 mg. Pregnancy bumps women's requirement up to 10 mg per day. Breast-feeding moms need 11 to 12 mg daily.

STAND BY ME: Since vitamin E is widespread in foods, deficiency is rare except in premature, very low–birth-weight babies and in people who cannot properly absorb fat.

Vegetable oils, margarine, and shortening are the most abundant vitamin E sources in the diet. Nuts and wheat germ are good sources, too. Vitamin E is sensitive to overprocessing, which makes the freshest foods richest in vitamin E. Too much cooking destroys vitamin E content.

- Sweet potato, 1 medium—6 mg
- Safflower oil, 1 tablespoon—5 mg
- Wheat germ, ¼ cup—4 mg

- Peanut butter, 2 tablespoons—3 mg
- Margarine, made with safflower oil, 1 tablespoon—2 mg

VITAMIN K

K IS FOR COAGULATION: Think all bacteria is bad? Not so. Certain bacteria in your intestinal tract produce vitamin K, which is required for making at least six blood-clotting proteins. Vitamin K was given new clout in 1989 when it was included for the first time in the National Research Council's RDA. Without vitamin K, your blood would not clot, and you would be susceptible to excessive bleeding that would not stop on its own.

RECOMMENDED DIETARY ALLOWANCES: Adult men over 24 years old need 80 micrograms (µg) of vitamin K daily, while women require 65 µg. Pregnancy and lactation do not increase dietary vitamin K requirements.

VITAMIN K IS WIDESPREAD: Like vitamin E, vitamin K is found in a variety of foods. Green, leafy vegetables are some of the richest food sources. Here are some specifics:

- Spinach, raw, 1 cup—148 µg
- Liver, beef, 3.5 ounces—104 µg
- Broccoli, raw, ½ cup—58 µg
- Tomato, raw, medium—28 µg
- Egg, 1 large—25 µg
- Milk, 8 ounces—10 µg

THE B VITAMINS

When health experts talk of B vitamins, they usually speak of a complex of vitamins that play closely related roles in good health. Most B vitamins are involved with energy metabolism. Put simply, your body needs B vitamins to liberate and use the energy trapped in food.

B IS FOR BALDERDASH: B vitamin supplements are touted as a panacea for stressful, low-energy life-styles, but when your diet suffers due to stress, chances are no amount of B vitamins will remedy the situation. Counting on one or two nutrients to correct dietary shortcomings is putting all your eggs in one basket. You need all of the vitamins, and you should get them from a varied diet.

Black-eyed peas and rice, aside from being a low-fat, high-fiber food choice, dish up healthy amounts of B vitamins.

THIAMIN (VITAMIN B$_1$): Thiamin is a key player in carbohydrate metabolism; that is, the processing of carbohydrates to release their potential as fuel for the body. Thiamin deficiency causes a disease called *beriberi,* a nervous system disorder. The symptoms include pain and paralysis of the legs and arms, swelling, and significant weight loss.

As with most nutrients, the RDA varies for different people: Men 25 to 50 years old require 1.5 mg per day; women in the same age group, 1.1 mg; pregnant women, 1.5 mg per day; and lactating women, 1.6 mg. Men over 50 should get 1.2 mg daily, and women over 51 should get at least 1 mg daily.

Good sources include unrefined cereals and grains, brewer's yeast, organ meats, pork, legumes, nuts, and seeds. Also, enriched and fortified grains, cereals, and baked goods contain certain amounts. Here are the specifics:

- Whole-wheat bread, 2 slices—0.2 mg
- Instant oatmeal, 1 packet—0.5 mg
- Egg noodles, enriched, cooked, 1 cup—0.3 mg
- Liver, beef, 3.5 ounces—0.2 mg
- Navy beans, boiled, ½ cup—0.2 mg
- Lentils, boiled, ½ cup—0.2 mg
- Milk, 1% fat, 8 ounces—0.1 mg

RIBOFLAVIN (B$_2$): Riboflavin plays a role in energy production similar to that of

thiamin and is also important to the health of the skin, lungs, and intestinal lining. Inadequate dietary B$_2$ results in tissue inflammation and breakdown and poor wound healing. Severe deficiency shows itself as a swollen, red tongue, burning, itching eyes, and scaly, greasy skin.

The RDA for men 25 to 50 years old is 1.7 mg; women in the same age group, 1.3 mg; pregnant women, 1.6 mg; lactating women, 1.7 to 1.8 mg. Men over 50 require 1.4 mg daily, and women over 50, 1.2 mg daily.

Meat, poultry, fish, and dairy products are good sources of riboflavin, as are enriched and fortified grains, cereals, and baked products.

- Milk, 1% fat, 8 ounces—0.4 mg
- Low-fat fruited yogurt, 8 ounces—0.4 mg
- Corn tortilla, enriched—0.10 mg
- Chicken, roasted, skinless, 3.5 ounces—0.10 mg
- Cheese, cheddar, 1 ounce—0.10 mg
- Whole-wheat bread, 2 slices—0.10 mg

HANDLE WITH CARE

Want to get the most nutrition for your money? Get close to the source. The least-processed foods often contain the most vitamins, and they're usually the cheapest. Knowing what foods to buy and how to handle them can boost nutrition.

- Go light on the cooking, especially when preparing vegetables. Cooking destroys nutrients. But you can't possibly eat all of your food raw—especially meat and seafood—so you must take care. Use as little nutrient-robbing heat as possible. Pressure cooking, light steaming, and microwaving head the list of nutrient-saving cooking techniques.

- Watch out for water. It steals nutrients. When your food comes into contact with fluid for long periods of time, such as when you cook carrots or potatoes in boiling water, you run the risk of losing precious vitamins. Steam, bake, or microwave to use as little water as possible when cooking vegetables. Save the nutrient-rich water to make soup.

- Buy the freshest produce. It has the most nutrients, although frozen fruits and vegetables are also right up there. They're usually picked ripe and are quickly frozen, so their vitamin content remains high. Canned fruits and vegetables have significantly fewer nutrients than their fresh or frozen counterparts.

- Opt for whole-grain bread, cereals, and pasta. Food made from refined grains, such as white bread, serve up fewer vitamins, minerals, and fiber. Refining strips the grain of its wheat germ and outer layers, which contain important nutrients.

For a source of B vitamins that is easy to incorporate into your daily routine, it's hard to beat a breakfast of fortified cereal.

NIACIN (B₃): Niacin is involved in the body's general metabolism, particularly in the use of fat. Sometimes, it is prescribed by doctors in megadoses to lower blood cholesterol levels, but only in a few cases and never without close monitoring. Niacin deficiency causes a disease called *pellagra* manifested by confusion, apathy, disorientation, nervous disorders, and skin disorders.

The RDA for men 25 to 50 years old is 19 mg daily; women in the same age group, 15 mg; pregnant women, 17 mg; lactating women, 20 mg. Men over 50 require 15 mg daily, and women over 50, 13 mg.

Meat, poultry, seafood, nuts, and fortified and enriched grain products are the major sources of this B vitamin.

- Chicken, roasted, skinless, 3.5 ounces—12 mg
- Tuna fish, water-packed, light, 3 ounces—11 mg
- Fortified breakfast cereal, per serving—about 5 mg
- Ground beef, broiled, 3.5 ounces—5 mg
- Peanut butter, 2 tablespoons, chunky—4 mg
- Rice, white, medium-grain, enriched, 1 cup—4 mg

PYRIDOXINE (B₆): Pyridoxine is needed primarily for protein and fat metabolism. Inadequate pyridoxine intake leads to anemia, irritability, and lack of energy.

The RDA is the same for adults of all ages: Men, 2 mg daily, and women, 1.6 mg daily. Pregnant women require 2.2 mg daily, and lactating women, 2.1 mg daily.

Meat, poultry, and seafood are rich in pyridoxine. Bananas are also an excellent source.

- Banana, 1 medium—0.7 mg
- Chicken, roasted, skinless, 3.5 ounces—0.6 mg
- Pork loin, broiled, 3.5 ounces—0.4 mg
- Tuna fish, water-packed, light, 3 ounces—0.3 mg
- Ground beef, cooked, 3.5 ounces—0.2 mg
- Mixed nuts, dry roasted, 2 ounces—0.2 mg
- Whole-wheat bread, 2 slices—0.1 mg

VITAMIN B₁₂: Vitamin B₁₂ is important in fat and carbohydrate metabolism and helps to make vital proteins for the body. Deficiencies result in pernicious anemia, which is usually caused by an inability to properly absorb vitamin B₁₂.

The RDA for adults over 24 years old is 2 µg. Pregnant women require 2.2 µg; lactating women need 2.6 µg.

Only animal products and seafood contain naturally occurring B₁₂. Fortified grain products are good sources, too.

- Clams, steamed, 3 ounces (19 small)—84 µg
- Salmon, Atlantic, cooked, 3 ounces—2.6 µg
- Tuna fish, water-packed, light, 3 ounces—2.5 µg
- Ground beef, cooked, 3.5 ounces—2.3 µg
- Breakfast cereal, fortified, per serving—1.5–2 µg
- Low-fat fruited yogurt, 8 ounces—1 µg
- Chicken, roasted, 3.5 ounces—0.34 µg

FOLATE: Folate (also known as *folic acid* and *folacin*) is vital for new cell production. It is known to prevent spina bifida and other spinal cord birth defects, which often occur during the first six weeks of pregnancy, usually well before a woman knows she's pregnant. For that reason, the U.S. Public Health Service recommends that all women in their childbearing years take a folate supplement of 400 µg daily, a practice which could cut the risk of birth defects in half. (For more about folate and birth defects, see pages 53–54.) Deficiencies also cause megaloblastic anemia, a blood disorder characterized by underdeveloped blood cells unable to carry sufficient oxygen to cells.

The RDA for men over 25 years old is 200 µg per day; women in the same age group, 180 µg. Pregnant

The word folate *comes from the same root as the word* foliage. *So it shouldn't come as much of a surprise that the best sources of folate are vegetables—especially green, leafy vegetables.*

women require 400 µg daily, and lactating women, 260–280 µg. Note: The U.S. Public Health Service recommendation of 400 µg daily supersedes the RDA for women who could become pregnant because of the serious risks of birth defects.

Sources include dark green, leafy vegetables (the term *folate* comes from the same root as *foliage*), fruit, whole grains, and fortified cereals.

- Spinach, cooked, 1 cup—262 µg
- Lentils, cooked, ½ cup—179 µg
- Chickpeas, cooked, ½ cup—141 µg
- Orange juice, 8 ounces—109 µg
- Broccoli, cooked, 1 cup—78 µg
- Corn, cooked, ½ cup—38 µg
- Avocado, raw, ¼ medium—34 µg

PANTOTHENIC ACID: This B vitamin is involved in carbohydrate, protein, and fat metabolism. Deficient intake may cause low energy levels.

There is no established RDA for this vitamin, largely because information about pantothenic acid is lacking. However, the Food and Nutrition Board of the National Academy of Sciences recommends that adults consume between 4 and 7 mg daily.

Widely distributed in many foods, good sources include animal products, organ meats, seafood, and whole-grain cereals.

- Low-fat fruited yogurt, 8 ounces—1 mg
- Chicken, skinless, roasted, 3.5 ounces—1.1 mg

- Milk, 1% fat, 8 ounces—0.8 mg
- Brown rice, medium grain, cooked, 1 cup—0.8 mg
- Avocado, raw, ¼ medium—0.6 mg
- Peanut butter, chunky, 2 tablespoons—0.3 mg
- Egg noodles, enriched, cooked, 1 cup—0.2 mg

BIOTIN: Biotin helps in fat and glucose production and the metabolism of amino acids, the building blocks of proteins. As with pantothenic acid, there is no established RDA, because information about biotin is lacking, and biotin deficiency is rare. However, the Food and Nutrition Board of the National Academy of Sciences recommends that adults consume between 30 and 100 µg daily.

Cereal and eggs are among the best sources.

- Egg, 1 large—10 µg
- Oat bran cereal, cooked, ⅔ cup—9 µg
- Wheat germ, ¼ cup—7 µg
- Noodles, enriched, cooked, 1 cup—4 µg
- Rice pilaf, prepared mix, 1 cup—4 µg

VITAMIN C

For being one of the most talked about vitamins, there are plenty of myths and misinformation surrounding it. Some of its powers have been blown way out of proportion, and others have been practically forgotten.

C IS NOT FOR CURE-ALL: When winter is in the air, people pop vitamin C pills to prevent colds and flu. If only it were that simple, none of us would get sick. Like so many other nutrients, vitamin C plays a formidable role in keeping your immune system strong so that it may repel the bacteria and viruses that would otherwise make you ill. But in the case of the common cold, viruses overpower your defenses, and there is little to do except ride it out. Colds and flu are caused by a number of germs insensitive to medication and vitamin C remedies.

BUT I FEEL BETTER: Research shows that consuming well over the RDA for vitamin C when you're under the weather may lessen the severity of your symptoms, but understand: Just because some extra vitamin C makes you feel better doesn't necessarily mean large doses are healthy.

As with some other vitamins (niacin, for example), vitamin C in large doses can have an effect that has little to do with its nutritive function. Sometimes, taking too much—upwards of 500 to 2,000 mg per day, for instance—results in bloating, gas, diarrhea, and kidney stones in some individuals.

NOT FOR COLDS ONLY: Vitamin C is versatile. Not only does it boost immunity, it may prevent cancer by heading off tissue damage in much the same way as vitamin E and beta-carotene. One of its most notable roles is in the production of collagen, a connective tissue that holds the body together. Vitamin C deficiency leads to a disease called scurvy. Symptoms include excessive tissue bleeding, swollen gums, loose teeth, and poor wound healing.

Vitamin C also promotes iron-rich blood by improving your body's ability to absorb iron, particularly

The benefits of vitamin C are only now beginning to be recognized. Citrus fruits and fruit juices are the best sources.

nonheme iron. Nonheme iron is primarily found in plant foods and has a lower absorption rate than animal-food iron, known as heme iron. Consuming vitamin C along with iron-rich foods boosts nonheme iron absorption by two to four times, which is of particular interest to vegetarians who shun animal products.

RECOMMENDED DIETARY ALLOWANCES: Nonsmoking adults of all ages need 60 mg of vitamin C daily. Pregnant women require 70 mg; breast-feeding moms need 90 to 95 mg. Smokers need more vitamin C than nonsmokers—at least 100 milligrams daily—because smoking depletes the body's vitamin C supply.

C IS FOR CITRUS: Citrus fruits contribute the most vitamin C to our diets. To satisfy your needs, include at least one vitamin C–rich food daily. Here are some excellent vitamin C sources:

- Orange juice, from frozen concentrate, 8 ounces—97 mg
- Strawberries, 1 cup—85 mg
- Kiwi, medium—75 mg
- Orange, medium—70 mg
- Cantaloupe, cubed, 1 cup—68 mg
- Green pepper, cooked, ½ cup—51 mg
- Grapefruit, pink and red, ½ medium—47 mg
- Potato with skin, medium, baked—26 mg
- Tomato, medium, raw—24 mg

Antioxidant Vitamins: The New Frontier

For years, scientists have known that vitamins are necessary to prevent deficiency diseases, but recent research has cast some vitamins in a new role.

Vitamins C and E, and beta-carotene (a form of vitamin A) are antioxidant vitamins that appear to be potent weapons in the body's ongoing battle with free radicals, destructive forms of oxygen that are thought to initiate diseases such as heart disease and cancer. The products of millions of chemical reactions that your body undergoes for survival, free radicals are roving marauders that wreak havoc on cells through a process known as oxidation.

When free radicals damage DNA, which is key to normal cell reproduction, they have crossed the line

ANTIOXIDANTS—NUTRIENT SUPER HEROES

There's lots of talk these days about how vitamin supplements may help stave off certain illness, including heart disease and cancer. You may have heard about beta-carotene, a form of vitamin A, and vitamins C and E. They've been attracting the most attention for their potential benefits. All the vitamins are crucial to good health, but only a few are antioxidants.

Antioxidants combat the structural damage committed by free radicals, which are destructive forms of oxygen created by your body during normal metabolism.

An oxygen atom is most stable when it contains four electrons in its outer shell, but when the body's normal metabolic processes render it one electron short, a free radical is created, and the oxygen atom goes from friend to foe.

When oxygen atoms lose electrons, they need to replace them in order to equalize themselves. To get what they need, free radicals steal electrons in a process known as oxidation. This becomes problematic when free radicals rob electrons from the membrane surrounding the cell, which may be thought of as a fortress needed to protect the cell's inner workings. It's particularly dangerous when free radicals tamper with DNA, the cells' blueprint for proper replication.

Antioxidants, including beta-carotene, vitamin C, and vitamin E, squelch free radical destruction by donating electrons to the unstable free radicals. In doing so, they halt the destructive forces in their tracks.

One important note: No amount of antioxidant vitamins will prevent aging, and whether taking vitamin supplements is worth it in the long run is unclear. The current research, while exciting, is limited, and the evidence is inconclusive. It may be years before we discover which antioxidant vitamins to take and the amounts that are safe. (For more information about antioxidant vitamins, see page 57.)

FOOD FIRST

It appears that vitamin supplementation is moving beyond correcting deficiencies into the realm of preventive medicine, but until health professionals know more, it is unwise to take vitamin pills haphazardly.

There is a downside to dietary supplements. For one, vitamin pills can be costly. But more importantly, when taken in excess, vitamins can produce unwanted and potentially dangerous side effects. For example, excessive beta-carotene can turn your skin orange; too much vitamin C interferes with the absorption of copper, an important mineral, and can cause diarrhea; and too much vitamin A and D can lead to liver failure, especially in children who process it less efficiently.

from potential pests to real threat. Altered DNA results in abnormal cell production and cell death that, when continued unchecked, may develop into a serious health problem.

Luckily, your body employs a complex system of enzymes to ward off the effects of free radicals. However, repeated exposure to environmental toxins and the inevitable toll of advancing age tax your sophisticated defense mechanism, and cellular destruction and alteration become more frequent. Enter the antioxidant vitamins. Theoretically, if you consume large amounts of beta-carotene and levels of vitamins C and E that far exceed the RDA, you may be able to postpone disease for a longer period.

Recent research suggests that long-term dietary supplementation of beta-carotene may help prevent heart attacks in men with a history of heart disease, and it may help prevent some forms of cancer. Vitamin C supplementation may decrease cataract risk and may decrease heart disease and cancer risk. Taking vitamin E supplements has been shown to reduce the risk of heart disease by 40 percent in men and women. Other research suggests that vitamin E boosts the immune system of the elderly.

Want to add vitamins to your life? Food is your best bet. Fruits, vegetables, and whole-grain products are packed with protective vitamins, fiber, and very little fat. An added bonus: Food contains a multitude of important disease-fighting chemicals other than vitamins that scientists are only beginning to discover. Who knows what other miracle nutrients will be discovered in broccoli or whole-wheat bread? You would miss out if you limited yourself to a handful of pills. Your best bet is still a well-balanced diet. (For more on planning a healthy diet, see chapter 3.)

Unsure about your diet? Have it evaluated by a trained health professional, preferably a registered dietitian. That way, you'll know whether you need a vitamin supplement or a better variety of foods to round out your diet. (For help finding a registered dietitian or just some answers to your specific questions, see the resource list on page 110.)

WATER

Water. How could something so devoid of color, odor, and taste be the elixir of life? Frequently overlooked as part of a healthy diet, water is perhaps the most indispensable of all the nutrients. You could go weeks without eating, but you could only survive a few days without water. That's because every life-sustaining bodily function and chemical process takes place in a watery environment.

WATER, WATER EVERYWHERE

Water is the most abundant component of the body. Water bathes cells, but it is also found on the inside of each cell, too. Every type of tissue contains water, some more than others. Blood is about 83 percent water, whereas more rigid bone tissue contains only about 22 percent. As a newborn, your body was nearly 80 percent water. As you get older, that percentage declines, settling at about 50 percent in older age.

All of life's functions happen in a medium of water. Keeping hydrated should be one of your highest dietary priorities.

A TALL ORDER

Water has many tasks. Not only does it help transport nutrients to, and waste products away from, cells, water also lubricates the digestive tract, moistens tissues, and cushions joints, organs, and the developing fetus. Water plays a leading role in ridding the body of waste products by providing the fluid necessary for urine production.

COOL IT

As if all that wasn't enough, water also serves as a coolant. Your internal temperature, which hovers around 98.6° Fahrenheit (give or take a degree) is regulated primarily through sweating. You sweat to get rid of body heat that would otherwise rise to deadly levels. When sweat, which is mostly water, evaporates from your skin, your body cools down.

Imagine your body as an engine that is always running. Working machines generate heat, and so does your body, even when you are still. You may be more aware of sweating in the summer months, because the air around you is warmer and may be more humid. When it is hot and humid outside, sweat evaporates more slowly, and you do not cool down as rapidly. But even if you don't notice it as much, your body has to sweat to dissipate heat even in the winter.

Without adequate water, your body would be unable to get rid of the heat generated by everyday living and physical activity, because it would be impossible to produce enough sweat.

WATER IN

Water and juice are among the most obvious, and most relied upon, fluid sources. Fluid is found in fruits and vegetables, too, but fatty foods contain little water. That's another reason why a low-fat diet rich in fruits and vegetables is beneficial.

Digestion produces usable water, too. Water is a by-product of the breakdown of carbohydrate, protein, and fat. Protein also requires water to metabolize, though, so there is no net gain of usable water from its breakdown.

WATER OUT

Your body has a mission that it must not fail: Get rid of the cells' waste products or risk a potentially deadly

WATER CONTENT OF COMMON FOODS

Health experts advocate drinking eight eight-ounce glasses of fluid daily. In addition to this, some of the food you eat contains some of the water your body craves, especially fruits and vegetables. High-fat foods, such as crackers, cookies, and oil, contain less.

Food	Percentage water by weight
Lettuce	96
Tomato	94
Green pepper, raw	90
Broccoli, cooked	90
Orange	87
Apricot	86
Blueberries	85
Apple	84
Kiwi	83
Banana	74
Corn, cooked	70
Potato, baked	65
Sweet potato, baked	62
Chicken, cooked	62
Bread, white	37
Vegetable oil	0

situation. To accomplish this task, your body makes up to two quarts of urine daily. Urine is the number one route of water loss. Water is also lost through the digestive tract, the skin, and through breathing.

HOW MUCH IS ENOUGH?

That depends on how much you eat, according to the National Academy of Sciences' Food and Nutrition Board. There is no RDA for water, but health experts have established a safe and adequate intake based on energy intake. You require about 32 ounces of fluid for every 1,000 calories you eat, with a minimum of about 48 ounces daily. In other words, if you take in 2,000 calories, you need to get 64 ounces of fluid a day; that's eight eight-ounce glasses. If you love water, go ahead and drink up. Because your body gets rid of the excess once it is completely hydrated, or has enough water on board, there is little chance of a water overdose. A tell-tale sign of good hydration is nearly, or completely, colorless urine.

DON'T GO DRY

Many people, including the elderly and the physically active, don't get enough water. They may be mistakenly relying on thirst to tell them when to drink. Or

they may not fully understand their body's fluid needs.

When your body needs water, thirst is the last to know. Thirst is not signaled until after water loss occurs, and it often shuts off before you have taken in enough water. That makes thirst an unreliable index of fluid needs. What's more, the thirst mechanism becomes even less reliable with age. Relying solely on thirst could spell trouble for seniors, who are prone to dehydration. The symptoms of dehydration include dark urine and, in may cases, disorientation, confusion, and exhaustion. Severe dehydration can be deadly.

THE DEHYDRATORS

You may be consuming cola, coffee, and tea in the hopes of satisfying fluid requirements. That's counterproductive, because these beverages contain caffeine, which is a diuretic, or dehydrator. Beer, wine, and hard liquor, all contain alcohol, which is also a potent diuretic.

STAY IN THE DRINK

Physical activity increases your body's internal temperature. Exercisers, particularly those who work out in hot weather, put themselves at risk for dehydration when they fail to drink fluid before, during, and after exercise. To stay cool, follow these suggestions:

- Exercise during the coolest parts of the day to avoid dehydration.

- Never restrict fluids during your workout—for any reason.

- Try to drink four to six ounces of cool, plain water every 15 minutes, especially in hot and humid weather.

- Consume a minimum of 16 ounces of water at least two hours before exercise. Follow up with the same amount 15 to 20 minutes before endurance exercise, such as running or biking.

- Stick with water, rather than a sports drink, when performing continuous aerobic activity under 90 minutes.

NUTRITION AND ILLNESS

The very young are particularly at risk for iron-deficiency anemia if they are not given iron-fortified formula.

ANEMIA

The Surgeon General's Report on Nutrition and Health, published in 1988, recognizes how important iron is to the health of children, teens, and women in the United States. The anemia that results from eating too little iron can make you tired, weaken your immune system, and make it difficult for you to concentrate. Children who are iron deficient may not perform as well in school.

IRON-POOR BLOOD

Iron-poor blood, officially known as *iron deficiency,* can afflict very young children, because they are born with only enough iron to last for their first six months. Premature infants have even lower stores when they are born. Breast milk and infant formula not supplemented with iron have very little iron. Bottle-fed infants should be given iron-fortified formula, and iron-fortified cereals should be their first solid food.

Most parents know how finicky toddlers can be about eating. Toddlers will often eat just a handful of foods that are not necessarily high in iron, like peanut butter sandwiches, oatmeal, and apple juice. Few parents are consistently successful at getting their toddler to eat beef and other meats that are good iron sources. The result may be iron deficiency and anemia, because a growing child's body often needs more iron than the child eats.

Iron deficiency also hits preteens and teens. They need more iron, because their bodies and their blood

supply are growing quickly. When teenage girls begin menstruating, they lose iron every month. Yet, the eating habits of teenaged girls often leave something to be desired.

Women in their childbearing years may not eat enough iron-rich foods to refill their iron storage depots after each period or birth of a child. When you have too little iron in your blood and body tissues, you feel and look tired. Even a mild deficiency can sap you of energy. People with full-blown iron-deficiency anemia feel woozy, because their blood has too little iron to carry oxygen from their lungs to the other tissues in their body.

WHY WOMEN NEED MORE THAN MEN

Menstruating women lose iron every month when they have their period. It is tough for women to get enough iron, even if they eat red meat (one of the best sources of iron) several times a week. Other foods that supply reasonable amounts of iron include legumes (dried peas and beans), fortified breakfast cereal, oysters, and dark meat poultry.

Particularly if you do not eat red meat, you should have your blood checked regularly for anemia. Your physician may prescribe iron supplements for you if you are consistently anemic.

Because of irregular eating habits and the onset of menstruation, teenage girls often find themselves deficient in iron.

TEST RESULTS FOR ANEMIA AND WHAT THEY MEAN

If your doctor suspects that you have anemia in some form, you will probably be given a blood test. The terminology of a blood test can seem confusing, but here is generally what the results mean:

If your test reveals:	Then you have:
Low ferritin or transferrin	Iron deficiency
Low ferritin or transferrin Low hemoglobin Low hematocrit Small-sized blood cells	Iron deficiency anemia
Low hemoglobin Low hematocrit Large-sized blood cells	Macrocytic anemia (too little vitamin B_{12})
High ferritin or transferrin	Hemochromatosis (too much iron)

GOODBYE IRON STOMACH

You start taking the iron supplements your physician recommended, and you feel even worse than you did when you were anemic. Your stomach is upset, constipation is a problem, and indigestion is your constant companion. If your iron supplements are not getting along with your gastrointestinal tract, notify your physician or a registered dietitian. They may be able to recommend a brand of supplement that is easier to tolerate. Add more fiber-rich foods to your diet or consider using a powdered fiber supplement if you become constipated, and don't forget to drink plenty of fluids.

IRON TO THE MAX FROM FOODS

Make the most of the iron in your food, and you may not need to rely on supplements. Cook sauces in cast iron pots; some of the iron leeches into your food. Have a glass of citrus or tomato juice when you eat a bowl of breakfast cereal, because the vitamin C in the juice makes the iron in the cereal easier to absorb.

CUT THE COFFEE

Both coffee and tea contain chemical compounds that make it harder for you to absorb iron. Washing down your multivitamin with a swig of tea or pairing your morning breakfast cereal with a cup of coffee blocks some of the iron from reaching your bloodstream. Orange juice is a better beverage choice, because it converts the iron into a form that is easy to absorb.

IRON-RICH BLOOD

Too little iron is bad for your health, but too much iron stored in your body leads to other problems. Preliminary studies have found that people with a lot of iron stored in their tissues are more likely to have heart disease. One explanation is that iron may damage low-density lipoprotein (LDL) cholesterol (sometimes called the *bad cholesterol*) in a process called oxidation. Oxidized LDL is more likely to stick to the inside of your blood vessels and begin the clogging process that is called *atherosclerosis*—one of the first steps toward heart disease.

It is important not to take iron supplements unless you need them. You may be told to stop taking iron supplements once you pass menopause. You do not lose much iron once your period stops, so your body stores the iron that it does not need. Too much iron can also contribute to problems such as liver disease and arthritis. Men rarely need iron supplements, because they do not routinely lose iron.

OTHER TYPES OF ANEMIA

Strict vegetarians can, after a few years of their restricted diet, experience a different type of anemia, called *macrocytic anemia*—meaning literally, large-cell anemia. In this anemia, your red blood cells become larger; in iron-deficiency anemia, red blood cells get smaller. Macrocytic anemia is caused by a deficiency of vitamin B_{12}, or folate.

Vitamin B_{12} is supplied only in animal foods such as milk, dairy products, eggs, meat, poultry, and fish. Vegetarians who completely avoid all animal products, including milk and eggs, can become anemic after several years.

Folate anemia is most common during the latter months of pregnancy, when your needs may be higher than your intake. However, even in the absence of folate anemia, women who are trying to conceive should be diligent about folate as it helps prevent birth defects when taken in the early weeks of pregnancy.

Good sources of folate include liver, dried beans, dark-green, leafy vegetables (especially spinach, asparagus, and broccoli), lean beef, potatoes, and whole-wheat bread.

ARTHRITIS

Almost 40 million American adults have arthritis. Far from being a single disease, *arthritis* is a general term for several bone and joint ailments. The most common types of arthritis include osteoarthritis (deterioration of the joints), rheumatoid arthritis (inflammation of the joints), gout (uric acid crystallization in the joints), and lupus (an immune system attack on joints and other parts of the body). Arthritis sufferers complain of pain, swelling in their joints, soreness, and overall fatigue.

What they have in common is that all types of arthritis attack a type of tissue called *connective tissue*. Cartilage, bones, tendons, ligaments, blood vessels, and the synovial tissues that cushion your joints are among the various types of connective tissues in your body.

TREATMENTS, NOT CURES

Thus far, no one has discovered a cure for arthritis. So, most arthritis treatments are designed to relieve symptoms but not to get rid of the disease. And whenever standard medicine cannot get rid of a disease, unproved "cures" become popular. Americans spend approximately one billion dollars a year on all sorts of arthritis remedies.

The food-arthritis link has been debated time and time again but remains unproved. Yet nutritional "cures" are among the most popular arthritis treatments. Why? Because changing your diet seems easy, and you're told that it has few risks and many benefits. Food is not the magic cure for arthritis that some would have you believe, but a couple of areas hold real promise for relieving the pain and other symptoms of arthritis and even for keeping some types of arthritis away to begin with.

Even working in the garden can be painful for arthritis sufferers, but some nutritional research holds promise.

A WEIGHTY ISSUE

If you are overweight, losing several pounds might help lower your risk of getting arthritis in your knees and back. An overweight body puts a lot of strain on the connective tissue in these two areas. After years of wear and tear, the structures in these joints can break down, resulting in osteoarthritis. Weight may play a role in arthritis of the hips and other joints, also.

If you already have arthritis, weight loss can help reduce joint discomfort. It can also make gout attacks less severe by reducing their intensity and by taking the extra weight off an already sore toe. Unfortunately, many arthritis sufferers find it difficult to chase away pounds, because their pain and discomfort limits their physical activity.

VERY VEGETARIAN

Over the years, vegetarian diets have been tried for arthritis relief. In a Norwegian study, a small group of people with rheumatoid arthritis were placed on a strict vegetarian diet that had no eggs, dairy products, sugar, citrus, or gluten (a protein found in wheat, barley, oats, and rye). Over the course of a few weeks, they had less joint swelling and were not as stiff in the morning. Many continued to feel better even after adding dairy products and grains back into their diet. The people in this study continued to have arthritis (a vegetarian diet doesn't cure the disease), but their symptoms were less severe.

This study was too small to be conclusive, but it is possible that vegetarian diets work because their fat content is different from that of a diet with meat

---

THE PROMISE OF VITAMIN C

Vitamin C had its heyday as an arthritis remedy in the 1940s. At that time, many people with rheumatoid arthritis were found to have low levels of vitamin C in their blood—hence, the thinking that giving them more vitamin C might help. Vitamin C also became popular because it is needed to form collagen, a protein found in connective tissue. However, vitamin C was not able to relieve arthritis symptoms. Therefore, health professionals advise against taking large doses of vitamin C as a treatment for arthritis.

and other animal products. Certain types of fatty acids affect the production of body hormones called *prostaglandins* that combat inflammation. Less inflammation means less pain.

Fishing for Relief

Omega-3 fatty acids are the type of fat found in fish. More than any other type of fat, these fatty acids may fight off inflammation by working with the body's prostaglandins. Some people say that fish-oil supplements help relieve their arthritis symptoms; however, the effects are not consistent.

Also, fish-oil supplements can thin out your blood and affect your blood's ability to clot, which can be dangerous, especially when combined with the blood-thinning effects of aspirin use. That is why you are better off getting your omega-3s from fatty fish like anchovies, bluefish, herring, mackerel, salmon, and sardines than you are by overdoing it with supplements.

Are You Allergic?

One of the symptoms of a food allergy is joint pain. Some people with rheumatoid arthritis have found that eliminating highly allergenic foods, such as soy, eggs, dairy products, oranges, beef, or pork, makes them feel better. But the relationship between arthritis and food allergies is not clear.

Do not completely eliminate a food until you are certain that it is the culprit for your pain. You increase your risk of nutrient deficiencies if you stop eating meats, dairy products, citrus fruits, or other foods that are key nutrient sources. Dairy products are high in calcium and riboflavin, meats provide iron and zinc, and citrus fruits supply vitamin C and folate. Replace these foods with other sources of the same nutrients, like canned salmon for calcium, fortified breakfast cereal for iron and zinc, and kiwi, potatoes, spinach, and other fruits and vegetables rich in vitamin C and folate.

Quelling the Swelling

Fluid retention, known as *edema*, in your joints is a common side effect of arthritis. It may result from a particular medication, or it can develop in a joint that is not moved very often because of arthritis pain. Cutting back on salt and salty foods may give you some relief.

The omega-3 fatty acids in fish may relieve some arthritis pain. Including more fish in your diet is not a bad idea.

The Triglyceride Link

Some arthritis sufferers have abnormally high blood levels of triglycerides, small "packages" of fat that travel through the bloodstream. Eating fewer simple carbohydrates (sugars) and fewer calories, and drinking little or no alcohol, may help lower your triglyceride levels and relieve your joint pain if you've been told by a physician that your triglyceride levels are too high. Your physician or a registered dietitian can advise you on the best diet for you to follow.

Unproved Remedies

Be wary of food and diet promises. Over the years, people with arthritis have been told that eliminating all acid fruits and vegetables (for example, oranges, grapefruits, pineapples, and tomatoes) or removing all meat, fruit, dairy products, egg yolks, acidic foods, and other specific foods and beverages would cure their disease. More recently, arthritis sufferers have shied away from peppers, white potato, eggplant, and tomatoes, the so-called *nightshade* vegetables. However, no curative powers have been proved for any food.

Common arthritis "cures" can be harmful. Alfalfa contains a type of protein that may worsen certain types of arthritis. High doses of zinc, another arthritis "treatment," can cause nausea, vomiting, and diarrhea and can block your body's absorption of copper. Be wary of miracle claims, and always check with your doctor or dietitian before starting on a "special" diet to make sure it isn't detrimental.

BIRTH DEFECTS

Before the 1990s, few people had heard of the B vitamin called *folate*. It was not one of the superstar nutrients and was not added to fortified bread. In fact, it wasn't even listed on food labels. Now, however, folate (also called *folic acid* or *folacin*; see page 43) is in the spotlight as the nutrient most important for preventing birth defects of the nervous system, defects called *neural tube defects*. Approximately seven percent of all infants are born with some kind of birth defect; a little over one percent have neural tube defects.

COMMON BIRTH DEFECTS

Two of the most common nervous-system birth defects are spina bifida and anencephaly. These result when the neural tube, which forms the brain and spinal column, does not close properly during the third or fourth week of pregnancy.

The neural tube of babies born with spina bifida does not close at the bottom, causing abnormalities at the base of the spine. Spina bifida often leads to paralysis and mental retardation.

Anencephaly—meaning literally, "without a brain"—develops when the fetus' neural tube does not completely close at the top. The newborn with anencephaly is missing part or all of its brain because of a problem with brain development early in the pregnancy. Anencephaly is always fatal. Sometimes,

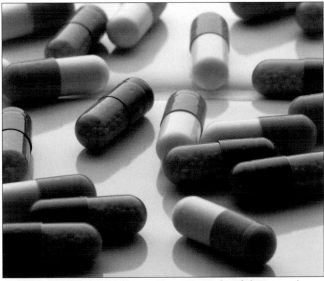

Taking vitamins is not always the answer, but folate supplements for women who may get pregnant may be a good idea.

the newborn can live a few days, but often the baby is stillborn.

THE VALUE OF VITAMINS

Taking a multivitamin during early pregnancy appears to help lower your risk of having a child with birth defects. In a 1989 study of over 22,000 women, Dr. Aubrey Milunsky and his colleagues at Boston University found that women who took a multivitamin had far fewer children born with neural tube defects.

FOCUSING ON FOLATE

Taking a multivitamin can reduce your risk of having a baby with birth defects, but it appears that one nutrient, folate, is the most important for preventing birth defects. To test the effects of folate on birth defects, researchers gave folate supplements to one group of women trying to get pregnant and a placebo to a second group of women. In one study, the protection from folate against birth defects was so great that the researchers stopped the study early, because it became clear that all women should receive folate while they are trying to become pregnant, and the study was unfair to the placebo group. Folate supplements had prevented almost three quarters of the neural tube birth defects.

If you are trying to become pregnant, check with your physician; he or she can recommend the appropriate vitamin supplement for you to take.

PRECAUTIONARY MEASURES

Nervous-system birth defects develop during the first few weeks of pregnancy, when the protective coating around the spinal nerves of the fetus closes. This is the time that you should be particularly careful about getting enough folate. However, many women do not even realize they are pregnant until they are well past the point where folate can make a difference. Taking folate after your seventh week of pregnancy has no protective effect against birth defects. Therefore, women should up their folate intake whenever there is a chance of getting pregnant.

Women in their childbearing years should be particularly diligent about getting enough folate, at minimum, the 180 micrograms (μg) daily suggested by the Recommended Dietary Allowance (RDA). If you are trying to get pregnant, you need more than twice as much.

THE EASIEST WAY—EAT RIGHT

Follow the guidelines of the Food Guide Pyramid (see page 102), and you will immediately increase the amount of folate you eat. To start, you'll be eating at least six daily servings of grain foods, many of which are or soon will be fortified with folate. (Traditionally, fortification meant adding a nutrient not normally present in a food, while enrichment added to a nutrient already in the food. Today the two terms are used interchangeably.) Then add five or more servings of fruits and vegetables; the top food sources of folate are fruits and vegetables, including leafy greens (especially the darker ones), legumes, bananas, and oranges.

GETTING THE MOST FOLATE FROM YOUR FOOD

Like other B vitamins, folate can be partially or totally destroyed by heat and water. To minimize folate loss, use as little water as possible when you cook fruits and vegetables, and cook them quickly; steam or microwave them, but don't boil them to death. If you buy canned vegetables, don't just throw away the folate-rich liquid—use it in soups, sauces, or in any other dish.

It is possible to get enough folate in your foods to meet or even exceed the RDA. An eight-ounce glass of orange juice teamed up with a spinach salad at

Eating right is crucial for a healthy pregnancy. A well-balanced diet and the avoidance of alcohol are very important.

lunch and a cup of steamed broccoli at dinner supplies you with over 280 µg of folate.

WHEN YOU NEED MORE

The U.S. Public Health Service recommends that women who are in their childbearing years should eat at least 400 µg of folate daily, but it is difficult for most women to eat enough folate-rich foods to meet the higher level.

Also, many women become pregnant before they have spoken to a physician regarding folate supplements. For this reason, folate enrichment of cereal, breads, and other foods was put into practice. Enrichment ensures that women automatically get more folate without making major changes in the way they eat.

JUST SAY NO TO ALCOHOL

Birth defects are more likely among the infants of women who drink alcoholic beverages during pregnancy. Since experts are not sure if even one drink can cause problems, they recommend that pregnant women completely avoid alcohol. And, of course, the use of any recreational and some therapeutic drugs can be dangerous to a developing fetus. Always check with your doctor before taking any medication.

FUNDAMENTALS OF FOOD FORTIFICATION

Food fortification and enrichment are inexpensive ways to prevent malnutrition. Diseases that have been virtually erased through food fortification and enrichment include pellagra (niacin deficiency), beriberi (thiamin deficiency), goiter (iodine deficiency), and rickets (vitamin D deficiency). Fortification in the United States includes salt fortified with iodine, margarine with vitamins A and D, and milk with vitamin D.

Flour and bread have been enriched for many years with four nutrients: thiamin, riboflavin, niacin, and iron. Folate enrichment was added in 1994.

The U.S. Public Health Service recommends that women of childbearing age consume 400 µg of folate per day. A diet rich in fruits and vegetables could supply close to this amount. However, fewer than ten percent of American women eat this much, and changing eating habits can take a long time. That's why folate fortification of grain products was initiated to help ensure that women consume adequate amounts of folate, particularly in their childbearing years.

CANCER

Between 35 and 60 percent of cancers may be influenced by what we eat. So, changing the way you eat today can have big health payoffs years from now. This does not mean turning your refrigerator into a medicine chest of food. Instead, you'll eat more of the foods that have protective benefits and less of those that contribute to cancer development.

FAT IS NOT WHERE IT'S AT

Cancers of the breast, colon, rectum, endometrium, and prostate tend to be more prevalent in countries where the diet is high in fat. The link is strongest for the hormone-related cancers: breast, endometrium, and prostate. The answer is simple—eat less fat.

Trim your own fat, also. Obesity increases your risk of the same cancers that seem to be related to the fat you eat. However, it is not clear whether eating too many calories or too much fat is to blame. Because fat is the most concentrated source of calories, cutting back on your intake means both less fat and far fewer calories.

KEEPING YOUR COLON HEALTHY

You can lower your risk of colon cancer by eating more fiber and less fat. High-fiber foods increase the bulk of your stool, helping it pass through your colon more rapidly. One anticancer benefit is that cancer-causing substances in your stool zip by your colon cells and are robbed of the opportunity to spark the cancer process. Fiber also hooks onto bile acids and other compounds that may contribute to colon cancer, pulling them out of your body before they can do any damage.

One way to study colon cancer is to look at precancerous lesions that may become cancerous. At the Harvard School of Public Health, Dr. Edward Giovannucci and others looked at the past eating habits of men with precancerous colon tumors. In general, men with precancerous tumors had eaten less fruit, vegetables, and grains than did men without tumors. And men who ate the least red meat, dairy fat, and saturated fat had the lowest cancer risk.

THE RED MEAT CONNECTION

In several studies, eating a lot of red meat increased a person's risk of colon cancer. Opinions are divided on

Red meat consumption has been associated with an increased risk of colon cancer in several studies. Moderation is indicated.

whether the amount of fat, saturated fat (the most likely suspect), or some other compound in red meat is the problem. Other foods with a lot of saturated fat are butter, cheese, and whole milk. It makes sense to switch to low-fat and nonfat dairy foods; they are still high in calcium (a mineral that may protect your colon against cancer), but they reduce your fat intake.

THE BREAST CANCER DEBATE

Some experts say that a high-fiber diet helps prevent breast cancer. Others say that it doesn't make a difference. Who is right?

Around the world, countries where the diet is high in fiber-rich foods have lower breast cancer rates. Several studies on individual groups of women have found that more fiber means less breast cancer.

Lower blood estrogen means lower breast cancer risk. Fiber may help lower breast cancer risk by binding with estrogen, a female hormone, in your intestinal tract to prevent it from being reabsorbed into your bloodstream. Also, lignin, a type of fiber found in whole grains and seeds, can make your body manufacture a type of protein that binds with estrogen. Other plant compounds called *phytoestrogens* block the formation of estrogen.

However, the naysayers swear by the results of a Harvard University School of Public Health study that found no relationship between fiber and breast cancer risk. Some fiber experts say that the Harvard study did not look closely enough at women who ate very-high-fiber diets. The bottom line: Eating more fiber can't hurt; it can only help.

MAKING VEGETABLES EASIER

Some people just put up with vegetables. Others love them. But regardless of where they rank in your personal opinion poll, vegetables are a must in the fight to prevent cancer. So move past the canned peas and explore the world of vegetables. Here are some tips for making the most of your vegetables:

- No time to cook? Prepare vegetables in minutes in your microwave. No time to chop? Buy pre-cut bagged or salad-bar vegetables.

- Get the most nutrition by cooking vegetables quickly and in very little water. Use a pressure cooker, and avoid overcooking.

- Love the idea of broccoli but cannot stand the smell? To reduce odor and improve taste, broccoli, cabbage, cauliflower, and other strongly flavored cruciferous vegetables should be cooked quickly and with the lid off the pot to allow the smelly compounds to escape.

- Add vegetables to soup, spaghetti sauce, casseroles, and stews. Use brightly colored fresh or frozen vegetables to decorate a pizza.

- Keep a bowl of washed, cut vegetables in your refrigerator, along with a yogurt dip for a quick snack or light meal.

- Don't undo the good nutrition of a salad by covering it with high-fat dressing. Use low-fat dressing, plain yogurt, or salsa instead to add flavor without too much fat.

- Use frozen vegetables when you can't use fresh ones.

FILLING UP WITH FIBER

Some people are fiber counters; they add up every smidgen of fiber from the poppy seeds on their morning bagel to the bran they sprinkle on their dinner salad. Others wisely take the easier road to fiber by just eating more whole grains, fruits, and vegetables.

The average American eats only half the amount of fiber recommended by the National Cancer Institute and endorsed by The American Dietetic Association. Why? Because we eat too few fruits, vegetables, and whole-grain breads and cereals. You need to eat just two servings of fruit, three of vegetables, and three of whole-grain products to reach your fiber goal. It's easy.

Insoluble fiber, found primarily in whole grains and in the skins and seeds of fruits and vegetables, is the most protective fiber against cancer. If you get fiber from a variety of different foods, you'll reap all the health benefits of fiber, from cancer protection to cholesterol lowering.

Another benefit of eating a high-fiber diet is that you tend to eat less fat. When you center your meal around fruits, vegetables, and grains, you have less room on your plate and in your stomach for meats, full-fat dairy products, and added fats such as butter and margarine.

MINDING YOUR PEAS AND CUKES

There is no doubt in anyone's mind that eating plenty of fruits and vegetables helps protect you from a multitude of different cancers, including lung, stomach, and cervical cancers. Eating even the less nutrient-rich vegetables, like lettuce and cucumbers, can lower your overall cancer risk.

CRUNCHING ON CRUCIFEROUS

Broccoli, brussels sprouts, cabbage, cauliflower—if it has a strong smell, it probably belongs to the cruciferous family of vegetables. Cruciferous vegetables are

Upping your fiber intake can reduce your risk of some cancers. Try to include more whole grains in your diet.

hailed for their ability to help ward off certain types of cancer with their hundreds of anticancer chemicals. One chemical in broccoli, called *sulforaphane,* helps your liver cells neutralize cancer-causing compounds, known as *carcinogens.* Other cruciferous vegetables such as cabbage, brussels sprouts, and cauliflower probably have the same chemical or other related compounds.

THE THREE MUSKETEERS

The three antioxidant nutrients, vitamin C, beta-carotene, and vitamin E, have unique properties that help ward off cancer. They can neutralize cancer-causing chemicals, strengthen your immune system, and block naturally occurring free radicals from starting the cancer process. (For more on the so-called antioxidant vitamins, see page 45.) Although each has its own turf to defend, all three are needed for optimal protection against cancer.

C FOR YOURSELF: Research findings overwhelmingly show that the more fruits and vegetables you eat, the lower your risk of lung cancer and cancers of the esophagus, larynx, mouth, and pancreas. Vitamin C seems to be the key nutrient in this finding. For lung cancer protection, eating lots of fruits and vegetables is crucial; in fact, one study showed that people who ate the most fruits and

The deep orange of carrots indicates that they are loaded with beta-carotene, which may prevent some forms of cancer.

vegetables were half as likely to get lung cancer as people who ate the least. That is quite a significant difference.

CARROTS—NOT FOR YOUR EYES ONLY: Carrots, spinach, and other orange or dark green vegetables dish up an abundance of beta-carotene, a plant color pigment that is a powerful cancer preventer. People who eat a lot of beta-carotene from fruits and vegetables have a lower risk of cancer of the lung, mouth, stomach, cervix, and esophagus. Conversely, your cancer risk goes up if beta-carotene–rich fruits and vegetables are not on your plate. Now is the time to start adding them to your diet.

Beta-carotene may also help prevent breast cancer. A Harvard University study of almost 90,000 women found that women who ate just one serving a day of a fruit or vegetable rich in beta-carotene were less likely to get breast cancer.

It may have a powerful effect on mouth cancer, too. Not only can eating lots of fruits and vegetables lower your risk of mouth cancer, but large daily doses of beta-carotene can even reverse the process, turning precancerous mouth lesions back to normal.

Popping beta-carotene supplements may not have the same effects as fruits and vegetables do. Experts are still sorting out whether beta-carotene or a combination of beta-carotene and other compounds in fruits and vegetables is the best cancer fighter. For now, stick with the food sources.

WHERE THE BETA-CAROTENE IS

Studies on the cancer-fighting properties of beta-carotene have used supplements instead of foods, up to 30 mg, compared with a recommended intake of approximately 6 mg. However, it is widely recommended that you get your nutrients from food instead of from pills until the role and safety of high-dose vitamins are better understood. Here are some of the foods highest in beta-carotene:

Food	Beta-carotene (mg)
Carrot juice, 1 cup	6.3
Carrots, cooked, ½ cup	2.9
Sweet potatoes, cooked, ½ cup	1.0
Mango, 1 medium	0.8
Butternut squash, cooked, ½ cup	0.7
Spinach, cooked, ½ cup	0.6
Kale, cooked, ½ cup	0.5
Apricots, canned in juice, 1 cup	0.4
Winter squash, cooked, ½ cup	0.4
Papaya, 1 cup	0.3
Broccoli, cooked, ½ cup	0.1

EATING MORE E: Vitamin E is the good soldier that helps protect you from all types of cancer. It runs interference against free radicals, blocking them before they can damage the cells in your body. Vitamin E also can stop cancer-causing free-radical reactions dead in their tracks. The best sources for vitamin E are nuts, sunflower seeds, vegetable oils, and the darker varieties of lettuce, such as romaine. Selenium, a mineral, works together with vitamin E in this process.

Folate Joins the Fight Against Cancer

Women who are not big fans of green, leafy vegetables and orange juice may have low levels of folate in their body. Without adequate folate, precancerous changes, resulting from exposure to a virus called *human papilloma virus (HPV),* are more likely to develop in your cervix. Folate fortification of breads and cereals may help boost folate intake and offer more protection against cervical cancer.

Summer Without Barbecues?

Barbecued meat is filled with compounds that can start the cancer process. The combination of the meat's fat and protein and heat from the grill create a chemical cocktail of bad guys. You don't have to ban the barbecue forever, though. Limit grilling to about once a week, pick lean cuts of meat, trim all visible fat, and limit your portion to three to four ounces cooked. Also, use a pan or some foil to catch the fat that drips; don't let it drip onto the hot coals.

In a Pickle

Eating fewer smoked and pickled foods can help lower your risk of stomach cancer. These foods tend to be rich in nitrites that can turn into cancer-causing chemicals called *nitrosamines* in your stomach. Stomach cancer is not common in the United States, in part because we eat enough fresh fruits and vegetables that block the formation of nitrosamines.

Peanut Butter Smarts

Peanuts that are contaminated with certain types of mold contain a cancer-causing chemical called *aflatoxin* that has been linked to liver cancer. Although peanuts are inspected for aflatoxin, some contaminated peanuts can slip through the cracks. To

Fatty meat and the hot, smoky cooking process can make barbecued meals loaded with carcinogenic compounds.

reduce your contact with aflatoxin, discard shriveled or moldy nuts. Also, buy only national brands of peanut butter, because local and health food store brands and fresh-ground peanut butter are less likely to be well inspected.

A Berry Good Idea

Ellagic acid is a naturally occurring acid found in strawberries, raspberries, cranberries, loganberries, cashews, pecans, walnuts, and brazil nuts. It may help fight cancer by neutralizing aflatoxin on nuts and grains and carcinogenic nitrosamines that form in cooked meat. Have a few walnuts on your hamburger, anybody?

Put Out Your Cigarette

If you smoke, you are far more likely to get cancer of the mouth, esophagus, lung, and stomach than a nonsmoker. Furthermore, people who smoke cigarettes tend to have lower blood levels of beta-carotene, vitamin C, and other protective nutrients.

Ban Booze

Although alcohol in moderation may be beneficial for your heart, it adds to your mouth and esophageal cancer risk. More than one drink a day is thought to make you more susceptible to breast cancer, as well.

CONSTIPATION

Do you ever wish that you were more regular? If nothing else, be comforted that you are not alone. Millions of Americans suffer from this annoying physical discomfort that is the most common digestive tract problem in the United States. Luckily, you can usually relieve constipation and get on the road to regularity just by making small changes in what you eat and drink.

How do you know if you're constipated?

Regularity may mean different things to different people. No two people are exactly alike in how often they have bowel movements. For young babies whose digestive tracts cannot completely digest and absorb the food and breast milk or formula they eat, regularity might be three, five, or even more bowel movements a day. By adulthood, regularity could be one bowel movement every one, two, or three days. Regardless of your schedule, however, you are constipated if your bowel movement is hard and pebbly and causes straining.

Sometimes constipated bowel movements are accompanied by bleeding; if you notice bleeding or a marked change in your normal bowel movements that lasts for more than a few days, be sure to consult your doctor.

How constipation happens

It takes between one and three days for your body to digest and absorb a meal and then eliminate the waste.

An adequate fluid intake and the proper amount of fiber are essential to normal digestive-tract functioning.

By the time food reaches your colon, most of its nutrients (protein, fat, carbohydrate, vitamins, and minerals) have been absorbed, and the colon simply absorbs water from the remaining food while pushing it down to your rectum. You become constipated when your colon pushes food too slowly. The longer your food stays in your colon, the more water gets pulled out, making the stool hard and difficult to eliminate.

What causes constipation?

The biggest cause of constipation is an improper diet. When you eat a lot of foods that are high in fiber, your stool becomes bigger and easier for your colon to push. If, like most Americans, you eat too little fiber, your stool can be small, and it can take a long time for your colon to move it through. People who go on strict diets to lose weight are likely to become constipated for the same reason: They eat too little, and their small stool is hard for the colon to move.

The amount of water and other fluids you drink is also important. People who do not drink enough fluids are more likely to have smaller, harder stools and constipation. You should drink at least eight cups of fluid each day.

Constipation is also one of the many side effects of getting too little activity. Physical activity helps improve muscle tone in your abdomen and strengthen the pushing contractions in your colon. Are you under stress? You might become constipated during stressful times, too.

EATING TO ELIMINATE CONSTIPATION

- Eat at least three servings of whole grains or foods made with whole grain, three servings of vegetables, and two servings of fruit every day.

- Increase fiber gradually to cut down on gas and discomfort.

- Switch to whole grains instead of just sprinkling bran onto your foods. Whole grains tend to cause less cramping and gas.

- Shop for breakfast cereals with at least five grams of fiber per serving.

- Make sure that you drink at least eight cups of water or other fluids daily. Add an extra half cup of water for every cup of coffee, tea, or other beverage with caffeine that you drink and for every ounce of alcohol, too.

The best fiber sources are the natural ones. Eat plenty of whole grains and fresh fruits, such as apples with the peel.

When you are tense, so are the muscles in your colon, and they cannot push as well. Finally, pregnant women are often constipated, because hormonal changes and the iron in prenatal vitamin supplements slow down the digestive tract.

Regardless of the cause, some people simply reach for a laxative for relief. Don't rely on them. Repeated use of laxatives can actually make constipation worse by weakening intestinal muscles.

Eating for Regularity

Here are a few ways to help you fight constipation simply by paying more attention to your eating habits. The changes you make don't have to be radical—take it slowly. Avoid switching from a low-fiber to a higher-fiber diet overnight. Also, be patient; getting bowel movements back to normal can take several days.

EAT REGULAR MEALS: It's easy to skip breakfast one day and maybe lunch the next, but this can worsen irregularity. By eating regular meals, you supply your colon with a large enough amount of food to push at one time. People who eat regular meals tend to have more regular bowel movements.

EAT MORE INSOLUBLE FIBER: Insoluble fiber, the type of fiber that is found primarily in whole grains, whole-wheat or bran cereals, and wheat bran, helps move food more rapidly through your large intestine. Fiber works by holding more water in the food in your intestines, increasing the size of your stool, and making it easier to push out. On average, Americans get only 10 to 15 grams of fiber daily; 20 to 30 grams daily is a healthier goal.

BECOME BREAD SMART: Whole grains have most of their fiber in their outer coating, called the *husk*. Consequently, breads made from whole-wheat flour, where the entire wheat kernel is ground and used, have more fiber than breads made from white flour, which has the husk removed from the wheat kernel before grinding. Look for bread that has visible pieces of whole grain on the crust or in the individual slices. Read ingredient lists to find breads that have some form of whole grain or bran as the first ingredient.

FOCUS ON FIVE-A-DAY: To prevent constipation, and for overall health, you should eat a minimum of five servings of fruits and vegetables daily. Make at least one of these servings a higher fiber fruit, such as an apple, a pear, berries, raisins, prunes, or other dried fruit. Your best vegetable bets for fiber include potatoes, sweet potatoes, peas, corn, and broccoli. Fans of juicing beware—unless you add back a lot of pulp, the juices you make are not good sources of fiber. The skins and seeds of most fruits and vegetables have much of the fiber.

LOAD UP ON LEGUMES: Beans and legumes, including split peas, kidney beans, and lentils, are among the foods with the most fiber. It is easy to add legumes to a meal, too. Toss them in a salad, add them to soup, or substitute them for ground meat in your favorite spaghetti sauce recipe.

The Lowdown on Fiber Supplements

Over-the-counter fiber supplements in powder form can help provide relief from constipation. Typically, they contain either cellulose, a common type of insoluble fiber, or psyllium, a high-fiber grain. Fiber supplements work by absorbing water and expanding in the large intestine. Remember to drink plenty of water if you go this route.

DENTAL HEALTH AND DISEASE

You probably take your teeth for granted. You may not brush as often or as well as you should. Flossing seems like a nuisance, and going to the dentist is one of your least favorite pastimes. No one is crazy about it. Yet, by caring for your teeth and your children's teeth now, you can prevent the two most common forms of dental disease—tooth decay and gum disease.

Strengthening Teeth You Can't See

A young child's teeth grow and develop below the gums long before you can feel or see them. It is during this time that eating right makes the biggest difference in how strong and healthy your child's teeth are. Children who eat a balanced diet with the right amount of calories, protein, calcium, zinc, and vitamins A, C, and D usually end up with baby and adult teeth that are strong and able to fight off damage from bacteria.

The Case for Fluoride

Before the widespread fluoridation of local water supplies and toothpastes, tooth decay was far more common. Today, a lot of tooth decay has been prevented in children and adults whose teeth come in contact with adequate amounts of fluoride. In fact,

---

> **DENTAL DEMONS**
>
> **These foods adhere to your teeth longest:**
> Chips
> Cookies
> Crackers
> Granola bars
> Ready-to-eat breakfast cereals
>
> **These foods are quite sticky:**
> Dried fruit
> Gumdrops
> Jelly beans
>
> **These foods stick a bit:**
> Bread
> Cake
> Candy bars with chocolate and caramel
>
> **These foods hardly stick:**
> Plain chocolate bars
> Fresh fruit
> Ice cream

---

water fluoridation is the most important preventive measure against tooth decay. Fluoride makes teeth stronger and helps block the formation of tooth plaque that is caused by bacteria that normally live in your mouth.

Too much fluoride, however, can turn your children's teeth a brownish color. To prevent this, squirt only a pea-sized portion of toothpaste on the toothbrush, teach children to spit out toothpaste instead of swallowing, and do not give your children a multivitamin with fluoride (available by prescription only) if your local water is fluoridated; fluoridated water provides plenty on its own.

Unless told otherwise, pregnant women should not take fluoride-supplemented multivitamins, because fluoride may cause permanent discoloration of their child's first set of teeth.

A Sticky Situation

Aristotle, the ancient Greek philosopher, was one of the first people to associate tooth decay with food—he put the blame on figs. Tooth decay, also known as *dental caries,* develops as the bacteria in your mouth feast on bits of food clinging to your teeth. The bacteria release acid that eats through your tooth enamel and eventually creates small pits and holes—cavities.

It is well known that sugary, sticky foods contribute to tooth decay. You would imagine that caramels, chewing gum, and candy bars are among the stickiest of all, right? Actually, starchy foods like chips and crackers stick to your teeth longer than candy does. Your saliva helps dissolve sugary foods and washes them off your teeth, but starchy foods are more stubborn. Starchy foods that stick to your teeth supply tooth-decaying bacteria with their favorite food to

Adequate amounts of fluoride, calcium, and vitamin D can make all the difference for a child's future dental health.

grow on, and bacteria growth means more acid eroding your tooth enamel.

Tooth-safe foods

Your mouth bacteria are not very fond of meats, eggs, and nuts. These foods have no starch for the bacteria to nibble on. Although dairy products contain a type of sugar called lactose (milk sugar), many cheeses may protect your teeth from bacterial attack if you eat them before eating something sugary or starchy. Dairy products also top the list of tooth-friendly foods, because they are so high in calcium and phosphorus—two minerals needed to build strong teeth.

Snack attacks

How many times a day do you and your family members snack? One, two, three? Every time you grab something to eat, you also feed the bacteria in your mouth. Having food clinging to your teeth almost all day could mean more cavities.

Snack less often, and when you do, choose snacks that are less likely to stick to your teeth. Also, add a defender food, like cheese, that can help fight off bacteria, or chew sugarless gum to scrub your teeth.

Try to brush your teeth after every snack to remove lingering food particles. Even a toothbrush just moistened with water can do the trick. Also teach your children to use a toothpaste-free toothbrush after a snack. Too much fluoridated toothpaste during the day, particularly if your child has not yet mastered the spitting-out phase of tooth brushing and if your water is fluoridated, could discolor your child's teeth.

When it comes to cavities, foods that stick in teeth and stay put for long periods, such as potato chips, are worse than sugar.

A little diligence in brushing and flossing and attention to good food choices can keep your smile beautiful for life.

Gum health

Periodontal (gum) disease is the most common cause of tooth loss in people over age 35. It is thought to be caused by plaque, a gelatinlike substance made from saliva and bacteria. When plaque builds up on your teeth, it causes your gums to swell and pull away from your teeth. Bacteria can then creep under your gums to create more plaque. In severe cases, you lose calcium and other minerals from the bone sockets that hold your teeth in place.

Eating right can help keep your gums healthy. It is thought that your gums need protein, zinc, vitamin C, and iron in order to block bacteria. Calcium helps keeps the bones in your tooth sockets strong.

Brush, brush, floss, floss

Less than ten minutes a day is all you need to take good care of your teeth and gums. Brush at least twice a day to remove food particles and plaque sticking to your teeth. Flossing gets rid of bits of food and plaque between your teeth and under your gums. Some dentists also recommend using a special rubber tip to jiggle your gums, making them more firm and helping them block creeping bacteria. Ask your dentist or dental hygienist for a refresher course at your next visit.

DIABETES

Although not the killer that heart disease is, diabetes has become a major health problem in the United States. Diabetes is a serious disease in itself and a risk factor for other health problems. Complications of diabetes include kidney failure, poor circulation, blindness, and stroke. And although approximately 14 million people in this country have diabetes, only half are aware that they have the disease. Diabetes rates are highest among African-Americans and Native Americans, and the disease is also closely linked to obesity.

A family history of diabetes may put you at higher risk, as can being Native American or African American.

INSULIN AND BLOOD SUGAR

Diabetes is a disease in which your blood sugar, called *glucose,* cannot get into the cells of your body. Glucose is the fuel that every cell needs, but in order to get into cells, glucose needs insulin, a hormone made in and dispatched by the pancreas. Insulin lowers the concentration of sugar in the blood by letting more glucose into your cells and regulating the amount of glucose released into the blood by the liver. When you have diabetes, either your pancreas is not making enough insulin or the cells in your body are not letting insulin unlock the door so that glucose can get in. The end result is that your blood sugar level is too high.

Your kidneys work overtime when your sugar level goes up. They try to flush out some of the extra glucose from your blood in your urine, making your urine more concentrated. Your kidneys then add more water to your urine to keep it at the right concentration. This is why you may feel unusually thirsty when you have diabetes; the extra sugar is causing your body to lose extra water in your urine.

TWO DIFFERENT DISEASES

Diabetes is actually two different diseases. Insulin-dependent diabetes usually is diagnosed in childhood and is the less common form of diabetes. People with this disease must take shots of insulin, because their pancreas cannot make enough. Only a small percentage of all people with diabetes need to take insulin.

Approximately 90 percent of the people with diabetes in the United States have non–insulin-dependent diabetes. It is a disease of middle age and tends to be found in adults over age 40. This type of diabetes is more common in people who have a family history of

the disease and who are overweight. In non–insulin-dependent diabetes, your pancreas usually works normally, producing enough insulin. The problem, instead, lies in the cells; suddenly, the insulin "key" no longer works to unlock the cell "door" to let glucose into the cells.

Before you have full-blown diabetes, your blood sugar levels may be higher than normal when you wake up in the morning. If your physician suspects diabetes, you will go through a fasting glucose test that measures your blood sugar before you have eaten in the morning.

DIET—THE FIRST LINE OF DEFENSE

What is the best advice for keeping a diabetic's blood sugar under control and reducing the risk of heart disease? The general consensus is that people with diabetes should limit the amount of fat, salt, alcohol, and sugar they eat, while increasing their intake of complex carbohydrates (the type found in bread, grains, pasta, fruits, and vegetables) and fiber. However, some people with diabetes have trouble keeping their blood sugar under control on a low-fat, high-carbohydrate diet. Blood levels of triglycerides, a type of fat that may increase heart disease risk, may rise. Everyone with diabetes should consult with a physician and a registered dietitian who can make diet recommendations based on blood sugar levels.

SOME MEDICATION CAN HELP

People with diabetes whose blood sugar stays high after a change in diet may need a medication called an oral hypoglycemic, a pill that helps lower glucose levels. Other people with diabetes might require

DIABETES DURING PREGNANCY

Gestational diabetes is a form of diabetes that develops during pregnancy in some women. Because of hormone changes, a pregnant woman's body suddenly may not react normally to insulin. This causes her blood sugar levels to go up. Infants born to mothers with poorly controlled gestational diabetes tend to be larger in size. You need to know that:

- You should gain weight slowly and steadily and control blood sugar by changing your diet. A registered dietitian can help you with your food choices.

- Some women require shots of insulin to keep their blood sugar levels normal.

- Diabetes during pregnancy disappears after the baby is born, but it is likely to return during the next pregnancy.

- Women who experience gestational diabetes are more likely to have diabetes later in life; it is especially important for these women to maintain a healthy weight and remain active.

insulin injections, even if they have non–insulin-dependent diabetes. However, losing weight is still one of the best ways to control your blood sugar, and it can even cause your non–insulin-dependent diabetes to disappear completely, as long as you keep the weight off.

A DOSE OF PREVENTION

According to the Surgeon General's Report on Nutrition and Health, the relationship between diabetes and what you eat is a strong one. People who keep their weight at a healthy level and eat according to the Dietary Guidelines for Americans dramatically reduce their risk of diabetes. (For more on the Dietary Guidelines, see page 97.) Here are some ways that you can lower your diabetes risk:

LOSE WEIGHT: It makes good health sense to keep your weight within a healthy range. People who are overweight may not respond as well to the insulin their pancreas makes, and they often have blood sugar levels that are too high. When you lose weight, your liver cells become more sensitive to insulin and do not release as much glucose into your blood. Even moderate weight loss by watching what you eat and increasing your physical activities can bring your blood glucose levels closer to normal.

GET A MOVE ON IT: Regular physical activity helps you keep your blood sugar under better control. During exercise, your muscles use up blood glucose for energy, and exercise builds more muscle that can lower your blood sugar even more. Exercise can

reduce your body's resistance to insulin, and when you exercise, losing weight is easier, too.

GET MORE COMPLEX: Foods high in complex carbohydrates, like cereals, bread, pasta, rice, corn, and peas, are less likely to send your blood sugar soaring. They take longer for your body to digest, turn into glucose, and absorb. Sugar and other simple carbohydrates, however, are digested and absorbed quickly. They can cause your blood sugar to get abnormally high after eating. Eating sugar will not cause diabetes; it only makes the symptoms more noticeable.

ADD MORE FIBER: Dietary fiber comes in two varieties, insoluble (found in wheat bran, whole grains, and vegetables) and soluble (found in oats, oat bran, barley, dried peas and beans, apples, pears, and carrots). Eating soluble fiber can help keep your blood sugar levels steady. It also can lower blood cholesterol and blood pressure. Soluble fiber seems to work by slowing the movement of food from your stomach to your intestine and allowing you to absorb glucose more slowly.

THE CHROMIUM CONNECTION

According to Richard Anderson, Ph.D., a researcher with the U.S. Department of Agriculture, people who have high blood sugar levels may be deficient in chromium. Chromium is a mineral that helps cells respond to insulin and lets blood sugar into cells. Without enough chromium, your blood sugar level can get too high. The best food sources of chromium include whole-wheat breads and cereals, brown rice, and broccoli.

ALLERGIC BEGINNINGS

Could some cases of diabetes be caused by food allergies? Studies in Finland, Canada, and the United States found that in families with a history of diabetes, infants who drank cow's milk during infancy were more likely to end up with diabetes than those fed breast milk or infant formula. The researchers suggest that the protein in cow's milk may trigger an immune reaction that shuts down the pancreas' ability to make insulin. These findings are only preliminary. The American Academy of Pediatrics still advocates giving milk to children older than one year.

FIBROCYSTIC BREAST DISEASE

Fibrocystic breast disease is an uncomfortable condition in which a woman's breast tissue is unusually lumpy and painful. Normal hormone fluctuations are to blame, but some women are more prone than others to having fibrocystic breasts. Close to one-third of women in this country are fellow sufferers of fibrocystic breast disease.

Women with fibrocystic breast disease may be at higher risk for developing breast cancer. Fibrocystic breasts are harder to examine for cancerous lumps; it is difficult to tell the difference between a benign fibrocystic lump and one that might be a tumor. Also, fibrocystic breast tissue looks cloudy on a mammogram, obscuring potentially cancerous lesions.

Although fibrocystic disease cannot be cured, what you do and do not eat may make a difference in how you feel.

CUT THE CAFFEINE

Caffeine is a type of chemical called a *methylxanthine*. Other methylxanthines include theophylline from tea and theobromine in chocolate. Some women

Caffeine, a methylxanthine, may be one of the chemicals that can increase the pain of fibrocystic breasts.

DISHES WITH OVER 1,000 mg OF SODIUM*

Chili con carne, canned, 1 cup†
Spaghetti with meat sauce, 1 cup†
Submarine sandwich made with cold cuts
Cheeseburger with catsup and pickle
Fast food breakfast muffin with cheese, egg, and ham
Soup, 1 cup, most flavors

* Dietary Guidelines recommend a daily limit of 2,400 mg.

† Homemade versions are not necessarily as high in sodium.

have less breast pain and lumpiness if they rid their diet of as much methylxanthine as possible. However, it's not as simple as just switching to decaffeinated coffee, tea, and cola. A few noncola soft drinks have caffeine, also; check the ingredient list to be sure that your favorite beverage is caffeine free. Also, look at the labels of over-the-counter cold remedies, diuretics, pain relievers, and stimulants, and select brands that do not list caffeine as an ingredient.

STOP THE SALT

Fibrocystic breasts tend to become more painful during the week before your period begins, and the pain may become worse if you eat a lot of salty or high-sodium foods. Staying clear of salt is a test of willpower when you find yourself craving high-salt foods such as pretzels and Chinese food. Still, successfully fighting back the urge can make you feel more comfortable.

AN *E*-ASY REMEDY?

Some women find that taking a vitamin E supplement reduces their breast soreness. A 1982 study found that 600 international units (IU) of vitamin E daily was associated with remission in 85 percent of patients with fibrocystic breast disease. Vitamin E has been studied in doses up to 1,200 IU per day, and thus far, has had no adverse side effects. Vitamin E has stirred up a lot of excitement for another reason too: It may help protect against heart disease. The preventive effects of vitamin E supplementation are not yet conclusive but are being actively studied.

WHEN TO SEE YOUR DOCTOR

All women should examine their breasts monthly, during the week after their period. Notify your physician of any changes, including development of a hard lump that does not move, tenderness in only one breast, or nipple discharge (unless you are nursing).

FLATULENCE

It's embarrassing and uncomfortable. It's unpre-dictable, unplanned, and unwanted. It's often blamed on the dog, the cat, or the new baby. And most of us would do *anything* to make it go away.

Flatulence, better known as gas, is one of life's necessary evils. Our bodies can digest and absorb most, but not all, of what we eat. The nutrients that we cannot break down, particularly certain types of fiber, travel unaltered through our intestinal tract to the large intestine. There, more than 400 different species of bacteria that live there wait to feast on what we've left behind. As the bacteria munch on our leftovers, they produce gas that we are stuck getting rid of.

THE FIBER-FLATULENCE CONNECTION

Health experts agree that eating more high-fiber foods should be one of your health priorities. However, fiber is notorious for fueling flatulence. Our bodies are missing the enzyme needed to break down fiber so that it can be converted to a form that we can absorb.

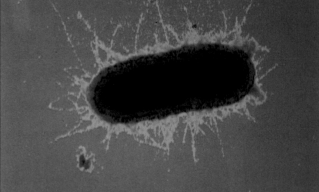

Escherichia coli *is the bacteria in your colon that produces gas by feeding off the food you did not digest.*

The result is that the fiber you eat gets passed on to the gas-forming bacteria that live in your colon. They digest the fiber and, in the process, release two gases, carbon dioxide and hydrogen.

Adding more fuel to the fire, when you eat a high-fiber diet, you help the gas-producing bacteria in your large intestine grow and multiply by giving them plenty to feast on. You might have gas regardless of the amount of fiber in your diet, but additional fiber will almost certainly increase your usual amount of gas.

SOME FOODS ARE GASSIER THAN OTHERS

It is hard to predict which foods will give you gas and which will not. Making the crystal ball even cloudier, a food that gives you gas one day may not have the same effect on a different day or at a different time of day. Proteins from animal muscle, like beef, lamb, pork, fish, poultry, and eggs, rarely, if ever, cause gas, but certain foods are almost a sure bet to cause flatulence. Here are some of the usual culprits:

LEGUMES: At the top of most people's list of troublemakers are legumes—dried peas and beans. It is unfortunate that a food with so many nutritional benefits can cause so much discomfort. Beans are high in fiber and low in fat, may help lower blood cholesterol levels, can help keep blood sugar levels under better control, are great sources of vitamins and minerals, and may help reduce cancer risk. However, they are

---

DEFUSING YOUR BEANS

You can make dried beans and peas less gassy by following a few simple preparation and cooking tips. Soak the beans for several hours or overnight to soften. Discard the soaking water (some of the carbohydrates that cannot be digested dissolve in water). Boil the beans until soft; then drain and rinse. If you have severe problems with gas, try draining and rinsing the beans after every half hour of boiling, and then replace the water with fresh water and repeat the cooking, draining, and rinsing process until the beans are ready.

VERY GASSY FOODS

Bran cereal
Broccoli
Brussels sprouts
Cabbage
Legumes
   (dried peas and beans)
Mushrooms
Onions
Potatoes
Radishes
Spinach
Turnips
Wheat bran

SOMEWHAT GASSY FOODS

Apples
Breads, baked goods made with
   wheat
Carbonated soft drinks
Eggplant
Fructose (fruit sugar)
Pretzels
Sorbitol- or xylitol-sweetened
   gum and candy

NONGASSY FOODS

Eggs
Meat
Poultry
Seafood

loaded with carbohydrates that your system cannot digest; so, plenty of people don't care a hill of beans about legumes because of their potentially gassy effects.

FRUITS AND VEGETABLES: Many fruits and vegetables follow closely behind legumes on the troublemaker list. Particularly troublesome are vegetables from the cabbage family, including broccoli, brussels sprouts, cabbage, cauliflower, and turnips. However, it's not a good idea to turn your nose up at these nutrition-packed vegetables—they've been linked to numerous health benefits, including cancer protection. Apples, melons, grapes, and dried fruit are the worst of the fruit offenders.

BREADS: Bread and other grain products may give you gas, regardless of whether they have a lot of fiber. For example, bagels and pretzels, two grain foods that are usually low in fiber, tend to cause flatulence. High-fiber breads and cereals are even more likely to add to your flatulence.

GAS GUZZLERS

You *can* eat a diet rich in grains, fruits, and vegetables without feeling like a gas station. The first step is to start slowly when adding potentially gassy foods to your usual diet. Your body may need several days or weeks to make the adjustment.

Foods high in fiber are the worst flatulence offenders, but don't avoid them—they are also packed with nutrients.

LOWDOWN ON LACTOSE

Most children have no trouble digesting lactose, the major carbohydrate in milk. However, as you get older, your body produces less and less lactase, the intestinal enzyme that is responsible for digesting lactose. The end result is that a large proportion of the lactose you consume in milk and other dairy products travels undigested down to the bacteria in your colon. As with fiber, undigested lactose becomes part of the next meal for the gas-producing bacteria.

If you suspect that dairy products are responsible for your gas, look for lactose-reduced milk and other low-lactose dairy products. Although not lactose-free, they are considerably lower in lactose and may allow you to enjoy dairy products with little discomfort. (For more on lactose intolerance, see pages 86–87.)

OVER-THE-COUNTER RELIEF

To break down those gas-causing foods that your body cannot digest, you can get help from several products. These products contain the enzymes that are missing from your digestive tract; so, they may be able to head off a gas attack by doing the work your body is not equipped to do.

Beano, a liquid that you sprinkle on gassy foods, is available at your local pharmacy or health-food store. Beano contains an enzyme called *alpha-galactosidase* that breaks down some of the undigestible fiber in vegetables and legumes. Once broken down, the fiber cannot be used by bacteria in the colon and, therefore, causes much less gas. Beano cannot be used in cooking or added to foods before cooking them, because heat destroys the enzyme.

If you're lactose intolerant, you can purchase liquid or tablets that contain lactase, the enzyme that breaks down the troublesome component of dairy products. The liquid can be added directly to a carton of milk, whereas the tablet can be chewed just before or after you consume a dairy product.

TABLE-SIDE TIPS

Try to avoid adding extra gas to your system. Swallowing air can add to a flatulence problem. Chew your food well and swallow slowly without gulping. Also, talk as little as possible when you eat. Finally, don't load up on carbonated beverages, and chew gum only in moderation.

FOOD ALLERGIES AND INTOLERANCE

Do you break out in hives during strawberry season? Does fish make you nauseous? Do lima beans make your lips swell? Do you describe yourself as having food allergies?

Although a lot of people say that they have food allergies, only one or two percent actually do. The rest have very real symptoms related to food, but they are not considered true allergies. Food allergies are most common in infants and young children; up to ten percent of children are affected, but most outgrow the allergy.

ALLERGY VERSUS INTOLERANCE

When you have a true food allergy, your immune system goes haywire after you eat the trigger food, called the *allergen*. Within a short period of time, you may get watery eyes, a runny nose, itchy skin, and even heart palpitations.

Many food-related symptoms that masquerade as allergies are called *food intolerances*. Food intolerance does not involve your immune system. Instead, there is another explanation of why the food is making you sick. For example, you probably have lactose (milk sugar) intolerance if you cannot drink milk because it gives you abdominal cramps and diarrhea. Some people are sensitive to sulfites, a food additive that prevents fruits, vegetables, and wine from turning brown. They may find it tough to breathe after they eat a food that has been treated with sulfites. You may get headaches as a reaction to the chemical monosodium glutamate (MSG), a flavor enhancer in Chinese food, soups, salad dressings, and other processed foods. These are food intolerances, not allergies.

ROUNDING UP THE USUAL SUSPECTS

Milk, eggs, nuts, legumes (dried peas and beans), and shellfish are the most highly allergenic foods. They contain a type of protein that can call your immune system into action. When your immune system attacks the invader, you get allergy symptoms. Other common problem foods include chocolate, fish, citrus fruit, wheat, bananas, tomatoes, and berries.

THE POWER OF THE MIND

Your mind may have more to do with your food reactions than you think. People who think they have food allergies often have negative results to allergy testing, even though they have allergy-like symptoms after eating a particular food. Some people who go through allergy testing have an allergic reaction to a placebo (a pill or injection that does not contain the allergenic food but a harmless nonallergenic substance), but they don't have a reaction to the food itself. These observations reinforce the role that your mind can play in causing very real reactions to foods.

CHEMICAL WARFARE

Should you worry about the almost 3,000 coloring agents, preservatives, and other compounds added to processed foods? Probably not. Only a small percentage of people appear to be sensitive to the most common offenders—yellow dye #5, the preservatives BHA and BHT, MSG, and sulfites. What makes detection more difficult is that you may react to one of these additives one day and not have a reaction the next.

It is hard to imagine what our food supply would be like without food additives. They slow down spoilage,

---

FOOD ALLERGY SYMPTOMS

Symptoms of a true food allergy develop up to two hours after eating the food you are allergic to. The most common symptoms include hives, swelling around your mouth and nose, and abdominal cramps. However, severe allergies may make breathing difficult and can lead to life-threatening shock. Here are some possible symptoms:

Skin
Itching
Rash
Redness
Hives
Swelling

Gastrointestinal tract
Vomiting
Diarrhea
Stomach pain

Respiratory system
Sneezing
Runny nose
Wheezing

Cardiovascular system
Palpitations
Shock

Eyes
Redness
Itching
Tearing

improve color, flavor, and texture, and add nutrients. Without additives, we would not be able to eat as wide a variety of foods year round, and we would have to rely on the food available locally.

Although it is difficult to avoid food additives in processed foods, you can reduce your exposure to additives like sulfites and MSG when you eat out. Don't be afraid to ask if vegetables or potatoes were treated with sulfites, or to request that your Chinese food be prepared without MSG. Many restaurants say right on their menus that they do not use MSG. Look for one of these.

It MIGHT BE FOOD POISONING

Stomach pain, diarrhea, nausea, and vomiting can be signs of a food allergy,

---

PREVENTING FOOD POISONING

Here are some simple ways to reduce your risk of food poisoning:

- Wash your hands well before you prepare or serve food to wash away some of the potentially harmful bacteria.

- Serve hot foods hot and cold foods cold.

- Do not keep prepared foods at room temperature for over two hours. Refrigerate leftovers promptly.

- Wash your cutting board well after cutting meat, poultry, or fish. Or keep one cutting board for meat and one for fruits, vegetables, and other foods.

- Cook meats and poultry to an *internal* temperature of at least 145° Fahrenheit. Check the temperature with a meat thermometer.

- Stay away from food that has not been kept at the right temperature, for example, a salad bar that is not chilled or a buffet that is not piping hot.

- Steer clear of raw fish and seafood—fish can carry bacteria and parasites; oysters and other mollusks may be infected with the virus that causes hepatitis.

---

but if these symptoms hit you out of the blue and up to a day after eating a particular food or dish, you may have food poisoning. Bacteria grow in food that has not been handled properly; for example, cold foods kept at too warm a temperature, meats that are not thoroughly cooked, or cooked meats that are left at room temperature can all be bacteria breeding grounds.

Testing, TESTING

Diagnosing a food allergy is easy if you react the same way to the same food over and over. You may be able to determine your own food culprits by keeping a food diary. Write down what you eat, what reaction you have, and how long after eating that the reaction occurred. Look for consistent reactions after eating similar types of foods, such as seafood or certain nuts.

In a physician's office, food allergies are often diagnosed using a skin-prick test called a *RAST* or *ELISA*. Small amounts of extracts of different suspect foods are injected under the skin. If you have a reaction, you are allergic to that food.

The problem is that you may be able to eat a food, even if your skin test says that you are allergic to it. Conversely, a food that gives you allergy symptoms may not turn up as one of the foods you are allergic to on the skin test. Allergy testing should be done by a board-certified allergist.

Many people have adverse reactions to monosodium glutamate—often found in Chinese and other prepared foods.

During the food challenge test, your physician gives you a pill that contains either an allergen that you may be allergic to or a placebo. Or, you may be asked to eat a number of disguised foods. Your physician may not know which pill or food is which. People who have an allergic reaction to an allergen but not to the placebo probably have a food allergy.

IF IN DOUBT, CUT IT OUT

One of the best ways to find out which food is causing you trouble is to go on an elimination diet. Under the guidance of a physician or registered dietitian, you start eliminating all possible allergenic foods from your diet. Then, you add foods back one by one and watch for an allergic reaction. After about three days, you add back another food. This process continues until you identify all the foods that you cannot eat. Once you know which foods you are allergic to or cannot tolerate, all you have to do is to stay away from them.

EYEING THE INGREDIENT LIST

People with food allergies or food intolerance become very skilled at reading food labels and scouting out

If you have an allergy or intolerance, read the labels carefully; you may be surprised where some ingredients are "hidden."

undesirable ingredients. For example, if you have lactose intolerance, you need to be on the lookout not only for foods with milk, but also those made with caseinate, whey, and other milk derivatives. Many foods have these "hidden" ingredients.

You may be able to handle small amounts of particular foods, even though larger portions cause trouble. The further down the list an ingredient is, the less of that ingredient is in the food.

PREVENTING FOOD ALLERGIES IN CHILDREN

The children of parents who have food allergies are more likely to be allergic also. It is possible, though, to delay the onset of their food allergies or even keep the allergies away entirely. Allergic mothers-to-be should stay away from allergenic foods during the third trimester of their pregnancy and while breast-feeding. This may spare the child the same allergy as the parent.

One explanation is that a mother's antibodies to allergenic foods can pass through the placenta to the fetus or through breast milk to the infant. The child's body then goes through an allergic reaction to fight off the antibodies. However, breast-feeding is not to be avoided. On the contrary, breast-feeding is very good for a child's immune system, and breast-fed infants, in general, have a lower incidence of food allergies.

Work with your pediatrician to set up a schedule for giving new foods to your young child. Watch for allergic reactions for three to five days after your child has tried a new food. If you see a reaction, hold off for several months before giving your child that food again. If your child has no reaction, move on to the next food. Children usually grow out of their food allergies. Their digestive tract and immune system mature and become better at combatting potentially allergenic foods.

WHEN ALLERGIES ARE SERIOUS

People with severe food allergies can experience life-threatening symptoms if they eat a food that they should not eat. The anaphylactic reaction of throat swelling, difficulty breathing, low blood pressure, and shock that some experience must be treated immediately with medication. Adults and children who suffer from these types of reactions should be diligent about carrying the medication, epinephrine, with them at all times.

GOUT

At one time, gout was considered an aristocratic disease. Only the well-off suffered from its painful effects. But there is nothing so regal about it. Gout is a type of arthritis that mostly causes trouble in your feet. It can cause pain and swelling in other parts of your body, but gout's main target is your big toe. For reasons that are not entirely clear, men are far more likely to have gout than women.

THE CAUSE IS CRYSTAL CLEAR

The symptoms of gout develop as uric acid, a naturally occurring compound in your body, builds up in your blood and eventually crystallizes in your joints. When people with gout eat a lot of foods high in a DNA building block called *purine,* their body makes more uric acid.

This excess uric acid builds up and the gout sufferer has trouble getting rid of the uric acid via normal routes, namely through their kidneys and urine. Instead, it builds up in their blood and then collects in crystalline form in their joints. Like cholesterol, though, only a small percentage of the uric acid in your body comes from what you eat; the rest is made by your body as a by-product of normal metabolism.

Although most gout sufferers don't have to change their diets, foods high in purines, such as anchovies, may be no-nos.

WHERE THE PURINES ARE

Although diet restrictions are generally no longer used to treat patients with gout, you may want to be aware of the foods that contain purines.

Foods high in purines:	Foods moderately high in purines:
sweetbreads	animal meat
fish eggs (roe)	seafood
anchovies	legumes
sardines	asparagus
liver	spinach
kidneys	peas
	mushrooms

DIET CHANGES

Back in the old days, beef, chicken, other animal meats, mushrooms, and asparagus were off limits for people with gout, because they are high in purines. A low-purine diet was widely prescribed but was difficult for men with gout, who often were big meat eaters, to stick with for any period of time.

Few people today have to restrict their diet, because medications have been developed that work better than diet does. Anti-gout medications can slow your body's production of uric acid or help it get rid of more uric acid through your kidneys.

WHAT I EAT DOESN'T MATTER?

Gout sufferers should not cast all dietary caution to the wind. Weight loss may make sense if you are overweight or obese (see pages 88–91). Diseases associated with obesity, such as heart disease, diabetes, and high blood pressure, are more common in people with gout. Overweight and obese people are more likely to have a bout with gout, and the stress and strain of a heavy body on a gout-ridden toe can be painful.

HOW ABOUT WHAT I DRINK?

Experts also advise that you cut down on or completely eliminate alcohol if you have gout. It can increase the amount of uric acid in your blood.

A final bit of good advice. Drink plenty of fluids— at least eight cups a day. Water and other fluids help your kidneys flush uric acid out into your urine. Fluid is particularly important if you are taking a medication that increases the amount of uric acid going to your kidneys.

HEADACHES

SOMETHING YOU ATE?

The food–headache relationship is difficult to sort out. Very few foods have been proven to cause headaches. Yet many people consistently get headaches from one or more foods or food additives.

Some people get headaches after eating foods rich in tyramine, an amino acid. Tyramine is thought to work by sparking a hormone called *norepinephrine* to constrict blood vessels in your brain, causing a migraine. Tyramine is even more likely to cause a headache if you are taking an antidepressant in the family called *monoamine oxidase (MAO) inhibitors.* Foods that are eliminated on a low-tyramine diet include red wine (particularly Chianti), aged cheese, aged or cured meats, chicken livers, and avocados.

Other similar food-related chemical reactions in your body can cause headaches. Some of the worst food offenders include chocolate, cheese, and alcohol.

SUBTRACTING FOOD ADDITIVES

The link between food additives and headaches is not well proved, nor is it well understood. Still, you may be plagued with headaches after eating foods with particular additives. Monosodium glutamate (MSG), the most widely used flavor enhancer in the United States, is added to commercial soup mixes, salad dressings, and other processed foods. It may cause headaches in susceptible people, particularly when eaten in concentrated amounts, as in Chinese-

Alcohol can give you a headache the morning after, but other chemicals in wine can also trigger a headache in some people.

Even though many people are scared to get near them, chili peppers contain a chemical that may stop headaches.

restaurant food. Avoiding MSG means asking restaurants to leave it out of the dishes you order and reading package labels carefully to check for MSG on the ingredient list. Another additive with a suspected headache link is FD&C yellow #5 (a food coloring).

CAFFEINE WITHDRAWAL

Caffeine—you can't live with it, and you can't live without it. Even in small amounts, caffeine can be addictive. If you are used to it, going without it in the morning almost guarantees that you will have a headache by midday. Likewise, drinking too much coffee can give you a headache. If you cannot do without your morning jolt of java, have a cup to avoid getting a headache. To kick the habit, don't go cold turkey. Gradually reduce the amount of coffee and other caffeinated beverages you drink to let your body, and your head, get accustomed to going without.

WHEN YOU'VE HAD TOO MUCH TO DRINK

You may feel perfectly fine after having more than a couple of drinks in one evening, but the next day's headache is enough to keep you in bed for the morning. The causes may be dehydration and the other by-products of alcohol metabolism commonly known as the *hangover.* You may be able to lessen the morning-after headache by drinking plenty of water to combat dehydration and by taking a nonaspirin over-the-counter pain reliever before you go to bed.

SPICE UP YOUR LIFE

Who would think that eating spicy food could chase away headaches, but a chemical in chili peppers, called *capsaicin,* may help reduce some types of headache pain.

HEARTBURN

You feel burning in your chest, almost like it is on fire. The pain travels from your stomach all the way up to your throat. Could it be a heart attack, or are you just suffering from heartburn?

Approximately half the adults in this country experience heartburn, an ailment that earned its name because of the pain and burning in the chest. For some people, heartburn, also called *indigestion,* is a minor inconvenience closely linked to eating or drinking too much. Others have heartburn after almost every meal, and women often experience heartburn during pregnancy.

As with other gastrointestinal disorders, see your doctor if your symptoms persist, if they occur long after you have eaten, or if you have trouble swallowing. Sometimes, angina or a heart attack can be mistaken for heartburn.

THE BEGINNING OF THE BURN

Under normal circumstances, the food you eat travels down your esophagus, a muscular tube that reaches

The "fizz-fizz" can be a welcomed sound to heartburn sufferers, but be aware that these antacids have a lot of sodium.

from your throat to your stomach. At the bottom of the esophagus is a ring of muscles called the *lower esophageal sphincter.* This "rubber band" is supposed to squeeze shut to keep the food and digestive juices in your stomach from squirting back into your esophagus. It's a one-way valve that stays closed unless food from your mouth knocks at the door, wanting to be let into the stomach—at least that's the way it is supposed to work.

When your lower esophageal sphincter loosens, it allows your stomach to push food and digestive juices back up the esophagus; this is called *gastroesophageal reflux,* literally meaning "stomach to esophagus backflow."

The burning sensation in your chest, throat, and even mouth is caused by burning chemicals like stomach acid, pepsin (a digestive enzyme that breaks down protein), and sometimes bile (a bitter-tasting substance needed to digest fat). These somewhat caustic digestive juices do not bother your stomach because your stomach lining has a special protective coating designed to withstand these harsh chemical substances; your esophagus, though, does not have this coating, and it is easily burned.

HOW DO YOU SPELL RELIEF?

Antacids come in several forms, formulas, and flavors. The shelf at the drug store can be very intimidating, and sorting out the different ingredients and indications can become a homework assignment in label reading. Here are some things to look for:

Liquid versus tablet: For quick relief, liquids usually work better. They seem to neutralize acid faster and also may coat your esophagus to help relieve pain. Tablets, though, are more convenient—it's hard to carry a liquid in your pocket.

Aluminum and magnesium: Several brand name and generic antacids contain a mixture of aluminum and magnesium. This prevents you from becoming constipated from the aluminum or having diarrhea from the magnesium. Long-term use of an aluminum-containing antacid can make your bones lose calcium and fluoride, though.

Calcium: Calcium antacids often double as calcium supplements. These antacids may cause constipation and can contribute to kidney stones in some people.

Sodium: Sodium antacids, like baking soda and commercial products with sodium bicarbonate, are extremely high in sodium. Persons who have been told to limit the amount of salt they eat should avoid these products as the sodium can really add up.

Simethicone: Simethicone helps reduce the amount of gas in your stomach, thus relieving the pressure that can cause stomach contents to reflux into the esophagus.

Natural Fire Extinguishers

Your saliva and some secretions in your stomach can help neutralize some of your stomach acid. Chewing gum may be a good fire fighter, because it increases the amount of saliva traveling from your mouth to your stomach to neutralize stomach acid and wash the harsh digestive juice back down into the stomach where it belongs.

Fight Fire with Less Fat

Heartburn sufferers often find that fatty foods make them more uncomfortable. One explanation is that high-fat foods stay in your stomach longer. More stomach churning can cause more gastric juices to push through your sphincter. Fat in your stomach also may weaken your lower esophageal sphincter. Try cutting back on fatty and fried foods and see if that helps put out the fire.

Eat and Drink in Moderation

Have you noticed that more people complain about heartburn around the holidays? Blame it on the overindulgence that is so common between Thanksgiving and New Year's Day. When you overeat, pressure inside your stomach increases and can force your sphincter to give way. Then add alcohol, which stimulates secretion of stomach acid, weakens your lower esophageal sphincter, and irritates the lining of your esophagus. All in all, it can be a pretty painful picture.

A note to those of you who take either Zantac (ranitidine) or Tagamet (cimetidine), two prescription drugs that lower stomach acid to relieve the burning of ulcers and other gastric problems: Alcohol may hit you harder and faster, because it is metabolized differently when you take one of these medications.

Spicy Sparks

Meatballs in marinara sauce, pepperoni pizza, enchiladas—some people get heartburn just thinking about spicy foods. Highly seasoned foods often dish up a painful combination of fat, cheese (a high-fat food), fiery spices, and tomato sauce or other tomato products that can irritate the lining of your esophagus. Worse yet, antacids may not put out the fire if your burn was caused by spicy ingredients instead of stomach juices.

For some, holiday feasting always brings on the burn. Too much food and alcohol often leads to reflux problems.

After-Dinner Myths

You've just finished dinner and your host brings out the coffee and after-dinner mints. Partake, and your chances of getting indigestion go up. Chocolate, peppermint, and coffee are notorious for causing your lower esophageal sphincter to relax, just the thing that you do not need after eating a large meal. Coffee, both regular and decaffeinated, can irritate the lining of your esophagus and increase your stomach acidity, also.

A Side Effect of Pregnancy

Most women experience heartburn at some point during pregnancy. In part, the position and size of the fetus are to blame. As the fetus grows and moves around, it puts pressure on the stomach, causing the stomach contents to put pressure on the sphincter. The end result is reflux and heartburn. This problem is compounded by the effects of two hormones that increase during pregnancy, estrogen and progesterone. They relax the lower esophageal sphincter, making reflux more frequent.

Additional Fire-Prevention Tips

- Identify and stay away from specific foods and combinations that bother you, like orange juice, chips and salsa, or a tuna sandwich with a cup of coffee.

- Eat smaller meals—large meals put pressure on your lower esophageal sphincter.

- Do not lie down or recline for several hours after eating.

- Wear comfortably loose clothing, instead of tight clothing.

HEART DISEASE

Heart disease is the number one killer in the United States. The good news is that you can make diet and lifestyle changes that reduce your risk of heart disease.

One goal is to lower your total cholesterol and low-density lipoprotein (LDL) cholesterol levels. LDL cholesterol, known as "bad" cholesterol, carries cholesterol to your arteries and deposits it on artery walls, leading directly to heart disease. Another goal is to raise your high-density lipoprotein (HDL) cholesterol level. HDL cholesterol, known as the "good" cholesterol, carries cholesterol away from your arteries and to your liver for disposal or repackaging, helping to reduce your heart disease risk.

Blue about your genes?

People who have close relatives with heart disease are more likely to have heart disease. You are at particularly high risk if your father, brother, grandfather, or uncle had a heart attack or died from heart disease before age 55 or if a close female relative was

The female hormone estrogen protects against heart disease, but after menopause, estrogen production virtually ceases.

stricken before age 65. By eating right and taking other preventive measures, though, you can delay or even prevent heart disease.

Protection with estrogen

Estrogen is a hormone produced in large amounts by a woman's body before she reaches menopause. Produced by the ovaries, estrogen is the major female reproductive hormone and is largely responsible for regulating the monthly menstrual cycle. But it has another function: Estrogen helps protect women, because it boosts HDL cholesterol levels. Estrogen also helps keep the walls of your arteries flexible and elastic. As you get older, your arteries stiffen; they have less give as blood flows through them. For this reason, blood pressure may creep up with age.

Your physician may recommend estrogen replacement therapy after menopause. By taking estrogen, you continue to get some protection against heart disease, but it may slightly increase your breast cancer risk. There are many pros and cons to estrogen replacement therapy that you should discuss with your doctor if you are at menopause.

Control your cholesterol

It is widely recommended that your total cholesterol levels be below 200

INEQUALITY BETWEEN THE SEXES

Heart disease is not for men only. Looking at all the research on heart disease, you would think that the disease afflicts only men, because very few studies have been done on women. But actually, heart disease is the leading killer of women, too.

Heart disease affects men and women differently. According to preliminary research findings, men and women may not respond the same way to diet changes. The following are some of the differences:

Men

- Heart disease develops at a young age.
- An immediate problem, like a heart attack, is often the first sign.
- Risk goes up moderately with age.
- High LDL cholesterol level greatly increases risk.
- High HDL cholesterol level moderately reduces risk.
- A diet high in soluble fiber tends to lower total and LDL cholesterol levels.

Women

- Heart disease develops at an older age, well past menopause.
- Chronic heart disease is an ongoing problem, not an acute episode.
- Risk is low until menopause and then goes up dramatically.
- High LDL cholesterol level moderately increases risk.
- High HDL cholesterol level greatly reduces risk.
- A diet high in soluble fiber lowers total and LDL cholesterol levels in postmenopausal women less than it does in men.

milligrams per deciliter (mg/dL). It is also important to keep your LDL cholesterol level down and to raise your HDL cholesterol level.

What you eat has a lot to do with how high or low your cholesterol level is. People who eat a lot of fatty foods, avoid vegetables and fruit whenever possible, and don't partake of whole-grain products are more likely to have higher levels of total and LDL cholesterol, and therefore, a higher risk of heart disease. On the other hand, by following dietary guidelines for healthy eating, you can lower your total cholesterol and LDL cholesterol (see chapter 3).

Dietary fat—how low to go?

No doubt you know that you can improve your health by lowering the amount of fat you eat to no more than 30 percent of your total calories. Some experts recommend that we severely restrict our intake of dietary fat to 10 percent of calories and cholesterol to fewer than 100 mg per day to stop heart disease progression and possibly reverse clogging of the arteries.

Minding your monos

Food has three major types of fat: saturated, polyunsaturated, and monounsaturated. Saturated fat is not good for your heart, because it causes your total blood cholesterol and artery-clogging LDL cholesterol levels to go up. Polyunsaturated fat is better for your heart. When substituted for saturated fat in a low-fat

diet, it lowers your total cholesterol but can also lower heart-protecting HDL levels. Better for your heart's health is the one-two punch of monounsaturated fats; they lower total cholesterol levels but don't lower HDL levels.

Olive oil is the classic example of an oil high in monounsaturated fat. Close behind is canola oil. Other foods with a lot of monounsaturated fat are avocados, some nuts (peanuts and almonds), and, surprisingly, many cuts of meat—but meats are also high in saturated fat. Of course, monounsaturated fats should not be added to your diet carelessly; in place of other fats, they are to be emphasized, but this is all in the context of a low-fat diet. Just because a fat is mono-unsaturated doesn't mean that it does not count in your total fat intake. Here, as elsewhere, moderation is the operative term.

Margarine, butter, margarine, butter

It is hard to know which one to use. Butter is high in naturally occurring saturated fat, which can raise your cholesterol levels. Margarine has *trans* fatty acids, a fat manufactured from vegetable oils that raises cholesterol levels, but not to the degree that butter does. Whichever one you choose should be used only in moderation.

Here fishy, fishy

One way to make your diet more heart healthy is to eat more fish. Many varieties of fish are extremely low in fat. Those that are not, including salmon, mackerel, sardines, and herring, have abundant supplies of a type of fat called *omega-3 fatty acid*. Omega-3s can really help reduce your risk of heart disease, in part because they make your blood platelets less sticky and therefore less likely to form artery-clogging clots.

In addition to this physical effect, omega-3s have a secondary dietary effect. Choosing fish for some of your meals may squeeze out some of the foods high in saturated fat that you would choose instead. Keep your portion size of fish to approximately three or four ounces before cooking, the same portion as for beef, chicken, and other meats.

Oats, Peas, Beans, and Barley Grow

These foods can help lower blood cholesterol levels, even if you are already following a low-fat diet. Their magic component is soluble fiber, a type of fiber that naturally binds to bile acids (a cholesterol derivative) in your intestine and helps your body get rid of them.

Look for soluble fiber in fruits and vegetables, including apples, apricots, okra, and brussels sprouts. As far as sprinkling oat bran on everything you eat—a craze started a few years ago by the overzealous media—you get more benefit from the multitude of different nutrients found in foods high in soluble fiber.

Your A-C-E in the Hole

Beta-carotene (a relative of vitamin A), vitamin C, and vitamin E help prevent heart disease through their role as antioxidants. These three antioxidant nutrients protect cells and tissues in your body from damage by naturally occurring chemicals and destructive forms

Soluble fiber, such as that found in oats, can lower your cholesterol by helping your body eliminate it before it's absorbed.

of oxygen called free radicals. A consequence of free radical damage can be cholesterol deposits in the arteries and heart disease. (For more on antioxidants, see pages 45–46.)

Several large studies have found that people who eat a lot of beta-carotene–rich fruits and vegetables are less likely to have heart disease. This lowering of heart disease risk seems to hold true for people who take beta-carotene supplements.

In the Physicians Health Study being conducted at the Harvard University School of Public Health, subjects taking 50 mg of beta-carotene in capsule form every other day had a far lower rate of heart attacks, deaths from heart disease, and strokes than did the subjects taking a placebo—a promising result for future prevention strategies.

Vitamin C appears to protect LDL cholesterol from being oxidized into an artery-clogging form. Also, people who eat a lot of foods rich in vitamin C tend to have lower blood pressure and higher HDL cholesterol levels. They also are less likely to die of heart disease.

A group of Harvard researchers found that people who took at least 100 international units (IU) of vitamin E every day, compared with the Recommended Dietary Allowance (RDA) of 10 IU, were far less likely to have a heart attack.

Although it is recommended that you get nutrients from foods instead of supplements, reaching this level of vitamin intake is possible only with pills. It is best to wait until more research on the effects of high-dose supplements is done, though, before you head to the drugstore to stock up.

The Weight Connection

You can lower your heart disease risk by losing weight. As you lose weight, your total and LDL cholesterol levels tend to go down. An added bonus is that your HDL cholesterol level usually goes up when you lose weight, giving you even more protection. But there are more advantages to losing weight than just a beneficial change in blood chemistry.

Losing weight reduces the amount of stress on your heart. To see the effect of losing even five pounds, pick up a heavy book or a five-pound sack of flour or sugar. Carry your extra load as you walk around. Or try jogging or climbing the stairs. You will feel the difference.

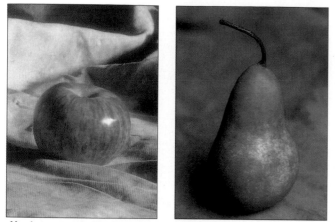

You're an apple if your waist is bigger than your hips; you're a pear if your hips are bigger than your waist.

WHICH FRUIT IS YOUR SUIT?

Are you an apple or a pear? That is, are you shaped more like an apple than a pear? The answer to this question says a lot about your risk of heart disease. To find out, use a tape measure to measure your waist and then your hips around the widest point. Compare the two measurements. Apples have a waist measurement that is close to or bigger than their hip measurement. Pears have bigger hips.

The problem with being an apple is that your risk of heart disease is higher. Fat that settles around your stomach is bad for your heart and can make you up to three times more vulnerable to heart disease. It is widely suggested that apples who are also above their recommended weight range lose weight by eating healthfully and exercising. Being an apple may also be a risk factor for diabetes (see pages 63–64).

SHAKE A LEG

And an arm, and a torso, and your whole body. If you do not exercise, you are a more probable candidate for heart disease. Physical exercise aids in the fight against heart disease on several fronts. Getting off your duff could be the best way to prevent heart disease.

Regular physical activity burns calories, helping you keep your weight at a healthy level. Also, as you exercise and build stamina and strength in your other muscles, so does your heart. Exercise raises the HDL cholesterol levels in your blood. By exercising, you also may help ward off diabetes and lower your blood pressure, two major heart disease risk factors. Best of all, it can make you feel great.

Exercise is a prescription for better health for people who have already suffered their first heart attack. According to the American Heart Association, exercisers live longer and are less likely to have a second heart attack.

STOP SMOKING

Cigarette smoking is very highly correlated with heart disease. It increases risk factors like high blood pressure and reduces your heart disease protection by lowering HDL cholesterol.

DRINK TO YOUR HEALTH

A daily glass of red wine has been shown to reduce heart disease risk in France and Italy. Wine and other alcohol can also elevate HDL, the good cholesterol, and may have an effect on total cholesterol. Recent studies have confirmed the findings from France and Italy.

Now the downside—diets in France and Italy have become higher in fat; many health experts expect heart disease rates to start going up, despite the red wine. Wine cannot undo the effects of a high-fat diet. You can't eat a high-fat diet and then go on a bender now and then to raise your HDL cholesterol level.

Additionally, because alcohol has significant health risks, experts recommend that men have no more than two drinks per day and women have no more than one per day. Don't forget, too, that alcohol is loaded with empty calories. Putting on excess pounds, especially around the waist, puts you at risk of heart disease. So, remember to use moderation.

Rowing is a demanding sport that is great for you, but you don't have to work that hard to get the benefits of exercise.

HEMORRHOIDS

Did you know that Americans spend more than $150 million a year on a problem that can often be helped by simple dietary changes? Did you know that simply by eating plenty of fruits, vegetables, and whole grains, you can avoid getting hemorrhoids?

What ARE THEY AND WHO GETS THEM?

If you have hemorrhoids, you know what they are and probably wish that you didn't. If you don't have them, you'll want to know how to avoid them.

VARICOSE VEINS OF THE INTESTINAL TRACT: Hemorrhoids are abnormally large, swollen pouches of blood vessels, tissues, and membranes that form inside your rectum and anus—the two lowermost parts of your intestinal tract. Hemorrhoids are a lot like the varicose veins that form in legs; they develop when the walls and valves of the veins in your rectum become weakened and can no longer push blood back to the heart, causing the blood to collect and build up pressure.

Hemorrhoids inside your anal canal are internal hemorrhoids. External hemorrhoids cause discomfort at the opening of the anus. Regardless of which type of hemorrhoid you have, hemorrhoids can be a pain to get rid of.

You may not even know that you have hemorrhoids until they start bothering you. Then, their typical symptoms of burning, itching, pain, and even bleeding can send you running for the closest over-the-counter remedy. (Consult your physician if you experience severe discomfort or notice any unusual bleeding.)

SITTING DUCK: Does your daily routine include spending a lot of hours in chairs, on a sofa, or at a desk? If it does, you may be a prime candidate for hemorrhoids. Sitting for long periods of time causes blood to collect in the veins of your rectum, much like the way it can collect in the veins of your legs. This increases pressure inside your rectal veins and can weaken and stretch the walls of the veins, causing even more blood to accumulate.

Catching up on your reading on the toilet can make hemorrhoids worse because you are sitting and adding extra pressure. Constipation also makes matters worse. When you strain to have a bowel movement, you push blood into your rectal and anal veins that

People whose jobs require them to sit all day are prime candidates for hemorrhoids. A little extra movement can help.

already may be under pressure from the hardened stool in your colon and rectum.

A PROBLEM OF PREGNANCY: Pregnant women often experience hemorrhoids. Constipation, one of the major causes of hemorrhoids, is a common side effect of pregnancy. Hemorrhoids can become even more problematic if the growing fetus presses against the veins that supply blood to the rectum and anus. This increases blood pressure in those veins, blocking the flow and making it harder for the blood to get back out.

A "BRAN" NEW APPROACH

People who eat more fiber are less likely to experience hemorrhoids. Fiber-rich foods help make your bowel movements larger, more regular, and easier to pass without straining. Fiber works by absorbing water into your stool, increasing its bulk and acting as a natural softener. But despite its benefits, most people's diets don't include enough of it; the average American eats only about half the amount of fiber recommended by The American Dietetic Association, National Cancer Institute, and other prominent health organizations.

An easy way to fiberize your diet is to make changes one meal at a time. At breakfast, switch from white bread to whole wheat or whole grain, and trade your low-fiber breakfast cereal for one with at least five grams of fiber per serving. Eat fruit instead of drinking juice—juice has almost no fiber. Top your favorite hot cereal with chopped dried apricots, prunes, raisins, or other dried fruit. Lacking at lunch? Sandwiches made on whole-wheat bread, rolls, bagels, or pita bread should be the rule. Add a cup of split-pea or bean soup for a quick fiber boost

Drinking plenty of fluids will insure that your lower intestinal tract will not be overstressed but will continue to run smoothly.

(legumes, dried peas and beans, are among the highest fiber foods). Include at least one serving of vegetables at lunch and two servings or more at dinner. You get the picture.

WATER, WATER EVERYWHERE

Drink plenty of fluids. Your stool needs water and other fluids in order to stay soft. Eating more fiber without drinking enough fluid actually could make you constipated. A good rule of thumb is to drink at least eight eight-ounce glasses every day.

DIET ALONE MAY NOT BE ENOUGH

Although changing your eating habits to include more fiber and enough fluid can go a long way toward preventing hemorrhoids, other changes in your life are also crucial.

AN EXERCISE A DAY: Daily exercise stimulates natural bowel contractions, helps blood flow through your veins (including the ones in your rectum), and strengthens your heart. Add short bursts of activity to your day by making small changes in your routine: Park your car farther away from the market or office and walk the extra distance, take the stairs, walk up the escalator instead of standing still, walk the long way, not the short cut.

RELAX: Learn to answer the call of nature. Holding in a bowel movement increases the blood pressure in your rectum and can worsen hemorrhoids. Get in

touch with your body's usual routine. If you normally do not have a bowel movement every day, do not force yourself to go on a daily basis. Straining can make the problem worse.

Set aside time after a particular meal to sit and relax. For many people, having a bowel movement after either breakfast or dinner is easiest. Eat a large enough meal to stimulate contractions in your colon. Additionally, have a warm beverage; warm drinks often help move things along. But if you drink coffee or tea, add extra fluids during the day, since coffee and tea act as diuretics, causing your body to eliminate more water.

OVER-THE-COUNTER RELIEF? Surprisingly, some over-the-counter remedies can make hemorrhoids worse. Laxatives that stimulate contractions of the muscles in your intestine can cause constipation if you take them for a prolonged period. Powdered fiber supplements that stimulate bowel movements by making your stool larger, softer, and easier to eliminate are better than laxatives that rely on altering intestinal muscles.

Staying active will help keep the muscles and blood vessels in your bowels toned and healthy, keeping hemorrhoids at bay.

HIATAL HERNIA

Hiatal hernia was once synonymous with heartburn. If you complained of heartburn, you were told that you had a hiatal hernia. Luckily, the problem is better understood now.

HOW IT'S SUPPOSED TO FIT TOGETHER

Your stomach is like a floppy sack with a pipe, your esophagus, coming out the top. The esophagus passes through an opening in your diaphragm, a set of muscles between your lungs and your stomach, just before it reaches the stomach. This opening is called the *hiatus*.

SO, WHAT'S THE PROBLEM?

If the whole area were static, there wouldn't be one, but your stomach is a pretty busy part of the body. It shakes and squeezes the food you eat for up to several hours after a meal. It serves as a holding tank for your food until the food passes into your small intestine, and it pumps your food full of acid and enzymes that begin the process of digestion.

During all of your stomach's shaking, rattling, and rolling, a portion of your stomach may get caught above the opening of your diaphragm, squeezing up through the hiatus. This is a hiatal hernia. When you have a hiatal hernia, the lower esophageal sphincter, the ring of muscles that usually keeps your esophagus and stomach separate, has trouble keeping the contents of the stomach from squeezing back up into your esophagus.

Hiatal hernias are a consequence of getting older, with a majority of adults having them by age 60. A hiatal hernia is not an illness; it is a condition.

THE PAIN, THE BURNING

A hiatal hernia can send you running to the doctor. Suddenly the pain and burning in your chest begin, and you are not sure if you ate the wrong thing or are having a heart attack. After a series of tests on your esophagus and stomach, you get your diagnosis—hiatal hernia.

You may have a hiatal hernia without knowing it. Many people never have pain or heartburn. Sometimes reflux (food you eat that escapes from your stomach and comes back up into your esophagus), or heartburn, may get worse when your hiatal hernia develops.

HOW DO YOU KNOW WHAT YOU HAVE?

The hallmark signs of a hiatal hernia are heartburn, reflux, pain, and possibly repeated burping. Always consult with your doctor if these symptoms last for more than a couple days. They could be the sign of a more serious illness.

PUTTING OUT THE FIRE

Can you and your hiatal hernia live together without bothering each other? Yes, if you make some simple changes in your habits.

EAT SMALL MEALS: When you have a big meal, your stomach works overtime. All the churning can push acidic stomach contents back up your esophagus and burn the tender esophageal lining.

CUT THE FAT: Foods high in fat stay in your stomach for a long time. Again, the more churning your stomach does, the more likely it is to either pop through your diaphragm or squirt its contents into your esophagus.

PLAINER IS BETTER: Spicy food can irritate the lining of your esophagus, which may already be sore.

REDUCE SMOKING AND DRINKING: Both habits can make your discomfort worse. Why not just quit?

Nothing can irritate an already bothersome hiatal hernia more than a spicy, high-fat food like pepperoni pizza.

HIGH BLOOD PRESSURE

High blood pressure, also called *hypertension,* is a chronic disease that is closely linked to what you eat. It is one of the most troublesome chronic diseases, because it increases your chances of heart disease, stroke, and some forms of kidney disease without showing any noticeable symptoms. Approximately one-quarter of American adults have high blood pressure.

High blood pressure develops when your arteries narrow or stiffen, losing some of their elastic quality. This forces your heart to pump harder to get blood through your vessels and increases the pressure of the blood within your arteries. Your blood pressure is considered high if it is consistently above 140 over 90 (140/90).

BLAME IT ON YOUR PARENTS

Heredity plays a role in hypertension. If one of your parents has high blood pressure, you are more likely to have the disease. Also, hypertension is more common among blacks than it is among whites or

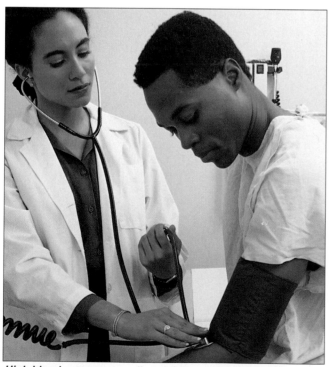

High blood pressure usually exhibits no symptoms. You must have it checked periodically if you want to keep a handle on it.

Asians. However, you do not have to follow in your parents' footsteps if you take the right preventive measures—watch the salt and sodium in your diet, eat plenty of high-calcium foods, keep your weight at a healthy level, and exercise regularly. You can keep your blood pressure normal despite your family's predisposition.

EFFECTS OF ALCOHOL AND SMOKING

Drinking too much alcohol can cause your blood pressure to go up. In fact, you are twice as likely to have hypertension if you are a heavy drinker (over three drinks a day) than if you do not drink at all.

Smokers are more likely to have hypertension than nonsmokers are. The nicotine in cigarette smoke hikes up your blood pressure. Smoking also thickens your blood and makes it clot more easily. These effects spell higher risk for a heart attack or stroke.

TRIM THE FAT

Being overweight increases your risk of hypertension, particularly if your surplus fat is around your waist instead of on your hips. People with too much abdominal fat are also at higher risk for heart disease. Losing weight can prevent your already high blood pressure from going too high and can actually lower your borderline high blood pressure, reducing or eliminating your need for medication.

In a large study, researchers at ten universities took more than 2,000 people with high-to-normal blood pressure and placed them alternately on a weight-loss program, a low-sodium diet, and a stress-management regimen. Weight loss lowered blood pressure better than either of the other two strategies.

What better way to start trimming the fat than to get regular physical exercise. Good choices include aerobic exercises like walking, jogging, swimming, bicycling, tennis, and skating. In addition, exercise, in and of itself, also lowers your risk of hypertension.

SHAKE THE SHAKER?

One line of attack against high blood pressure is a low-salt diet. When you have hypertension, your body may start to retain fluid and sodium (the main element in salt). The extra fluid collects outside your blood vessels and your blood vessels become less elastic. This increases blood pressure. Cutting down on salt

Some people turn to alcohol to relax, but drinking too much can make your blood pressure go up.

can help your body get rid of fluid and lower blood pressure. A diuretic, a medication that promotes the excretion of fluids, may also assist in this process.

You can cut your salt intake by simply avoiding the habit of adding salt during cooking or at the table. Avoiding very salty foods, such as commercial soup, chips, olives, pickles, and tomato sauce, is also a good strategy.

A large amount of the sodium you eat comes from processed foods, not from the salt that you shake on your food. High-sodium ingredients to look for on the label include salt, baking powder, baking soda, monosodium glutamate (MSG), sodium benzoate, sodium caseinate, sodium citrate, sodium nitrate, and sodium saccharine. Salt or sodium containing ingredients high on the list usually mean that the food is high in sodium.

Experts are not sure if eating a lot of salt actually *causes* high blood pressure. They also do not know if a low-sodium diet will ward off hypertension if your blood pressure is normal. In any case, a smart move is to limit the salt and high-sodium foods in your diet to the Dietary Guidelines for Americans recommendation of 2,400 mg of sodium per day. The average American adult eats almost twice that much.

THE PRESSURE OF AGING

The older you are, the more you may benefit from cutting back on sodium. Your body becomes sensitive to sodium as you age, increasing your chances of having hypertension later in life, even if your blood pressure is normal now.

Compounding the problem, your aging kidneys may be less efficient at filtering out extra water and sodium, and when you retain fluid, your blood pressure goes up.

COUNTING CALCIUM

Approximately half the adults with high blood pressure do not improve when they cut their salt intake. Instead, their blood pressure goes down after they add more high-calcium foods to their daily diet. The process by which calcium helps is extremely complex. Suffice it to say, a good health measure is to make sure you eat at least two servings of foods high in calcium daily.

ADD MORE FRUITS AND VEGETABLES

You need potassium to keep your blood pressure under control. Be even more diligent about eating bananas, apricots, oranges, cantaloupe, and other potassium-rich foods if you take diuretics to help control your blood pressure. Diuretics, which cause you to lose more water, drain some of the potassium from your body.

HOW 2,400 mg OF SODIUM ADD UP

Breakfast

¾ cup of bran flake cereal	227 mg
1 cup of 1% milk	123 mg
1 banana	1 mg
1 slice of wheat toast	153 mg
1 teaspoon of unsalted butter	1 mg
1 teaspoon of jam	1 mg

Lunch

Sandwich with 3 slices of ham, 2 slices of white bread, mayonnaise	1279 mg
½ cup of coleslaw	16 mg
Tossed salad with 1 tablespoon of dressing	140 mg
1 apple	1 mg

Dinner

1 cup of spaghetti, ½ cup of low-sodium tomato sauce, 3 ounces of ground meat	77 mg
Steamed broccoli	40 mg
1 slice of Italian bread, unsalted butter	153 mg

Snacks

1 cup of low-fat yogurt	133 mg
1 ounce of unsalted, whole-wheat pretzels	58 mg
TOTAL	2,403 mg

IRRITABLE BOWEL SYNDROME

First you're constipated. Then you have diarrhea. Then you're constipated again. And then the diarrhea is back. Is something seriously wrong with your bowels? Probably not. You may just be suffering from a case of irritable bowel syndrome, also known as *spastic colon.*

When it hits you for the first time, irritable bowel syndrome may look a lot like food poisoning or the flu, because it can cause cramping, bloating, gas, nausea, and vomiting. However, these symptoms are hardly a one-time occurrence; unfortunately, a spastic colon tends to act up again and again.

THE CASE OF THE SCHIZOPHRENIC COLON

Irritable bowel syndrome means that your colon is not pushing food down your intestinal tract normally. On some days, your colon works too quickly, propelling foods without removing enough water to form a firm bowel movement, resulting in diarrhea. At other times, your colon slows down and has enough time to pull too much water out of your stool, making it hard and pebbly and leaving you feeling bloated and constipated. If your colon tightens up in a spasm, your bowel movements may become extremely thin. With a culprit like irritable bowel syndrome, anything can happen, and it is hard to predict what your colon will do next.

Figuring out what triggers are to blame in your case of irritable bowel syndrome is an exercise in deductive reasoning.

BECOMING A DIETARY SHERLOCK HOLMES

Many people find that their attacks of irritable bowel syndrome don't come out of nowhere. Usually the episodes are triggered by something—a food they've eaten, their mood, a change in work load at the office, family problems, or stress. You can be a detective on your own case by keeping a food diary to identify possible suspects.

Each day, write down what you eat at each meal and snack, how your colon is acting, what type of mood you are in, and whether anything in your work, home, or social life is particularly stressful. Of course, you may have to keep a diary for several days or weeks if your colon suddenly decides to behave normally. Keep writing down even little things. Every clue might help.

Don't become obsessed with your diary. The added stress can worsen your spastic colon. Instead, take a very unemotional and nonjudgmental approach to keeping a record of what you eat and how you feel. Write down your foods and moods without trying to figure out immediately what is setting your colon off.

Make your diary easy to carry with you. A large binder is not very portable;

BOWEL DISORDERS THAT REQUIRE MEDICAL CARE

Some bowel disorders share the same symptoms with irritable bowel syndrome but are more serious. These include colitis (inflammation of the colon), ulcerative colitis (inflammation and ulcers in the colon), and Crohn's disease. People who suffer from colitis or Crohn's disease have almost constant inflammation of their large intestine; Crohn's disease also hits the small intestine.

These severe bowel diseases are more likely to surface between ages 10 and 30, and then again between ages 50 and 60. Their symptoms resemble those of spastic colon and can include diarrhea, bleeding, abdominal pain, and weight loss. See your physician if you have fever or anemia (low blood iron) in addition to these symptoms. You may have a form of colon disease that requires medical treatment.

As with irritable bowel syndrome, colitis and Crohn's disease are affected by stress. However, diet rarely is to blame; changing your diet may not have any effect on your symptoms.

you're better off with a small note pad that you can tuck into your purse or pocket without too much trouble, and always keep a pen or pencil handy.

Round up the usual suspects

After a few weeks of detective work, you should have a better idea of which foods trigger your colon spasms. It may even be elementary, Watson. Caffeine, alcohol, and in some cases, warm beverages stimulate colon contractions and can exacerbate discomfort and diarrhea. If they give you trouble, stay away from them. Fatty or fried foods also are trouble makers for some people; it doesn't hurt to avoid them for other health reasons, too.

Bigger may not be better

Large meals increase contractions throughout your entire gastrointestinal tract, including your colon. If you are in the diarrhea phase of irritable bowel syndrome, you may be more comfortable after eating small meals.

Include some small snacks if you are losing weight. Many people with irritable bowel syndrome eat less when their colon acts up, because pain and spasms make eating too uncomfortable, but be sure to get the nutrients your body needs.

During the constipation phase, a larger meal may help jump start your colon, stimulate contractions, and cause you to have a more normal bowel movement. Other ways to relieve constipation include having regular meals, keeping meals calm and relaxed, and allowing yourself a bit of time to relax after you have eaten.

Fight with fiber

Fighting your spastic colon with fiber, a food component that stimulates bowel movements, may not seem to make sense. However, a diet rich in fiber can help normalize your colon and your bowel movements. High-fiber meals provide your colon with enough bulk to stimulate normal and regular contractions. Your bowel movements will become more regular.

Fiber absorbs water in your colon. So, it works well to combat diarrhea by making your bowel movement more firm. When you are constipated, fiber holds onto water, and your stool becomes softer, easier for the colon to push, and easier for you to eliminate without pain and strain.

The last thing you need is additional stress from figuring out what to eat. That is why you should follow the principles of the USDA's simple Food Guide Pyramid (see page 102). Start with grain products—bread, grains, cereals, pasta, and rice. Make sure that at least three of your daily grain servings are made from whole grain and are high in fiber (read the ingredient list and fiber listing on the label). Good choices include whole-wheat bread, bulgur wheat, oatmeal, and brown rice, all of which are great fiber and energy sources.

Have at least five servings of fruits and vegetables every day, too. Include an apple or some figs in the afternoon for a quick fiber fix. Voilà, you've added fiber without stress. If you are used to a diet low in fiber, up your intake slowly to avoid cramping and bloating. With fiber on your side, you colon may finally fall in line.

Steadily upping your fiber intake may be one way to tame your colon. Try including more legumes in your menu.

LACTOSE INTOLERANCE

You stopped drinking milk years ago. To this day, you do not know why, although you tell your friends and family that the taste bothers you. The real reason you don't drink milk could be that it gives you gas and diarrhea. If milk, in fact, does not agree with you, you're in good company; a majority of adults around the world have the same problem you do—lactose intolerance.

SIMPLE SUGAR—NOT SO SIMPLE TO DIGEST

Lactose is the type of carbohydrate found in milk and other dairy products. It is a sugar called a *disaccharide,* because it is made up of two single sugars—in this case, glucose and galactose. An enzyme called *lactase,* which is made in your small intestine, breaks up lactose into glucose and galactose for absorption.

Most infants and young children can drink milk without any discomfort. Their intestines make enough lactase to break down all the lactose that they get from breast milk, cow's milk formula, or straight

Dairy foods are too important to just give up. Try yogurt with active cultures, aged cheeses, and lactose-reduced products.

cow's milk. However, as you get older, you make less and less lactase; many children begin to have trouble tolerating lactose.

WHO IS LACTOSE INTOLERANT?

Over half the adults in the world cannot make enough lactase. Adults who are most likely to have trouble with lactose are those of African, Asian, Jewish, Native American, or Hispanic descent. Northern Europeans and Scandinavians are best able to handle lactose.

If you continue drinking milk and eating other dairy products throughout your childhood and adult years, you may not have any trouble with milk. The villi in your intestines manufacture more lactase when they are exposed to the lactose in dairy products. Even people who are lactose intolerant may be able to drink approximately half a cup of milk without any discomfort, and having milk products as part of a meal, rather than on an empty stomach, makes them easier to tolerate, too.

SIGNS AND SYMPTOMS

How do you know if you have lactose intolerance? You might experience gas, gurgling, cramping, and diarrhea shortly after eating dairy products. What happens is that the lactose you cannot digest in your small intestine travels down to the bacteria that live in your colon. They can and gladly do digest the lactose, giving off gas in the process and causing flatulence in some people. Lactose intolerance can also cause diarrhea because your intestine pours water into your stool to dilute the lactose that it doesn't know how else to handle.

Some adults are not always lactose intolerant. For example, you may have more discomfort from milk and dairy products after a bad intestinal virus, because your villi, the small folds in your intestines, temporarily produce less lactase. In most cases, they return to normal within a few days.

DON'T SAY NO TO DAIRY

Why not just skip dairy products altogether? Because they are one of the best food sources of essential vitamins like riboflavin and minerals like calcium. Although you can get enough riboflavin in your diet without dairy products, getting adequate amounts of

Be careful about foods that are made with milk products, such as pancakes or pudding. Read ingredient lists carefully.

calcium is more difficult. The average eight-ounce glass of milk supplies over one third of the total amount of calcium you need in a day. You would have to eat seven sardines with bones, over half a cup of canned salmon, or four cups of cooked broccoli to get the same amount. Another option is calcium-fortified beverages like orange juice or fruit juice drinks that have calcium added to them. (Ordinarily, juices and juice drinks have little or no calcium.) Check to see if your brand has added calcium.

Say cheese... and yogurt

Many adults who cannot drink milk are able to eat hard cheese and yogurt. Hard cheeses, which are often aged, have less than ten percent of the lactose found in milk. Only people who are extremely lactose intolerant have trouble with hard cheeses.

You may be able to eat refrigerated or frozen yogurt. Yogurt that has plenty of live bacteria cultures is easy for some people to tolerate, because the bacteria break down the lactose before it causes trouble. Frozen yogurt is a different story, because most brands have only a fraction of the live cultures that you get in regular yogurt. Look for brands that say "live and active cultures" on the label.

Fighting lactose with lactase

Look for lactose-reduced milk and other low-lactose dairy products. Most lactose-reduced dairy products are not lactose-free, but they are considerably lower in lactose and may allow you to enjoy dairy products with little discomfort. Your pharmacy, supermarket, or health-food store also may have lactase-containing pills and tablets that help you digest lactose.

Look at the label

You should pay careful attention to the ingredient list on food package labels. Dairy ingredients, such as milk, nonfat milk powder, milk solids, whey, casein, and whey protein concentrate, have lactose. Expect the unexpected—your favorite brand of bread, muffins, soup, salad dressing, or even hot dogs may have lactose-containing ingredients that won't agree with you. Watch out for foods that are made with milk, like pancakes, waffles, muffins, and pudding. Also, many medications, both prescription and nonprescription, contain lactose as a base.

DEALING WITH DAIRY PROBLEMS

Lactose intolerance has become much easier to tolerate with the increasing availability of two types of products—dairy products that have been treated with the lactase enzyme and lactase "supplements" that you can put into your dairy food or take in tablet form.

Many of the lactase-treated dairy products have only 30 percent of their original lactose remaining. However, if you are extremely sensitive to lactose, you still may experience discomfort. The next step is to use a lactase supplement. Brands that are available in liquid form can be added directly to milk. By adding a designated amount and then leaving the milk in the refrigerator for one to two days, you can eliminate almost all of the lactose. Your other option is to take one or two lactase-containing tablets whenever you eat dairy products.

FOOD	APPROX. LACTOSE (*IN GRAMS*)
Milk, 1 cup	10–11
Ice cream or ice milk, ½ cup	6–9
Yogurt, 1 cup	5
Milk, commercial, treated to remove 70% of lactose	3–4
Cottage cheese, ½ cup	2–3
American cheese, 1 ounce	2
Cheddar, swiss, other hard cheeses, 1 ounce	1
Half and half, 1 ounce	1
Milk, treated to remove all lactose	<1

Source: *American Journal of Clinical Nutrition* 1988, 48:1099–1104.

OVERWEIGHT AND OBESITY

Almost two thirds of American women and approximately one half of American men are trying to lose weight or maintain weight that they've lost—and at a high cost. Americans spend over $30 billion every year on weight-loss foods, formulas, programs, and products that usually do not work.

The health cost of being overweight is high. Your risk of chronic diseases, including heart disease, high blood pressure, diabetes, and some forms of cancer, goes up as your weight goes up. However, determining whether you are overweight involves more than just stepping on the scale. Many factors need to be considered in the determination. Your healthy weight range depends on how much of your weight is fat (based on your weight and your height), where your fat is located on your body (namely, around your waist or on your hips and thighs), and which particular weight-related health problems you have or are at particularly high risk for.

SHAPED LIKE AN APPLE?

According to the U.S. Department of Agriculture's (USDA's) Dietary Guidelines for Americans, people whose waist measurement is close to or greater than their hip measurement (giving them an "apple" shape) are more likely to have heart disease, diabetes, and certain types of cancer. That is why apple-shaped people who are above their healthy weight range should try to "pear" down.

Pear-shaped adults have bigger hips than waist and are at much lower risk for chronic disease. A word of advice to women who are pears: Weight loss may be difficult for you, because your female hormones want to put fat into long-term storage on your hips and thighs.

YOU CAN'T CHOOSE YOUR RELATIVES

Are your parents, grandparents, or aunts and uncles overweight or obese? If so, you are more likely to weigh in above your healthy range. According to one estimate, you have a 40-percent chance of being overweight if you have one overweight parent and an 80-percent chance if both parents are above their healthy weight. Sometimes the tendency to be overweight skips a generation or crosses family lines.

Families usually share the same shape. If your relatives are overweight, your chances of being overweight go up.

That is why you may be overweight even though your parents are not.

COUCH POTATOES GROW TATER TOTS

Overweight and obese children are more common today than they were a generation ago. One theory is that Americans are much less active. We drive instead of walking, spend hours in front of the television, work at desk jobs, and get little exercise. Our children are following in our footsteps.

DIETING IS NOT ALWAYS THE ANSWER

A recent study by the National Institutes of Health (NIH) found that most people who lose weight on diet programs gain back most, if not all, of their lost pounds. Maintaining weight at a healthy level works best in the context of your overall lifestyle, including the way you eat and the amount of regular activity you get.

EAT LIKE AN EGYPTIAN

The Food Guide Pyramid developed by the USDA depicts a balanced eating plan that can fit all ages and lifestyles (see page 102). By following the guidelines of the Pyramid, you know how much and which types of foods you should eat to improve your health. The Food Guide Pyramid ensures that you get the calories and nutrients you need in a low-fat, high-fiber eating plan that you can follow for the rest of your life.

High fiber, low fat

Eat a lot of high-fiber foods and you may find it easier to watch your weight. Whole-grain breads and cereals, fruit, and vegetables can fill you up, not out, since they are satiating without having a lot of calories. They also take longer to chew and eat.

According to current research, you may be able to lose weight by switching from higher-fat foods to their lower-fat counterparts, without making any other change in the way you eat. For example, instead of having regular mayonnaise on your turkey sandwich, use fat-free mayonnaise, or have fat-free frozen yogurt in place of the regular version.

David Levitsky, M.D., a nutrition professor at Cornell University in Ithaca, New York, found that a group of 13 women ate fewer calories per day and lost more weight when they were on a low-fat diet (20 to 25 percent of their calories from fat) than on a standard diet (35 to 40 percent fat calories). As long as you do not eat more food to make up for the fat calories that you cut out, you, too, may be able to drop a few pounds simply by trimming the fat from your food. (For more information on planning a low-fat, high-fiber diet, see pages 102–107.)

Changing your ways

What you eat is not the only factor to consider in trying to lose weight. *How* you eat can be just as important. One method of weight loss and weight control involves modifying your food-related behaviors. For example, if you tend to overeat at dinner because you eat too quickly, you might modify your behavior by eating more slowly. Instead of preparing another forkful while chewing the last one, put your fork down until you swallow. If you snack on vending machine cuisine every afternoon, you could walk to the water fountain instead. According to the National Institutes of Health (NIH), behavior modification has been shown to work in the short term, but it may not keep your weight off over a period of years. Its long-term effectiveness is still being studied, but it wouldn't hurt to start changing your ways now.

The NIH found that behavior modification by itself usually is not enough. You may also need to learn how to cope with emotional and social situations without overeating; many people automatically start eating when stressed. Solving problems and reducing the stress in your life are also important parts of the weight-control solution. Behavior modification in combination with a healthy diet and regular physical activity can be the most effective—but only if you keep it up.

SHOULD YOU LOSE WEIGHT?

First, compare your weight to this table of suggested weights from the Dietary Guidelines for Americans. Measure your height and weight when you are not wearing shoes or clothing.

Height	Weight (19–34 years)	Weight (35+ years)
5′	97–128	108–138
5′1″	101–132	111–143
5′2″	104–137	115–148
5′3″	107–141	122–157
5′4″	111–146	122–157
5′5″	114–150	126–162
5′6″	118–155	130–167
5′7″	121–160	134–172
5′8″	125–164	138–178
5′9″	129–169	142–183
5′10″	132–174	146–188
5′11″	136–179	151–194
6′	140–184	155–199
6′1″	144–189	159–205
6′2″	148–195	164–210

If you are muscular, your weight may be at the high end of the range for your height, but in most cases, even people with much less body fat than muscle will fall well within the suggested weight range.

Next, find out where more of your fat is located. Measure your waist near your belly button and your hips around the widest part of your buttocks. Then divide your waist measurement by your hip measurement. For example, if your waist measures 30 inches and your hips are 36 inches, your ratio would be 0.83. If your ratio is greater than one, you are at the highest risk for some chronic diseases.

Finally, look at your overall health. Do you have a weight-linked medical problem, such as high blood pressure, diabetes, or heart disease? Has a doctor told you to lose weight?

Think twice about losing weight if you are within the suggested range for your height, if your hips are bigger than your waist, and if you have no significant medical problems related to weight.

Ban the browsing

Do you ever catch yourself browsing through the refrigerator, taking a nibble of this and a spoonful of that? Or standing in front of the pantry cupboard with a box of crackers in one hand and a bag of cookies in the other? This type of shelf-shopping can add extra calories to your diet and unwanted fat to your body.

Instead, make your kitchen as boring as possible by covering and tightly wrapping leftovers, putting favorite foods out of immediate sight, and best yet, keeping mostly low-fat, high-fiber snacks in the cupboard.

Are you trigger happy?

Research by Marie Simonson, Ph.D., in the Health, Weight, and Stress Clinic at the Johns Hopkins Medical Institutions has found that colors, music, and other "triggers" in the environment can stimulate you to eat more. She discovered that the colors orange, yellow, and red make people feel hungrier than the cooler colors, blue and green. In music, a faster tempo meant faster eating (and possibly eating more, since your brain needs time to register when you are full). Changes in season can also affect your weight; it is normal to put on a few pounds in the late fall and winter months and to shed them relatively easily in the spring.

TV, or not TV?

According to a study of 800 adults by Steven L. Gortmaker, Ph.D., and his colleagues at the Harvard

Research shows a correlation between watching a lot of TV and being obese. Pick a more active family activity.

School of Public Health, people who watch more television are more likely to be obese. Television watching can make weight management much more difficult, because it diverts you from doing calorie-burning physical activities. Your body also slows down during TV time. When you watch television, your metabolism drops, and you burn calories at a low rate, similar to the sluggish rate during sleep.

You may be packing in more calories than you realize if you snack in front of the television. The bottom line is limit the amount of television that you and your children watch, keep healthy snacks around the house, and find physical activities that the entire family can enjoy.

Is your engine too slow?

How many times have you heard someone blame their weight gain on slow metabolism? Could there be some truth to the excuse? Maybe there is, especially if they've been on and off diets over and over. When you repeatedly go on low-calorie diets, your metabolism may slow down because your body is anticipating getting too little food. In this situation, weight loss becomes more difficult. The second problem arises when you resume eating a normal number of calories. You actually may gain weight, because your motor is still running at the lower calorie level.

Keeping the rate up

Two of the best ways to jump start your metabolism are to eat regular-sized meals and to exercise. When you eat a moderate amount of food at one time, your metabolism speeds up and burns more calories while it digests and absorbs the food. Some experts feel that your metabolism does not increase as much if you snack your way through the day.

Even more dramatic is the effect that exercise has on your metabolism; it hikes your metabolism while you are exercising and for a couple of hours after. Regular exercise can really help you control your weight. Activity burns calories and builds muscle, which uses more calories than fat does. By increasing the muscle on your body, you increase the number of calories your body burns even at rest. Among the other benefits of exercise are higher blood levels of high-density lipoprotein (HDL) cholesterol (the "good" cholesterol) and a reduced risk of heart disease and diabetes. Exercise can also help you cope with stress and make your feel more energetic.

Regular exercise is an often overlooked, but essential, part of any weight-loss program. Diet alone cannot keep the pounds off.

Very Low Calorie... Very Low Success

A 1993 study of 255 people on a six-month, low-calorie, liquid-diet regimen discovered that although almost everyone lost weight on the program, most had gained back at least two-thirds of the weight after two years. However, those people who exercised regularly found it easier to keep the pounds off.

The American Dietetic Association feels that although very-low-calorie diets can promote rapid weight loss, these diets have health risks. People on programs that supply very few calories, usually using special drinks, should be under the supervision of a team of health professionals, including a doctor and a registered dietitian. You cannot stay on the drinks forever. Programs should teach you how to eat normally once you've stopped the drinks.

CONSIDERATIONS WHEN CHOOSING A WEIGHT-LOSS METHOD

What should you look for in a weight-loss program? The National Institutes of Health (NIH) list some considerations:

- Which foods you like to eat
- How much structure and guidance you want
- Whether you prefer a group or one-on-one setting
- Time and money
- How well the program will fit into your lifestyle
- How successful others have been at losing and maintaining weight using the method you are considering
- Whether you will be working with physicians, dietitians, and other qualified health professionals
- Whether the method includes diet, exercise, and behavior modification

WARNING

A word of caution: If you are severely overweight, pregnant, breast-feeding, over age 65, or are under a physician's care for an ongoing medical problem, do not embark on a weight loss program without first notifying your doctor.

The Lowdown on Diet Pills

Wouldn't it be easier to pop a pill and give up the fight against food? We are always looking for the quick fix, the easy short cut. As with other too-good-to-be-true weight-control methods, pills usually are not the answer to shedding pounds forever. Some claims, such as the miracle of grapefruit, are completely false. Over-the-counter diet pills do act as mild appetite suppressants. However, they often contain stimulants that can make you feel jumpy and cause you to have trouble sleeping.

Herbal remedies are not any better. Despite their "natural" reputation, herbs are not always harmless. Herbs can have side effects just like any other drug. Ma Huang, for example, a Chinese stimulant used in many herbal remedies, can give you heart palpitations, nervousness, and jitters.

A newer appetite suppressant, fenfluramine, is available by prescription only. Fenfluramine increases your brain levels of a hormone called serotonin, which makes you feel full. It also reduces carbohydrate cravings. However, fenfluramine's effects on appetite and weight loss usually disappear when the medication is stopped. Experts do not recommend fenfluramine for people who are only moderately overweight. It is a serious drug for serious medical problems.

A Formula for Serious, Lasting Success

Slow and steady wins the race. The NIH panel on weight loss and weight control has suggested that people who set reasonable weight goals and shed their pounds slowly are more likely to succeed at weight loss and maintenance. If you are serious about weight loss, you have to change your eating habits and physical activity permanently to keep your weight off.

OSTEOPOROSIS

Even though you've made it into adulthood without breaking a bone, you are not guaranteed a cast-free lifetime. In fact, women who have passed menopause are among those at the highest risk of breaking bones. Why? Because of osteoporosis, a disease in which you lose calcium and other essential minerals from your bones.

In osteoporosis, your bones become more porous and fragile and break more easily. Even minor falls and twisted ankles can cause fractures for osteoporotic bones. Hip fractures can be particularly common and debilitating for sufferers of osteoporosis.

Bones are built when calcium and other minerals are attached to a type of protein called *collagen*. You build bone rapidly during your childhood and teen years. Then your bones grow slowly until you reach your mid-thirties. Bone loss then takes over, particularly in women who have reached or passed menopause.

A WOMAN'S DISEASE

Osteoporosis is far more prevalent among women than men because of changes in the level of the female hormone estrogen. Estrogen promotes the deposition of calcium in women's bones. In this regard, women have a protector early in life. During menopause, a woman's estrogen level drops dramatically, causing her bones to lose calcium rapidly. Another strike against women is the amount of bone-building calcium in their diet. Women tend to eat fewer calcium-rich foods than men do. Also, men have bigger bones that lose calcium more slowly.

YOU CAN BE TOO THIN

Thin women are more likely to have problems with osteoporosis, which is a good reason to keep your weight within the healthy range for your height. Other risk factors include smoking, inactivity, and light skin color.

STOPPING THE LOSS

In the first five years after menopause, bone loss is dramatic and occurs because of hormonal changes, not because of a lack of dietary calcium. However, after these five years, eating more calcium can slow your loss of calcium and may even help increase bone mass.

For this reason, it has been recommended that postmenopausal women get at least 800 mg of calcium every day, the recommended dietary allowance (RDA) for women. Although the exact amount is still a matter of debate, some experts feel that women should have 1,200 to 1,500 mg, a level that is difficult to attain without taking calcium supplements.

STOCKPILING CALCIUM

Your bones are your chief storage depot for calcium. In fact, almost all of the calcium in your body is stored in your bones. One of the best ways to avoid the problems of osteoporosis in the future is to make sure that those storage depots are full. Hoarding the mineral can help you make up for deficiencies later.

Women who built up stronger bones in their teen years may be less likely to experience osteoporosis when they get older. They can build these strong bones by eating a lot of calcium-rich foods, but teens are notorious for their poor eating habits. A large percentage of teenage girls do not come close to meeting their RDA for calcium of 1,200 mg. Few have the three or more servings of milk and other dairy products that would

---

MAKING THE MOST OF CALCIUM SUPPLEMENTS

- Women who have not yet reached menopause who take calcium supplements should take them between meals to prevent calcium from blocking absorption of other key minerals, like iron. Men, seniors, and postmenopausal women, who tend to get enough iron to meet their needs, can have their supplements at mealtime.

- If you take iron supplements, don't take iron and calcium at the same time.

- You may absorb more calcium if you split up your daily dose into two or three smaller doses.

- Make sure that the supplement you choose will be easy for your body to absorb. Drop a tablet into a small amount of vinegar. If the tablet does not fall apart within 30 minutes, it will be difficult to absorb. Try a different brand.

- Pick a calcium supplement with a lot of calcium per tablet. Otherwise, you will be taking a lot of tablets each day to get enough calcium.

HOW MUCH CALCIUM IS IN YOUR SUPPLEMENT?

Different calcium sources and different pill sizes can make supplementation a confusing area. As a rule, the higher the percentage of calcium, the fewer pills you need to take. The following are approximate percentages of calcium:

		In a 600 mg pill:
Calcium carbonate	40% calcium	240 mg
Calcium gluconate	9% calcium	54 mg
Calcium lactate	13% calcium	78 mg
Calcium phosphate	30% calcium	180 mg

bring them to this level, and some experts think that teens need even more calcium than that to increase their bone strength.

Although women in their twenties have stopped growing taller, their bones can continue to get stronger. The key is to get regular weight-bearing physical activity, like walking or jogging, and to meet the 800-mg RDA for calcium. Once you hit age 35, calcium starts trickling out of storage, gradually weakening your bones—so don't delay.

MORE THAN MILK

For many adults, getting enough calcium can be difficult. You may not be able to tolerate lactose, the sugar in milk; every time you drink milk, you get cramps, gas, and diarrhea. If dairy products are a problem for you, think juice. Several brands of orange juice and juice drinks are fortified with as much calcium as you would get in milk, 300 mg in an eight-ounce glass. However, remember that dairy products supply other important nutrients that you do not find in juice.

Planning a few minutes a day to soak up some sun is one way to get your vitamin D and help your bones stay strong.

GOOD DAY SUNSHINE

You can lower your risk of osteoporosis by spending time outside as often as possible, particularly in the spring and summer months. When you are out in the sunlight, your body manufactures vitamin D that helps your body absorb calcium. (You also get vitamin D from dairy products, eggs, and fatty fish.)

Without enough vitamin D, your body has trouble absorbing enough calcium to build bone or to perform its other everyday functions. Your body then takes calcium out of your bones, making them weaker.

Seniors have reason to be concerned about how much vitamin D they eat. They spend less time in the sun, and their skin is not as efficient at making vitamin D.

EXERCISE, EXERCISE

Take a big step toward preventing osteoporosis by taking a step. Weight-bearing exercise, such as walking, jogging, and aerobics, helps boost your bone strength during your childhood and teen years and into your twenties and thirties. Once you've passed menopause, exercise can slow bone loss only if you also eat enough calcium.

Other types of exercises that may suit you better also build stronger bones. Try lifting light weights to strengthen your arm bones and muscles. No weights in the house? Too tough to get to the gym? Look no further than your kitchen cabinet. Cans of soup and bottles of water work just as well and are more convenient.

A CASE FOR SUPPLEMENTS

Postmenopausal women may need more vitamin D from fall to early spring when they are not exposed to as much sunlight. Bess Dawson-Hughes, M.D., a researcher at the U.S. Department of Agriculture Human Nutrition Research Center at Tufts University in Boston gave 249 post-menopausal women either a vitamin D supplement with twice the RDA or a placebo, in addition to calcium supplements. After a year, the women who had received the vitamin D supplement lost less bone than the women on the placebo. Taking more than the RDA of vitamin D can be dangerous, because relatively small excesses can be toxic.

STROKE

Approximately 500,000 people in the United States suffer from strokes every year. The Surgeon General's Report on Nutrition and Health, published in 1988, estimated that approximately two million Americans with stroke-related disabilities generate health-care and disability costs of over 11 billion dollars annually.

A HEART ATTACK OF THE BRAIN

A stroke is your brain's equivalent of a heart attack. The blood vessels in your head and neck are subject to the same problems as the arteries in your chest. Plaque builds up, blocking the flow of blood through the arteries to your brain.

Age is also a factor. The blood vessels become stiffer as you get older, and your blood pressure goes up. When one of these stiffer arteries to your brain becomes clogged, a portion of your brain loses its oxygen supply and becomes damaged with potentially disastrous results.

LOWERING YOUR BLOOD PRESSURE

High blood pressure (hypertension) is the major risk factor for having a stroke. Just lowering your blood pressure by five percent can dramatically reduce your stroke risk. For this reason, getting your blood pressure to come down should be your top priority in stroke prevention (see pages 82–83).

One line of attack is to lose weight; being overweight increases your risk of having high blood pressure, whereas losing weight helps lower your blood pressure. Also, eat less sodium. If you drink alcohol, you should drink only in moderation.

OTHER DISEASES AND CONDITIONS CAN INCREASE YOUR STROKE RISK

Diabetes: People with diabetes are highly susceptible to blood-vessel damage and heart disease. The standard treatment regimen for diabetes includes dietary change, weight loss, exercise, and possibly, medication.

Obesity: People who are obese are more likely to have strokes, even if their blood pressure is normal and they do not smoke.

Stress: Stress can increase blood pressure and contribute to heart disease. People under stress may also smoke and have a poor diet.

GET THEM WHILE THEY'RE YOUNG

The earlier you catch hypertension in yourself or your family members, the easier it is to prevent complications like stroke. If you have a strong family history of stroke, get your own and your family's blood pressure checked sooner rather than later. Sometimes, some simple intervention can make a big difference.

TIPS ON SLASHING SODIUM

Sodium is abundant in the American diet. The average American eats between four and six grams a day, at least twice the amount recommended in the Dietary Guidelines for Americans and up to 16 times the amount your body needs.

Speak to your physician or a registered dietitian about reducing your sodium intake if you have high blood pressure, have a family history of high blood pressure, or are black. (For reasons that are not well-understood, salt-sensitive high blood pressure and strokes are extremely common among blacks.)

Cutting down on sodium means more than just tossing out the shaker:

- The biggest source of sodium in our diet is processed food. Compare labels to find brands with less sodium, or switch from convenience foods to more basic ingredients.

- Packaged or canned soups can be extremely high in sodium. Look for lower-salt alternatives. Another way to have your soup and eat it, too, is to combine a low-sodium and a regular soup.

- Go easy on high-sodium meats like bacon, ham, luncheon meats, frankfurters, and smoked meats. For a smoky taste without the sodium, use a smoke-flavored seasoning liquid in stews, soups, and vegetables.

- Some other common sodium sources are pickles, olives, salted snacks, and soy sauce.

A HEALTHY APPROACH TO WEIGHT LOSS

Obesity is a major cause of high blood pressure and, therefore, a risk factor for stroke. Even overweight children can have higher blood pressure than their lean friends do. The good news is that

Besides being in salt and prepared foods, sodium can also be found in meats, such as pork and smoked products.

your blood pressure is likely to drop when you lose weight. Therefore, it makes sense to help your entire family reach a healthy weight, particularly those members whose blood pressure is high.

Dieting is out. Instead, the U.S. Department of Agriculture's Food Guide Pyramid depicts a healthy way of eating for Americans of all ages (see page 102).

ALCOHOL IN MODERATION

Drinking more than a couple of drinks a day can push up your blood pressure. It also adds unnecessary calories if you are trying to lose weight. The best advice is to drink only in moderation—one to two drinks a day—if you drink at all.

LISTEN TO YOUR HEART

People with heart disease have more than double the risk of stroke of their healthy counterparts. The best preventive measure is to do all you can to lower your heart-disease risk or improve your heart health if you already have heart disease. Lower your cholesterol by eating more fiber and less fat and saturated fat.

STOP SMOKING

Cigarette smoking increases stroke risk by damaging your blood vessels, increasing your blood pressure, lowering the amount of oxygen that is carried in your blood, and making your blood stickier and more likely to clot.

THE IMPORTANCE OF EXERCISE

It is hard to ignore the numerous benefits of exercise. Your blood pressure will come down, extra pounds

start to melt away, your heart becomes stronger, you are less likely to get diabetes and heart disease, and you feel better.

WHERE AND WHEN

The southeastern portion of the United States is known as the *stroke belt,* because strokes are more common there than anywhere else in the country. Time of year also makes a difference. Strokes are more common in either very hot or very cold weather.

A DOUBLE WHAMMY

Oral contraceptives by themselves do not increase your risk of having a stroke, but taking birth control pills and smoking may increase your risk considerably.

CONTACT YOUR DOCTOR

The warning signs of a stroke include sudden weakness or numbness in your face, arm, or leg; dimming of your vision in one eye; difficulty speaking; a sudden headache; and dizziness or falling, especially in combination with other symptoms.

Smoking raises your blood pressure, significantly increasing your risk of stroke. Quitting as soon as possible is crucial.

GUIDELINES FOR HEALTHY EATING

DIETARY GUIDELINES FOR AMERICANS

The prevalence of heart disease, diabetes, high blood pressure, stroke, obesity, and cancer in this country is a major health problem that costs billions of dollars each year in lost productivity, health-care costs, and disability. However, improving the way you eat can reduce your chances of experiencing these chronic diseases.

Slowly, the American diet is changing for the better, but we still eat too many calories and too much fat, saturated fat, cholesterol, and sodium. We fall short by not eating enough of the protective nutrients like complex carbohydrate and fiber.

A BRIEF HISTORY

The American Heart Association (AHA) was one of the first health organizations to recognize the importance of diet to health. In fact, today's Dietary Guidelines for Americans are based on many of the diet–health links recognized by AHA years ago. In 1961, the AHA recommended that Americans eat fewer calories and less fat, cholesterol, and saturated fat. Sound familiar?

The earliest government version of the Dietary Guidelines was published in the mid-1970s, under the

The U.S. Department of Agriculture Dietary Guidelines are simple recommendations designed to teach Americans eating habits to insure a life of good health.

title, *Dietary Goals for the United States*. They included the AHA guidelines on fat and cholesterol, along with broad recommendations on starch, refined sugars, and sodium.

The 1990 U.S. Department of Agriculture Dietary Guidelines for Americans in use today are the most widely accepted nutrition guidelines for health. They represent the nutrition advice of a number of different authorities—the Surgeon General, National Research Council of the National Academy of Sciences, American Heart Association, American Cancer Society, and other organizations and experts in health and nutrition.

The beauty of today's dietary recommendations is that they are so consistent. The more the messages are the same, the easier they are for you to remember. All of these major health organizations agree on these few simple guidelines.

CHANGING WITH THE TIMES

When you need to know which general nutrition principles to follow for good health, look no further than the Dietary Guidelines. Every five years, the Guidelines are reviewed by a panel of experts, in light of the newest and most widely agreed upon information about diet and health. Sometimes, the experts

---

DIETARY GUIDELINES FOR AMERICANS

- Eat a variety of foods.
- Maintain a healthy weight.
- Choose a diet low in fat, saturated fat, and cholesterol.
- Choose a diet with plenty of vegetables, fruits, and grain products.
- Use sugars only in moderation.
- Use salt and sodium only in moderation.
- If you drink alcoholic beverages, do so in moderation.

change or modify recommendations; sometimes, just the wording of the recommendations changes. For example, we now are told, "use salt and sodium in moderation," instead of the 1985 version, "avoid too much sodium." The panel chooses its words carefully.

The 1990 Dietary Guidelines reinforce two major food messages—eat less fat and eat more carbohydrate and fiber. These two pieces of dietary advice are probably the most important for helping to make your future a healthy one.

It is important to note that the Dietary Guidelines were developed for Americans over the age of two. The nutrition needs of infants and toddlers differ from those of adults. For adults, though, we will review each guideline in more detail.

EAT A VARIETY OF FOODS

Variety is the spice of life. Imagine how boring eating would be if you ate the same few foods over and over. While it's true that toddlers and preschoolers do not suffer nutritionally when they go on food jags of only oatmeal, peanut butter sandwiches, apples, and juice for a few days, adults cannot get away with that type of eating for very long. Without a lot of different types of foods, you can miss out on the vitally important nutrients that your body needs to function at its best.

Foods are divided into five food groups (see the section on the Food Guide Pyramid later in this chapter) with recommended numbers of servings from each group. For example, apples, canned fruit cocktail, and orange juice all belong to the fruit group, from which you should have three to five servings each day. The group that beef fits in is a little more diverse, because it includes many plant and animal foods that are good sources of protein. In the meat group, you'll also find poultry and fish, and nonmeat protein sources, such as legumes (dried peas and beans), eggs, nuts, and seeds.

Variety also means picking different foods from within each food group. For example, you should not eat just one or two types of vegetables. Instead, have several different vegetables during the week, like sweet potatoes on Monday, spinach salad on Tuesday, raw carrots, celery, and cherry tomatoes on Wednes-

---

FIGURING OUT YOUR BODY MASS INDEX (BMI)

1) Measure your weight in pounds, without shoes or clothing, and your height in inches, without shoes.
2) Divide your weight in pounds by 2.2 to get your weight in kilograms.
3) Multiply your height in inches by 0.0254 to get your height in meters. Then multiply your height in meters by itself. This is your height squared.
4) Divide your weight by your height squared to get your BMI.
5) A healthy BMI is between 19 and 25 for men and women aged 19 to 34 and between 21 and 27 for people 35 and older.

An example:
1) A 36-year-old woman weighs 130 pounds and is 65 inches tall.
2) $130 \div 2.2 = 59$ kilograms
3) $65 \times 0.0254 = 1.65$ meters
   $1.65 \times 1.65 = 2.73$ meters squared
4) $59 \div 2.73 = 22$ (a healthy BMI)

---

day, and so on. Sure it would be easier to just alternate between peas and carrots, but you would miss out on important vitamins and minerals that are in one vegetable but not in another.

MAINTAIN A HEALTHY WEIGHT

Not long ago, you could find out whether you were "overweight" by comparing your weight to a height and weight table developed by a life insurance company. When the Dietary Guidelines were revised in 1990, the expert committee decided that using the insurance company tables did not make sense. All that the tables told you was whether your weight was in the same range as people who were your height and had applied for life insurance. What you need to know is what you should weigh to be healthy.

NEW WEIGHT TABLES: Now, you evaluate how healthy your weight is by using three criteria. First, you determine your body mass index (BMI), a number that relates your weight to your height squared. You can figure out your own BMI with a tape measure, a scale, and a calculator, or you can take the short cut by referring to the Dietary Guidelines suggested weights (see page 89).

What is interesting about the new weight tables is that they are not divided into weights for men and for women, only for adults under age 35 and adults 35 and over. You'll also notice that you can weigh a bit more when you are older and still stay within your healthy weight range.

PICKING YOUR FRUIT: When you overeat, where do the extra pounds land, in your spare tire or as extra

There are so many delicious and nutritious food choices. Eating more vegetables is one way to fill up without all the excess fat and calories.

padding on your hips? If you answered spare tire, you probably are shaped like an apple, meaning that your waist is big relative to your hips. If your hips are larger than your waist, then you are a pear.

The location of your extra fat is the second consideration when deciding whether or not your weight is healthy. Apple-shaped people have a higher risk of diabetes, gall bladder disease, high blood pressure, high cholesterol levels, and heart disease.

Take a tape measure and measure your waist and your hips at the widest part. If your waist measurement is the same as or bigger than your hips, you are an apple. Check with your doctor to find out whether you should lose weight to lower your disease risk. You are a pear if your waist is smaller than your hips. For pears, losing weight may not be necessary to improve your health. In general, a waist-to-hip measurement ratio of 1:1 is appropriate for men, and a ratio of 0.8:1 is appropriate for women.

DOCTOR, DOCTOR: Your weight is within the suggested range for your height, and you are a pear. Good news? Not always. Some people are advised by their doctors to lose or gain weight for medical reasons, such as heart or lung disease or some arthritis conditions, regardless of their weight and body shape. Your doctor can address the specifics.

A STRATEGY TO LOSE WEIGHT: First and foremost, the Dietary Guidelines recommend exercise as the best way for you to lose weight. It burns calories and boosts overall health and fitness. Dieting, especially going under 1,200 calories per day, is not advocated, because you may not meet all of your nutrient needs on a diet that low in calories.

Be patient. You should lose only a half pound to a pound per week. Rapid weight loss of more than two

pounds per week means that you are either eating too little or exercising too much. In fact, you may be losing muscle and water instead of fat. Also, slow weight loss may make it easier for you to keep the pounds off. The Dietary Guidelines recommend that you lose weight slowly by:

- eating less fat and fatty foods.

- eating more fruits, vegetables, and breads and cereals—without fats and sugars added during cooking or at the table.

- eating less sugars and sweets.

- drinking little or no alcohol.

- eating smaller portions and limiting second helpings.

CHOOSE A DIET LOW IN FAT, SATURATED FAT, AND CHOLESTEROL

These three nutrients shoulder much of the blame for the amount of heart disease in the United States—the nation's number one killer. Fat has also been implicated because of its links to obesity and some types of cancer.

MORE BANG FOR YOUR CALORIE BUCK: One benefit of eating less fat is that you can eat more food. Ounce for ounce, fat has more than twice the number of calories that protein and carbohydrate do. So, when you eat less fat, you free up a lot of calories to be spent on other foods. For example, a mere tablespoon of butter is approximately 100 calories. You can use those same calories on a salad with fat-free dressing plus a small whole-grain roll, or a small scoop of low-fat cottage cheese and a half cup of melon—a much more satisfying lunch.

FIGURING OUT TOTAL FAT: Fat should account for no more than 30 percent of the calories you eat in a day. However, the 30-percent mark should not be used to evaluate individual foods. During the course of the day, some foods you eat may be over 50 percent fat, like nuts, whereas others may have little or no fat. You can't and you shouldn't avoid all high-fat foods. Over several days, the higher-fat and lower-fat foods balance each other out. What is most important is that your overall diet is at or below 30 percent.

You can figure out how much fat is the maximum you should eat in a day: Multiply the approximate number of calories you eat (see the Food Guide Pyramid, or use the 2,000-calorie standard that appears on food labels) by 0.3 to get the number of calories contributed by fat. For example, 2,000 times 0.3 equals 600 calories from fat. Then divide by 9—the calories in a gram of fat. The number you end up with, 67, is the maximum number of grams of fat you should eat in a day; you can eat much less, of course.

LABEL LINGO: The Nutrition Facts food labels can help you make smart food choices by helping you to keep tabs on the fat, saturated fat, and cholesterol in your diet. The first place you find fat information is near the top of the nutrition panel, next to the information on total calories. There, you can learn how many calories per serving come from fat in the food that you've picked. For example, two tablespoons of a salad dressing might have 72 fat calories. Compare that to the total calories to get a sense of how high in fat the food is. If two tablespoons of that salad dressing have 80 total calories, almost all of its calories come from fat.

The second and more useful numbers to look at are the ones on total fat. The label will tell you how many grams are in a serving of the food and, most important, what percentage that is of the daily fat allotment for someone eating 2,000 calories. If the number is high, you've picked a food with a lot of fat. (For more on food labels, see pages 108–110.)

Pasta, once thought to be the dieters' downfall, is really one of the best food choices. It's packed with complex carbohydrate, and if you go easy on the sauce, it is deliciously low fat.

EAT LESS MEAT: Beef, pork, veal, lamb, poultry, and even some types of fish can be relatively high in fat. We also eat far larger portions than we need for nutrition and health. You should be eating no more than six to seven ounces of meat, poultry, or fish daily. That is the equivalent of two pieces, each the size of the palm of your hand or a deck of cards.

SATURATED WITH FAT: The Dietary Guidelines also recommend that you get no more than ten percent of your total calories from saturated fat. This means that less than one third of the fat in your diet should be saturated.

Don't let the thought of more calculations boggle your mind. Saturated fat will fall into place without much thought if you choose lower-fat foods, go easy on foods with a lot of saturated fat (meat, whole-milk dairy products, and hydrogenated vegetable oils), and plan your meals using the principles of the Food Guide Pyramid (see page 102).

CURBING CHOLESTEROL: Animal products are the only source of cholesterol in your diet. They are also

---

FOLLOWING THE DIETARY GUIDELINES AND FOOD GUIDE PYRAMID TO EAT LESS FAT, SATURATED FAT, AND CHOLESTEROL

- Use fats and oils sparingly in cooking.
- Use small amounts of regular salad dressings and spreads, such as butter, margarine, and mayonnaise, or substitute fat-free products.
- Choose liquid vegetable oils for cooking most often, because they are lower in saturated fat than solid fats.
- Have a maximum of two or three servings of meat, poultry, fish, dry beans, and eggs, with a daily total of six ounces cooked, or the equivalent in beans (½ cup cooked or canned per ounce of meat) or eggs (one egg per ounce of meat).
- Trim fat from meat; take the skin off poultry.
- Have cooked, dry beans and peas instead of meat occasionally.
- Moderate the use of egg yolks and organ meats.
- Have two or three servings daily of milk and milk products.
- Choose skim or low-fat milk and fat-free or low-fat yogurt and cheese most of the time.
- Eat snack foods and desserts only in moderation, since many are high in fat.

the main source of fat and saturated fat. When you eat smaller portions of animal products and choose lean meat and skinless poultry, you automatically eat less cholesterol. Remember, it's the cholesterol and saturated fat from your diet that work together to elevate your cholesterol levels.

CHOOSE A DIET WITH PLENTY OF VEGETABLES, FRUITS, AND GRAIN PRODUCTS

Do you eat at least three half-cup servings of vegetables and two of fruit every day? Sadly, few Americans do. Eating fruits and vegetables is one of the best ways to improve your diet and live healthier. Fruits and vegetables are packed with complex carbohydrates, fiber, and protective nutrients and other compounds. They tend to be low in fat and calories. Furthermore, you get cancer protection from some vegetables, such as those in the cruciferous family: cabbage, broccoli, cauliflower, brussels sprouts, and kale.

You should also eat at least six daily servings of breads, cereals, pasta, rice, legumes, and starchy vegetables like potatoes and corn. The fiber from these foods and other grains and grain products lowers your risk of heart disease, constipation, hemorrhoids, and numerous other ailments. When you eat more starchy foods, you tend to eat less fat and saturated fat.

EAT FOOD FOR YOUR FIBER: Fruits, vegetables, grains, and starches supply you with innumerable nutrients and protective compounds that you do not get in a fiber supplement. Large doses of fiber supplements or bran can cause gastrointestinal problems and can block your absorption of essential minerals. Stick to the food sources.

USE SUGARS ONLY IN MODERATION

It is virtually impossible to cut all sugars out of your diet. They enhance the flavor of many foods; they serve as natural thickeners and food preservatives; and they are necessary for taste and texture in baked goods. Commonly used sugars are table sugar, brown sugar, raw sugar, dextrose, fructose, corn syrup, honey, and fruit juice concentrate.

You should eat sugars only in moderation for two reasons. The first is that they add calories without contributing other nutrients. By spending some of your daily calories on sugars, you have less to spend

HOW SUGAR ADDS UP

Food	Teaspoons of sugar added*
Fresh fruit	0
Fruit, canned in juice, ½ cup	0
Fruit, canned in light syrup, ½ cup	2
Fruit, canned in heavy syrup, ½ cup	4
Fruit punch, 6 ounces	4
Fruit-flavored soda, 6 ounces	4
Fruit pie, 1 slice	6
Lemonade, 6 ounces	6

*not including the sugar that occurs naturally.

on foods with more nutrition value. For example, a 12-ounce can of regular soda pop has approximately 150 calories and no other nutrients, whereas the same 150 calories of orange juice provide well over the Recommended Dietary Allowance (RDA) for vitamin C and close to the RDA for folate. However, people who are extremely active or need to eat a lot of calories may use sugars as a source of some of their extra calories.

The second reason applies to sugars and starchy foods. Both can increase tooth decay, particularly

Honey may be all natural, but it adds only calories and very few nutrients to your diet. As with all sugars, use honey only in moderation.

when they are snacked on between meals. That is why the Dietary Guidelines discuss the importance of protective measures like fluoridated water and toothpaste and a conscientious program of regular brushing and flossing.

USE SALT AND SODIUM ONLY IN MODERATION

Most people use the terms salt and sodium interchangeably. Salt is a more familiar term, is easier to understand, and is the source of most of the sodium in our foods and beverages.

In the United States, approximately one out of every three adults has high blood pressure. Around the world, high blood pressure is less common among groups of people who eat less salt than we do. If you have high blood pressure and begin to eat less sodium, chances are good that your blood pressure will go down.

Even if your blood pressure is not high, eating less salt and sodium cannot hurt and may help prevent high blood pressure in the future.

TIPS FOR CUTTING BACK: You can eat less salt and sodium without having to resort to buying low-sodium foods. Here are a few tips that will help limit your sodium intake without drastic changes:

- Use salt sparingly in cooking, and don't add any at the table.

- Choose fresh or frozen vegetables instead of canned.

- Cook cereals, pasta, and rice without salt.

- Pick fresh meat, poultry, and fish over canned and processed varieties.

- Watch out for high-salt prepared foods like frozen dinners, canned soup, salad dressing, soy sauce, pickles, olives, catsup, and mustard; read the labels carefully.

- Eat salty snacks sparingly.

A FINAL WORD ABOUT SODIUM: Get your blood pressure checked to find out whether it is high. If you have high blood pressure, consult with your doctor and a registered dietitian regarding changes you should make in your diet. Congratulations to people with normal blood pressure—keep it that way by maintaining a healthy weight, exercising regularly, and cutting down on sodium.

The Guidelines don't prohibit any food outright, but for many reasons, they do recommend that alcohol be used only in moderation.

IF YOU DRINK ALCOHOLIC BEVERAGES, DO SO IN MODERATION

Alcohol has more negatives than positives. It is a major contributor to liver disease, automobile accidents, and other types of accidents. Alcohol drains your body of water and B vitamins and is full of empty calories—calories without other nutrients.

MODERATION IS NOT THE SAME FOR EVERYONE: Moderate drinking is no more than two drinks a day for men and one a day for women. Take out your measuring cups and spoons; one drink is 12 ounces of regular beer, 4 ounces of wine, or 1 ounce of 100-proof liquor.

Complete abstinence is best for women who are pregnant or trying to conceive because of the relationship between alcohol and birth defects. Because your body does not shake the effects of alcohol for three to five hours after moderate drinking, you should not drink if you will be driving or operating machinery. When you are taking medications, alcohol may be a no-no; check with your doctor.

FINAL WORDS ON THE DIETARY GUIDELINES

You need more than just food to keep you healthy. Other factors that influence your health are your genes and your lifestyle. However, by following the Dietary Guidelines, you have a better chance of holding onto and improving your health. The best way to put the Guidelines into practice is by using the Food Guide Pyramid.

THE FOOD GUIDE PYRAMID

The Food Guide Pyramid is a graphic depiction of the Dietary Guidelines for Americans. Using the Food Guide Pyramid, you will know what and how much to eat from each of the food groups. Your diet will not be too high in calories, fat, saturated fat, cholesterol, sugars, sodium, or alcohol. It will have plenty of complex carbohydrates and fiber. Overall, the Food Guide Pyramid is your picture of health.

LAY YOUR FOUNDATION

At the base of the Pyramid, you'll find the food group that is the foundation of healthful eating. This group is the bread, cereal, rice, and pasta group. Foods in this group supply you with the complex carbohydrates that you need for energy, plus B vitamins, minerals, and fiber.

Depending on your calorie needs, you should eat between 6 and 11 servings from this group; half of these should be high-fiber, whole-grain products like cracked wheat bread, bran cereal, and brown rice. What is a serving? A slice of bread, an ounce of

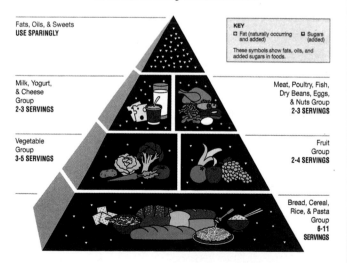

Food Guide Pyramid
A Guide to Daily Food Choices

A serving is: for grains, 1 slice of bread, ½ a bagel, or ½ cup of cooked rice or pasta; for vegetables, 1 cup of raw leafy vegetables or ½ cup of cooked vegetables; for fruits, 1 medium piece of fruit or ½ cup of chopped fruit; for dairy, 1 cup of milk or yogurt or 1½ to 2 ounces of cheese; for the meat group, 3 ounces of meat (an egg or ½ cup of beans counts as 1 ounce).

ready-to-eat cereal (usually between a half and one cup; check the label of your favorite brands), one small tortilla, a half-cup of cooked cereal, pasta, or rice, three cups of popped popcorn, or half of a medium bagel, English muffin, or pita bread.

GOING WITH THE GRAIN

Try a new approach to meal planning. Start with the bread group and then plan the rest of your meal around the grain that you choose. Here's how you might begin: You start off the morning with a cup of oatmeal (two servings) plus a slice of whole-wheat toast (one serving). You have a bagel at lunch (two servings), a small bag of unsalted pretzels for a snack (one serving), a cup of pasta for dinner (two servings), along with a small roll (one serving). That takes care of your bread group servings for the day.

GREENING OF YOUR PLATE

The next level of the Pyramid, right on top of the bread group, includes the vegetable group and its close cousin, the fruit group. It's tough to find fault with vegetables. They are your best source of beta-carotene, vitamin C, and folate. Vegetables also stock you with iron, magnesium, and other key minerals. For a high-fiber, low-fat food, look no further than vegetables.

Eating just one small serving of vegetables each day? If you answered yes, your diet needs an immediate overhaul. According to the Pyramid, you should eat between three and five servings of vegetables daily. A serving is one cup of lettuce, raw spinach, or other raw, leafy vegetables, a half-cup of cooked or chopped vegetables, or six ounces of tomato or vegetable juice.

GREEN, YELLOW, RED: Use the colors of the traffic light to remind you to eat at least three colors of vegetables. Go with the green, particularly dark green—romaine lettuce, spinach, kale, and broccoli—for plenty of beta-carotene and vitamin C. Be careful to include the yellow and orange vegetables like carrots, sweet potatoes, and winter squash to fill your tank with more beta-carotene. Then, stop for red vegetables like tomatoes and red peppers that have vitamin C plus vegetable pigments that may help protect your health. In general, the darker the color, the more vitamins and minerals a vegetable contains. Iceberg lettuce and celery, for example, add water and crunch to your diet but little else, but romaine is loaded with nutrients.

Potatoes are an excellent food choice. Not only do they provide the energy of complex carbohydrates, but they're also loaded with vitamins—especially if you leave the skins on.

INCLUDE STARCHY VEGETABLES: Potatoes, corn, and peas supply you with plenty of complex carbohydrates for energy, along with important vitamins, minerals, and fiber. Be bean smart, too. Legumes, which include split peas, kidney beans, lentils, and chickpeas, are rich in vitamins and minerals and abundant in complex carbohydrates. They also supply both the soluble fiber that may help prevent heart disease and the insoluble fiber needed to keep your colon healthy. (Legumes are listed in both the vegetable and meat groups.)

WATCH THE SALT: Vegetables are naturally low in sodium, but regular canned vegetables are swimming in a salty sea. The sauce that bathes some types of frozen vegetables can be full of salt. Furthermore, you may be topping your vegetables with salt or high-sodium sauces. Instead, get accustomed to the flavor of vegetables *au natural* or with just a light dash of herbs, spices, or lemon juice.

TUTTI-FRUITY

Most people love fruit, so meeting the Pyramid's recommendation of two to four fruit servings daily should be relatively easy. What counts as a serving? A medium piece of fruit, like an apple, banana, orange, or peach, a half-cup of cooked, chopped, or canned fruit, or six ounces of juice.

Fruit is packed with many of the same nutrients that you find in vegetables, especially fiber, vitamin C, and the mineral potassium. As with vegetables, you should eat a variety of fruits to ensure that you are getting a good mix of different nutrients. For example,

an apple with skin provides fiber but almost no vitamin C, while an orange has fiber plus vitamin C.

THE SWEET TRUTH: Fruit is sweet, and it does contain sugar naturally. The sugar adds up even more quickly if you buy fruit canned in light or heavy syrup, frozen fruit packed with sugar, sweetened fruit punch, or other fruit products processed with sugars.

Flavored, sweetened seltzers made with fruit juice are no nutrition bargain. Many use highly concentrated grape or apple juice that has been stripped of its flavor. These sweeteners are virtually nutrient free and are just as sweet as sugar is.

JUICES AND JUICING: When possible, eat whole fruit more often than you drink juice. While juice has the same vitamins as the fruit that it came from, it is missing fiber and some minerals that went out with the pulp. Juice also adds calories quickly without filling you up. A six-ounce glass of orange juice is gone in a couple of gulps; a whole orange takes longer to eat, supplies you with fiber, and can help you feel satiated.

Fruit juice made with a juicer does not have special healing or energizing powers. It is an expensive way

Juices are not the same as the whole fruit. Although most of the vitamins and minerals remain in the juice, the fiber from the pulp is lost.

to get your nutrients from fruit and has little or no fiber unless you add back the pulp.

Moving up a Level

At the next level, the Pyramid becomes much narrower for a reason: you should eat less from the two food groups at this level than of the three groups closer to the base. That does not make these two food groups—the milk, yogurt, and cheese group (the milk group) and the meat, poultry, fish, dry beans, eggs, and nuts group (the meat group)—any less important to your health.

Your body still benefits from these nutrient-rich foods; it just doesn't need as many servings from these groups. Foods in these two food groups also tend to be higher in fat, saturated fat, and cholesterol and very low in fiber, with the exception of legumes, which are quite the opposite.

MAKE ROOM FOR MILK: One serving from the milk group is a cup of milk or yogurt, one and a half ounces of hard cheese like cheddar or Swiss, or two ounces of processed cheese like American. In addition to protein, B vitamins, and minerals, foods from this group supply you with the calcium you need for strong bones.

Some foods in the milk group are smarter nutrition choices than others. Skim and low-fat milk and low-fat and nonfat yogurt give you the most nutrition with the least amount of fat. Frozen yogurt is not as wise a choice, because it is heavily sweetened and lower in calcium. Lower-fat cheeses and ice creams have less fat, saturated fat, cholesterol, and calories than their full-fat counterparts, but they should not be relied on to provide significant amounts of calcium and other important dairy nutrients.

THE MEAT OF THE MATTER: Next to the milk group is the meat group. It is the most diverse group, because it contains not only meats, poultry, and fish, but also dried peas and beans, eggs, nuts, and peanut butter. These foods are grouped together in the meat group, because they supply similar nutrients. All supply protein and B vitamins. Many are good sources of iron, zinc, and other minerals. With dried beans and peas, you have the added bonus of lots of fiber.

To get a sense of portion size, take out a scale or deck of cards, or use the palm of your hand. A portion of cooked meat, poultry, or fish weighs two to three

Eggs are included in the meat group on the third level of the Pyramid. Eggs, like meat, fish, and poultry, are excellent protein sources.

ounces and is the same size and thickness as a deck of cards or the palm of your hand. For other foods, a half cup of cooked or canned legumes, one egg, or two tablespoons of peanut butter is equivalent to one ounce of meat.

LEAN ON MEAT: Lean meats have less fat, saturated fat, and cholesterol than higher-fat cuts do. To go lean and low fat:

- Choose lean cuts, like beef round, loin, and sirloin; pork tenderloin; lamb leg and loin; chicken and turkey without the skin; and fish canned in water instead of oil.

- Use low-fat preparation and cooking techniques like trimming away all visible fat and broiling, grilling, or roasting instead of frying, which adds lots of extra fat.

- Eat more beans—they are cholesterol free, naturally low in fat, and high in fiber.

The Top of the Pyramid—Fats, Oils, and Sweets

These high-calorie, low-nutrient foods reside at the top of the Pyramid and in the smallest space. Use them only sparingly, to add flavor, texture, and some calories to your diet.

It is widely recommended that you get no more than 30 percent of your calories from fat. If you were to follow the Pyramid guidelines, choose foods low in fat, and add no extra fat, your diet probably would be too low in calories. It also would be extremely low in fat, probably closer to 20 percent than 30 percent. Therefore, you can have prudent amounts of extra fat, approximately one to three teaspoons per meal. However, if you pick higher-fat foods, you may not have room to add extra fat or calories.

STRETCHING YOUR FAT DOLLAR:
The shelves at your local supermarket are bursting with lower-fat alternatives to traditional fats. From reduced-fat margarine to low-fat cream cheese to low-fat, and even fat-free salad dressing, you can get the taste of fat at a lower calorie and fat cost. The biggest advantage is that your small allotment of fat for the day goes farther. Two teaspoons of reduced fat margarine may be the same as one teaspoon of regular margarine. You get a similar bargain with salad dressings: Switch to lower fat, and you may be able to double your portion.

FOR YOUR SWEET TOOTH: You should limit your extra sugars to between 6 and 18 teaspoons per day. At first glance, this sounds like a lot, but remember

THE FOOD GUIDE PYRAMID AT DIFFERENT DAILY CALORIE LEVELS			
FOOD GROUP	**1,600 CALS**	**2,200 CALS**	**2,800 CALS**
Bread (*servings*)	6	9	11
Vegetable (*servings*)	3	4	5
Fruit (*servings*)	2	3	4
Milk (*servings*)	2–3	2–3	2–3
Meat (*ounces*)	5	6	7
Total fat (*grams*)	53	73	93
Total added sugar (*teaspoons*)*	6	12	18

*not including the sugar that occurs naturally.

that some of the added sugar is hidden in sweetened foods. Here are the sugar equivalents for some favorite foods:

- a serving of sweetened breakfast cereal—2 or 3 teaspoons of sugar
- a doughnut—2 teaspoons
- a cup of chocolate milk—3 teaspoons
- a cup of fruit yogurt—3 to 7 teaspoons
- a half-cup bowl of gelatin dessert— 4 teaspoons
- a 12-ounce can of regular soda—9 teaspoons

PUTTING IT ALL TOGETHER

How do you know how many servings you should have of each food group? Should you have 6 bread servings, 11 bread servings, or something in between? When should you have three dairy servings instead of two? The answer depends on your age, sex, and activity level. At the very least, though, you should get the lowest number of servings from each group.

Sedentary women and older adults need the fewest calories, approximately 1,600 daily, according to surveys of how many calories Americans are eating. This calorie level corresponds to the lowest serving numbers for each food group.

The next level, 2,200 calories, is recommended for most children over the age of two, teenage girls, active women, and sedentary men. Servings fall in the middle of the range for these groups.

Finally, if you are a teenage boy, active man, or very active woman, you should eat according to the high end of the range—11 servings from the breads, 5 from the vegetables, and so on. (For more on figuring energy needs, see pages 7–9.)

The Pyramid suggests that you limit the amount of added sugar in your diet. One 12-ounce cola contains as much as 9 teaspoons of added sugar.

MEAL PLANNING USING THE PYRAMID

Now you are ready to plan a day's menu using the Food Guide Pyramid. You may feel a bit confused about how all this information translates into actual meals, but it is quite simple really. First, find your calorie level. For this example, we will use the middle level of 2,200 calories per day. Start by distributing your bread group servings over three meals and a snack. You may feel like you are turning meal planning upside down, since most people think about their meats first, but working first with the bread group reinforces their importance as the foundation of a healthy diet.

BREAD: Let's return to the bread example used earlier in the chapter and begin to fill in a menu for the day. Take a sheet of paper and divide it into meals and snacks across the top. Along the left margin, list the food groups plus the number of daily servings you'll be having from each. Fill the bread group in first:

Food Group (servings)	Breakfast	Lunch	Snack	Dinner
Bread (9)	1 cup oatmeal	1 bagel	1 small bag pretzels	1 cup pasta 1 small wheat roll
Vegetable (4)		Large salad		½ cup peas ½ cup carrots
Fruit (3)				
Milk (2)				
Meat (6 oz.)				
Added Fat	1 tsp. butter	1 tbsp. dressing		

VEGETABLE: Next, move to the four servings from the vegetable group. Because most people do not eat vegetables for breakfast, it makes sense to divide the four servings into two servings of vegetables each at lunch and at dinner. A large lettuce and mixed vegetable salad could use up your two vegetable servings at lunch. For dinner, you might want two half-cup servings of two different vegetables. Or you could have vegetable soup plus a small salad. The combinations are endless.

You may not want or be able to eat two servings of vegetables at lunch. At a diner or coffee shop, for example, it might be better passing on the cooked vegetables rather than eating vegetables swimming in added butter or margarine. If time is tight, hunting around for a fast food outlet that serves vegetables is not always the best use of your time.

In any case, what's most important is to try to hit your target number of servings by the end of the day. So, you can have vegetables for your snack or a lot of vegetables at dinner. If occasionally you do not hit the goal number of servings, try again tomorrow by adding some extra servings.

FRUIT: Follow the same basic process for fruit as you did for vegetables. Decide where to put your fruit servings based on your eating habits and schedule. You can divide up your servings among breakfast, lunch, and dinner, eat fruit only between meals as a snack, or have some at meals and some for a snack. Fruit is easy to carry along if you are going someplace where fruit may not be available.

MILK: Many Americans do not have their two daily servings from the milk group, even though including them in your diet is relatively easy. A good place to start is at breakfast; you can pour milk over ready-to-eat cereal, drink a glass of milk, make a yogurt parfait with fruit, or whip up a yogurt-fruit shake. Without milk at breakfast, it may be more difficult for you to hit your goal.

When should you fit the second milk serving in? Lunch or a snack may be the best time to grab a carton of milk or a yogurt. Or, maybe your family drinks milk at dinner.

Young children need calcium and vitamin D for strong bones and growing teeth. The dairy group is one of the key sources of calcium in the diet, and milk is often fortified with vitamin D, too.

You should set your goal at three servings a day if you are pregnant, breast-feeding, in your teen years, or early twenties. Because of their strengthening bones, young adults up through age 24 need more calcium than children and adults do.

MEAT: Allocating your meat servings appears to be easy—just have three ounces, cooked, at lunch and another three at dinner. Four ounces of raw meat cooks down to about three ounces. The problem is that many Americans are accustomed to eating much larger portions of meat, often twice the recommended size.

You can handle your meat servings in several ways. One way is to have two three-ounce portions. However, if you eat out, your portion is likely to be bigger than three ounces. So, put your hand next to your plate, palm side up, and estimate how much extra meat is on your plate. Either take the extra in a doggy bag, leave it on your plate, or eat the whole thing and compensate accordingly at the next meal.

You may decide to skip a meat group choice at lunch and have a larger portion at dinner. On the weekend, your meat dollars can buy two eggs at brunch, leaving four ounces to have at dinner. Or you can have a meatless meal, like vegetarian chili or a peanut butter sandwich. No matter how you divide up your meat group servings, lean and low fat should be the rule whenever possible.

FATS, OILS, AND SWEETS: Now add in the extras—butter or margarine on your toast, a bit of low-fat salad dressing on your lunch salad, olive oil on your pasta. Fats, oils, and sweets used in cooking and baking count, also.

THE FOOD GUIDE PYRAMID—YOUR STRATEGY

The Food Guide Pyramid was not designed to make you a food slave. It is just a guide to healthy eating, not an absolute.

Take a couple of days to jot down what you eat. Then compare your eating pattern to the Food Guide Pyramid to see where you need to make changes. If possible, use the information on food labels and at your market to estimate how much total fat and added sugar you are eating. Compare your diet evaluation with the food group, fat, and sugar goals for your calorie level. Then make changes gradually until your eating plan meets the Pyramid guidelines and becomes a habit instead of a chore.

The picture of a healthy diet: The Pyramid is built on a broad foundation of grains and decreases in size as it rises through fruits and vegetables, meats and dairy until it ends with just a small tip of added fats and sugar.

NATIONAL CANCER INSTITUTE AND AMERICAN CANCER SOCIETY GUIDELINES

THE FIGHT AGAINST CANCER

Much like the American Heart Association (AHA), the National Cancer Institute (NCI) and the American Cancer Society (ACS) developed more detailed guidelines than those published by the U.S. Department of Agriculture. Although the spirit of all the guidelines is the same, the guidelines developed by NCI and ACS talk more about issues specific to cancer prevention.

FAT, FAT, AND LESS FAT

By now you know that you should limit your fat to no more than 30 percent of your calories for the day. The importance of a low-fat diet appears to be as important to cancer prevention as it is to prevention of other chronic diseases. However, one nagging thought remains in the minds of many cancer experts. Maybe 30 percent of calories from fat is too high to ward off breast and other cancers. Of course, they realize that the first step toward a really low-fat diet is the 30-percent mark. Once you've done that well, 20 percent may be around the corner for cancer prevention.

Once again, the Food Guide Pyramid and its concepts of low-fat food choices can help you eat the type of low-fat diet recommended by NCI.

The Fuss over Fiber

Want to know how much fiber you should be eating? Turn to NCI. They recommend that Americans eat between 20 and 30 grams of fiber per day (with a maximum of 35 grams to prevent problems with mineral absorption and intestinal distress). The bad news is that the average American eats approximately half the recommended amount. You can jack up your fiber intake by using the Food Guide Pyramid to plan your meals.

According to NCI, you should get your fiber from a variety of foods, including vegetables, fruits, and whole-grain cereals. Sounds like the Dietary Guidelines again.

Variety in Vegetables and Fruits

The ACS has taken the lead with its recommendations on the types of fruits and vegetables that you should be eating. They highlight those fruits and vegetables associated with cancer prevention—ones high in beta-carotene and vitamin C—and the cruciferous vegetables (cabbage, broccoli, cauliflower, and brussels sprouts). The vitamin A (retinol) found in milk, butter, liver, and other animal products may also play a role.

In a Pickle

The salt recommendations for cancer prevention are quite different from the recommendations in the Dietary Guidelines. True, eating fewer salt-cured, pickled, and smoked foods will lower the amount of

Pickles and other cured foods are suspected in the formation of nitrosamines and other cancer-causing compounds. They are also very high in sodium, so go easy on them.

sodium in your diet, but the concern in terms of cancer is not the salt itself. The problem with pickled and cured foods is that they may spark the formation of nitrosamines and other cancer-causing compounds in your stomach.

Many experts are not all that concerned about pickled and cured foods. We have very low rates of stomach cancer in the United States. However, for overall control of the amount of sodium in your diet, you probably are better off telling them to hold the pickle.

THE "NUTRITION FACTS" FOOD LABEL

Today's food package labels represent the efforts of government agencies, Congress, the food industry, and health and professional groups to create a label to help Americans make wise food choices. Nutrient and ingredient information on the label enable you to reduce your disease risk and improve your health profile through the foods you purchase and eat. Using the food label, you will be able to plan your meals according to the Dietary Guidelines for Americans, the Food Guide Pyramid, and other guidelines.

Out with the Old

Food labels used to be difficult to use. You could not compare information on different brands of the same product because each label listed a different portion size. You needed a calculator to figure out whether a food was high in fat or not. Figuring out how a food would fit into a healthy eating plan was virtually impossible. Also, labels were so full of hype that it was tough to believe anyone.

In with the New

Once you get used to the Nutrition Facts labels, you will find it easy to rely on them as your main tool for selecting foods. Products now have standardized portion sizes, like two tablespoons for salad dressing. You can compare two different brands.

The Percent Daily Value lets you know how the fat, saturated fat, carbohydrate, fiber, and protein in a food measure up to what you should be eating for the whole day.

Health claims are now believable—*fat free* means fat free, not that the manufacturer listed too small a portion size to have any fat. Remember the one-teaspoon serving of salad dressing and the tiny slice of reduced-fat cake?

The ingredient list is more complete so that you know what is really in a food. No more unpleasant reactions from eating caseinate and other milk derivatives that were not listed as being milk products.

GENTLE REMINDERS

No need to take a memory improvement course to remember how much fat, saturated fat, sodium, total carbohydrate, or fiber you should eat. No need to remember how many calories are in each gram of fat. Label space permitting, manufacturers list the Daily Values for these nutrients, based on a 2,000-calorie and a 2,500-calorie diet.

The Daily Value generally is the upper limit for the above nutrients and the RDA for vitamin A, vitamin C, calcium, and iron. For example, the Daily Value for fat on a 2,000-calorie diet is 65 grams. This is the equivalent of 30 percent of calories from fat. The Daily Values for protein, total carbohydrate, and fiber agree with the recommendations of the National Cholesterol Education Program and NCI.

If you eat fewer than 2,000 calories a day, as many women and older men do, you need to scale down the Daily Values for fat, saturated fat, total carbohydrate, and fiber. The upper limits for cholesterol (300 mg) and sodium (2,400 mg) remain the same for all adults.

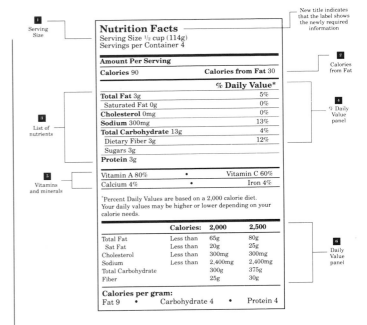

The Nutrition Facts label is easier to digest if broken into its six component parts.

THE SEARCH FOR PROTECTIVE NUTRIENTS

The food label can help you spot the nutrition bad guys—fat, saturated fat, cholesterol, sodium, and for some people, sugar. It lists fiber, a good guy. But what about other protective nutrients?

Directly below the information on Daily Values is information on vitamin A, vitamin C, calcium, and iron. Now, it is easier to find foods that have higher amounts of these nutrients that may lower your risk of heart disease, cancer, osteoporosis, high blood pressure, and anemia.

WHERE HAVE ALL THE VITAMINS GONE?

The only vitamin and mineral information that is mandatory is on vitamins A and C and the minerals calcium and iron. The B vitamins, thiamin, riboflavin, and niacin, once appeared on every food label. When food labeling began, our major nutrition concern was vitamin deficiency, not heart disease and cancer. Now that vitamin deficiencies are rare in this country, those nutrients are not required on the food label.

LEARNING BY DOING
A LESSON IN COMPARISON SHOPPING

Now it is time to put your newfound label knowledge into practice. For this example, your goal is to pick a yogurt that is highest in calcium and lowest in fat and sugar. You can repeat this activity with other foods and nutrients.

Step 1	Go to the yogurt section of the dairy case in your market.
Step 2	Select a variety of different yogurts: plain, fruit-flavored, low-fat, fat-free, artificially sweetened, and organic.
Step 3	Locate the % Daily Value for calcium. Pick the five yogurts with the highest % Daily Value; these have the most calcium.
Step 4	Now locate the % Daily Value for fat. Pick the three yogurts with the lowest fat value.
Step 5	Of the three remaining yogurts, which has the least amount of sugar? Usually, the winner is a low-fat or nonfat plain yogurt.

PROMISES, PROMISES

Believe it or not, you can believe the label. If it says *good source of vitamin C*, it supplies between 10 and 19 percent of the vitamin C Daily Value in a standard serving. A sweet potato dish that says *high in vitamin A* has at least 20 percent of the Daily Value. And *extra lean* meat truly is extra lean. These phrases—*good source*, *high in*, and *extra lean*—have been standardized by law. In the case of the Nutrition Facts label, you can believe what you read.

COULD THIS FOOD HELP KEEP ME HEALTHY?

You can believe the claim on the label. Only seven claims have been approved, the very ones that you would expect: Calcium protects against osteoporosis; fiber-containing grain products, fruits, and vegetables protect against cancer; all fruits and vegetables provide some protection against cancer (because of beta-carotene, vitamin C, and fiber); fiber-containing grain products, fruits, and vegetables protect against heart disease; a low-fat diet protects against cancer; a diet low in saturated fat and cholesterol protects against heart disease; and a diet low in sodium protects against high blood pressure. Here is what a claim might look like:

- A diet with enough calcium helps women maintain good bone health and may reduce their risk of osteoporosis later in life.

- Development of heart disease depends on many factors. Eating a diet low in saturated fat and cholesterol and high in fruits, vegetables, and grain products that contain fiber may lower blood cholesterol levels and reduce your risk of heart disease.

- Development of cancer depends on many factors. A diet low in total fat may reduce the risk of some cancers.

LABELING AN APPLE

You will not find nutrition information stamped or pasted onto the skin of an apple. Nor will you find a nutrition label dangling from a drumstick. The produce section of your market should have nutrition information handy on the 20 most popular fruits and vegetables. Some packages in the meat case will be labeled with nutrition information. Otherwise, look for labeling materials like posters or brochures nearby.

GETTING STARTED

At first glance, the food label is overwhelming, but the label is the best tool for planning a diet for health. Don't try to tackle the whole label at once. Instead, pick the two or three nutrients that are most important to you. If you have a family history of heart disease, concentrate on fat, saturated fat, and cholesterol. Do female relatives have osteoporosis? Then start with calcium. Have you been told that you are anemic? Iron would be the place to start.

Look closely at the information on the nutrients or ingredients you picked. Compare products to locate better choices. Once you've mastered one nutrient or ingredient, move onto another one and another one until you've conquered the entire label.

WHERE TO TURN FOR MORE INFORMATION

- U.S. Department of Agriculture. *The Food Guide Pyramid*. Home and Garden Bulletin Number 252

- U.S. Department of Agriculture. *Nutrition and Your Health: Dietary Guidelines for Americans*. Home and Garden Bulletin Number 232

- U.S. Department of Agriculture. *Dietary Guidelines and Your Diet* pamphlets and bulletins. Home and Garden Bulletins Number 232-1 through 232-11

Order all of the above through:
The U.S. Department of Agriculture
Human Nutrition Information Service
6505 Belcrest Road
Hyattsville, MD 20782

or through:
Consumer Information Center
Department 514-X
Pueblo, CO 81009

- The American Cancer Society, 1-800-4 CANCER

- Your local American Heart Association chapter

- The National Center for Nutrition and Dietetics Consumer Nutrition Hot Line, 1-800-366-1655

- The National Center for Nutrition and Dietetics dietitian referral service, 1-800-366-1655

- Cooperative Extension System
Look under your county name in a local phone book.

HEALTHFUL FOODS

Now you have all the rules and tools, right? You've got the best advice from the leading professional organizations and governmental agencies, and you even know how to read food labels. But wait a minute. What does all of it mean? How does this translate into specific foods?

It's one thing to know the rules about limiting fat and increasing fiber; it's another thing to recognize which foods contain which nutrients. This chapter's chart is designed to put that information at your fingertips. The following 101 foods are among the most common and the most packed with nutrients. Use this chart to find out which foods are low in fat or low in sodium and which provide good amounts of the important protective nutrients, such as beta-carotene and fiber.

In the last column, you will find numbers that correspond to the recipes that begin on page 145.

These recipes give you a healthy way to serve up the foods that you select from the chart. Some of the items don't have corresponding recipes, because they are already prepared, such as fig cookies or bagels, or because they are the kind of food you eat by itself, like popcorn. Of course, you can create your own recipes and combinations—variety is good for you—but remember to limit the added fats and try to keep the added salt and sugar to a minimum.

A few notes of explanation: The information for vegetables assumes that you are using the fresh or frozen varieties; canned vegetables or those packaged with sauces or special seasonings are often less nutrient rich or higher in fat and sodium. Also, be careful not to undo the nutritive benefits of these foods with your cooking technique. Overcooking vegetables can destroy some of the vitamins that you chose the food for. For example, you can destroy folate simply by boiling too long instead of quickly steaming or microwaving.

One other word of warning: When looking for foods that are lactose free, read the labels carefully. Some foods with multiple ingredients (bagels, for example) can have hidden lactose. Different brands use different formulas; it's best to check for yourself.

FOOD	LOW IN:				GOOD SOURCE OF:							
	FAT	SATURATED FAT	CHOLESTEROL	SODIUM	SOLUBLE FIBER	INSOLUBLE FIBER	CARBOHYDRATE	PROTEIN	IRON	CALCIUM	BETA-CAROTENE	FOLATE
Angel food cake	X	X	X				X					
Apple	X	X	X	X	X	X	X					
Apricot	X	X	X	X	X		X				X	
Asparagus	X	X	X	X								X
Avocado		X	X	X	X	X						X
Bagel	X	X	X	X			X					
Banana	X	X	X	X	X	X	X					X
Barley	X	X	X	X	X	X	X					
Bean sprouts	X	X	X	X								X
Beans, green	X	X	X	X								X
Beef, lean				X				X	X			
Berries	X	X	X	X	X	X	X					X
Bread, whole wheat	X	X	X	X		X	X					

VITAMIN C	VITAMIN E	LACTOSE FREE	HEALTH BENEFITS	RECIPE NUMBERS
		X	A diet low in fat, saturated fat, and cholesterol may help prevent **cancer** and **heart disease** and may help relieve **heartburn** and **hiatal hernia** symptoms.	262, 276, 292
		X	Soluble fiber may help prevent **heart disease** and **diabetes**. Insoluble fiber may help protect you from **cancer**, **constipation**, **irritable bowel syndrome**, and **hemorrhoids**.	47, 59, 62, 77, 92
X		X	Beta-carotene and vitamin C may play a role in **cancer** and **heart disease** prevention. Vitamin C may also prevent **high blood pressure**.	66, 102, 162, 206, 264
X	X	X	Folate is important for **immunity** and may help prevent **birth defects** and **cancer**. Vitamins C and E may also help prevent **cancer** and **heart disease**.	83
	X	X	Folate may prevent **birth defects** and **cancer**. Vitamin E may help ward off **cancer**, **heart disease**, and **fibrocystic breast disease**.	
		X	A diet low in fat, saturated fat, and cholesterol may help prevent **cancer and heart disease** and can help relieve **heartburn** and **hiatal hernia** symptoms.	
		X	Folate may help prevent **birth defects** and **cancer**. A low-sodium diet reduces your risk for **heart disease**, **high blood pressure**, and **stroke**, and can help relieve the symptoms of **fibrocystic breast disease**.	51, 246, 248, 251, 285
		X	Soluble fiber may help ward off **heart disease** and **diabetes**. Insoluble fiber may help protect you from **cancer**, **constipation**, **irritable bowel syndrome**, and **hemorrhoids**.	222, 239
		X	A diet low in fat, saturated fat, and cholesterol may protect against **cancer** and **heart disease** and can help relieve **heartburn** and **hiatal hernia** symptoms.	97, 225
		X	A low-sodium diet reduces your risk for **heart disease**, **high blood pressure**, and **stroke** and can help relieve the symptoms of **fibrocystic breast disease**. Folate may help prevent **birth defects** and **cancer**.	89, 214, 218
		X	Iron combats **anemia**. Protein is important for **immunity**.	67, 68, 120, 121, 127
X		X	Folate may help prevent **birth defects** and **cancer**. Vitamin C may protect against **cancer**, **heart disease**, and **high blood pressure** and is, with folate, needed for **immunity**.	4, 32, 51, 216, 261
			Insoluble fiber may help protect you from **cancer**, **constipation**, **hemorrhoids**, and **irritable bowel syndrome**.	146, 150, 225, 227, 252

FOOD	LOW IN:				GOOD SOURCE OF:								
	FAT	SATURATED FAT	CHOLESTEROL	SODIUM	SOLUBLE FIBER	INSOLUBLE FIBER	CARBOHYDRATE	PROTEIN	IRON	CALCIUM	BETA-CAROTENE	FOLATE	
Broccoli	X	X	X	X		X				X		X	
Brussels sprouts	X	X	X	X		X						X	
Bulgur wheat	X	X	X	X		X	X						
Cabbage	X	X	X	X								X	
Canola oil		X	X	X									
Cantaloupe	X	X	X	X			X				X	X	
Carrots	X	X	X	X	X	X	X				X		
Cauliflower	X	X	X	X		X						X	
Cereal, bran flake, fortified	X	X	X			X	X		X				
Cheese, reduced fat								X		X			
Chicken, skinless	X	X		X				X					

VITAMIN C	VITAMIN E	LACTOSE FREE	HEALTH BENEFITS	RECIPE NUMBERS
X		X	Folate may help prevent **birth defects** and **cancer**. Calcium helps fight off **dental disease, osteoporosis,** and **high blood pressure**. Vitamin C may help prevent **heart disease** and **high blood pressure** and, with folate, is needed for **immunity**.	60, 80, 84, 91
X		X	Folate may help prevent **birth defects** and **cancer**. Vitamin C may help prevent **cancer, heart disease,** and **high blood pressure** and is, with folate, needed for **immunity**.	105, 107, 112
		X	A diet low in fat, saturated fat, and cholesterol and high in insoluble fiber may help prevent **cancer** and **heart disease**, and help relieve **heartburn, constipation, irritable bowel syndrome,** and **hemorrhoids**.	160, 208, 225
X		X	A low-fat, low-sodium diet reduces your risk for **cancer, heart disease, high blood pressure,** and **stroke**, and can help relieve the symptoms of **fibrocystic breast disease**.	47, 63, 67, 109
	X	X	Fats low in saturated fat and cholesterol used in moderation can help protect against **heart disease**. Vitamin E may help ward off **cancer, heart disease,** and **fibrocystic breast disease**.	49, 126, 115, 234, 237
X		X	Beta-carotene and vitamin C may play a role in preventing **cancer, heart disease,** and **high blood pressure**.	34, 35, 43
		X	Beta-carotene may play a role in preventing **cancer** and **heart disease**. Soluble fiber may help prevent **heart disease** and **diabetes**. Insoluble fiber may help prevent **cancer, constipation, irritable bowel syndrome,** and **hemorrhoids**.	18, 77, 80, 93
X		X	Folate may help prevent **birth defects** and **cancer**. Vitamin C may help prevent **cancer, heart disease,** and **high blood pressure** and, with folate, is needed for **immunity**.	91, 110, 219
		X	A diet low in fat, saturated fat, and cholesterol may help prevent **cancer** and **heart disease**. Insoluble fiber may help protect you from **cancer, constipation, irritable bowel syndrome,** and **hemorrhoids**. Iron combats **anemia**.	241, 242
			Calcium helps fight off **dental disease, osteoporosis,** and **high blood pressure**.	145, 146, 153, 170, 207
		X	Protein is important for **immunity**. A low-sodium diet reduces your risk of **heart disease, high blood pressure,** and **stroke** and can help relieve the symptoms of **fibrocystic breast disease**.	40, 157, 158

FOOD	LOW IN:				GOOD SOURCE OF:								
	FAT	SATURATED FAT	CHOLESTEROL	SODIUM	SOLUBLE FIBER	INSOLUBLE FIBER	CARBOHYDRATE	PROTEIN	IRON	CALCIUM	BETA-CAROTENE	FOLATE	
Collards	X	X	X	X						X			
Cookie, fig bar	X	X	X	X		X	X						
Corn	X	X	X	X		X	X					X	
Corn oil		X	X	X									
Cottage cheese, 1% fat	X	X	X					X					
Crab	X	X						X				X	
Crackers, rye crisp	X	X	X			X	X						
Dates	X	X	X	X		X	X						
Egg, whole				X				X				X	
Eggplant	X	X	X	X								X	
Egg white	X	X	X	X				X					
Figs	X	X	X	X		X	X						
Fish, tuna, canned in water	X	X						X					

VITAMIN C	VITAMIN E	LACTOSE FREE	HEALTH BENEFITS	RECIPE NUMBERS
		X	A diet low in fat, saturated fat, and cholesterol may help prevent **cancer** and **heart disease**. Beta-carotene may play a role in preventing **cancer** and **heart disease**.	
		X	A low-sodium diet reduces your risk for **heart disease**, **high blood pressure**, and **stroke** and can help relieve **fibrocystic breast disease**.	
		X	Insoluble fiber may help protect you from **cancer**, **constipation**, **irritable bowel syndrome**, and **hemorrhoids**. Folate is important for **immunity** and may help prevent **birth defects** and **cancer**.	1, 125, 138, 141
X	X		Fats low in saturated fat and cholesterol used in moderation can help protect against **heart disease**. Vitamin E may help ward off **cancer**, **heart disease**, and **fibrocystic breast disease**.	55, 69
			Protein is important for **immunity**.	11, 100, 170, 196, 207
		X	A diet low in fat and saturated fat helps protect against **heart disease** and **cancer**. Protein is important for **immunity**.	192
		X	A diet low in fat, saturated fat, and cholesterol and high in insoluble fiber may help prevent **cancer**, **constipation**, **heart disease**, **hemorrhoids**, and **irritable bowel syndrome**.	
		X	A diet low in fat, saturated fat, and cholesterol and high in insoluble fiber may help prevent **cancer**, **constipation**, **heart disease**, **hemorrhoids**, and **irritable bowel syndrome**.	
		X	Folate may help prevent **birth defects** and **cancer** and, along with protein, is important for **immunity**.	221, 233, 248
		X	A diet low in fat, saturated fat and cholesterol may help prevent **cancer** and **heart disease**. Folate is important for **immunity** and may prevent **birth defects** and **cancer**.	90, 99, 104
		X	A diet low in fat, saturated fat, and cholesterol may help prevent **cancer** and **heart disease**.	177, 221, 233, 248, 250
		X	A diet low in fat, saturated fat, and cholesterol and high in insoluble fiber may help prevent **cancer**, **constipation**, **heart disease**, **hemorrhoids**, and **irritable bowel syndrome**.	
		X	Protein is important for **immunity**.	100, 187, 188

FOOD	LOW IN:				GOOD SOURCE OF:							
	FAT	SATURATED FAT	CHOLESTEROL	SODIUM	SOLUBLE FIBER	INSOLUBLE FIBER	CARBOHYDRATE	PROTEIN	IRON	CALCIUM	BETA-CAROTENE	FOLATE
Fish, filet of sole	X	X		X				X				
Fish, salmon				X				X				
Fish, salmon, canned								X		X		X
Frozen yogurt, low-fat	X	X	X	X			X			X		
Grapefruit	X	X	X	X	X	X	X					
Honeydew melon	X	X	X	X			X					X
Ice milk	X	X	X	X			X			X		
Juice, cranberry	X	X	X	X			X					
Juice, orange	X	X	X	X			X					X
Juice, tomato, low sodium	X	X	X	X								X
Kale	X	X	X	X							X	
Kiwifruit	X	X	X	X		X	X					
Legumes, dried	X	X	X	X	X	X	X	X	X			X

VITAMIN C	VITAMIN E	LACTOSE FREE	HEALTH BENEFITS	RECIPE NUMBERS
		X	Protein is important for **immunity**. A low-sodium diet reduces your risk for **heart disease**, **high blood pressure**, and **stroke** and can help relieve the symptoms of **fibrocystic breast disease**.	177, 182, 186, 193
		X	Protein is important for **immunity**. A low-sodium diet reduces your risk for **heart disease**, **high blood pressure**, and **stroke** and can help relieve the symptoms of **fibrocystic breast disease**.	195, 199
	X	X	Protein is important for **immunity**. Calcium helps fight off **dental disease**, **osteoporosis**, and **high blood pressure**. Vitamin E helps ward off **cancer**, **heart disease**, and **fibrocystic breast disease**.	199
			Calcium helps fight off **dental disease**, **osteoporosis**, and **high blood pressure**.	292
X		X	A diet low in fat, saturated fat, and cholesterol and high in insoluble fiber may help prevent **cancer**, **constipation**, **heart disease**, **hemorrhoids**, and **irritable bowel syndrome**. Vitamin C may help prevent **cancer**, **heart disease**, and **high blood pressure**, and is needed for **immunity**.	258
X		X	Folate may prevent **birth defects** and **cancer**. Vitamin C may help prevent **cancer**, **heart disease**, and **high blood pressure**.	21, 216
			Calcium helps fight off **dental disease**, **osteoporosis**, and **high blood pressure**.	33
X		X	Vitamin C may help prevent **cancer**, **heart disease**, and **high blood pressure**, and is needed for **immunity**.	4, 26, 95, 289
X		X	Vitamin C may help prevent **cancer**, **heart disease**, and **high blood pressure**, and is needed for **immunity**. Some brands are fortified with calcium for protection against **osteoporosis**.	5, 70, 112, 275
X		X	Folate may prevent **birth defects** and **cancer**. Vitamin C may help prevent **cancer**, **heart disease**, and **high blood pressure**.	
X	X	X	Beta-carotene, vitamin C, and vitamin E may play a role in preventing **cancer**, **heart disease**, and **high blood pressure**. Vitamin C is also needed for **immunity**, and vitamin E may help ward off **fibrocystic breast disease**.	
X		X	Vitamin C may help prevent **cancer**, **heart disease**, and **high blood pressure** and is needed for **immunity**.	66, 216
		X	A diet low in fat, saturated fat, and cholesterol and high in insoluble fiber may help prevent **cancer**, **heart disease**, **constipation**, **hemorrhoids**, and **irritable bowel syndrome**.	79, 85, 124, 148, 158

FOOD	LOW IN:				GOOD SOURCE OF:							
	FAT	SATURATED FAT	CHOLESTEROL	SODIUM	SOLUBLE FIBER	INSOLUBLE FIBER	CARBOHYDRATE	PROTEIN	IRON	CALCIUM	BETA-CAROTENE	FOLATE
Lettuce	X	X	X	X								X
Liver	X	X		X				X	X			X
Lobster	X	X						X				
Mango	X	X	X	X	X	X					X	X
Milk, 1% fat or skim	X	X	X	X			X	X		X		
Milk, soy, fortified		X	X	X			X	X		X		
Mollusks (clams, mussels, oysters)	X	X						X				
Muffin, bran						X	X					X
Nuts, unsalted		X	X	X				X				X
Oatmeal, plain	X	X	X	X	X		X					
Olive oil		X	X	X								
Onions	X	X	X	X								

VITAMIN C	VITAMIN E	LACTOSE FREE	HEALTH BENEFITS	RECIPE NUMBERS
		X	A diet low in fat, saturated fat, and cholesterol may help prevent **cancer** and **heart disease**, and help relieve **heartburn** and **hiatal hernia** symptoms. A low-sodium diet further reduces your risk for **heart disease**, **high blood pressure**, and **stroke**.	46, 71, 146, 162
		X	Protein is important for **immunity**. Folate is also important for **immunity** and may help prevent **birth defects** and **cancer**. Iron combats **anemia**.	
		X	Protein is important for **immunity**.	189
X		X	Insoluble fiber may help protect you from **cancer**, **constipation**, **irritable bowel syndrome**, and **hemorrhoids**. Folate helps prevent **birth defects** and **cancer**. Beta-carotene may play a role in preventing **cancer** and **heart disease**, as does vitamin C.	199
			Calcium helps fight off **dental disease**, **osteoporosis**, and **high blood pressure**.	41, 85, 166
	X	X	Calcium helps fight off **dental disease**, **osteoporosis**, and **high blood pressure**. Vitamin E may ward off **cancer**, **heart disease**, and **fibrocystic breast disease**. Lactose-free foods can be helpful for **food allergies**, **lactose intolerance**, and **flatulence**.	
		X	Protein is important for **immunity**.	176
	X		Insoluble fiber may help protect you from **cancer**, **constipation**, **irritable bowel syndrome**, and **hemorrhoids**. Folate may help prevent **birth defects** and **cancer**. Vitamin E may help ward off **cancer**, **heart disease**, and **fibrocystic breast disease**.	241
	X	X	A low-sodium diet reduces your risk of **heart disease**, **high blood pressure**, and **stroke**. Folate is important for **immunity** and may help prevent **birth defects** and **cancer**. Vitamin E may help ward off **cancer**, **heart disease**, and **fibrocystic breast disease**.	160, 225, 241, 269, 276
		X	A diet low in fat, saturated fat, and cholesterol may help prevent **cancer** and **heart disease** and help relieve **heartburn** and **hiatal hernia** symptoms. Soluble fiber may also protect against **diabetes**.	240, 241, 243, 245, 251
	X	X	Vitamin E may help ward off **cancer**, **heart disease**, and **fibrocystic breast disease**.	152, 162, 197
		X	A low-sodium diet reduces your risk for **heart disease**, **high blood pressure**, and **stroke**, and can help relieve the symptoms of **fibrocystic breast disease**.	78, 90, 99, 163, 185

FOOD	LOW IN:				GOOD SOURCE OF:							
	FAT	SATURATED FAT	CHOLESTEROL	SODIUM	SOLUBLE FIBER	INSOLUBLE FIBER	CARBOHYDRATE	PROTEIN	IRON	CALCIUM	BETA-CAROTENE	FOLATE
Orange	X	X	X	X	X	X	X					X
Papaya	X	X	X	X		X	X				X	X
Pasta	X	X	X	X			X					
Peach	X	X	X	X		X	X					
Peanut butter			X					X				X
Pear	X	X	X	X		X	X					
Peas	X	X	X	X	X	X	X	X				X
Pepper, green	X	X	X	X								
Pineapple	X	X	X	X			X					
Plum	X	X	X	X			X					
Popcorn, plain unsalted	X	X	X	X		X	X					
Pork, lean				X				X				

VITAMIN C	VITAMIN E	LACTOSE FREE	HEALTH BENEFITS	RECIPE NUMBERS
X		X	Vitamin C may help prevent **cancer**, **heart disease**, and **high blood pressure**, and is needed for **immunity**. Folate adds possible protection from **birth defects**. A diet high in soluble and insoluble fiber may help prevent **cancer**, **heart disease**, **diabetes**, **constipation**, **irritable bowel syndrome**, and **hemorrhoids**.	198, 294
X		X	Folate and vitamin C are important for **immunity** and help prevent **cancer**; folate may help prevent **birth defects**, also. Beta-carotene may also play a role in preventing **cancer**. Beta-carotene and vitamin C may protect against **heart disease**.	199
		X	A diet low in fat, saturated fat, and cholesterol may help prevent **cancer** and **heart disease** and relieve **heartburn** and **hiatal hernia**.	199, 203, 204, 209
		X	A diet low in fat, saturated fat, and cholesterol and high in insoluble fiber may help prevent **cancer**, **constipation**, **heart disease**, **hemorrhoids**, and **irritable bowel syndrome**.	10, 15, 33, 42, 69
	X	X	Protein and folate are important for **immunity**, and folate may help prevent **birth defects** and **cancer**. Vitamin E may also help ward off **heart disease** and **fibrocystic breast disease**.	30
		X	Insoluble fiber may help protect you from **cancer**, **constipation**, **irritable bowel syndrome**, and **hemorrhoids**.	27, 36, 38, 50, 52
X		X	A diet high in soluble and insoluble fiber may help prevent **cancer**, **constipation**, **diabetes**, **heart disease**, **hemorrhoids**, and **irritable bowel syndrome**. Folate adds protection from **birth defects** and, together with protein and vitamin C, is needed for **immunity**.	49, 146, 209, 233
X		X	Vitamin C may help prevent **cancer**, **heart disease**, and **high blood pressure** and is needed for **immunity**.	58, 71, 90, 138, 163
X		X	Vitamin C may help prevent **cancer**, **heart disease**, and **high blood pressure** and is needed for **immunity**.	48, 63, 70, 136, 143
		X	A diet low in fat, saturated fat, and cholesterol may help prevent **cancer** and **heart disease**.	19, 26, 95, 99
		X	A diet low in fat, saturated fat, and cholesterol and high in insoluble fiber may help prevent **cancer**, **constipation**, **heart disease**, **hemorrhoids**, and **irritable bowel syndrome**.	
		X	Protein is important for **immunity**.	119, 122, 133

FOOD	LOW IN:				GOOD SOURCE OF:								
	FAT	SATURATED FAT	CHOLESTEROL	SODIUM	SOLUBLE FIBER	INSOLUBLE FIBER	CARBOHYDRATE	PROTEIN	IRON	CALCIUM	BETA-CAROTENE	FOLATE	
Potato, baked with skin	X	X	X	X		X	X						
Pretzels	X	X	X	X			X						
Prunes	X	X	X	X		X	X						
Pumpkin	X	X	X	X		X	X				X		
Raisins	X	X	X	X		X	X		X				
Rice cakes	X	X	X	X			X						
Rice, brown	X	X	X	X		X	X						
Rice, white	X	X	X	X			X						
Salsa	X	X	X									X	
Sardines, with bones		X						X		X			
Scallops	X	X						X					
Shrimp	X	X						X					
Sorbet	X	X	X	X			X						
Soup, split pea	X	X	X		X	X	X	X	X				

VITAMIN C	VITAMIN E	LACTOSE FREE	HEALTH BENEFITS	RECIPE NUMBERS
X		X	A diet low in fat, saturated fat, and cholesterol and high in insoluble fiber may help prevent **cancer**, **constipation**, **heart disease**, **hemorrhoids**, and **irritable bowel syndrome**.	132, 228
		X	A diet low in fat, saturated fat, and cholesterol may help prevent **cancer** and **heart disease**.	25
		X	A diet low in fat, saturated fat, and cholesterol and high in insoluble fiber may help prevent **cancer**, **constipation**, **heart disease**, **hemorrhoids**, and **irritable bowel syndrome**.	253
		X	Beta-carotene may play a role in preventing **cancer** and **heart disease**. A diet low in fat, saturated fat, and cholesterol and high in insoluble fiber may help prevent **cancer**, **constipation**, **heart disease**, **hemorrhoids**, and **irritable bowel syndrome**.	269
		X	A diet low in fat, saturated fat, and cholesterol and high in insoluble fiber may help prevent **cancer**, **constipation**, **heart disease**, **hemorrhoids**, and **irritable bowel syndrome**. Iron combats **anemia**.	47, 63, 168, 241, 256
		X	A diet low in fat, saturated fat, and cholesterol may help prevent **cancer** and **heart disease**. A low-sodium diet further reduces your risk of **high blood pressure** and **stroke** and can help relieve the symptoms of **fibrocystic breast disease**.	25
		X	A diet low in fat, saturated fat, and cholesterol and high in insoluble fiber may help prevent **cancer**, **constipation**, **heart disease**, **hemorrhoids**, and **irritable bowel syndrome**.	96, 175, 180, 183, 206
		X	A diet low in fat, saturated fat, and cholesterol may help prevent **cancer** and **heart disease**.	67, 138, 157, 190, 205
X		X	Vitamin C may help prevent **cancer**, **heart disease**, and **high blood pressure** and is needed for **immunity**.	14
		X	Calcium helps fight off **dental disease**, **osteoporosis**, and **high blood pressure**. Protein is important for **immunity**.	
		X	Protein is important for **immunity**.	185
		X	Protein is important for **immunity**.	72, 180, 190
		X	A diet low in fat, saturated fat, and cholesterol may help prevent **cancer** and **heart disease**.	248, 268, 290
		X	Protein is important for **immunity**. Iron combats **anemia**. A diet high in soluble and insoluble fiber may help prevent **cancer**, **constipation**, **diabetes**, **heart disease**, **hemorrhoids**, and **irritable bowel syndrome**.	148

FOOD	LOW IN:				GOOD SOURCE OF:							
	FAT	SATURATED FAT	CHOLESTEROL	SODIUM	SOLUBLE FIBER	INSOLUBLE FIBER	CARBOHYDRATE	PROTEIN	IRON	CALCIUM	BETA-CAROTENE	FOLATE
Spinach	X	X	X	X	X	X			X	X	X	X
Squash, winter	X	X	X	X		X	X				X	
Sunflower seeds		X	X	X								X
Sweet potato	X	X	X	X		X	X				X	X
Tofu, with calcium		X	X	X				X		X		X
Tomato	X	X	X	X								
Tortilla, corn	X	X	X	X			X					
Turkey, breast, no skin	X	X		X				X				
Turkey, dark meat, no skin				X				X	X			
Walnuts		X	X	X				X				X
Watermelon	X	X	X	X			X					
Wheat germ		X	X	X		X	X					X
Yogurt, low-fat or nonfat	X	X	X				X	X		X		X

VITAMIN C	VITAMIN E	LACTOSE FREE	HEALTH BENEFITS	RECIPE NUMBERS
X		X	Beta-carotene, folate, and vitamin C help prevent **cancer** and **heart disease**. Iron combats **anemia**. Calcium helps fight off **dental disease**, **osteoporosis**, and **high blood pressure**.	56, 61, 64, 123, 152
		X	Beta-carotene may play a role in preventing **cancer** and **heart disease**. Insoluble fiber may help prevent **cancer**, **constipation**, **irritable bowel syndrome**, and **hemorrhoids**.	86
	X	X	Folate is important for **immunity** and may help prevent **birth defects** and **cancer**. Vitamin E may help ward off **cancer**, **heart disease**, and **fibrocystic breast disease**.	244
X	X	X	Beta-carotene, folate, and vitamins C and E may help prevent **cancer** and **heart disease**. Folate also protects against **birth defects**.	16, 140, 174, 279
	X	X	Calcium helps fight off **dental disease, osteoporosis,** and **high blood pressure**. Protein and folate are important for **immunity**. Folate may also help prevent **birth defects** and **cancer**. Vitamin E may help ward off **heart disease** and **fibrocystic breast disease**.	88, 236
X		X	Vitamin C may help prevent **cancer**, **heart disease**, and **high blood pressure**, and is needed for **immunity**.	78, 79, 99, 100, 169
		X	A diet low in fat, saturated fat, and cholesterol may help prevent **cancer** and **heart disease** and can help relieve **heartburn** and **hiatal hernia** symptoms.	1
		X	Protein is important for **immunity**. A low-sodium diet reduces your risk for **heart disease, high blood pressure,** and **stroke**, and can help relieve the symptoms of **fibrocystic breast disease**.	55, 145, 153, 155, 163
		X	A low-sodium diet reduces your risk for **heart disease, high blood pressure,** and **stroke**, and can help relieve **fibrocystic breast disease**.	156
	X	X	Insoluble fiber may help protect you from **cancer, constipation, irritable bowel syndrome,** and **hemorrhoids**. Folate is important for **immunity** and may help prevent **birth defects** and **cancer**. Vitamin E may add protection from **heart disease** and **fibrocystic breast disease**.	51, 63, 209, 234, 246
		X	A diet low in fat, saturated fat, and cholesterol may help prevent **cancer** and **heart disease** and can help relieve **heartburn** and **hiatal hernia** symptoms.	32, 92
	X	X	Insoluble fiber may help protect you from **cancer, constipation, irritable bowel syndrome,** and **hemorrhoids**. Vitamin E may help ward off **cancer, heart disease,** and **fibrocystic breast disease**.	19, 241, 249
			Calcium fights **dental disease, osteoporosis,** and **high blood pressure**.	41, 43, 51, 113, 114

THE PICTURE OF HEALTH

Good health. We all want it. But what is health, and how do we hold on to it?

Health is a state of wellness in which you are living up to your full physical potential. Your present state of health may be viewed as the sum total of your heredity, your medical history, how much you exercise, whether you smoke, what you eat and drink, and your stress level.

Some people dismiss health as the luck of the draw: You either have good genes, or you don't. It is true that genetics plays a formidable role in whether or not you will have a chronic illness, including heart disease and cancer, but there is overwhelming evidence that suggests lifestyle choices largely determine not only how long you'll live, but how well you will live.

EXERCISE

You are getting older. That's inevitable, but you don't have to take it lying down. In fact, if you do, you're likely to age less than gracefully. The earlier you begin exercising, the better, but it's never too late to reap the benefits of physical activity. Studies show that even 80- and 90-year-olds can increase their muscle strength. And you can, too.

A healthy lifestyle holds benefits for people of every age. Your chronological age is merely a number; don't let it dictate how you feel or your overall health goals.

Inactivity is the curse of a hectic lifestyle. When you don't exercise, your muscles shrink, and your body becomes fattier. Not only an unsightly inconvenience, but being out of shape can spell trouble.

TIME MARCHES ON

It's largely up to you to control the toll that time takes on your health. Unfortunately, we lose muscle as we age, and as a consequence, we burn fewer calories, because muscle burns more calories than fat. We lose bone tissue, too, and have a harder time making the vitamin D that is central to bone strength.

Enough with the bad news, though. The good news is that you can fight these changes. Exercise is your best defense against the aging process.

YOU'RE AS OLD AS YOU FEEL

Do you act your age? We hope not, because it doesn't matter how old you are. Just how fit you are. Health experts are putting less emphasis on chronological age and more on biological age. Biological age is determined primarily by heredity and medical history, and perhaps even more importantly, lifestyle choices.

Why the emphasis on biological age? Because the numbers don't always have a bearing on health, nor do they tell the whole story. Also, as we age, we become very different from one another depending on what has happened to us during our lifetimes. Take the case of a 60-year-old woman who moves, acts, and thinks like she's 90. Then, consider the 75-year-old woman who is still running in road races. We all know both types of people.

AN OUNCE OF PREVENTION

At this stage in your life, you may be active and busy. Perhaps that's why you are putting off doing what needs to be done to preserve your quality of life for longer. Getting regular exercise now is particularly crucial for preventing and postponing illness later on. Along with a healthy diet and proper medical care, exercise helps to keep debilitating diseases at bay, including heart disease and osteoporosis, which are typically symptomless until an advanced stage.

You don't have to be slumped over an exercise bike huffing and puffing to get your exercise. A brisk walk three or four times a week is all you need to get started.

FAT BURNER

Want to get rid of some fat? Try exercise. You know that exercise burns calories, and when combined with a reduction in calories, exercise usually promotes the loss of body fat.

Exercise can also change your body composition by actually burning fat during activity, provided that you exercise long enough. Here's how it works: To tap into your fat stores for energy, exercise at a lower intensity for at least 30 minutes. For example, instead of running for 20 minutes, try walking for 35 or 40. The longer you exercise, the greater the amount of fat used, and a pleasant walk is a lot more attractive than an agonizing jog. Isn't it nice to know that the easier alternative has its benefits, too? Another example of a fat-burning regimen: If you have a total of three hours per week to devote to exercise, you will burn more fat by walking four times a week for 45 minutes each rather than walking six times a week for 30 minutes. This regimen may fit your schedule better.

BASAL METABOLISM BOOSTER

Because exercise preserves and builds muscle tissue, it increases your basal metabolic rate (BMR), the rate at which you burn calories to sustain life. Muscle tissue burns more calories than fat tissue even when it is not exercising. The faster you burn calories, the easier it is to fight the battle of the bulge, which gets harder to do with each passing decade.

EXERCISE HELPS YOU EAT RIGHT

At first glance, this may seem like an odd claim, but it's true. Exercisers may be able to eat more without gaining weight, because they burn more calories. The more calories you eat, the greater your chances of meeting all of your nutrient needs. In addition, involving yourself in regular activity may help you control eating binges that make keeping your weight in line difficult. If you're out walking in the afternoon, you won't be in the kitchen munching on high-fat snacks.

ALL ABOUT INTENSITY

About 15 to 20 minutes into aerobic activity, stop to take your pulse. It only takes ten seconds to find out whether you are working too hard or not hard enough. Don't know how to figure out your target heart rate? Begin by subtracting your age from 220. That's your maximum number of beats per minute, also called *maximal heart rate*. When you're exercising, strive for about 70 percent of your maximal heart rate, more if you are well-conditioned, and less if you are just beginning. After you have subtracted your age from 220, multiply that number by 0.7 to get 70 percent of your maximal heart rate. Then divide that number by 6 to get your goal pulse rate for a ten-second period.

If you don't want to mess with the math, use these examples to best determine how high your pulse should be.

Age	Maximal Heart Rates	Target Zones 60%	75%	Ten Second Pulse Counts 60%	75%
25	195	117	146	20	24
30	190	114	143	19	24
35	185	111	139	19	23
40	180	108	135	18	23
45	175	105	131	18	23
50	170	102	128	18	23
55	165	99	124	17	21
60	160	96	120	17	21
65	155	93	116	16	20
70	150	90	113	16	19
75	145	87	109	15	19
80	140	84	105	14	18

GIVE YOUR HEART A BREAK

Exercise strengthens muscles, including your heart. Stronger muscles can do more work with less effort, and a healthy heart works smart: It beats less often to pump out the same amount of blood to the rest of the body. Physical activity can lower blood pressure and keep it low. Exercise can also decrease total blood cholesterol levels and increase high-density lipoprotein (HDL) cholesterol levels. HDL cholesterol is considered beneficial, because it helps rid the body of artery-clogging cholesterol deposits.

MOOD BOOSTER

Exercise can actually improve your outlook on life. Activity may brighten your mood and allow you to think more clearly by increasing circulation and releasing tension. Exercise is often prescribed as part of the treatment for depression. A daily walk, jog, or bike ride may help you to relax and sleep more restfully, too. And exercise can be fun. You may actually look forward to it as a welcome distraction from a hectic day.

BODY CONFIDENCE

Clothes a bit snug? Do you weigh the same, but need a larger size? Put exercise on the case. If your weight hasn't changed, then your body composition probably has. Exercise tones muscles. It helps tighten up the muscles in flabby areas so that your clothes fit better. Stronger muscles may help you feel stronger and

Getting enough exercise and staying active doesn't have to be a chore. In fact, exercise can have great benefits for your mood and your self-image—you may even enjoy it.

better able to perform daily physical feats, such as bending to pick up a small child or bringing in the groceries from the car.

LIMBER UP

Physical activity improves flexibility and decreases stiffness, particularly when it involves a warm-up and cool-down stretching period. Movement is often recommended to improve mobility in arthritis sufferers, who frequently experience joint pain and stiffness.

DIABETES BUSTER

Diabetes affects about 13 million Americans; the majority of them received the diagnosis of non–insulin-dependent diabetes later in life. Where does exercise fit in?

Exercise makes muscle. The more muscle you have, the better use your body makes of insulin, the hormone that facilitates the transfer of glucose from the blood into the cells.

Because muscle is a major calorie burner, you're less likely to become overweight, which also decreases your chances of developing diabetes. Dieting alone has a poor long-term success rate, but when it is paired up with an exercise regimen, the outlook gets brighter.

The risk of glucose intolerance, or higher-than-normal blood sugar levels, goes up with advancing age. Activity enhances the effectiveness of insulin and decreases your risk of experiencing glucose intolerance.

People with insulin-dependent diabetes who exercise may need less insulin to control their blood glucose levels. If you take insulin to control your diabetes, ask your doctor about how exercise can help and what the proper program would be for you.

IMPROVED BONE HEALTH

Exercise strengthens the muscles, tendons, and ligaments surrounding your bones. Women begin to lose more bone tissue than they make in their mid-30s; men start to lose significant amounts of bone tissue much later in life. Exercise can help mitigate the effects of age by promoting calcium deposition in your bones. Experts are unsure about exactly why this occurs, but studies confirm that regular exercisers have thicker and stronger bones.

Women, in particular, should take care to stay active. Exercise at all ages can be helpful in warding off the debilitating bone disease osteoporosis later in life.

WHICH EXERCISE IS BEST FOR YOU?

There are two categories of exercise: Aerobic, which means with oxygen, and anaerobic, meaning without oxygen.

Aerobic exercise is continuous and repetitive in nature. This is the kind that gets you huffing and puffing. It uses the large muscle groups, and increases your heart rate, mainly because your body uses oxygen to provide your working muscles with the energy they need to sustain the activity. Aerobic exercise improves circulation, strengthens the heart, lowers blood pressure, and aids in weight management. Examples include walking, jogging, biking, and climbing stairs.

Anaerobic exercise is more the stop-and-go variety, including weight training, calisthenics, and yoga. Anaerobic activities burn some, but not a lot of, calories. More often than not, they are used to tone and build specific muscle groups, such as the biceps in your arms and the hamstrings in your legs. The energy pathways that support anaerobic exercise do not use oxygen. Particular muscle groups cannot be exercised in this way for much longer than a few seconds or minutes.

HOW MUCH IS ENOUGH?

For optimal health, the American College of Sports Medicine (ACSM) recommends a combination of aerobic and anaerobic exercise for peak performance. You should get 20 to 60 minutes of aerobic activity

three to five days per week. You should exercise hard enough to increase your heart rate to within your target heart zone, or between 60 and 90 percent of your maximum heart rate; 70 percent is considered moderate. If you can talk during exercise, then you are working at just the right level. Nonathletic adults and beginners should exercise for longer at a lower intensity to get the same conditioning benefits.

Strength training is now considered an important part of the exercise mix. According to the ACSM, you should perform at least 8 to 12 repetitions of eight to ten exercises designed to condition the major muscle groups. Do that at least two days per week.

COUCH POTATOES, REJOICE!

Exercise is no longer considered an all-or-nothing affair. Only 22 percent of us get enough exercise, according to the ACSM, but there is hope for couch potatoes.

In an attempt to get more people moving, ACSM and the U.S. Centers for Disease Control and Prevention developed more realistic guidelines for activity. After a careful review of the scientific evidence, exercise experts say that even moderate activity, such as gardening, strolling, and stair climbing, may help reduce the risk of disease, including heart disease.

Try to accumulate at least 30 minutes of activity daily. For example, take two ten-minute walks, and climb five flights of stairs three or four times a day. You don't have to huff and puff to reap the rewards of activity, but you do have to get off your duff and move it. The more the better, of course.

GUIDELINES FOR GETTING STARTED

Have you been sidelined for a number of years without much physical activity? The first thing you should do if you are contemplating a new exercise routine is seek your doctor's approval. Then read on.

- Start slowly. Devote a few minutes three to four times a week to your chosen activity. Don't go all out the first week. That's one sure route to injury and disillusionment with your new routine.

- Always warm up. Don't overlook stretching and other exercises that stimulate blood flow. Stretching prepares your body for activity and prevents injury.

- Wear sensible clothing and shoes appropriate for the activity and the season. For example, if you join

Keeping yourself hydrated is very important when you exercise. Be sure to drink plenty of fluids before and after exercise.

an aerobics class, invest in a new pair of sneakers designed specially for aerobics.

- Don't forget to drink. Exercisers need more fluid. Make sure you get at least one to two eight-ounce glasses of water before exercising and the same amount afterwards.

FOOL YOURSELF INTO MORE MOVEMENT

Can't seem to find the time or the drive to exercise? You have more opportunity than you think to sneak in some activity. Here's how:

- Always take the stairs instead of the elevator. If you are out of shape, start with a few flights at a time.

- Meet a friend to exercise. That way you can kill two birds with one stone.

- Make exercise a social occasion. Get together with friends for doubles tennis and eat a healthy breakfast afterwards.

- Bring the groceries from the car one bag at a time.

- Don't do drive-thrus. Park in the lot and get out of your car when you go to the bank or to get a quick cup of coffee.

- Walk or take your bike, don't drive, whenever possible, especially for those errands that required a trip of only a few blocks.

- At the office, use your feet instead of the telephone. Walk to see a coworker rather than calling.

STICK-TO-IT TIPS

Make exercise a part of your daily schedule. When you treat exercise like any other important task, it's less likely to get lost in the shuffle. If you need to move your exercise time around, be flexible enough to reschedule, but try not to skip any more than two days in a row.

- Cut back on boredom by reading, watching TV, or listening to tapes while riding your stationary bike or while walking on the treadmill.

- Reward yourself. Take yourself to the theater or to a movie, or buy yourself some jewelry or clothing as a visual reminder of your progress.

Making exercise a family affair makes it easier to stick with. Good company and mutual support make staying active fun.

- Make exercise a family affair. Ride bikes or walk with the kids or your spouse.

- Pick a convenient time and an enjoyable activity. For example, if you loathe jogging, then don't try to make it a part of your life. Remember, the best time to exercise is when it is right for you. What good does an exercise regimen do if you can't get yourself to do it?

- Try shorter exercise bouts. Even ten minutes of walking three times daily contributes to good health. There is no need to work out to the point of exhaustion to receive the benefits of an exercise program.

DOES YOUR EXERCISE ROUTINE GO SOUTH WHEN WINTER APPROACHES?

It may, if you live in the Northeast or Midwest. Dark and wintery days make it difficult to get outside and keep up with the same warm weather routine. The solution? Flexibility coupled with creativity.

While the impulse to hibernate is strong, resist ditching your workout. It's not healthy to stop activity cold when the warm weather ceases. Try these tips:

- Walk during the warmest times of the day.

- Ski or skate with your kids, or take up ballroom dancing.

- Seek indoor walking groups. There are indoor tracks at many gyms, and some shopping malls allow groups to walk before business hours. Call your local mall or YMCA for more information.

- Invest in a stationary bike, treadmill, or join a health club.

- Check out exercise videotapes to use at home. Pick up a few from your local video store and try them out before making your final decision. Purchase tapes with a combination of aerobic exercise and stretching and toning moves. Beginners, stick with stretching and low-impact routines, and move up to more vigorous programs with time.

- Participate in your own home exercise class by watching a televised daily exercise show.

- Try water aerobics. The water can be very invigorating and easy on the joints, especially if you usually avoid physical activity because of arthritis pain. Be aware, though, that water offers more resistance than you are used to; so, go easy at first.

DIET
PUTTING MODERATION INTO PRACTICE

Remember the dietitians' mantra: There are no good or bad foods, just good and bad diets. Balance, variety, and moderation are the keys to a healthy lifestyle. You can have your cake and eat it too, but not all the time.

In theory, moderation sounds great. You don't have to curb all of your food cravings. Nor must you take the straight and narrow path all the time. You don't have to exercise to exhaustion seven days a week, either. That's music to most people's ears.

But what exactly do health experts mean when they prescribe moderation, and how does that translate to your life? If you're like most people, you crave the hard facts, like how much red meat you're allowed and how often, and whether ice cream, eggs, and butter are good or bad for you. Pegging foods as "good" and "bad" takes much of the joy out of eating, however. It may lead to feelings of deprivation that won't do you any good in the long run.

A healthy lifestyle doesn't have to be hard line, but it should be balanced. It must involve eliminating dangerous health practices, such as cigarette smoking and alcohol abuse.

The older we get, the harder it can be to meet our nutritional requirements and to get out for some exercise, but don't give up. There are many simple ways to better health at any age.

THE TERRIBLE *TOOS*

At one time, we were mainly concerned with people not getting enough of certain nutrients. Now, however, generally speaking, many of our health problems stem from dietary excesses, rather than deficiencies. As a nation, we eat too many calories and too much fat. Some people drink too much alcohol; many smoke cigarettes (any number is too many); and, according to surveys of our exercise habits, most people spend altogether too much time reclining in their easy chairs.

There are still some concerns about deficiency, though. Despite an abundant food supply fortified to the hilt with vitamins and minerals, we fall short on some nutrients. For instance, many Americans get too little iron, calcium, and fiber. This is a particular concern in regard to certain risk groups. Older adults, for example, may be getting less-than-adequate levels of a multitude of nutrients.

SUMMON YOUR SUPERMARKET SMARTS

Half the battle for good nutrition is keeping healthy foods on hand. Even the most creative cook would be hard pressed to create something out of nothing. Keeping these staples on the shelves will prevent you from ordering fast food or snacking on less-than-healthy fare. Copy this page to use as a modified shopping list.

- Whole-grain bread
- Low-fat (less than two grams per serving) breads, rolls, bagels, and English muffins
- Safflower, sunflower, corn, olive, or canola oil
- Rice, preferably not in pre-packaged flavored mixes (The seasoning packets are high in sodium and may require fat in preparation.)
- Breakfast cereals with at least two grams of fiber per serving
- Graham crackers, gingersnaps, or animal crackers
- Low-fat microwave popcorn or pretzels
- Frozen fruit or juice bars or frozen yogurt

- Frozen vegetables without added sauces or sodium
- Nonfat or low-fat milk
- Nonfat or low-fat yogurt
- Reduced-fat cheese
- 100% fruit juice
- Lean deli meats, such as turkey and ham
- Fresh fruit
- Fresh vegetables
- Skinless poultry
- Lean red meat
- Peanut butter
- Ground turkey or chicken (Make sure it's at least 90% fat free.)
- Pasta
- Canned beans (chickpeas, kidney beans, and so on)

BRIDGING THE GAP

Several studies suggest that we are losing the battle of the bulge. Despite the hundreds of delicious and nutritious nonfat and low-fat foods on the market today, Americans of all ages are getting heavier. Yet our collective consciousness about the importance of diet has never been higher. So, why the gulf between knowing that we should eat better and exercise more, and actually doing what we know it takes to stay our healthiest?

A survey of eating habits conducted by The American Dietetic Association sheds some light on this complex subject. According to the poll, many Americans recognize the importance of good nutrition, but few are taking the simple steps necessary to improve their diets.

What are the obstacles? Many say they don't want to give up their favorite foods. Others cite a lack of time as a reason for not keeping track of what they eat. Many others are just plain confused by the conflicting nature of nutrition information.

A PROBLEM OF PERCEPTION

Health experts dole out an endless stream of lifestyle advice. Diet plan manufacturers with their own agenda add misinformation to the confusion. You may find it particularly tough to sift through it all to figure out what *you* should eat and drink, and how much *you* should exercise. The barrage of suggestions from health organizations and government agencies may have led you to believe that unless you completely overhaul your life, you may as well make no changes at all. Nothing could be further from the truth. Take heart. Even the seemingly small steps that require little effort will help you on your way to better health.

CONQUERING CONFUSION

No single food or food group will make or break a diet, no matter what anyone says. Always consider the source of a study or report—especially when you see a sensational headline. There are plenty of groups that want you to adhere to their one theory or study "finding." Health professionals do not base public health recommendations on the results of a single study. You shouldn't put too much stock in them, either.

It appears that researchers frequently change their minds about what you should eat. For example, one day the TV and newspaper reports say that coffee increases blood cholesterol. The next week, you may see a report suggesting it has no effect. What should you believe? Nutrition is an evolving science. The recommendations health professionals make are based on decades of well-designed research; suggestions are not made on a whim. Making radical changes in your diet because of what you read in a magazine one day is not the best policy.

It's tempting to believe claims made about a product or a study result, but remember: If it sounds too good to be true, it probably is. Claims about many nutritional products, such as amino acids, or bee pollen, arc largely unsubstantiated. At best, they are untrue. At worst, they are dangerous, and occasionally life-threatening.

The more you know, the better your chances of spotting faulty claims or conclusions about scientific studies or products. Use this book as a reference to educate yourself about the basics of good health, and depend on reliable sources for information, including The American Dietetic Association, the American Heart Association, and governmental agencies like the U.S. Department of Agriculture and the Food and Drug Administration. Even if the headlines about some nutrients appear to change with the wind, the basic tenets of a healthy diet do not.

DITCH THE ALL-OR-NOTHING APPROACH

It's self-defeating. Take lofty New Year's resolutions, for example. Does this sound familiar? On December 31st, you resolve to lose 25 pounds and to exercise three times weekly, right after you join your local gym and buy all the right clothes.

Hold it! You have overlooked one thing: your hectic schedule. Where will you find the time to concentrate on all of those changes at once? Better bring your expectations in line with your lifestyle to make them as attainable as possible. That way, you'll improve your chances of success in the long term, instead of chucking all of your ambitious goals in the first month.

One Big Mac attack does not mean the end of your new lifestyle. Even after a double bacon cheeseburger, a large fries, and a shake, you can get back on track.

KEEP IT SIMPLE

Here's one way to simplify. Pick a few high-fat foods you eat consistently, such as whole or two-percent milk, ice cream, and blue cheese salad dressing. Then substitute lower fat versions like skim or one-percent milk, low-fat frozen yogurt, and nonfat blue cheese dressing. Sounds too easy, right? We know, it doesn't look like much of an improvement, but it will result in huge fat and calories savings over a year's time.

Instead of spending precious resources on a gym membership you may use only a few times, invest in a comfortable pair of walking shoes and stroll with a friend for 30 minutes a day at lunch time. Yes, this is a more modest plan than an exercise regimen at the gym, but it may yield as many, or more, benefits. Why? Because it is realistic, and it is designed to withstand the test of time. Try these additional tips for success:

- Don't make too many drastic changes all at once. For example, trying to lose weight and to quit smoking at the same time is probably not a good idea. Try one major change at a time. (Quit smoking first. It's more important.)

- Don't give up on good taste. The more you equate good nutrition with sacrifice, the weaker your resolve. Change to delicious, lower-fat alternatives instead, but don't forget to indulge yourself with your favorite foods on occasion.

- Strive for five. Eat five servings of fruits and vegetables daily. That way, you'll crowd out more

Grain products, especially whole-grain breads and cereals, should be the focus of your healthy diet. Complex carbohydrates provide satisfying amounts of energy and nutrients without the fat.

The days of sitting down to three meals are gone for many busy families. More women than ever are in the work force, a trend that is unlikely to change. With two working parents, just having dinner with the kids can be a monumental feat.

Busy lifestyles breed on-the-go feeding styles. We are a nation of fast-food eaters. In consuming more meals on the fly, we may consume more calories, fat, and sodium, and fewer vitamins, minerals, and fiber than we need. With little time for food preparation, we often resort to commercially prepared and highly refined meals.

Breakfast Benefits

Breakfast is often cited as the most important meal of the day, but you'd never know it by how many people pass it up. A 1991 National Restaurant Association poll found that a third of 25- to 34-year-olds missed breakfast five to seven times a week. Skipping breakfast may mean missing out on calcium, iron, and B vitamins, never mind the calories you need to get through a busy morning.

Waist watchers take note: Eating breakfast burns calories. According to research conducted by C. Wayne Callaway, M.D., of George Washington University,

high-fat, refined foods, such as cookies, crackers, and chips, and you will pack more complex carbohydrate, fiber, and important vitamins and minerals into your day.

- Go for the grain. Depending on your age and calorie needs, you need from 6 to 11 servings of breads, cereals, and grains daily. Focusing on enough servings of fruits, vegetables, and grains saves time and energy over tabulating the number of calories and grams of fat you eat every day.

Say Good-Bye to the Three Squares

Life has changed rapidly since the beginning of the 20th century. We are more sure than ever of the link between how we live, our risk of disease, and the quality of life. Rapid changes in technology and social movements have left their mark on the when, how, and what we eat.

NIBBLERS TAKE NOTE

Appetite wreckers. Dietary saboteurs. Just plain bad. These are some of the insults that have been hurled at snacks. But snacks are merely light meals, nothing else. And when snacking is done right, it can be quite nutritious. The key is to keep calorie and fat levels in check.

According to a U.S. Department of Agriculture consumption study, snacks can contribute a significant number of nutrients to your diet. Women aged 19 to 50 consumed nearly 20% of their daily carbohydrate, 15 percent of their calcium, and 11 percent of their iron in snacks, nutrients that might otherwise have been missed.

Many people who don't eat full meals tend to "graze" their way through the day with several small snacks. Despite the fact that your mother may have lectured you about the importance of three meals a day, grazing is not detrimental. It may even be healthier. Some studies show that eating more than three meals daily keeps weight down, provided you don't eat more calories than you need.

It's when snacking goes wrong that your diet suffers. Snacking is unhealthy when you consistently pick high-fat, high-calorie foods, such as chips, soft drinks, or donuts. Too many high-fat snacks could result in weight gain when not balanced by physical activity. And depending on what you are snacking on, you could exceed your daily fat, cholesterol, and sodium quotas.

A bowl of cereal with low-fat milk and some fresh fruit is an easy and nutritious way to start your day off right.

breakfast eaters burn four to five percent more calories during the day than those that skip breakfast.

Can't face food in the early A.M.? Don't despair. You don't have to eat breakfast at the crack of dawn. You don't even have to eat traditional breakfast foods. There is no rule that says you must have bacon and eggs first thing in the morning. Rise and dine whenever you want with these breakfast tips:

- Whip up a fruity shake. Blend eight ounces of low-fat milk or yogurt with fruit and ice for a frothy beginning to your day.

- Pack up an eight-ounce container of yogurt and ½ to ¾ cup of ready-to-eat cereal to bring to work. When you're hungry, mix the cereal into the yogurt to munch at your desk.

- Grab a bagel and some juice on your way to work. Top the bagel with peanut butter, jelly, or fat-free cream cheese.

- Wrap up a few pieces of leftover pizza to eat while you dash to work.

- Keep a box of cereal at work. Purchase milk and fruit on the way.

- Spread peanut butter on graham crackers and nibble them while you enjoy eight ounces of low-fat milk or yogurt.

- Stop at a convenience store to pick up a bagel, a single serving pack of string mozzarella cheese, and fruit or fruit juice to eat later on.

- When the cold weather comes, keep packets of instant oatmeal on hand. Microwave and top with dried or fresh fruit.

WHO'S MINDING THE KITCHEN?

Kids are making more food decisions these days. According to a poll conducted by The American Dietetic Association and the International Food Information Council, half of all children said they decided what food to buy for their snacks and meals. Sixty-five percent of children aged 9 to 15 choose their own breakfast, and nearly three quarters said they decide what to eat for snacks.

NO MORE DINING OUT DILEMMAS

We love to dine out. According to the National Restaurant Association, the average American over the age of eight dines away from the home 198 times a year. Luckily, more restaurants—even fast-food chains—are bending to consumer demand for healthier fare. You're more likely than ever to find egg substitutes, margarine, and lower-fat milk on the menu. Chefs and waitstaff are more accommodating, too. Many are willing to prepare and serve menu items with less fat and sodium. Even burger joints are joining in, adding salads, baked potatoes, and low-fat shakes to their menus.

We spend nearly half of our food dollars on dining out. With such an investment of financial resources, you expect tasty food. You should also invest some time to learn how to pick the healthiest restaurant fare possible.

You may dine out only once or twice a month, and you probably look forward to eating whatever you want, like a juicy steak, baked potato slathered with sour cream, and a gooey dessert. That's your choice, but most people dine away from the home a lot more frequently, as the statistics bear out, so it pays to be aware of some of the most prominent pitfalls.

- **Problem**: Portions are larger than what you would eat at home. **Solution**: Ask for a doggy bag at the beginning of the meal. Remove half the food from your plate. That way, you won't be tempted to pick at your food and wind up eating twice as much as you should. Eat the leftovers for lunch the next day. Or split a large entree or oversized dessert with your dining companion to curb calorie and fat consumption.

- **Problem**: Hidden fat. Many dishes, including fettucini Alfredo, or baked seafood are prepared with hidden fat. **Solution**: Avoid entrees described as creamed, buttery, pan-fried, or fried. Go for grilled, steamed, poached, and braised dishes instead. Stay away from food covered in a cream or cheese sauce or gravy.

- **Problem**: Not enough fiber. **Solution**: Capitalize on fiber by ordering extra vegetables or a salad on the side (with reduced calorie dressing, of course). Forgo french fries in favor of a baked potato. Order a fruit cup for dessert, and a fresh vegetable platter with dip as an appetizer.

- **Problem**: Alcoholic beverages. Alcohol has nearly twice the calories of carbohydrate or protein. And when you mix it with soda or sour mix, the calorie content soars. **Solutions**: Order a nonalcoholic beverage for starters. That way you won't gulp your drink and need to order another before your meal. Stick with light beer or wine spritzers made with no more than four ounces of wine. Steer clear of cream-based drinks; they have nearly four times the calories of wine or beer.

IMPROVE YOUR SITUATION

The key to good nutrition is planning. Investing an hour or two thinking about meals and shopping for food can set you on your way to better nutrition in no time. Having healthy ingredients on hand enhances your chances for eating better. It can also save money, because it prevents you from ordering out, buying your lunch at work, and making frequent stops at a convenience store for something on the way home.

Here's what to do. On the weekend, mull over your family's commitments for the upcoming week. Think of a few quick and easy dishes you can prepare on the weekend or throw together on a weeknight. Jot down

Quick, simple dishes that you can prepare in advance and that focus on pasta and vegetables will help you to stay on track even in the middle of a busy week.

the necessary ingredients on your shopping list. Don't forget to add breakfast and lunch foods, beverages, and snacks.

Here are more easy ways to improve nutrition:

- Choose low-fat snacks to stock your kitchen shelves and your desk at work. Purchase raisins, graham crackers, flavored rice cakes, pretzels, low-fat popcorn, juice, or yogurt for quick pick-me-ups.

- Dish up frozen fruits and vegetables if you don't like to buy fresh because you're afraid they will spoil before you get around to using them. Canned vegetables are the lowest in nutrients.

- Prepare one or two dishes, such as roasted chicken or a bean soup, on the weekend. Reheat, adding a salad or steamed vegetables, bread or rolls, milk, and fruit for a nourishing, quick mid-week meal.

- Good intentions are hard to keep when you're hungry, tired, and aggravated after a long day at work. If this is a vulnerable time for you, make plans to stay away from food. You might want to use the time after work to exercise to relieve some of the day's stress.

- Pack low-fat, nourishing snacks to munch on in the car or have them ready to eat as soon as you get home to tide you over until dinner is ready. Try fruit, unsalted pretzels, and yogurt.

BACK TO BASICS

Concentrate on reducing fat and increasing complex carbohydrate and fiber. If you changed two meals a week and kept all of your other eating habits the same, you could make a big difference over the course of your lifetime.

FORGET ABOUT DIETING

It doesn't work. That's been proved. It's even more likely to fail when you severely restrict your intake—that's dangerous, too. Many people try to lose weight on "crash" or "fad" diets only to gain the weight back time and again.

Weight cycling, or yo-yo dieting, can be particularly hazardous to your health. Studies show that weight cycling increases the risk of heart disease and premature death. Health professionals say that it's probably in your best interest to carry around a few extra pounds rather than diet repeatedly to lose the same 20 pounds over and over again.

GOING SOLO

You may find yourself eating alone for any number of reasons. And you may be enjoying it less. If you live alone, there's a good chance you're not getting all the nutrients you need, according to some studies. But don't skimp on good nutrition just because you're not cooking for a crowd. Here are the dos and don'ts of dining alone:

- Do prepare hot meals for yourself. For example, roast a chicken or small turkey one day. Heat the leftovers along with some vegetables and some rice, pasta, or potatoes for quick, nourishing meals later in the week.

- Do shop with a list. Stock up on frozen fruits and vegetables when you think fresh will only go to waste. Or buy small amounts of fresh fruits and vegetables to have on hand.

- Don't keep tempting foods in the house, such as snack chips and baked goods. If you live alone, you may end up eating all of them yourself.

- Don't skip breakfast. Breakfast presents an excellent opportunity to bolster your nutrient intake. Even something as simple as cereal, milk, and fruit provides significant nutrition.

- Do make sure you have the ingredients for sandwiches on hand to eat for lunch or dinner. Keep cans of tuna fish and a jar of peanut butter in your cupboards. Or purchase small amounts of deli meats such as turkey breast and lean ham. Round out your meal by adding a serving of vegetables or fruit, and milk, yogurt, or cheese.

Get rid of the guilt

Has this ever happened to you? You've resolved to eat better. You buy all the right "health" foods, and you do well for a while on your new regimen. Then one day, you spy some cookies. You figure you've been good; why not have one? So, you do. Moments later, you begin to feel as if you've ruined your diet. You eat another cookie, and another, and maybe one more. Now you feel guilty and figure you're a failure.

We have news for you. One cookie does not ruin an otherwise healthy diet. And missing one day, or even one week of exercise will not forever ruin your fitness plans, as long as you start back on your healthy pursuits as soon as you are able. Wallowing in guilt, on the other hand, will probably sabotage your plans for eating better and exercising more. Guilt may lead to depression, which can result in overeating. So, try not to feel bad when you indulge; carry on as it if never happened.

STRESS

Under stress? Who isn't? Most people recognize losing a job, the death of a friend or family member, and the constant pursuit of perfection as particularly stressful. But joyful events, such as getting married, having a baby, or moving into your dream house may produce stress, too.

You know that you feel stressed out, but you may not know why. When confronted with danger or any sort of threat, your body shifts into the stress response. Stress stimulates the secretion of hormones that prepare your body to fight or flee the scene. As a result, your muscles tense, your heart races, your breath quickens, and your blood pressure rises.

Hormones to the rescue

The fight-or-flight reaction to danger is common in nearly every animal. In humans, the stress response was more useful back in the caveman days, when the need to flee the scene at a moment's notice was more common than it is now. Granted, there are times when that hormonal jolt benefits us, like when we need to dodge an oncoming car or rush to catch a falling child.

The fast pace of our society and the stress it creates can leave its mark on your health. Finding ways to deal with your stress is crucial to your well-being.

However, for the most part, the stresses of modern life are ones that we cannot run away from, and sometimes, cannot confront—like when your boss is breathing down your neck and you'd like to tell him a thing or two, or when you are racing to get to work, only to be delayed in a major traffic jam.

Where does that rage and frustration go? Right back at you, that's where. If you could yell at your boss or drive right over those cars to make it to work on time, then you would probably feel better. Your body would begin to calm down, eventually returning to its normal state, but more often than not, we have no outlet for the irritations of the day.

When the relief from stress is scarce, it may take its toll on you in the form of insomnia, headaches, high blood pressure, back pain, and stomach aches, to name a few. Prolonged stress may weaken your immune system, too.

Physical stress

The body attempts to shield itself from injury of any sort. So when it's confronted with a stressor, such as a fever, a broken bone, or a burn, it launches into a cascade of reactions designed to maintain balance. Typically, your metabolic rate is revved up to meet the demands of healing. When physical stress is serious, nutritional requirements soar. This most often occurs

Don't let the aggravations of everyday life eat away at you. After an hour in bumper-to-bumper traffic, try channeling your frustration into something constructive—like a good workout.

when you are hospitalized or diagnosed with a major illness that warrants additional nutrition. Fractures and burns also increase your nutritional needs.

Emotional stress

Most of us endure this sort of stress on a day-to-day basis. Your mind and body respond in much the same way they would to physical stress; only when it comes to emotional stress, your mind may fight back with learned, rather than in-born, responses to mental duress. For example, in order to ward off psychological injury, you may resort to several techniques in the name of insuring balance, including rationalization and suppression of your feelings.

Experts say that reactions to external events differ from person to person. For instance, your friend may not mind flying, but it scares you to death. Your way of handling what happens to you is related to the amount of stress you feel. The good news is that you can learn to change the way you react to people and events that you find stressful.

A gray area

One of the major problems with assessing the effects of emotional stress on health is defining and measuring it. For one, emotional stress is largely a matter of perception and is difficult to quantify, which makes it hard to study. Secondly, stress can be positive. Some people need to be under the gun to get work done, or they feel vibrant only when the pressure is on. The lasting effects of stress are still difficult to assess in different people.

Diet and stress

When you're under stress, you may eat more. Or you may eat less. In either case, you may not be getting all the nutrients you need.

A stressful lifestyle may translate into more sugar, more caffeine, more alcohol, and fewer vitamins and minerals than you need. You might skip fruits and vegetables in favor of highly refined fast food. To add insult to injury, you probably don't get enough sleep, and you may not have the time or energy to exercise. Weight gain may result.

The effects of emotional stress on individual nutrients is unclear. It may depend on the nature and the duration of the stress, as well as who it is affecting. For example, younger people can tolerate more stress

MIND YOURSELF

You don't know your blood cholesterol level. You can't remember when you last had your blood pressure checked. You don't weigh yourself, and you have no idea what your body fat content is. You are playing with fire.

The National Cholesterol Education Adult Treatment Panel recommends that all adults know their total cholesterol and high-density lipoprotein (HDL) cholesterol levels to determine their heart-disease risk. Your total cholesterol and HDL cholesterol values are telling. For instance, if your blood cholesterol level is too high and your HDL cholesterol level is too low, then you should cut back on saturated fat, cholesterol, and calories. And your should exercise regularly.

Knowing your body weight and fat composition gives you even more information about your fitness level. For example, you may be within range for body weight, but out of the acceptable fat-tissue limit; or you could weigh more and have much less fat, which is definitely the healthier situation of the two.

Don't forget to see your doctor regularly and have periodic screening tests, including mammograms for women over 35. Men, in particular, put off seeing their doctors. That's usually because they don't feel sick, so they figure, why bother? But this is not a valid reason for anyone to skip yearly physical exams. Doctors can educate you about how to perform self-examinations for cancer and can help you recognize warning signs for certain medical conditions. Seeing your doctor can give you a clearer picture of your health status.

with fewer physical ramifications. Older people, in particular, respond to stress differently, because they have weaker defense systems, including a weaker immune system.

When going through particularly stressful times, try to eat as regularly as possible, choose low-fat foods, exercise as much as possible, avoid excess caffeine and alcohol, and try to get more sleep. To cover your bases, you may want to take a multivitamin that does not exceed the Recommended Dietary Allowances (RDA) for any nutrient, but don't expect this to make up for poor eating habits.

THE CAFFEINE CONNECTION

Caffeine is found in coffee, tea, and soft drinks, as well as in chocolate and some over-the-counter medication, such as certain brands of aspirin and antacid, that you may be taking to counteract the effects of stress.

Caffeine stimulates your central nervous system, making you more alert and preventing fatigue and sleepiness. It may even increase your blood pressure temporarily. Caffeine is considered safe when used in moderation, but chronic caffeine consumption can result in dependence, nervousness, anxiety, and

sleeplessness, none of which reduces the stress in your life. The more caffeine you have, the more you need to produce the effects. People who consume the least caffeine get the greatest jolt from it.

If you want to cut down but don't want to go cold turkey, try these tips:

- Alternate caffeine-free coffee, tea, or soft drinks with regular. This will cut caffeine consumption by half.

- Keep cold, refreshing water on your desk to sip throughout the day to cut back on caffeine consumption and insure proper hydration.

- Rely on juice to get you through the mid-afternoon slump instead of a caffeinated beverage, but remember, juice is not without calories.

- Check your medications. They may contain caffeine.

WHAT ABOUT ALCOHOL?

When you're under stress, you may rely on alcohol to unwind. Healthy people can consume all foods in moderation with very little chance of hurting their health, and that includes alcohol, unless your doctor tells you otherwise. Alcohol becomes problematic when you have too much on a regular basis and when you are pregnant.

According to the National Academy of Sciences 1989 *Diet and Health* report, moderate drinking is defined as no more than two drinks a day. A drink is 12

Many people mistakenly think that alcohol can magically melt away their stress. Alcohol can do quite the opposite, creating additional stress for your relationships and your health.

ounces of beer, 4 ounces of wine, or 1 ounce of 100-proof alcohol.

Despite some studies and media reports suggesting that moderate drinking lowers heart-disease risk, you should not take up drinking in the hopes of heading off a heart attack. Alcohol has not been sufficiently studied in a controlled environment.

Excessive and habitual alcohol consumption increases the risk of heart disease, high blood pressure, liver damage, and certain forms of cancer, among other health problems. Alcohol causes your body to lose B vitamins and can lead to nutrient deficiencies generally.

Pregnant women should avoid alcohol altogether. Women who drink during pregnancy risk delivering babies with Fetal Alcohol Syndrome (FAS). Alcohol prevents sufficient oxygen and glucose from getting to the developing fetus. It also crosses the placenta and wreaks havoc on brain development. As a result, children can be born with mental and physical retardation and facial deformities.

LIGHTS OUT

Sleep. If you haven't had enough in a while, you'd give your right arm for a good night's sleep. How much sleep you get can play a role in your stress level.

Nearly everyone has had a sleepless night. That's normal. But insomnia is different. It's a sleep disorder that runs rampant in our society. Insomniacs may toss and turn their way through sleepless nights every day of the week. Or they may find themselves staring at the clock wondering when sleep will come. One of the reasons for insomnia is stress; sleep is often disturbed by what's on your mind.

A lack of sleep does nothing for your ability to handle stress. In fact, it can put you on edge all day and make you more vulnerable to minor irritations. Most of us don't take it seriously enough. Night after night we stay up to watch the late news and the late-night talk shows. Then, we drag ourselves around like zombies the next day.

Most adults need about eight hours of sleep, although that varies from person to person. A very few can get by with a remarkable three or four hours a night and be perfectly productive and cheerful during the day, but more often than not, people become sleep deprived, which is often corrected by getting an hour or so more of sleep a night. Your stress level may benefit from a little more down time.

With all the dangers that stress presents to your health and well-being, it is vitally important to create some time for relaxation. You may find that setting aside a few moments to read or meditate will make a world of difference.

KEEP IT CALM

In our fast-paced society, relaxation is at a premium. Leisure time is seen as unproductive and wasteful. Sadly, relaxing is not held in as high esteem as some health professionals would have it. Nor does it come easily to most people who are juggling work, home, and all the activities of a growing family.

Yet, relaxation is key to good health. Studies show that relaxing activities can decrease pulse rate, lower blood pressure, and decrease muscle tension.

Finding a way to unwind is the first step in the right direction. It may be as easy as taking a hot bath at the end of the day or pampering yourself with a massage or facial. Meditation and deep breathing exercises are gaining acceptance, particularly because they help improve circulation and may help lower your pulse rate. Exercise is another option, because it improves circulation and relieves muscle tension.

Take up a hobby that you enjoy. You may want to read a little each day, do needlepoint, or play tennis or golf. Try to devote some time to your hobby every week. That way, you'll be spending some stress-free time on yourself.

Above all, simplify your life whenever possible. You probably can't quit your job, but you can give up on keeping your house or apartment immaculately clean all the time or volunteering for every community activity that presents itself.

SMOKING

According to the American Cancer Society, smoking results in 400,000 deaths every year in this country. No doubt everyone knows about the strong relationship between smoking and lung cancer, but did you know that smoking also increases the risk of mouth, pancreas, and uterine cancer, stroke, and heart disease? Smokers have more colds and upper respiratory infections, too. Women who smoke during pregnancy may give birth to low-birth-weight babies, and smokers' babies are also more likely to die from sudden infant death syndrome (SIDS).

THE POWER OF PUFFING

The nicotine in cigarettes is what gets you hooked. Nicotine addiction is powerful. It's been likened to other dependencies such as heroine and cocaine addiction. That's why it is so difficult for smokers to quit, even though they may want to.

CAUSE FOR ALARM

Even if you don't smoke, smoking may be threatening your health or that of your children. Just breathing cigarette fumes, or secondhand smoke, can increase your risk of disease, especially if you live with a smoker. The American Cancer Society says that children exposed to secondhand smoke run a greater risk of suffering from infections of the respiratory tract, have poorer lung function, and experience more middle ear infections.

SMOKING AND FERTILITY

Men, listen up. Your unhealthy habits may affect the health of your child. Cigarette smoke, and other environmental toxins, can damage sperm and may lead to birth defects. If you smoke more than a half a pack of cigarettes daily, your baby is more likely to die at birth, and your child may suffer later on as a result of delayed brain development thought to be caused by cigarette smoke.

THE QUESTION OF WEIGHT GAIN

When you quit, you may put on a few pounds. In fact, many women still smoke for that very reason. Why the extra pounds? There is the obvious answer, of course. When smokers quit, they often substitute food for cigarettes. To make matters worse, nicotine increases your metabolic rate, so when you smoke, you burn more calories. But take heart: The weight gain may be only temporary, especially if you start exercising regularly. Just remember the threat of lung and heart disease far outweighs the irritation you may feel at carrying around a few extra pounds, and it's easier to get rid of five pounds than it is to get rid of cancer.

AFTER YOU QUIT

You have made the choice to kick the habit. Undoubtedly, many of your other lifestyle habits will improve,

---

WHEN SMOKERS QUIT
Within 20 minutes of smoking that last cigarette, the body begins a series of changes that continues for years.

20 MINUTES
- Blood pressure drops to normal
- Pulse rate drops to normal
- Body temperature of hands and feet increases to normal

8 HOURS
- Carbon monoxide level in blood drops to normal
- Oxygen level in blood increases to normal

24 HOURS
- Chance of heart attack decreases

48 HOURS
- Nerve endings start regrowing
- Ability to smell and taste is enhanced

2 WEEKS to 3 MONTHS
- Circulation improves
- Walking becomes easier
- Lung function increases up to 30 percent

1 to 9 MONTHS
- Coughing, sinus congestion, fatigue, shortness of breath decrease
- Cilia regrow in lungs, increasing ability to handle mucus, clean the lungs, reduce infection
- Body's overall energy increases

1 YEAR
- Excess risk of coronary heart disease is half that of a smoker

5 YEARS
- Lung cancer death rate for average former smoker (one pack a day) decreases by almost half
- Stroke risk is reduced to that of a nonsmoker 5-15 years after quitting
- Risk of cancer of the mouth, throat and esophagus is half that of a smoker's

10 YEARS
- Lung cancer death rate similar to that of nonsmokers
- Precancerous cells are replaced
- Risk of cancer of the mouth, throat, esophagus, bladder, kidney and pancreas decreases

15 YEARS
- Risk of coronary heart disease is that of a nonsmoker

Used by permission. © American Cancer Society, Inc. Centers for Disease Control and Prevention

In addition to the myriad of deadly health problems that smoking entails, smokers are often deficient in vitamin C. They require nearly double the RDA of this vitamin, because smoking depletes the body's supply.

too. Your diet will probably get better, largely because food will be tastier now. Smokers typically have poorer diets, because they may not eat enough, and they may eat too many high-fat foods and too little produce. On top of that, smokers need nearly double the Recommended Dietary Allowance (RDA) for vitamin C, according to the National Academy of Sciences' Food and Nutrition Board, because smoking depletes vitamin C from the body.

After you quit, your chances for starting a moderate exercise program soar. Smokers usually don't exercise regularly, primarily because they have a hard time breathing. Now that you have stopped, check with your doctor to see what type and how much exercise is appropriate for you, and start using your new-found lung power.

ON YOUR WAY TO A LONGER AND BETTER LIFE

Now that you have decided to change your lifestyle for the better, make a list of your goals. Concentrate on making one change a week—or more if you're

really ambitious. Incorporating as little as one change a month into your life translates into 12 new healthy habits in the course of the year. It's probably even better not to change your routine too fast. If you completely upend your lifestyle, there is a good chance that you won't stick with it. Gradual and lasting is better than radical and temporary.

PATIENCE MAKES PERFECT

A better life evolves with time—there is no quick fix. There will be periods in your life when you cannot exercise as much as you would like, or eat as well as you should. Life events often get in the way of our best intentions. For example, the birth of a child, moving to an unfamiliar new city, the death of a loved one, a hectic work schedule can throw a monkey wrench into your best-laid fitness and dietary plans. But you know what? That's OK. As long as you keep focused on healthy habits and know that you're in it for the long haul, then momentary slips mean relatively little in the course of an entire lifetime.

Of course, there will also be times when you want to ditch your resolve for a healthier life. Especially after a momentary slip up, it can be tempting to throw your hands up and quit the whole thing. And who can blame you? It's not always easy. Too much denial or too much guilt is the quickest route to giving up.

Here's where the question of quality comes in. There will be times when desire overrules common sense, like when you really want ice cream instead of nonfat frozen yogurt, or when you go on vacation and have more fatty foods and alcohol than you would at home. Fine. Go ahead once in a while. Better to give in to a bowl of ice cream than drive yourself crazy with self-denial.

The bottom line is this: It is your life. You call the shots. As long as you stick to the basics and keep moderation in mind, you'll live a longer, and better, life.

WHO CAN I ASK?

If you have a nutrition question, contact the Consumer Nutrition Hot Line at The American Dietetic Association's National Center for Nutrition and Dietetics at 800-366-1655. You can speak directly with a registered dietitian or listen to recorded messages for information about food, nutrition, and health. Ask them about a free referral to a registered dietitian in your area for additional counseling about your own personal eating style. (For more information sources, see page 110.)

RECIPES FOR SMART EATING

Now that a direct correlation between diet and health has been established, it is easy to see why it is important to eat well to stay well. In addition to proper exercise, eating foods that are lower in fat, sodium and cholesterol helps maintain a healthy lifestyle. The recipes that follow have been selected because they're easy to prepare, taste great and fit easily into the dietary parameters that promote good health.

It is widely known that most Americans' diets are too high in fat. As described earlier in the book, a low fat diet reduces the risk of getting certain diseases and helps to maintain a healthy weight. Nutrition experts recommend diets that contain 30% or less of total daily calories from fat. The "30% of calories from fat" goal applies to a total diet over time, not to a single food, serving of a recipe or meal.

NUTRITIONAL ANALYSIS

Along with fat, there are other nutrients in recipes that are important, including saturated fat, sodium, cholesterol, protein, carbohydrates and several vitamins and minerals. Daily values for these nutrients have been established by the government and reflect current nutritional recommendations for a 2,000 calorie reference diet (see page 102). Each recipe in *Live Longer & Live Better* is followed by a nutritional analysis block that lists certain nutrient values for a single recipe serving.

- The analysis of each recipe includes all the ingredients that are listed in the recipe, *except* ingredients labeled as "optional" or "for garnish."

- If a range is given in the yield of a recipe ("Makes 6 to 8 servings" for example), the *lower* yield was used to calculate the per serving information.

- If a range is offered for an ingredient ("¼ to ⅛ teaspoon" for example), the *first* amount given was used to calculate the nutrition information.

- If an ingredient is listed with an option ("2 cups hot cooked rice or noodles" for example), the *first* item listed was used to calculate the nutritional information.

- Foods shown in photographs on the same serving plate and offered with "serve with" suggestions at the end of the recipe are *not* included in the recipe analysis unless they are listed in the ingredient list.

- Meat should be trimmed of all visible fat since this is reflected in the nutritional analysis.

- In recipes calling for cooked rice or noodles, the analysis was based on rice or noodles prepared without added salt or fat unless otherwise mentioned in the recipe.

- There are some recipes that call for "defatted broth." To defat broth, chill the can thoroughly. Open, and use a spoon to lift out the solid fat on the surface of the broth.

The recipe nutrition information was calculated by an independent nutrition consulting firm. Every effort has been made to check the accuracy of these numbers. However, because numerous variables account for a wide range of values in certain foods, all analyses should be considered approximate.

The recipes in this publication are *not* intended as a medically therapeutic program, nor as a substitute for medically approved diet plans for people on fat, cholesterol or sodium restricted diets. You should consult your physician before beginning any diet plan. The recipes offered here can be a part of a healthy lifestyle that meets recognized dietary guidelines. A healthy lifestyle includes not only eating a balanced diet, but engaging in proper exercise as well.

When cooking these delicious low fat recipes, you will find some techniques or ingredients are different from traditional cooking. Fat serves as a flavor enhancer and gives foods a distinctive and desirable texture. In order to compensate for the lack of fat and still give great-tasting results, many of the recipes call for a selection of herbs or combination of fresh vegetables. A wide variety of grains and pastas are also used. Many of the recipes call for alternative protein sources, such as dried beans or tofu. Often meat is included in a recipe as an accent flavor rather than the star attraction. These simple changes are easy to make and incorporate into a diet that reflects the smarter eating choices of a healthier lifestyle.

APPETIZERS & BEVERAGES

1 Tortilla Pizza Wedges

Not only are these pizza wedges great tasting but they're high in complex carbohydrates as well.

1 cup frozen whole kernel corn, thawed
1 cup thinly sliced fresh mushrooms
4 (6-inch) corn tortillas
¼ cup low sodium spaghetti sauce
1 to 2 teaspoons chopped jalapeño pepper*
¼ teaspoon dried oregano leaves, crushed
¼ teaspoon dried marjoram leaves, crushed
½ cup (2 ounces) shredded part-skim mozzarella cheese

Preheat oven to 450°F. Coat large skillet with nonstick cooking spray; heat over medium heat. Add corn and mushrooms. Cook and stir 4 to 5 minutes or until vegetables are tender.

Place tortillas on baking sheet. Bake about 4 minutes or until edges start to brown. Combine spaghetti sauce, jalapeño, oregano and marjoram in small bowl. Spread over tortillas. Arrange corn and mushrooms on top of tortillas. Sprinkle with cheese. Bake 4 to 5 minutes or until cheese melts and pizzas are heated through. Cut into wedges.

Makes 4 servings

**Chili peppers can sting and irritate the skin; wear rubber gloves when handling peppers and do not touch eyes. Wash hands after handling chili peppers.*

Nutrients per Serving:

Calories	155	(23% of calories from fat)			
Total Fat	4 g	Dietary Fiber	3 g	Thiamin	<1 mg
Saturated Fat	2 g	Protein	7 g	Riboflavin	<1 mg
Cholesterol	8 mg	Calcium	143 mg	Niacin	2 mg
Sodium	136 mg	Iron	1 mg	Vitamin A	80 RE
Carbohydrate	24 g	Folate	22 µg	Vitamin C	4 mg

Dietary Exchanges: 1½ Starch/Bread, ½ Meat, ½ Fat

2 Chinatown Stuffed Mushrooms

Lean ground pork replaces the usual ground beef in this popular appetizer. A hint of soy and ginger gives the mushrooms a pleasant Oriental flavor.

24 large fresh mushrooms (about 1 pound)
½ pound ground pork or turkey
1 clove garlic, minced
¼ cup fine dry bread crumbs
¼ cup thinly sliced green onions
3 tablespoons low sodium soy sauce, divided
1 teaspoon minced fresh ginger
1 egg white, slightly beaten
⅛ teaspoon crushed red pepper flakes (optional)

Remove stems from mushrooms; finely chop enough stems to equal 1 cup. Reserve remaining stems for use in salads, soups or stews, if desired. Cook pork, chopped mushroom stems and garlic in medium skillet over medium-high heat until pork is no longer pink, stirring to separate pork. Drain off fat.

Stir in bread crumbs, onions, 2 tablespoons soy sauce, ginger, egg white and red pepper flakes; mix well.

Brush mushrooms lightly on all sides with remaining 1 tablespoon soy sauce; spoon about 2 teaspoons stuffing into each mushroom cap. Place stuffed mushrooms on rack of foil-lined broiler pan. Broil 4 to 5 inches from heat 5 to 6 minutes until hot.

Makes 2 dozen appetizers

Nutrients per Serving:

Calories	22	(28% of calories from fat)			
Total Fat	1 g	Dietary Fiber	<1 g	Thiamin	<1 mg
Saturated Fat	<1 g	Protein	2 g	Riboflavin	<1 mg
Cholesterol	4 mg	Calcium	4 mg	Niacin	1 mg
Sodium	80 mg	Iron	<1 mg	Vitamin A	4 RE
Carbohydrate	2 g	Folate	5 µg	Vitamin C	1 mg

Dietary Exchanges: ½ Meat

Tortilla Pizza Wedges

Iced Mocha

3 Iced Mocha

The combination of coffee and chocolate flavors are referred to as mocha. Try this cool mocha recipe instead of after-dinner coffee.

2 cups strongly brewed coffee
¾ cup skim milk
1 tablespoon packed brown sugar
½ teaspoon cocoa powder

Add coffee, milk, sugar and cocoa to blender. Process until smooth. Pour over ice and serve immediately, or refrigerate, stir well and serve over ice.   Makes 2 servings

---

Nutrients per Serving:

Calories	64	(3% of calories from fat)		
Total Fat	<1 g	Dietary Fiber	<1 g	Thiamin <1 mg
Saturated Fat	<1 g	Protein	3 g	Riboflavin <1 mg
Cholesterol	2 mg	Calcium	125 mg	Niacin 1 mg
Sodium	54 mg	Iron	1 mg	Vitamin A 56 RE
Carbohydrate	12 g	Folate	5 μg	Vitamin C 1 mg

Dietary Exchanges: ½ Milk, ½ Fruit

4 Nectarine Punch Cooler

This fresh and fruity punch is so delicious you can serve it at your next party.

1 pint fresh strawberries
2 medium fresh California nectarines, halved, pitted and cut into wedges
1 can (6 ounces) frozen pineapple or cranberry juice concentrate
12 ice cubes, cracked
1 to 2 cups sparkling water
Additional nectarine wedges for garnish

Hull strawberries. Reserve 6 whole strawberries for garnish. Add remaining strawberries, nectarines and frozen juice concentrate to blender. Process until smooth. Add ice and process until smooth. Pour into punch bowl or large container. Stir in sparkling water. Ladle into glasses. Serve with reserved strawberries and some additional nectarine wedges threaded onto stirrers.   Makes 6 servings

Nutrients per Serving:

Calories	102	(4% of calories from fat)				
Total Fat	<1 g	Dietary Fiber	2 g	Thiamin	<1 mg	
Saturated Fat	<1 g	Protein	1 g	Riboflavin	<1 mg	
Cholesterol	0 mg	Calcium	29 mg	Niacin	1 mg	
Sodium	2 mg	Iron	1 mg	Vitamin A	37 RE	
Carbohydrate	25 g	Folate	13 μg	Vitamin C	46 mg	

Dietary Exchanges: 1½ Fruit

5 Orange-Pineapple Breakfast Shake with Yogurt and Honey

This drink is packed with vitamins, minerals and protein to get your morning off to a great start.

1 cup orange or tangerine juice
½ cup unsweetened pineapple juice
½ cup plain low fat yogurt
1 teaspoon honey
Orange twists or fresh mint leaves for garnish (optional)

Add orange juice, pineapple juice, yogurt and honey to food processor or blender. Process until smooth.

Pour into two glasses. Garnish with orange twists or fresh mint sprigs, if desired. Serve immediately.
          Makes 2 servings

Nutrients per Serving:

Calories	137	(8% of calories from fat)				
Total Fat	1 g	Dietary Fiber	1 g	Thiamin	<1 mg	
Saturated Fat	1 g	Protein	4 g	Riboflavin	<1 mg	
Cholesterol	4 mg	Calcium	128 mg	Niacin	1 mg	
Sodium	42 mg	Iron	<1 mg	Vitamin A	36 RE	
Carbohydrate	28 g	Folate	89 μg	Vitamin C	69 mg	

Dietary Exchanges: ½ Milk, 1½ Fruit

6 Today's Slim Line Dip

By preparing this traditional onion dip with cottage cheese and buttermilk instead of sour cream, you'll get all the flavor but a lot less fat.

1 cup dry curd cottage cheese
½ cup buttermilk
¼ teaspoon lemon juice
1 package dry onion soup mix

Add cottage cheese, buttermilk, lemon juice and onion soup mix to food processor or blender. Process until smooth. Refrigerate. Serve with raw vegetables.   Makes 16 servings (about 2 cups)

Nutrients per Serving:

Calories	40	(15% of calories from fat)				
Total Fat	1 g	Dietary Fiber	1 g	Thiamin	<1 mg	
Saturated Fat	<1 g	Protein	3 g	Riboflavin	<1 mg	
Cholesterol	1 mg	Calcium	26 mg	Niacin	1 mg	
Sodium	883 mg	Iron	<1 mg	Vitamin A	2 RE	
Carbohydrate	6 g	Folate	3 μg	Vitamin C	<1 mg	

Dietary Exchanges: ½ Starch/Bread

7 Herbed Stuffed Tomatoes

The fat content of cottage cheese varies widely. Creamed cottage cheese can have as much as 4% fat, low fat cottage cheese ranges from 1% to 2% fat and dry curd cottage cheese, made without added cream, has less than ½% fat. In this recipe the 1% cottage cheese adds a little richness to the filling without adding a lot of fat.

15 cherry tomatoes
½ cup 1% low fat cottage cheese
1 tablespoon thinly sliced green onion
1 teaspoon chopped fresh chervil or
 ¼ teaspoon dried chervil leaves, crushed
½ teaspoon chopped fresh dill or
 ⅛ teaspoon dried dill weed
⅛ teaspoon lemon pepper

Cut thin slice off bottom of each tomato. Scoop out pulp with small spoon; discard pulp. Invert tomatoes on paper towels to drain.

Combine cottage cheese, green onion, chervil, dill and lemon pepper in small bowl. Spoon into tomatoes. Serve at once or cover and refrigerate up to 8 hours.

Makes 15 stuffed tomatoes (3 per serving)

Nutrients per Serving:

Calories	27	(12% of calories from fat)			
Total Fat	<1 g	Dietary Fiber	<1 g	Thiamin	<1 mg
Saturated Fat	<1 g	Protein	3 g	Riboflavin	<1 mg
Cholesterol	1 mg	Calcium	18 mg	Niacin	<1 mg
Sodium	96 mg	Iron	<1 mg	Vitamin A	39 RE
Carbohydrate	3 g	Folate	9 μg	Vitamin C	9 mg

Dietary Exchanges: Free food

8 Sparkling Punch

This delicious sparkling beverage packs a giant vitamin C punch.

2 cups orange juice
 Juice of one lemon (optional)
6 ounces unsweetened pineapple juice
1 cup unsweetened apple juice
12 ounces lemon or lime sparkling mineral water

Combine orange juice, lemon juice, pineapple juice, apple juice and sparkling water in large pitcher. Serve over ice. Makes 4 (10-ounce) servings

Nutrients per Serving:

Calories	109	(2% of calories from fat)			
Total Fat	<1 g	Dietary Fiber	1 g	Thiamin	<1 mg
Saturated Fat	<1 g	Protein	1 g	Riboflavin	<1 mg
Cholesterol	0 mg	Calcium	33 mg	Niacin	1 mg
Sodium	4 mg	Iron	1 mg	Vitamin A	25 RE
Carbohydrate	26 g	Folate	79 μg	Vitamin C	72 mg

Dietary Exchanges: 2 Fruit

9 Breakfast Lassi

This fruity drink provides lots of protein and tastes great too.

1 cup buttermilk
2 fresh California nectarines, halved, pitted and cubed
1 teaspoon honey
3 ice cubes, cracked

Add buttermilk, nectarines and honey to food processor or blender. Process until smooth. Add ice; process until frothy. Serve immediately.

Makes 2 servings

Nutrients per Serving:

Calories	127	(11% of calories from fat)			
Total Fat	2 g	Dietary Fiber	2 g	Thiamin	<1 mg
Saturated Fat	1 g	Protein	5 g	Riboflavin	<1 mg
Cholesterol	5 mg	Calcium	150 mg	Niacin	1 mg
Sodium	129 mg	Iron	<1 mg	Vitamin A	112 RE
Carbohydrate	25 g	Folate	11 μg	Vitamin C	9 mg

Dietary Exchanges: ½ Milk, 1 Fruit, ½ Fat

10 Peach Fizz

*A refreshing drink to serve at your next gathering;
it's loaded with nutrients too.*

**3 fresh California peaches, peeled,
halved, pitted and sliced
1 can (6 ounces) pineapple juice
¼ cup frozen limeade or lemonade
concentrate
¼ teaspoon almond extract
Finely crushed ice
3 cups club soda, chilled**

Add peaches to food processor or blender. Process
until smooth to measure 2 cups. Stir in pineapple
juice, limeade and almond extract. Fill 12-ounce
glasses ⅔ full with crushed ice. Add ⅓ cup peach
base to each. Top with club soda. Stir gently. Serve
immediately.   Makes 6 servings

Nutrients per Serving:					
Calories	53	(1% of calories from fat)			
Total Fat	<1 g	Dietary Fiber	1 g	Thiamin	<1 mg
Saturated Fat	<1 g	Protein	<1 g	Riboflavin	<1 mg
Cholesterol	0 mg	Calcium	11 mg	Niacin	1 mg
Sodium	24 mg	Iron	<1 mg	Vitamin A	23 RE
Carbohydrate	13 g	Folate	8 µg	Vitamin C	7 mg

Dietary Exchanges: 1 Fruit

11 Vegetable Dip

*This colorful recipe provides vitamins, delicious
flavor and very little fat.*

**1 cup 1% low fat cottage cheese
2 tablespoons finely chopped green bell
pepper
2 tablespoons finely chopped onion
2 tablespoons finely chopped radish
¼ teaspoon celery salt
Assorted vegetable dippers (optional)**

Drain cheese, reserving liquid. Add drained cheese
to food processor or blender. (Add 1 to 2 teaspoons
of reserved liquid for easier blending.) Process until
smooth. Transfer mixture to small bowl; stir in bell

pepper, onion, radish and celery salt. Cover;
refrigerate at least 1 hour to allow flavors to blend.
Serve with vegetable dippers.
Makes 10 (1-tablespoon) servings

Nutrients per Serving:					
Calories	18	(12% of calories from fat)			
Total Fat	<1 g	Dietary Fiber	<1 g	Thiamin	<1 mg
Saturated Fat	<1 g	Protein	3 g	Riboflavin	<1 mg
Cholesterol	1 mg	Calcium	15 mg	Niacin	<1 mg
Sodium	131 mg	Iron	<1 mg	Vitamin A	4 RE
Carbohydrate	1 g	Folate	4 µg	Vitamin C	3 mg

Dietary Exchanges: ½ Meat

12 Egg Drop Soup

*The simplicity and delicious flavor of this soup is
what makes it a Chinese classic.*

**2 cans (14 ounces each) ⅓-less-salt
chicken broth
1 tablespoon low sodium soy sauce
2 teaspoons cornstarch
1 carton no cholesterol egg substitute
¼ cup thinly sliced green onions**

Bring broth to a boil over high heat in large
saucepan; reduce heat to a simmer.

Blend soy sauce and cornstarch in cup until smooth;
stir into broth. Cook and stir 2 minutes or until
soup boils and thickens slightly.

Stirring constantly in one direction, slowly pour egg
substitute in thin stream into soup.

Ladle into soup bowls. Sprinkle with onions.
Makes 4 appetizer servings (about 3½ cups)

Nutrients per Serving:					
Calories	45	(7% of calories from fat)			
Total Fat	<1 g	Dietary Fiber	<1 g	Thiamin	<1 mg
Saturated Fat	<1 g	Protein	7 g	Riboflavin	<1 mg
Cholesterol	0 mg	Calcium	31 mg	Niacin	1 mg
Sodium	243 mg	Iron	2 mg	Vitamin A	334 RE
Carbohydrate	3 g	Folate	34 µg	Vitamin C	2 mg

Dietary Exchanges: 1 Meat

13 Easy Wonton Chips

These chips are so easy to make and are a great accompaniment to soups or dips.

1 tablespoon low sodium soy sauce
2 teaspoons peanut or vegetable oil
½ teaspoon sugar
¼ teaspoon garlic salt
12 wonton wrappers

Preheat oven to 375°F.

Combine soy sauce, oil, sugar and garlic salt in small bowl; mix well.

Cut each wonton wrapper diagonally in half. Place wonton wrappers on 15×10-inch jelly-roll pan coated with nonstick cooking spray. Brush soy sauce mixture lightly but evenly over both sides of each wonton wrapper.

Bake 4 to 6 minutes or until crisp and lightly browned, turning after 3 minutes. Transfer to cooling rack; cool completely.

Makes 4 servings

Nutrients per Serving:

Calories	96	(29% of calories from fat)			
Total Fat	3 g	Dietary Fiber	1 g	Thiamin	<1 mg
Saturated Fat	1 g	Protein	3 g	Riboflavin	<1 mg
Cholesterol	18 mg	Calcium	6 mg	Niacin	1 mg
Sodium	264 mg	Iron	1 mg	Vitamin A	6 RE
Carbohydrate	12 g	Folate	6 µg	Vitamin C	0 mg

Dietary Exchanges: ½ Starch/Bread

14 Oriental Salsa

This salsa recipe is low in calories but high in vitamins and flavor. Use it instead of Mexican salsa for an Oriental flair.

1 cup diced, unpeeled cucumber
½ cup chopped red bell pepper
½ cup thinly sliced green onions
⅓ cup coarsely chopped cilantro
1 clove garlic, minced
1 tablespoon rice vinegar
2 teaspoons soy sauce
½ teaspoon Oriental sesame oil
¼ teaspoon crushed red pepper flakes
   Easy Wonton Chips (recipe above) or
   Chinese crackers

Combine cucumber, bell pepper, onions, cilantro, garlic, rice vinegar, soy sauce, sesame oil and red pepper flakes in medium bowl until well blended.

Cover and refrigerate until serving. Serve with Easy Wonton Chips for dipping. Or, serve with broiled fish, chicken or pork.

Makes 12 (2-tablespoon) servings

Nutrients per Serving:

Calories	4	(24% of calories from fat)			
Total Fat	<1 g	Dietary Fiber	<1 g	Thiamin	<1 mg
Saturated Fat	<1 g	Protein	<1 g	Riboflavin	<1 mg
Cholesterol	0 mg	Calcium	4 mg	Niacin	<1 mg
Sodium	29 mg	Iron	<1 mg	Vitamin A	17 RE
Carbohydrate	1 g	Folate	4 µg	Vitamin C	6 mg

Dietary Exchanges: Free food

15 The Luscious Pink One

Buttermilk is made from low fat or skim milk and is usually more easily digested than other types of milk.

4 fresh California peaches, peeled,
   halved, pitted and sliced
1 cup buttermilk
½ cup strawberries (or other red berries)
1 tablespoon lemon juice
   Strawberries for garnish

Add peaches, buttermilk, strawberries and lemon juice to food processor or blender. Process until smooth. Pour into 4 mugs. Freeze until slushy. Top each serving with strawberry, if desired. Serve immediately with long-handled spoons and straws.

Makes 4 servings

Nutrients per Serving:

Calories	68	(8% of calories from fat)			
Total Fat	1 g	Dietary Fiber	2 g	Thiamin	<1 mg
Saturated Fat	<1 g	Protein	3 g	Riboflavin	<1 mg
Cholesterol	2 mg	Calcium	78 mg	Niacin	1 mg
Sodium	64 mg	Iron	<1 mg	Vitamin A	52 RE
Carbohydrate	14 g	Folate	10 µg	Vitamin C	19 mg

Dietary Exchanges: 1 Fruit

Microwave Sweet Potato Chips

16 Microwave Sweet Potato Chips

Sweet potatoes are an excellent source of beta-carotene. One ½ cup of mashed sweet potato has more beta-carotene than a medium carrot.

2 cups thinly sliced sweet potatoes
1 tablespoon packed brown sugar
2 teaspoons margarine

Place sweet potatoes, in single layer, in microwavable dish. Sprinkle with water. Microwave at HIGH (100% power) 5 minutes. Stir in brown sugar and margarine. Microwave at HIGH (100% power) 2 to 3 minutes. Let stand a few minutes before serving.

Makes 4 servings

Nutrients per Serving:

Calories	98	(18% of calories from fat)			
Total Fat	2 g	Dietary Fiber	2 g	Thiamine	<1 mg
Saturated Fat	<1 g	Protein	1 g	Riboflavin	<1 mg
Cholesterol	0 mg	Calcium	22 mg	Niacin	<1 mg
Sodium	30 mg	Iron	<1 mg	Vitamin A	1,469 RE
Carbohydrate	19 g	Folate	15 µg	Vitamin C	16 mg

Dietary Exchanges: 1 Starch/Bread, ½ Fat

17 Fresh Fruit Cubes

This is a great dessert idea for kids because not only is it nutritious, but it tastes great too.

3 cups fresh California peaches, plums and nectarines, peeled, halved, pitted and chopped *or* Bartlett pears, peeled cored and chopped
1 tablespoon lemon juice

Add peaches, plums, nectarines and lemon juice to food processor or blender. Process until smooth. Pour into ice cube trays; freeze. Insert toothpicks and serve.

Makes 18 cubes

Nutrients per Serving:

Calories	12	(2% of calories from fat)			
Total Fat	<1 g	Dietary Fiber	<1 g	Thiamin	<1 mg
Saturated Fat	<1 g	Protein	<1 g	Riboflavin	<1 mg
Cholesterol	0 mg	Calcium	1 mg	Niacin	<1 mg
Sodium	<1 mg	Iron	<1 mg	Vitamin A	15 RE
Carbohydrate	3 g	Folate	1 µg	Vitamin C	2 mg

Dietary Exchanges: Free food

18 Lemon and Fennel Marinated Vegetables

Although most vegetables lose vitamins during cooking, carrots are an exception. Cooking breaks down cell walls in carrots, releasing far more beta-carotene (a precursor of vitamin A) than raw carrots.

1 cup water
2 medium carrots, diagonally sliced
        ½ inch thick
1 cup small whole fresh mushrooms
1 small red or green bell pepper, cut into
        ¾-inch pieces
3 tablespoons lemon juice
1 tablespoon sugar
1 tablespoon olive oil
1 clove garlic, minced
½ teaspoon fennel seeds, crushed
½ teaspoon dried basil leaves, crushed
¼ teaspoon black pepper

Bring water to a boil over high heat in small saucepan. Add carrots. Return to a boil. Reduce heat to medium-low. Cover and simmer about 5 minutes or until carrots are crisp-tender. Drain and cool.

Place carrots, mushrooms and bell pepper in large resealable plastic food storage bag. Combine lemon juice, sugar, oil, garlic, fennel, basil and black pepper in small bowl. Pour over vegetables. Close bag securely; turn to coat. Marinate in refrigerator 8 to 24 hours, turning occasionally.

Drain vegetables; discard marinade. Place vegetables in serving dish. Serve with toothpicks.

Makes 4 servings

Nutrients per Serving:

Calories	47	(24% of calories from fat)		
Total Fat	1 g	Dietary Fiber	2 g	Thiamin	<1 mg
Saturated Fat	<1 g	Protein	1 g	Riboflavin	<1 mg
Cholesterol	0 mg	Calcium	18 mg	Niacin	<1 mg
Sodium	15 mg	Iron	1 mg	Vitamin A	1,058 RE
Carbohydrate	9 g	Folate	19 µg	Vitamin C	44 mg

Dietary Exchanges: 2 Vegetable

Lemon and Fennel Marinated Vegetables

19 Plum Purple Frappé

Wheat germ is the embryo of the wheat plant. It is loaded with vitamin E, iron, riboflavin and protein.

3 fresh California plums, halved, pitted
        and coarsely chopped
½ cup plain low fat yogurt
2 tablespoons wheat germ
2 tablespoons honey
3 ice cubes, cracked

Add plums, yogurt, wheat germ, honey and ice cubes to food processor or blender. Process until smooth. Serve immediately.   Makes 2 servings

Nutrients per Serving:

Calories	207	(10% of calories from fat)		
Total Fat	2 g	Dietary Fiber	3 g	Thiamin	<1 mg
Saturated Fat	1 g	Protein	6 g	Riboflavin	<1 mg
Cholesterol	4 mg	Calcium	113 mg	Niacin	1 mg
Sodium	42 mg	Iron	1 mg	Vitamin A	58 RE
Carbohydrate	44 g	Folate	30 µg	Vitamin C	14 mg

Dietary Exchanges: ½ Milk, 2½ Fruit, ½ Fat

20 Iced Swiss Chocolate Peppermint

The classic combination of chocolate and mint turn this coffee drink into a candy-like treat.

2 cups strongly brewed Swiss Dutch
        Almond coffee
2 tablespoons low fat milk
½ teaspoon cocoa powder
1 drop peppermint extract
2 teaspoons sugar

Add coffee, milk, cocoa, peppermint extract and sugar to blender. Process until smooth. Pour over ice and serve immediately, or refrigerate, stir well and serve over ice.   Makes 2 servings

Nutrients per Serving:

Calories	28	(10% of calories from fat)		
Total Fat	<1 g	Dietary Fiber	<1 g	Thiamin	<1 mg
Saturated Fat	<1 g	Protein	1 g	Riboflavin	<1 mg
Cholesterol	1 mg	Calcium	24 mg	Niacin	1 mg
Sodium	13 mg	Iron	<1 mg	Vitamin A	9 RE
Carbohydrate	6 g	Folate	1 µg	Vitamin C	<1 mg

Dietary Exchanges: ½ Starch/Bread

21 Honeydew Melon Shake

The honeydew melon in this drink adds fiber and potassium and also makes it sweet and refreshing.

½ cup vanilla low fat yogurt
2 teaspoons sugar
1 cup honeydew melon chunks, chilled

Add yogurt, sugar and melon to food processor or blender. Process until smooth and frothy. Serve immediately.   Makes 2 servings

Variation: For strawberry-melon flavor blend in 1 cup frozen strawberries and add another teaspoon sugar.

Nutrients per Serving:

Calories	105	(9% of calories from fat)			
Total Fat	1 g	Dietary Fiber	1 g	Thiamin	<1 mg
Saturated Fat	<1 g	Protein	3 g	Riboflavin	<1 mg
Cholesterol	3 mg	Calcium	88 mg	Niacin	1 mg
Sodium	49 mg	Iron	<1 mg	Vitamin A	3 RE
Carbohydrate	21 g	Folate	6 µg	Vitamin C	21 mg

Dietary Exchanges: ½ Milk, 1 Fruit

22 Red Grape Cooler

Red grapes are high in antioxidants, which are molecular compounds that attack cell-destroying free radicals.

2 cups club soda
1 cup red grapes
1 tablespoon sugar

Add club soda, grapes and sugar to food processor or blender. Process until smooth. Strain. Serve over ice.   Makes 2 servings

Variation: For a bubbly drink, blend 1 cup club soda with grapes and sugar. Strain. Add remaining 1 cup club soda to strained liquid.

Nutrients per Serving:

Calories	52	(2% of calories from fat)			
Total Fat	<1 g	Dietary Fiber	1 g	Thiamin	<1 mg
Saturated Fat	<1 g	Protein	<1 g	Riboflavin	<1 mg
Cholesterol	0 mg	Calcium	15 mg	Niacin	<1 mg
Sodium	49 mg	Iron	<1 mg	Vitamin A	5 RE
Carbohydrate	14 g	Folate	2 µg	Vitamin C	2 mg

Dietary Exchanges: 1 Fruit

23 Party Punch

Zesty and sweet, this punch is just the thing to quench any thirst.

1 cup Time-Saver Sugar Syrup (page 167)
1 cup orange juice
1 cup pineapple juice
4 cups seltzer water

Mix syrup, orange juice, pineapple juice and seltzer in large bowl or pitcher. Serve over ice.
                    Makes 8 servings

Nutrients per Serving:

Calories	208	(0% of calories from fat)			
Total Fat	<1 g	Dietary Fiber	<1 g	Thiamin	<1 mg
Saturated Fat	<1 g	Protein	<1 g	Riboflavin	<1 mg
Cholesterol	0 mg	Calcium	11 mg	Niacin	<1 mg
Sodium	7 mg	Iron	<1 mg	Vitamin A	6 RE
Carbohydrate	54 g	Folate	24 µg	Vitamin C	19 mg

Dietary Exchanges: 3½ Fruit

24 Iced Tea

Sweetened freshly brewed iced tea is thirst-quenching refreshment on long summer days.

2½ tablespoons Time-Saver Sugar Syrup (page 167)
1 cup double-strength hot tea

Add syrup to tea; stir well. Pour over crushed ice.
                    Makes 2 servings

Nutrients per Serving:

Calories	87	(0% of calories from fat)			
Total Fat	0 g	Dietary Fiber	0 g	Thiamin	0 mg
Saturated Fat	0 g	Protein	0 g	Riboflavin	<1 mg
Cholesterol	0 mg	Calcium	<1 mg	Niacin	0 mg
Sodium	8 mg	Iron	<1 mg	Vitamin A	0 RE
Carbohydrate	23 g	Folate	12 µg	Vitamin C	0 mg

Dietary Exchanges: 1½ Fruit

Peppy Snack Mix

25 **P**eppy Snack Mix

*If you are closely watching the sodium in your diet,
make this recipe with sodium free rice cakes and low
sodium pretzels.*

**3 plain rice cakes, broken into bite-size
  pieces**
**1½ cups bite-size frosted shredded wheat
  biscuit cereal**
¾ cup pretzel sticks, halved
**3 tablespoons reduced calorie margarine,
  melted**
**2 teaspoons low sodium Worcestershire
  sauce**
¾ teaspoon chili powder
⅛ to ¼ teaspoon ground red pepper

Preheat oven to 300°F. Combine rice cakes, wheat
biscuits and pretzels in 13×9-inch baking pan.
Combine margarine, Worcestershire sauce, chili
powder and pepper in small bowl. Drizzle over
cereal mixture; toss to combine. Bake, uncovered,
20 minutes, stirring after 10 minutes.

Makes 6 servings (4 cups)

Nutrients per Serving:					
Calories	118	(25% of calories from fat)			
Total Fat	3 g	Dietary Fiber	1 g	Thiamin	<1 mg
Saturated Fat	1 g	Protein	2 g	Riboflavin	<1 mg
Cholesterol	0 mg	Calcium	12 mg	Niacin	3 mg
Sodium	156 mg	Iron	1 mg	Vitamin A	266 RE
Carbohydrate	20 g	Folate	51 μg	Vitamin C	11 mg

Dietary Exchanges: 1½ Starch/Bread, ½ Fat

26 Plum Slush

Plums are full of potassium, a mineral that aids in carbohydrate and protein metabolism.

6 fresh California plums, halved, pitted and coarsely chopped
1 can (6 ounces) frozen cranberry juice concentrate
20 ice cubes, cracked

Add plums, juice concentrate and ice cubes to food processor or blender. Process until smooth. Serve immediately.   Makes 8 servings

Nutrients per Serving:

Calories	80	(5% of calories from fat)			
Total Fat	<1 g	Dietary Fiber	1 g	Thiamin	<1 mg
Saturated Fat	<1 g	Protein	1 g	Riboflavin	<1 mg
Cholesterol	0 mg	Calcium	5 mg	Niacin	<1 mg
Sodium	1 mg	Iron	<1 mg	Vitamin A	24 RE
Carbohydrate	20 g	Folate	2 μg	Vitamin C	24 mg

Dietary Exchanges: 1½ Fruit

27 Pear Grapefruit Drink

Use pink grapefruit juice in this recipe for extra vitamin C and a shot of vitamin A.

1 fresh California Bartlett pear, peeled, cored and diced
1 can (6 ounces) unsweetened grapefruit juice
1 cup ice cubes, cracked

Add pears, juice and ice to food processor or blender. Process until smooth. Serve immediately.
Makes 2 servings

Nutrients per Serving:

Calories	81	(4% of calories from fat)			
Total Fat	<1 g	Dietary Fiber	2 g	Thiamin	<1 mg
Saturated Fat	<1 g	Protein	1 g	Riboflavin	<1 mg
Cholesterol	0 mg	Calcium	15 mg	Niacin	<1 mg
Sodium	1 mg	Iron	<1 mg	Vitamin A	2 RE
Carbohydrate	20 g	Folate	15 μg	Vitamin C	28 mg

Dietary Exchanges: 1½ Fruit

28 Shantung Twin Mushroom Soup

Two kinds of mushrooms—dried black and button—make up the twins in this delightful soup. Or, simply use all button mushrooms if you don't mind sacrificing some of the flavor.

1 package (1 ounce) dried black Chinese mushrooms
2 teaspoons vegetable oil
1 large yellow onion, coarsely chopped
2 cloves garlic, minced
2 cups sliced fresh mushrooms
2 cans (about 14 ounces each) chicken broth
2 ounces cooked ham, cut into thin strips (½ cup)
½ cup thinly sliced green onions
1 tablespoon low sodium soy sauce
1 tablespoon dry sherry
1 tablespoon cornstarch

Place dried mushrooms in small bowl; cover with warm water. Soak 20 minutes to soften. Drain; squeeze out excess water. Discard stems; slice caps.

Heat large saucepan over medium heat. Add oil; heat until hot. Add chopped yellow onion and garlic; cook 1 minute. Add Chinese mushrooms and fresh mushrooms; cook 4 minutes, stirring occasionally.

Add broth; bring to a boil over high heat. Reduce heat to medium-low. Cover; simmer 15 minutes.

Stir in ham and green onions; heat through. Blend soy sauce and sherry into cornstarch until smooth. Stir into soup. Cook 2 minutes or until soup thickens, stirring occasionally. Ladle into soup bowls.   Makes 6 servings (about 5½ cups)

Nutrients per Serving:

Calories	92	(30% of calories from fat)			
Total Fat	3 g	Dietary Fiber	1 g	Thiamin	<1 mg
Saturated Fat	1 g	Protein	7 g	Riboflavin	<1 mg
Cholesterol	6 mg	Calcium	19 mg	Niacin	4 mg
Sodium	626 mg	Iron	1 mg	Vitamin A	33 RE
Carbohydrate	9 g	Folate	22 μg	Vitamin C	8 mg

Dietary Exchanges: ½ Meat, 2 Vegetable, ½ Fat

29 Pinwheel Appetizers

These delicious appetizers can be made way ahead; the longer they sit in the refrigerator, the more the flavors will blend.

3 cups cooked wild rice
1 package (8 ounces) nonfat pasteurized process cream cheese product
⅓ cup grated Parmesan cheese
1 teaspoon dried parsley flakes
½ teaspoon garlic powder
½ teaspoon Dijon-style mustard
2 to 3 drops hot pepper sauce (optional)
3 (12-inch) soft flour tortillas
2½ ounces thinly sliced corned beef
9 fresh spinach leaves

Combine wild rice, cream cheese, Parmesan cheese, parsley, garlic powder, mustard and pepper sauce. Spread evenly over tortillas, leaving ½-inch border on one side of each tortilla. Place single layer corned beef over rice and cheese mixture. Top with layer of spinach. Roll each tortilla tightly toward ½-inch border. Moisten border of tortilla with water; press to seal roll. Wrap tightly in plastic wrap. Refrigerate several hours or overnight. Cut into 1-inch slices.   Makes 36 appetizers

Nutrients per Serving:

Calories	37	(21% of calories from fat)			
Total Fat	1 g	Dietary Fiber	<1 g	Thiamin	<1 mg
Saturated Fat	<1 g	Protein	2 g	Riboflavin	<1 mg
Cholesterol	4 mg	Calcium	20 mg	Niacin	<1 mg
Sodium	91 mg	Iron	<1 mg	Vitamin A	19 RE
Carbohydrate	5 g	Folate	9 µg	Vitamin C	1 mg

Dietary Exchanges: ½ Starch/Bread

30 Peanutty Nog

A nutty twist to the traditional eggnog, try it during the holidays.

1 cup skim milk
2 teaspoons creamy peanut butter
2 teaspoons granulated sugar
Pinch pumpkin pie spice

Add all ingredients to food processor or blender. Process until smooth and frothy. Serve immediately.   Makes 2 servings

Nutrients per Serving:

Calories	89	(28% of calories from fat)			
Total Fat	3 g	Dietary Fiber	<1 g	Thiamin	<1 mg
Saturated Fat	1 g	Protein	5 g	Riboflavin	<1 mg
Cholesterol	2 mg	Calcium	153 mg	Niacin	1 mg
Sodium	89 mg	Iron	<1 mg	Vitamin A	75 RE
Carbohydrate	11 g	Folate	11 µg	Vitamin C	1 mg

Dietary Exchanges: ½ Meat, ½ Milk, ½ Fat

31 Iced French Roast

Imagine yourself at a European cafe when you sip this aromatic mocha beverage.

2 cups strongly brewed French Roast coffee
2 tablespoons 2% low fat milk
2 teaspoons sugar
½ teaspoon cocoa powder
Dash ground cinnamon

Add coffee, milk, sugar, cocoa and cinnamon to blender. Process until smooth. Pour over ice and serve immediately, or refrigerate, stir well and serve over ice.   Makes 2 servings

Nutrients per Serving:

Calories	28	(10% of calories from fat)			
Total Fat	<1 g	Dietary Fiber	<1 g	Thiamin	<1 mg
Saturated Fat	<1 g	Protein	1 g	Riboflavin	<1 mg
Cholesterol	1 mg	Calcium	24 mg	Niacin	1 mg
Sodium	13 mg	Iron	<1 mg	Vitamin A	9 RE
Carbohydrate	6 g	Folate	1 µg	Vitamin C	<1 mg

Dietary Exchanges: ½ Starch/Bread

32 Raspberry Watermelon Slush

Watermelon is a good source of vitamin A and is very low in calories.

1 cup frozen raspberries
1 cup cubed seeded watermelon
1 cup lemon-lime seltzer
1 tablespoon sugar

Add raspberries, watermelon, seltzer and sugar to food processor or blender. Process until smooth. Serve immediately.   Makes 2 servings

Nutrients per Serving:

Calories	120	(5% of calories from fat)				
Total Fat	1 g	Dietary Fiber	3 g	Thiamin	<1 mg	
Saturated Fat	<1 g	Protein	1 g	Riboflavin	<1 mg	
Cholesterol	0 mg	Calcium	21 mg	Niacin	1 mg	
Sodium	7 mg	Iron	<1 mg	Vitamin A	37 RE	
Carbohydrate	30 g	Folate	18 μg	Vitamin C	23 mg	

Dietary Exchanges: 2 Fruit

33 Peach-Lemon Frost

For easy seed removal, try to purchase Freestone peaches for this recipe.

3 fresh California peaches, peeled, halved, pitted and quartered
1 cup 2% low fat milk
2 teaspoons grated lemon peel
½ cup fresh lemon juice
3 ice cubes, cracked
½ pint vanilla ice milk

Add peaches to food processor or blender. Process until smooth to measure 2 cups. Add low fat milk, lemon peel, lemon juice and ice cubes. Process until smooth. Continue processing at low speed; slowly add ice milk until well blended. Pour into glasses. Serve immediately.   Makes about 5 cups

Nutrients per Serving:

Calories	90	(20% of calories from fat)				
Total Fat	2 g	Dietary Fiber	1 g	Thiamin	<1 mg	
Saturated Fat	1 g	Protein	3 g	Riboflavin	<1 mg	
Cholesterol	7 mg	Calcium	100 mg	Niacin	1 mg	
Sodium	46 mg	Iron	<1 mg	Vitamin A	69 RE	
Carbohydrate	16 g	Folate	8 μg	Vitamin C	16 mg	

Dietary Exchanges: ½ Starch/Bread, ½ Fruit, ½ Fat

Top to bottom: Peach-Lemon Frost and Raspberry Watermelon Slush

34 Cantaloupe Strawberry Shake

This drink will add fiber and vitamin C to your diet without adding much fat.

1 cup hulled strawberries
1 cup cubed cantaloupe
⅔ cup skim milk
2 teaspoons sugar

Add ingredients to food processor or blender. Process until smooth and frothy. Serve immediately.   Makes 2 servings

Nutrients per Serving:

Calories	87	(6% of calories from fat)				
Total Fat	1 g	Dietary Fiber	3 g	Thiamin	<1 mg	
Saturated Fat	<1 g	Protein	3 g	Riboflavin	<1 mg	
Cholesterol	1 mg	Calcium	95 mg	Niacin	1 mg	
Sodium	39 mg	Iron	<1 mg	Vitamin A	298 RE	
Carbohydrate	19 g	Folate	30 μg	Vitamin C	77 mg	

Dietary Exchanges: 1½ Fruit

35 Nectarine Cantaloupe Smoothie

Lots of beta-carotene and vitamin A make this delicious drink good for you too.

1 fresh California nectarine, halved, pitted and cubed
1 cup cubed cantaloupe
½ cup plain low fat yogurt
1 teaspoon honey
3 ice cubes, cracked

Add nectarine and cantaloupe to food processor or blender. Process until smooth. Stir in yogurt, honey and ice just until blended. Serve immediately.

Makes 2 servings

Nutrients per Serving:

Calories	108	(11% of calories from fat)				
Total Fat	1 g	Dietary Fiber	2 g	Thiamin	<1 mg	
Saturated Fat	1 g	Protein	4 g	Riboflavin	<1 mg	
Cholesterol	4 mg	Calcium	116 mg	Niacin	1 mg	
Sodium	47 mg	Iron	<1 mg	Vitamin A	319 RE	
Carbohydrate	22 g	Folate	22 μg	Vitamin C	38 mg	

Dietary Exchanges: ½ Milk, 1 Fruit

36 Pear Berry Crush

This recipe is an easy way to get your daily supply of vitamin C and fiber.

1 package (10 ounces) unsweetened frozen raspberries or strawberries
1 fresh California Bartlett pear, peeled, cored and coarsely chopped
12 ice cubes, cracked

Combine frozen berries, pear and ice in blender. Process until smooth and frothy. Serve immediately.

Makes 2 servings

Nutrients per Serving:

Calories	118	(8% of calories from fat)			
Total Fat	1 g	Dietary Fiber	8 g	Thiamin	<1 mg
Saturated Fat	<1 g	Protein	2 g	Riboflavin	<1 mg
Cholesterol	0 mg	Calcium	40 mg	Niacin	1 mg
Sodium	0 mg	Iron	1 mg	Vitamin A	20 RE
Carbohydrate	29 g	Folate	43 µg	Vitamin C	39 mg

Dietary Exchanges: 2 Fruit

37 Nectarine Mocktail

Nectarines and strawberries add lots of vitamin C and fiber to this delicious drink.

3 fresh California nectarines, halved, pitted and diced
1 container (10 ounces) unsweetened frozen strawberries, partially thawed
1 bottle (28 ounces) club soda or sugar-free ginger ale
8 mint sprigs (optional)

Add nectarines, strawberries and 1 cup club soda to blender. Process until smooth. Pour into chilled glasses about ⅔ full. Top with remaining club soda. Garnish with mint, if desired.   Makes 8 servings

Nutrients per Serving:

Calories	37	(6% of calories from fat)			
Total Fat	<1 g	Dietary Fiber	2 g	Thiamin	<1 mg
Saturated Fat	<1 g	Protein	1 g	Riboflavin	<1 mg
Cholesterol	0 mg	Calcium	12 mg	Niacin	1 mg
Sodium	22 mg	Iron	<1 mg	Vitamin A	39 RE
Carbohydrate	9 g	Folate	8 µg	Vitamin C	17 mg

Dietary Exchanges: ½ Fruit

38 Spiced Pear-Cranberry Soup

Ginger has been used for centuries in Asia. It seems to have many curative properties including an anti-nausea remedy.

2 fresh California Bartlett pears, peeled, cored and chopped
¼ teaspoon ground cinnamon
⅛ teaspoon ground cloves
2 thin slices fresh ginger
1½ cups low calorie cranberry juice cocktail
Plain low fat yogurt (optional)

Add pears, cinnamon, cloves and ginger to food processor or blender; process until smooth. With machine running, slowly add cranberry juice. Ladle into serving bowls. Garnish each serving with dollop of yogurt, if desired. Soup may be served warm or cold.   Makes 4 servings

Nutrients per Serving:

Calories	70	(4% of calories from fat)			
Total Fat	<1 g	Dietary Fiber	2 g	Thiamin	<1 mg
Saturated Fat	<1 g	Protein	<1 g	Riboflavin	<1 mg
Cholesterol	0 mg	Calcium	11 mg	Niacin	<1 mg
Sodium	8 mg	Iron	<1 mg	Vitamin A	2 RE
Carbohydrate	17 g	Folate	6 µg	Vitamin C	34 mg

Dietary Exchanges: 1 Fruit

39 Lemonade

Nothing tastes as good as old-fashioned homemade lemonade on a hot summer day.

1 cup Time-Saver Sugar Syrup (recipe follows)
1⅓ cups freshly squeezed lemon juice
4 cups water

Prepare Time-Saver Sugar Syrup; set aside. Combine Time-Saver Sugar Syrup, lemon juice and water. Mix thoroughly; serve over ice.

Makes 1½ quarts

Lemonade

Time-Saver Sugar Syrup

1 cup water
1½ cups sugar
1 teaspoon grated lemon peel

Combine water, sugar and lemon peel in medium
saucepan. Over medium heat, dissolve sugar. Cool
to room temperature and strain. Refrigerate.

Makes about 2 cups

Nutrients per Serving:

Calories	117	(0% of calories from fat)			
Total Fat	0 g	Dietary Fiber	<1 g	Thiamin	<1 mg
Saturated Fat	0 g	Protein	<1 g	Riboflavin	<1 mg
Cholesterol	0 mg	Calcium	10 mg	Niacin	<1 mg
Sodium	9 mg	Iron	<1 mg	Vitamin A	1 RE
Carbohydrate	32 g	Folate	8 µg	Vitamin C	28 mg

Dietary Exchanges: 2 Fruit

40 Spicy Orange Chicken Kabob Appetizers

Chicken has a lot of copper, which the body uses to build red blood cells. Shellfish, whole grains and nuts are also good sources of copper.

2 boneless, skinless chicken breast halves
1 small red or green bell pepper
24 small whole fresh mushrooms
½ cup orange juice
2 tablespoons low sodium soy sauce
1 tablespoon vegetable oil
1½ teaspoons onion powder
½ teaspoon Chinese five-spice powder

Cut chicken and bell pepper each into 24 (¾-inch) square pieces. Place chicken, bell pepper and mushrooms in large resealable plastic food storage bag. Combine orange juice, soy sauce, oil, onion powder and five-spice powder in small bowl. Pour over chicken mixture. Close bag securely; turn to coat. Marinate in refrigerator 4 to 24 hours, turning frequently.

Preheat broiler. Coat broiler pan with nonstick cooking spray. Drain chicken and vegetables; reserve marinade. Place marinade in small saucepan and bring to a full boil. Thread 1 piece of chicken, bell pepper and 1 mushroom on wooden toothpicks. Place on broiler pan. Brush with marinade. Broil 4 inches from heat 5 to 6 minutes or until chicken is no longer pink in center, turning and brushing once with marinade; discard remaining marinade. Serve immediately.

Makes 24 appetizers (3 appetizers per serving)

Nutrients per Serving:

Calories	15	(26% of calories from fat)			
Total Fat	<1 g	Dietary Fiber	<1 g	Thiamin	<1 mg
Saturated Fat	<1 g	Protein	2 g	Riboflavin	<1 mg
Cholesterol	5 mg	Calcium	2 mg	Niacin	1 mg
Sodium	19 mg	Iron	<1 mg	Vitamin A	3 RE
Carbohydrate	1 g	Folate	3 µg	Vitamin C	4 mg

Dietary Exchanges: ½ Meat

41 O.J. Yogurt Shake

Try something a little different than your usual orange juice tomorrow morning. Not only do you get vitamin C but protein as well.

1 cup milk
1 carton (8 ounces) plain or vanilla low fat yogurt
1 can (6 ounces) frozen orange juice concentrate
2 cups ice cubes, cracked

Add milk, yogurt and orange juice concentrate into food processor or blender. Process until smooth and frothy. Add ice; process until smooth and frothy.

Makes 5 (1-cup) servings

Nutrients per Serving:

Calories	107	(14% of calories from fat)			
Total Fat	2 g	Dietary Fiber	<1 g	Thiamin	<1 mg
Saturated Fat	1 g	Protein	5 g	Riboflavin	<1 mg
Cholesterol	6 mg	Calcium	153 mg	Niacin	<1 mg
Sodium	57 mg	Iron	<1 mg	Vitamin A	49 RE
Carbohydrate	18 g	Folate	60 µg	Vitamin C	53 mg

Dietary Exchanges: ½ Milk, 1 Fruit

42 Ahaina Sunset

Transport yourself to Hawaii with this frozen fruity fantasy.

2 fresh California peaches, peeled, pitted and halved
1 cup 2% low fat milk
¼ cup pineapple juice
3 ice cubes, cracked
1 teaspoon rum extract

Add peaches, milk and pineapple juice to food processor or blender. Process until smooth. Add ice and rum extract; process until smooth and frothy. Serve immediately.
Makes 3½ cups

Nutrients per Serving:

Calories	35	(18% of calories from fat)			
Total Fat	1 g	Dietary Fiber	<1 g	Thiamin	<1 mg
Saturated Fat	<1 g	Protein	1 g	Riboflavin	<1 mg
Cholesterol	3 mg	Calcium	45 mg	Niacin	<1 mg
Sodium	18 mg	Iron	<1 mg	Vitamin A	35 RE
Carbohydrate	6 g	Folate	5 µg	Vitamin C	3 mg

Dietary Exchanges: ½ Fruit

Spicy Orange Chicken Kabob Appetizers

SALADS

43 Turkey, Mandarin and Poppy Seed Salad

Both the red leaf lettuce and spinach in this recipe are very high in vitamin A.

5 cups torn stemmed red leaf lettuce
2 cups torn stemmed washed spinach
½ pound honey roasted turkey, cut into
    ½-inch julienne strips
1 can (10½ ounces) mandarin oranges,
    drained
¼ cup orange juice
1½ tablespoons red wine vinegar
1½ teaspoons poppy seeds
1½ teaspoons olive oil
1 teaspoon Dijon-style mustard
⅛ teaspoon ground pepper

In large bowl, combine lettuce, spinach, turkey and oranges. In small bowl, combine orange juice, vinegar, poppy seeds, oil, mustard and pepper. Pour dressing over turkey mixture. Serve immediately.

Makes 4 servings

Nutrients per Serving:

Calories	143	(20% of calories from fat)			
Total Fat	3 g	Dietary Fiber	2 g	Thiamine	<1 mg
Saturated Fat	2 g	Protein	15 g	Riboflavin	<1 mg
Cholesterol	43 mg	Calcium	119 mg	Niacin	4 mg
Sodium	727 mg	Iron	3 mg	Vitamin A	347 RE
Carbohydrate	14 g	Folate	115 µg	Vitamin C	49 mg

Dietary Exchanges: 1½ Meat, ½ Fruit, 1 Vegetable

44 Wild Rice Seafood Salad

Most imitation crabmeat is made from ground pollack which is flavored and then shaped. It is a good source of protein and can have up to 75% less cholesterol than real shellfish.

⅓ cup low fat mayonnaise
⅓ cup nonfat sour cream
¼ cup low sodium chili sauce
1 tablespoon lemon juice
1 teaspoon Dijon-style mustard
3 cups cooked wild rice
½ cup thinly sliced green onions
1 large tomato, peeled, seeded and diced
1 cup thinly sliced celery
½ pound imitation crabmeat
    Salt and pepper (optional)
    Lettuce cups (optional)
    Chopped fresh parsley (optional)

In medium bowl blend mayonnaise, sour cream, chili sauce, lemon juice and mustard to make dressing. Refrigerate. Combine rice, onions, tomato, celery and seafood. Season to taste.

Place salad in individual lettuce cups and garnish with parsley, if desired. Serve with dressing.

Makes 6 servings

Nutrients per Serving:

Calories	186	(21% of calories from fat)			
Total Fat	4 g	Dietary Fiber	2 g	Thiamine	<1 mg
Saturated Fat	1 g	Protein	9 g	Riboflavin	<1 mg
Cholesterol	12 mg	Calcium	22 mg	Niacin	1 mg
Sodium	372 mg	Iron	1 mg	Vitamin A	57 RE
Carbohydrate	28 g	Folate	32 µg	Vitamin C	9 mg

Dietary Exchanges: 1½ Starch/Bread, 1 Meat, ½ Fat

Turkey, Mandarin and Poppy Seed Salad

45 Sun Country Chicken Salad

Cantaloupes are a good source of fiber, potassium and beta-carotene.

1 large cantaloupe
2 cups cubed cooked chicken
1 cup cucumber chunks
1 cup green grapes
½ cup chopped green onions
2 tablespoons chopped fresh parsley
1 cup plain nonfat yogurt
3 tablespoons prepared chutney
¼ teaspoon grated lemon peel
1 tablespoon lemon juice
¼ cup whole blanched California Almonds,* toasted
1 large bunch watercress

Cut cantaloupe into 12 wedges, removing seeds and peel. Combine chicken, cucumber, grapes, onions and parsley. Blend together yogurt, chutney, lemon peel and lemon juice. Toss lightly with chicken mixture. Fold in almonds. Arrange watercress on 4 salad plates. Stand 3 wedges of cantaloupe on each plate. Spoon chicken salad mixture over cantaloupe.

Makes 4 servings

*To toast, spread almonds in single layer on baking sheet. Toast at 350°F, 5 to 8 minutes, stirring occasionally, until lightly browned. Cool.

Nutrients per Serving:

Calories	356	(23% of calories from fat)			
Total Fat	9 g	Dietary Fiber	6 g	Thiamine	<1 mg
Saturated Fat	2 g	Protein	25 g	Riboflavin	<1 mg
Cholesterol	49 mg	Calcium	206 mg	Niacin	10 mg
Sodium	154 mg	Iron	2 mg	Vitamin A	1,283 RE
Carbohydrate	47 g	Folate	25 μg	Vitamin C	132 mg

Dietary Exchanges: 3 Meat, 3 Fruit

46 Chilean Grapes and Greens

The darker green the lettuce leaves, the more nutrition they contain. They are excellent sources of vitamin C and beta-carotene.

1 cup seedless or halved, seeded Chilean grapes (red, green or combination)
2 tablespoons water
1 tablespoon raspberry or white wine vinegar
1 tablespoon lemon juice
1 shallot, chopped
2 teaspoons prepared mustard
2 teaspoons olive oil or vegetable oil
¼ teaspoon dried tarragon leaves, crushed
Pepper to taste
1 quart lightly packed torn salad greens (butter, curly, romaine, red leaf lettuces, escarole, curly endive, watercress sprigs)
2 teaspoons toasted walnut pieces
2 tablespoons Parmesan cheese shavings
4 slices French bread

Rinse grapes, remove stems and set aside. In small bowl, whisk together water, vinegar, lemon juice, shallot, mustard, oil, tarragon and pepper. In salad bowl combine greens, grapes and walnuts. Sprinkle cheese on bread slices and broil until toasted and cheese melts. Toss salad with dressing and serve with Parmesan toasts.

Makes 4 servings

Nutrients per Serving:

Calories	182	(28% of calories from fat)			
Total Fat	6 g	Dietary Fiber	2 g	Thiamine	<1 mg
Saturated Fat	1 g	Protein	6 g	Riboflavin	<1 mg
Cholesterol	2 mg	Calcium	108 mg	Niacin	2 mg
Sodium	291 mg	Iron	2 mg	Vitamin A	124 RE
Carbohydrate	27 g	Folate	71 μg	Vitamin C	14 mg

Dietary Exchanges: 1 Starch/Bread, 1 Vegetable, ½ Fruit, 1 Fat

Sun Country Chicken Salad

47 Confetti Appleslaw

There are over 7,000 varieties of apples grown in the world; try a new one for this recipe.

2 tablespoons frozen orange or apple juice concentrate, thawed
1 unpeeled red apple, cored and diced
4 cups shredded cabbage
2 small red onions, finely shredded
1 red or green bell pepper, thinly sliced
3 tablespoons raisins
½ cup plain low fat yogurt
1 tablespoon reduced calorie mayonnaise
½ teaspoon dry mustard
Paprika to taste
Freshly ground black pepper to taste

In large bowl, combine juice concentrate and diced apple. Add cabbage, onions, bell pepper and raisins. In small bowl, combine yogurt, mayonnaise, mustard, paprika and black pepper. Add to vegetable mixture. Cover tightly and refrigerate until ready to serve.   Makes 7 servings

Nutrients per Serving:

Calories	70	(13% of calories from fat)			
Total Fat	1 g	Dietary Fiber	2 g	Thiamine	<1 mg
Saturated Fat	<1 g	Protein	2 g	Riboflavin	<1 mg
Cholesterol	2 mg	Calcium	64 mg	Niacin	<1 mg
Sodium	24 mg	Iron	1 mg	Vitamin A	19 RE
Carbohydrate	14 g	Folate	45 μg	Vitamin C	42 mg

Dietary Exchanges: 1½ Vegetable, ½ Fruit

48 Turkey Ham and Pineapple Boats

When choosing a pineapple, select one with a strong pleasant pineapple fragrance. The scent suggests the pineapple is ripe which is important because pineapples don't ripen after they're picked.

1 package (3 ounces) chicken-flavored instant Oriental noodle soup, prepared according to package directions
1⅓ cups turkey ham, cut into 2 × ¼-inch strips
⅓ cup thinly sliced green onions
⅓ cup prepared mango chutney, chopped
¼ cup water chestnuts, sliced
¼ teaspoon ground red pepper
2 small pineapples
2 tablespoons almonds, toasted

Combine soup, turkey ham, onions, chutney, water chestnuts and ground red pepper in medium bowl. Cover and refrigerate overnight.

Just before serving, cut pineapples in half lengthwise. With grapefruit knife remove pineapple from skin; reserve skins for serving. Cut pineapple meat into ½-inch cubes. Add 3 cups pineapple cubes to turkey mixture.

To serve, spoon turkey mixture into reserved pineapple shells; top with almonds.

Makes 4 servings

Nutrients per Serving:

Calories	280	(25% of calories from fat)			
Total Fat	8 g	Dietary Fiber	2 g	Thiamine	<1 mg
Saturated Fat	1 g	Protein	11 g	Riboflavin	<1 mg
Cholesterol	33 mg	Calcium	37 mg	Niacin	3 mg
Sodium	903 mg	Iron	3 mg	Vitamin A	46 RE
Carbohydrate	44 g	Folate	19 μg	Vitamin C	21 mg

Dietary Exchanges: 1 Starch/Bread, 1 Meat, 2 Fruit, ½ Fat

49 Artichoke Wild Rice Salad

Artichokes are a member of the thistle family. They are high in protein and are delicious to eat.

1 jar (6 ounces) marinated artichoke hearts
2 cups cooked wild rice
1 cup frozen peas, thawed
1 can (8 ounces) sliced water chestnuts, drained
4 ounces shredded mozzarella cheese (optional)
1 jar (2 ounces) diced pimiento, drained
2 tablespoons canola oil
2 tablespoons reserved liquid from artichokes
1 tablespoon balsamic vinegar
½ teaspoon dried tarragon leaves, crushed
½ teaspoon Dijon-style mustard
2 to 3 drops hot pepper sauce (or to taste)

Drain artichokes, reserving liquid. In large bowl, combine artichokes, rice, peas, water chestnuts, cheese and pimiento. In small bowl, combine oil, reserved liquid from artichokes, vinegar, tarragon, mustard and hot pepper sauce; pour over salad and toss. Refrigerate 4 hours or overnight to allow flavors to blend. Makes 6 to 8 servings

Nutrients per Serving:

Calories	129	(22% of calories from fat)			
Total Fat	4 g	Dietary Fiber	3 g	Thiamine	<1 mg
Saturated Fat	<1 g	Protein	4 g	Riboflavin	<1 mg
Cholesterol	0 mg	Calcium	21 mg	Niacin	1 mg
Sodium	48 mg	Iron	1 mg	Vitamin A	37 RE
Carbohydrate	22 g	Folate	37 µg	Vitamin C	11 mg

Dietary Exchanges: 1 Starch/Bread, 1 Vegetable, ½ Fat

50 Indonesian Chicken and Pear Salad

Pears are a good source of boron—a trace mineral needed for strong bones.

Curry Dressing (recipe follows)
1½ cups cubed cold cooked chicken
3 fresh California Bartlett pears, halved, cored, divided
½ cup macadamia nuts or peanuts, coarsely chopped (optional)
½ cup sliced cucumber
3 tablespoons crystallized ginger, slivered (optional)
2 tablespoons thinly sliced green onion
Lemon juice
Iceberg lettuce cups
Toasted shredded coconut (optional)

Prepare Curry Dressing. Place chicken in large bowl. Cube 1 pear; add to chicken with nuts, cucumber, ginger and onion. Add Curry Dressing; mix gently. Dip remaining 4 pear halves into lemon juice and arrange in lettuce cups on salad plates. Spoon salad onto pear halves. Sprinkle with coconut, if desired. Makes 4 servings

Curry Dressing: Combine ½ cup plain low fat yogurt, ½ teaspoon curry powder and ¼ teaspoon *each* dry mustard, ground allspice and garlic powder; mix well. Make about 20 minutes before using to allow flavors to blend. Makes about ⅔ cup.

Nutrients per Serving:

Calories	180	(21% of calories from fat)			
Total Fat	4 g	Dietary Fiber	4 g	Thiamine	<1 mg
Saturated Fat	1 g	Protein	15 g	Riboflavin	<1 mg
Cholesterol	38 mg	Calcium	78 mg	Niacin	6 mg
Sodium	50 mg	Iron	1 mg	Vitamin A	33 RE
Carbohydrate	22 g	Folate	16 µg	Vitamin C	7 mg

Dietary Exchanges: 1½ Starch/Bread, 1½ Meat

Artichoke Wild Rice Salad

51 Fruited Lamb Salad

To retain the vitamin C in strawberries, don't remove the stems and caps until just before serving.

3 cups cooked American lamb, cubed or cut into slices
3 cups cooked brown and wild rice, chilled
1½ cups sliced strawberries
1½ cups orange slices, cubed
¾ cup green grapes
½ cup sliced bananas
¼ cup walnuts
2 tablespoons honey
2 tablespoons lemon juice
1 tablespoon orange juice
12 large Romaine lettuce leaves

Combine lamb, rice, fruit and nuts large bowl. Combine honey, lemon juice and orange juice in small bowl; toss with lamb mixture. Refrigerate. Serve on lettuce leaves.   Makes 12 servings

Nutrients per Serving:

Calories	167	(27% of calories from fat)			
Total Fat	5 g	Dietary Fiber	2 g	Thiamine	<1 mg
Saturated Fat	1 g	Protein	13 g	Riboflavin	<1 mg
Cholesterol	33 mg	Calcium	24 mg	Niacin	3 mg
Sodium	31 mg	Iron	1 mg	Vitamin A	13 RE
Carbohydrate	18 g	Folate	43 µg	Vitamin C	25 mg

Dietary Exchanges: ½ Starch/Bread, 2 Meat, ½ Fruit

52 Nectarine and Pear Melange

There are many varieties of pears available at the grocery store. They are sweet and juicy, low in calories and high in fiber.

¼ cup lemon juice
1 tablespoon packed brown sugar
1½ teaspoons finely chopped fresh mint or ½ teaspoon dried mint
1 teaspoon finely chopped garlic
¼ teaspoon pepper
3 fresh California Bartlett pears, cored and halved
2 fresh California nectarines, halved and pitted
½ cup chopped red onion

Combine lemon juice, brown sugar, mint, garlic and pepper in cup. Slice pears and nectarines (about ½ inch thick). Arrange pear and nectarine slices in shallow dish. Sprinkle onion over fruit. Drizzle dressing over salad. Marinate in refrigerator 2 hours.
        Makes 6 servings

Nutrients per Serving:

Calories	88	(5% of calories from fat)			
Total Fat	1 g	Dietary Fiber	3 g	Thiamine	<1 mg
Saturated Fat	<1 g	Protein	1 g	Riboflavin	<1 mg
Cholesterol	0 mg	Calcium	18 mg	Niacin	1 mg
Sodium	1 mg	Iron	<1 mg	Vitamin A	37 RE
Carbohydrate	22 g	Folate	12 µg	Vitamin C	12 mg

Dietary Exchanges: 1½ Fruit

53 Applesauce Berry Salad

One ½-cup serving of strawberries supplies 100% of the Recommended Daily Allowance of vitamin C plus more fiber than a slice of whole wheat bread.

1 package (3 ounces) sugar-free strawberry gelatin
1 cup boiling water
1 package (10 ounces) frozen strawberries, thawed
1 cup applesauce
1 cup plain low fat yogurt or low fat sour cream

Dissolve gelatin in boiling water; add thawed strawberries and applesauce. Pour into 10 × 6-inch dish; refrigerate until set. Spread yogurt over gelatin mixture. Cover and refrigerate 2 hours. Cut into squares.   Makes 6 to 8 servings

Nutrients per Serving:

Calories	78	(6% of calories from fat)			
Total Fat	4 g	Dietary Fiber	1 g	Thiamine	<1 mg
Saturated Fat	<1 g	Protein	8 g	Riboflavin	<1 mg
Cholesterol	2 mg	Calcium	58 mg	Niacin	<1 mg
Sodium	251 mg	Iron	<1 mg	Vitamin A	8 RE
Carbohydrate	9 g	Folate	9 µg	Vitamin C	15 mg

Dietary Exchanges: ½ Fruit

Greek Pasta and Vegetable Salad

54 Greek Pasta and Vegetable Salad

Everyone knows you should eat your spinach, but why? Spinach is a wonderful source of vitamin A, phosphorus and calcium.

⅔ **cup corkscrew macaroni**
⅓ **cup lime juice**
2 **tablespoons honey**
1 **tablespoon olive oil**
1 **clove garlic, minced**
4 **cups torn washed stemmed spinach**
1 **cup sliced cucumber**
½ **cup thinly sliced carrot**
¼ **cup sliced green onions**
2 **tablespoons crumbled feta cheese**
2 **tablespoons sliced pitted ripe olives**

Prepare macaroni according to package directions, omitting salt; drain. Rinse under cold water; drain. Combine lime juice, honey, oil and garlic in large bowl. Stir in macaroni. Cover; marinate in refrigerator 2 to 24 hours.

Combine spinach, cucumber, carrot, onions, cheese and olives in large bowl. Add macaroni mixture to salad; toss to combine.   Makes 4 servings

Nutrients per Serving:					
Calories	188	(28% of calories from fat)			
Total Fat	6 g	Dietary Fiber	2 g	Thiamine	<1 mg
Saturated Fat	1 g	Protein	5 g	Riboflavin	<1 mg
Cholesterol	3 mg	Calcium	94 mg	Niacin	2 mg
Sodium	230 mg	Iron	3 mg	Vitamin A	794 RE
Carbohydrate	30 g	Folate	121 μg	Vitamin C	27 mg

Dietary Exchanges: 1 Starch/Bread, 3 Vegetable, 1 Fat

[55] Curried Turkey Salad with Celery and Brown Rice

Skinless turkey breast has one of the lowest percentages of fat among meats. One 3½-ounce serving has less than 1 gram of fat.

1½ cups quick-cooking brown rice (uncooked)
2 cups cubed cooked turkey or chicken breast
2 cups sliced celery
1 cup diced red bell pepper
¼ cup sliced pitted ripe olives
¼ cup plain nonfat yogurt
2 tablespoons lemon juice
1 tablespoon corn oil
1 teaspoon salt
1 teaspoon curry powder
⅛ teaspoon black pepper

Bring 1¾ cups water to a boil in medium saucepan. Add rice; reduce heat and simmer, covered, until tender and water is absorbed, about 10 minutes. Combine rice, turkey, celery, bell pepper and olives in large bowl. Combine yogurt, lemon juice, oil, salt, curry powder and black pepper in small bowl. Pour over rice mixture; toss to coat. Serve at room temperature or cover and refrigerate until ready to serve.   Makes 4 servings

Nutrients per Serving:

Calories	470	(18% of calories from fat)			
Total Fat	9 g	Dietary Fiber	6 g	Thiamine	<1 mg
Saturated Fat	1 g	Protein	33 g	Riboflavin	<1 mg
Cholesterol	71 mg	Calcium	98 mg	Niacin	10 mg
Sodium	924 mg	Iron	3 mg	Vitamin A	45 RE
Carbohydrate	63 g	Folate	51 μg	Vitamin C	58 mg

Dietary Exchanges: 3½ Starch/Bread, 3½ Meat, 1 Vegetable

[56] Fruit and Green Salad

This tasty recipe is filled with protein, fiber and vitamins.

2 tablespoons plain low fat yogurt
1 teaspoon lemon juice
1 teaspoon sugar
1½ cups torn lettuce
1 orange, cubed
1 apple, cubed
1 teaspoon walnuts

In small bowl combine yogurt, lemon juice and sugar. In salad bowl toss lettuce, orange and apple. Pour dressing over salad and top with nuts.
                                    Makes 2 servings

Nutrients per Serving:

Calories	102	(11% of calories from fat)			
Total Fat	1 g	Dietary Fiber	4 g	Thiamine	<1 mg
Saturated Fat	<1 g	Protein	2 g	Riboflavin	<1 mg
Cholesterol	1 mg	Calcium	66 mg	Niacin	<1 mg
Sodium	14 mg	Iron	<1 mg	Vitamin A	34 RE
Carbohydrate	22 g	Folate	48 μg	Vitamin C	42 mg

Dietary Exchanges: 2 Vegetable, 1 Fruit

[57] Cucumber Salad

Cucumbers are low in calories and high in water content which makes this salad very refreshing if served chilled on a hot summer day.

2 cucumbers
½ cup plain nonfat yogurt
1 teaspoon dried mint
½ teaspoon sugar

Slice cucumbers. Combine yogurt, mint and sugar in small bowl. Toss cucumbers in yogurt mixture. Serve immediately.   Makes 4 servings

Nutrients per Serving:

Calories	37	(6% of calories from fat)			
Total Fat	<1 g	Dietary Fiber	2 g	Thiamine	<1 mg
Saturated Fat	<1 g	Protein	2 g	Riboflavin	<1 mg
Cholesterol	1 mg	Calcium	78 mg	Niacin	<1 mg
Sodium	25 mg	Iron	<1 mg	Vitamin A	10 RE
Carbohydrate	7 g	Folate	24 μg	Vitamin C	8 mg

Dietary Exchanges: 1½ Vegetable

58 Grilled Chicken and Florida Grapefruit Salad

Grapefruit's fiber comes in the form of pectin, a water-soluble ingredient used in thickening food for canning or preserving.

½ cup frozen Florida grapefruit juice
    concentrate, thawed
¼ cup finely minced green onions
1 ripe banana, mashed
2 tablespoons chopped fresh dill
1 tablespoon olive oil
2 teaspoons red wine vinegar
2 cloves garlic, minced
1 teaspoon packed brown sugar
½ teaspoon salt
¼ teaspoon ground black pepper
4 boneless, skinless chicken breast
    halves
4 cups mixed salad greens (Boston,
    romaine, red leaf)
1 pint cherry tomatoes, halved
1 green bell pepper, cut into strips
2 Florida grapefruit, peeled and cut into
    ½-inch-thick wheels
    Additional green onions and dill
    (optional)

Preheat grill or broiler. In medium bowl, combine grapefruit juice concentrate, ¼ cup onions, banana, dill, oil, vinegar, garlic, sugar, salt and black pepper; stir to combine. Place chicken in resealable plastic food storage bag. Divide marinade mixture and pour half over chicken. Marinate in refrigerator 30 minutes, turning breasts over once. Place chicken on grill or broiler, 4 inches from heat. Cook 5 to 7 minutes on each side or until chicken is no longer pink in center. Remove to plate; set aside 5 minutes.

Divide and arrange salad greens, tomatoes, bell pepper and grapefruit on plates. Slice chicken diagonally and place 1 chicken half on each plate. Drizzle juices and remaining dressing over chicken and salad greens. Garnish with additional green onions and dill, if desired.   Makes 4 servings

Nutrients per Serving:

Calories	296	(21% of calories from fat)			
Total Fat	7 g	Dietary Fiber	3 g	Thiamine	<1 mg
Saturated Fat	1 g	Protein	29 g	Riboflavin	<1 mg
Cholesterol	73 mg	Calcium	83 mg	Niacin	13 mg
Sodium	338 mg	Iron	2 mg	Vitamin A	212 RE
Carbohydrate	30 g	Folate	100 µg	Vitamin C	98 mg

Dietary Exchanges: 3 Meat, ½ Vegetable, 2 Fruit

59 Golden Fruit Salad

Bananas are the most popular fruit in the U.S. They're a good source of potassium and fiber.

Orange Yogurt Dressing (recipe follows)
1 Golden Delicious or Crispin apple, cored
    and sliced
1 Red Delicious or Empire apple, cored
    and sliced
1 banana, peeled and sliced
½ cup red or green grapes
    Lettuce

Prepare Orange Yogurt Dressing. Combine fruit; mix well. Serve on lettuce-lined salad plates with Orange Yogurt Dressing.   Makes 3 servings

Orange Yogurt Dressing: Combine ½ cup plain low fat yogurt, 2 to 3 tablespoons orange juice and dash nutmeg in small bowl; mix well.

Nutrients per Serving:

Calories	137	(8% of calories from fat)			
Total Fat	1 g	Dietary Fiber	3 g	Thiamine	<1 mg
Saturated Fat	1 g	Protein	3 g	Riboflavin	<1 mg
Cholesterol	2 mg	Calcium	82 mg	Niacin	<1 mg
Sodium	28 mg	Iron	<1 mg	Vitamin A	19 RE
Carbohydrate	31 g	Folate	21 µg	Vitamin C	17 mg

Dietary Exchanges: 2 Fruit

*Grilled Chicken and
Florida Grapefruit Salad*

60 Greens and Broccoli Salad with Peppy Vinaigrette

Broccoli receives rave reviews for its nutritional content. It is rich in vitamin C and also contains vitamin A, thiamin, riboflavin, calcium and iron.

4 sun-dried tomato halves (*not* packed in oil)
3 cups torn washed red-tipped or plain leaf lettuce
1½ cups broccoli flowerets
1 cup sliced fresh mushrooms
⅓ cup sliced radishes
2 tablespoons water
1 tablespoon balsamic vinegar
1 teaspoon vegetable oil
¼ teaspoon chicken bouillon granules
¼ teaspoon dried chervil, crushed
¼ teaspoon dry mustard
⅛ teaspoon ground red pepper

Pour enough boiling water over tomatoes in small bowl to cover. Let stand 5 minutes; drain. Chop tomatoes. Combine tomatoes, lettuce, broccoli, mushrooms and radishes in large salad bowl.

Combine 2 tablespoons water, vinegar, oil, bouillon granules, chervil, mustard and ground red pepper in jar with tight-fitting lid. Cover; shake well. Add to salad; toss to combine.   Makes 4 servings

Nutrients per Serving:

Calories	54	(23% of calories from fat)		
Total Fat	2 g	Dietary Fiber	2 g	Thiamine <1 mg
Saturated Fat	<1 g	Protein	3 g	Riboflavin <1 mg
Cholesterol	0 mg	Calcium	57 mg	Niacin 2 mg
Sodium	79 mg	Iron	2 mg	Vitamin A 406 RE
Carbohydrate	9 g	Folate	51 µg	Vitamin C 48 mg

Dietary Exchanges: 2 Vegetable

61 Health Club Chicken Salad

Alfalfa sprouts are highly nutritious and are almost without calories. One cup of sprouts has only 10 calories, but they're high in protein, B vitamins and vitamin C.

2 cans (16 ounces each) California cling peach halves in juice or extra light syrup
1 cup seeded sliced peeled cucumber
½ cup sliced green onions
2 tablespoons olive oil
1 carton (8 ounces) plain nonfat yogurt
1 clove garlic, minced
1 tablespoon grated fresh ginger
½ teaspoon lemon pepper
½ teaspoon dill weed
3 cups shredded cooked chicken
1 cup sliced celery
½ cup chopped roasted red peppers
3 quarts chopped stemmed washed spinach
1½ quarts alfalfa sprouts

Drain peaches, reserving liquid for other use. Refrigerate peaches. Add cucumber, onions, oil, yogurt, garlic, ginger and pepper to food processor or blender; process until smooth. Stir in dill weed. Combine chicken, celery and roasted red peppers. Place spinach on individual serving plates. Top with alfalfa sprouts, peach halves and chicken mixture. Serve with cucumber dressing.

    Makes 6 servings

Nutrients per Serving:

Calories	261	(23% of calories from fat)		
Total Fat	7 g	Dietary Fiber	6 g	Thiamine <1 mg
Saturated Fat	1 g	Protein	24 g	Riboflavin <1 mg
Cholesterol	44 mg	Calcium	232 mg	Niacin 7 mg
Sodium	181 mg	Iron	5 mg	Vitamin A 852 RE
Carbohydrate	29 g	Folate	253 µg	Vitamin C 61 mg

Dietary Exchanges: 3 Meat, 2 Vegetable, 1 Fruit

Greens and Broccoli Salad with Peppy Vinaigrette

62 Curry Rice Salad with Apples

The combination of yogurt, curry and cloves gives this dish an exotic Indian flair.

⅓ cup plain or vanilla low fat yogurt
1½ tablespoons dry sherry or cider vinegar
1 to 2 teaspoons curry powder
⅛ teaspoon ground cloves
  Salt and pepper to taste
¾ cup finely diced celery
¼ to ½ cup currants or raisins
2 apples, unpeeled, cored, cubed and mixed with a little lemon juice to prevent browning (Empire, McIntosh, or Cortland)
4 cups cooked brown rice

In large bowl, combine yogurt, sherry, curry, cloves, salt and pepper; mix well. Stir in celery, currants and apples. Add rice; mix well.

Salad keeps well for a few days, covered, in the refrigerator. Makes 6 servings

Nutrients per Serving:

Calories	226	(4% of calories from fat)			
Total Fat	1 g	Dietary Fiber	3 g	Thiamine	<1 mg
Saturated Fat	<1 g	Protein	5 g	Riboflavin	<1 mg
Cholesterol	1 mg	Calcium	63 mg	Niacin	2 mg
Sodium	30 mg	Iron	2 mg	Vitamin A	9 RE
Carbohydrate	48 g	Folate	13 μg	Vitamin C	6 mg

Dietary Exchanges: 1½ Starch/Bread, 2 Fruit

63 Fruited Slaw

Cabbage is high in fiber and vitamin C. Studies have also shown that it may have cancer-prevention potential.

1 can (8¼ ounces) pineapple chunks, in syrup
1 carton (8 ounces) orange low fat yogurt
1 tablespoon lemon juice
3 cups finely shredded cabbage
1 can (11 ounces) mandarin orange sections, drained
1 cup thinly sliced celery
½ cup chopped walnuts
¼ cup raisins
1 medium banana, sliced

Drain pineapple, reserving 2 tablespoons syrup. In small bowl, combine reserved syrup, yogurt and lemon juice. In large bowl, combine pineapple, cabbage, oranges, celery, nuts and raisins; fold in yogurt mixture. Gently fold in banana. Cover; refrigerate. Makes 8 servings

Nutrients per Serving:

Calories	141	(30% of calories from fat)			
Total Fat	5 g	Dietary Fiber	2 g	Thiamine	<1 mg
Saturated Fat	1 g	Protein	5 g	Riboflavin	<1 mg
Cholesterol	1 mg	Calcium	84 mg	Niacin	1 mg
Sodium	38 mg	Iron	1 mg	Vitamin A	27 RE
Carbohydrate	22 g	Folate	44 μg	Vitamin C	33 mg

Dietary Exchanges: ½ Milk, 1 Fruit, 1 Fat

64 Spinach Chickpea Salad

Chickpeas, also called garbanzo beans, are a good source of protein.

2 tablespoons red wine vinegar
2 tablespoons water
1 teaspoon sesame oil
1 teaspoon lite soy sauce
1 teaspoon sugar
3 cups washed torn stemmed spinach
2 carrots, sliced
1 cup canned chickpeas, drained and rinsed
1½ tablespoons sesame seeds

In small bowl, mix vinegar, water, oil, soy sauce and sugar to make dressing. In salad bowl toss dressing with spinach, carrots and chickpeas. Sprinkle with sesame seeds. Makes 4 servings

Nutrients per Serving:

Calories	114	(30% of calories from fat)			
Total Fat	4 g	Dietary Fiber	6 g	Thiamine	<1 mg
Saturated Fat	1 g	Protein	5 g	Riboflavin	<1 mg
Cholesterol	0 mg	Calcium	107 mg	Niacin	1 mg
Sodium	324 mg	Iron	3 mg	Vitamin A	1,295 RE
Carbohydrate	17 g	Folate	89 μg	Vitamin C	18 mg

Dietary Exchanges: ½ Starch/Bread, 1 Vegetable

Hearty Healthy Chicken Salad

65 **H**earty Healthy Chicken Salad

Tomatoes and red bell peppers are a good source of vitamin A, which is vital for maintaining good vision.

1 broiler-fryer chicken, cooked, skinned, boned and cut into chunks
1 cup small macaroni, cooked and drained
3 tomatoes, cubed
1 cup sliced celery
½ cup chopped red bell pepper
3 tablespoons chopped green onions
1 teaspoon salt
½ teaspoon black pepper
¼ teaspoon dried oregano leaves, crushed
1 cup low sodium chicken broth
1 clove garlic, minced
¼ cup white wine vinegar

Combine chicken, macaroni, tomatoes, celery, bell pepper and onions in large bowl. Sprinkle with salt, black pepper and oregano. Place chicken broth and garlic in small saucepan. Bring to a boil over high heat for 10 minutes or until broth is reduced to ½ cup. Add wine vinegar. Pour over salad; mix well. Refrigerate until cold.   Makes 6 servings

Nutrients per Serving:

Calories	266	(30% of calories from fat)			
Total Fat	9 g	Dietary Fiber	2 g	Thiamine	<1 mg
Saturated Fat	2 g	Protein	35 g	Riboflavin	<1 mg
Cholesterol	101 mg	Calcium	39 mg	Niacin	11 mg
Sodium	482 mg	Iron	2 mg	Vitamin A	83 RE
Carbohydrate	11 g	Folate	27 µg	Vitamin C	31 mg

Dietary Exchanges: ½ Starch/Bread, 3½ Meat, 1 Vegetable

66 California Apricot Fruit Salad

Apricots are rich in beta-carotene, which your body converts into vitamin A.

**2 cups sliced pitted fresh California
  apricots
1½ cups sliced fresh strawberries
1½ cups peeled and sliced kiwi
¼ cup California apricot nectar
¼ cup flaked coconut, lightly toasted
1 tablespoon finely chopped fresh mint**

In medium bowl, combine all ingredients and refrigerate. Serve as salad or thread onto wooden skewers for fresh fruit kabobs.   Makes 5 servings

Nutrients per Serving:					
Calories	115	(17% of calories from fat)			
Total Fat	2 g	Dietary Fiber	5 g	Thiamine	<1 mg
Saturated Fat	2 g	Protein	2 g	Riboflavin	<1 mg
Cholesterol	0 mg	Calcium	33 mg	Niacin	1 mg
Sodium	16 mg	Iron	1 mg	Vitamin A	267 RE
Carbohydrate	24 g	Folate	35 µg	Vitamin C	83 mg

Dietary Exchanges: 1½ Fruit, ½ Fat

67 Japanese Steak Salad

Snow peas are a good source of protein, iron, vitamin C, potassium and iron.

**Sesame Marinade and Dressing
  (recipes follow)
1 pound trimmed beef top sirloin steak,
  cut 1 inch thick
3 cups sliced napa cabbage
3 cups torn romaine lettuce
½ cup diagonally sliced carrots
½ cup thinly sliced radishes
½ cup thinly sliced cucumber
1 cup cooked rice
24 pea pods, blanched**

Prepare Sesame Marinade and Dressing. Place beef in resealable plastic food storage bag; add reserved Sesame Marinade, turning to coat. Close bag securely and marinate in refrigerator 2 hours,

turning once. Remove steak from marinade; place on rack in broiler pan. Broil 3 to 4 inches from heat. Broil 14 to 16 minutes, turning once. Let stand 5 minutes. Carve steak into thin slices. Combine cabbage, lettuce, carrots and radishes; place equal amounts of each on 4 individual plates. Arrange equal numbers of cucumber slices in a circle at top of salad greens on each plate. Mound ¼ cup rice on top of each cucumber circle. Fan pea pods around both sides of rice. Arrange steak slices in spoke fashion on salad greens, radiating down from rice. Serve Dressing with salad.

Makes 4 servings

Sesame Marinade and Dressing

**3 tablespoons *each* dry sherry, reduced
  sodium soy sauce and rice wine
  vinegar
2 tablespoons hoisin sauce
½ teaspoon grated fresh ginger
¼ cup water
2 tablespoons chopped green onion
1 tablespoon *each* sugar and Oriental
  dark-roasted sesame oil**

Combine sherry, soy sauce, vinegar, hoisin sauce and ginger. Reserve ⅓ cup for Marinade. To prepare Dressing, combine remaining sherry mixture with water, onion, sugar and sesame oil.

Makes ⅓ cup Marinade and ¾ cup Dressing

Nutrients per Serving:					
Calories	308	(30% of calories from fat)			
Total Fat	10 g	Dietary Fiber	4 g	Thiamine	<1 mg
Saturated Fat	3 g	Protein	24 g	Riboflavin	<1 mg
Cholesterol	57 mg	Calcium	81 mg	Niacin	5 mg
Sodium	527 mg	Iron	5 mg	Vitamin A	534 RE
Carbohydrate	21 g	Folate	120 µg	Vitamin C	64 mg

Dietary Exchanges: 1 Starch/Bread, 3 Meat, 2 Vegetable, ½ Fat

California Apricot Fruit Salad

68 | Spicy Beef and Rice Salad

*Beef is very dense in its concentration of nutrients,
It's loaded with iron, zinc and B vitamins.*

**2 teaspoons Spicy Seasoning Mix (recipe
   follows), divided
2 cups Spicy Cooked Rice (recipe follows)
1 pound boneless beef top sirloin steak,
   cut 1 inch thick
   Salt (optional)
1 medium red apple, cored and cut into
   pieces
2 to 3 green onions, thinly sliced
¼ cup coarsely chopped walnuts, toasted
   Leaf lettuce and apple (optional)**

Prepare Spicy Seasoning Mix and Spicy Cooked
Rice. Heat large nonstick skillet over medium heat
5 minutes. Meanwhile, rub 1 teaspoon Spicy
Seasoning into sides of steak. Place steak in skillet
and cook 12 to 14 minutes, turning once. Season
with salt, if desired. Meanwhile combine rice, apple,
onions and walnuts. Carve steak into thin slices;
arrange over rice mixture. Garnish with lettuce and
apple, if desired.   Makes 4 servings

Spicy Seasoning Mix

**3 tablespoons chili powder
2 teaspoons ground cumin
1½ teaspoons garlic powder
¾ teaspoon dried oregano leaves, crushed
½ teaspoon ground red pepper**

Combine all ingredients. Store, covered, in airtight
container. Shake before using to blend. Makes about
⅓ cup.

Spicy Cooked Rice: Prepare ⅔ cup rice
according to package directions; add 1 teaspoon
Spicy Seasoning Mix to water before cooking.

Nutrients per Serving:

Calories	379	(25% of calories from fat)			
Total Fat	10 g	Dietary Fiber	2 g	Thiamine	<1 mg
Saturated Fat	3 g	Protein	35 g	Riboflavin	<1 mg
Cholesterol	72 mg	Calcium	31 mg	Niacin	6 mg
Sodium	68 mg	Iron	5 mg	Vitamin A	17 RE
Carbohydrate	35 g	Folate	20 µg	Vitamin C	3 mg

Dietary Exchanges: 2 Starch/Bread, 4 Meat

69 | Insalata Rustica

*Peaches are a good source of potassium, vitamin A
and fiber. Ripen peaches at room temperature, after
which they should be stored in the refrigerator.*

**Mustard Dressing (recipe follows)
1 quart iceberg lettuce, torn
1 quart romaine lettuce, torn
1 bunch watercress, stems removed and
   leaves torn
2 tomatoes, sliced
6 radishes, sliced
2 large fresh California peaches, peeled,
   halved, pitted and cut into wedges**

Prepare Mustard Dressing; set aside. Combine
iceberg lettuce, romaine lettuce and watercress in
large salad bowl. Arrange tomatoes, radishes and
peaches in attractive pattern on top. Drizzle with
Mustard Dressing.   Makes 6 servings

Mustard Dressing: Combine ¼ cup corn oil,
3 tablespoons white wine vinegar, 4 teaspoons
Dijon-style mustard, 2 teaspoons minced garlic and
½ teaspoon sugar in jar with tight-fitting lid. Cover;
shake well.   Makes about ½ cup

Nutrients per Serving:

Calories	77	(30% of calories from fat)			
Total Fat	3 g	Dietary Fiber	3 g	Thiamine	<1 mg
Saturated Fat	<1 g	Protein	2 g	Riboflavin	<1 mg
Cholesterol	0 mg	Calcium	38 mg	Niacin	1 mg
Sodium	60 mg	Iron	1 mg	Vitamin A	192 RE
Carbohydrate	12 g	Folate	81 µg	Vitamin C	27 mg

Dietary Exchanges: ½ Fruit, 1 Vegetable, ½ Fat

70 Blueberry-Peach Salad

Buttermilk is creamy, tangy and more easily digested than regular milk.

- **1 package (6 ounces) orange-flavored gelatin**
- **⅓ cup sugar**
- **1 teaspoon finely shredded orange peel**
- **2¼ cups orange juice, divided**
- **2 cups buttermilk**
- **1 can (8 ounces) crushed pineapple, drained**
- **1 cup chopped pitted halved peeled peaches**
- **1 cup fresh or frozen unsweetened blueberries, thawed**
- **1 carton (8 ounces) dairy sour cream**

In medium saucepan combine gelatin and sugar; stir in orange peel and 2 cups orange juice. Cook and stir until gelatin is dissolved; cool. Stir in buttermilk. Refrigerate until partially set. Fold in fruit; spoon into 10 individual molds. Refrigerate 6 hours or until firm. Combine sour cream and remaining ¼ cup orange juice; refrigerate. Unmold salad; serve with sour cream mixture.

Makes 10 servings

Nutrients per Serving:

Calories	204	(23% of calories from fat)			
Total Fat	5 g	Dietary Fiber	1 g	Thiamine	<1 mg
Saturated Fat	3 g	Protein	5 g	Riboflavin	<1 mg
Cholesterol	12 mg	Calcium	95 mg	Niacin	1 mg
Sodium	114 mg	Iron	<1 mg	Vitamin A	82 RE
Carbohydrate	36 g	Folate	38 μg	Vitamin C	34 mg

Dietary Exchanges: ½ Milk, 2 Fruit, ½ Fat

71 Green Chili Vegetable Salad

Using nonfat mayonnaise in place of regular mayonnaise in this wonderfully creamy dressing reduces the fat by more than 10 grams per serving and the cholesterol by 8 grams.

- **4 cups torn washed romaine lettuce**
- **1 large green bell pepper, cut into strips**
- **1 cup halved cherry tomatoes**
- **3 tablespoons shredded low fat colby or Cheddar cheese**
- **¼ cup nonfat mayonnaise or salad dressing**
- **2 tablespoons plain low fat yogurt**
- **1 can (4 ounces) diced green chilies, drained**
- **¼ teaspoon ground cumin**

Combine lettuce, bell pepper, tomatoes and cheese in large bowl. Combine mayonnaise, yogurt, green chilies and cumin in small bowl. Add dressing to salad; toss to combine.

Makes 4 servings

Nutrients per Serving:

Calories	81	(18% of calories from fat)			
Total Fat	2 g	Dietary Fiber	4 g	Thiamine	<1 mg
Saturated Fat	1 g	Protein	4 g	Riboflavin	<1 mg
Cholesterol	4 mg	Calcium	86 mg	Niacin	1 mg
Sodium	168 mg	Iron	2 mg	Vitamin A	238 RE
Carbohydrate	14 g	Folate	102 μg	Vitamin C	132 mg

Dietary Exchanges: 3 Vegetable

Blueberry-Peach Salad

72 Japanese Petal Salad

The sesame seed oil used in this recipe adds flavor and is also highly monounsaturated.

1 pound medium shrimp, cooked, or
   2 cups chicken, cooked and shredded
Romaine lettuce leaves
2 fresh California nectarines, halved, pitted and thinly sliced
2 cups sliced cucumber
2 celery stalks, cut into 3-inch matchstick pieces
⅓ cup shredded red radishes
   Sesame Dressing (recipe follows) or low calorie dressing
2 teaspoons sesame seeds (optional)

Center shrimp on 4 lettuce-lined salad plates. Fan nectarines to right side of shrimp; overlap cucumber slices to left side. Place celery at top of plate; mound radishes at bottom of plate. Prepare dressing; pour 3 tablespoons over each salad. Sprinkle with sesame seeds, if desired.

Makes 4 servings

Sesame Dressing: In small bowl, combine ½ cup rice wine vinegar (*not* seasoned type), 2 tablespoons low sodium soy sauce, 2 teaspoons sugar and 2 teaspoons dark sesame oil. Stir to dissolve sugar. Makes about ⅔ cup.

Nutrients per Serving:

Calories	192	(18% of calories from fat)			
Total Fat	4 g	Dietary Fiber	2 g	Thiamine	<1 mg
Saturated Fat	1 g	Protein	25 g	Riboflavin	<1 mg
Cholesterol	222 mg	Calcium	67 mg	Niacin	4 mg
Sodium	573 mg	Iron	4 mg	Vitamin A	130 RE
Carbohydrate	15 g	Folate	22 µg	Vitamin C	11 mg

Dietary Exchanges: 3 Meat, ½ Fruit

73 California Brown Rice Salad

Brown rice contains the rice germ and bran which makes it much more nutritious than white rice.

1 can (16 ounces) California fruit cocktail in juice or extra light syrup
1 cup brown rice
1 medium tomato, diced
1 cup sliced celery
½ cup sliced green onions
2 tablespoons red wine vinegar
1 tablespoon vegetable oil
1 tablespoon Dijon-style mustard
½ teaspoon dried tarragon leaves, crushed
⅛ teaspoon garlic powder

Drain fruit cocktail, reserving ¼ cup liquid; save remainder for other uses. Prepare rice according to package directions; refrigerate thoroughly. Toss rice with fruit cocktail, tomato, celery and onions. Combine reserved fruit cocktail liquid with vinegar, oil, mustard, tarragon and garlic powder. Stir into rice mixture; refrigerate to allow flavors to blend.

Makes 6 servings

Nutrients per Serving:

Calories	182	(17% of calories from fat)			
Total Fat	3 g	Dietary Fiber	3 g	Thiamine	<1 mg
Saturated Fat	1 g	Protein	3 g	Riboflavin	<1 mg
Cholesterol	0 mg	Calcium	31 mg	Niacin	2 mg
Sodium	58 mg	Iron	1 mg	Vitamin A	72 RE
Carbohydrate	35 g	Folate	18 µg	Vitamin C	10 mg

Dietary Exchanges: ½ Starch/Bread, 2 Fruit, ½ Fat

Japanese Petal Salad

74 Fruity Turkey Salad

Wild rice is really a grass seed and not a grain. It is high in protein, low in fat and a good source of B vitamins.

1 cup plain low fat yogurt
¼ cup light mayonnaise
2 tablespoons honey
1 teaspoon ground ginger
½ teaspoon salt (optional)
¼ teaspoon curry powder
2 cups cooked wild rice
2 cups cubed cooked turkey breast
1 cup diced pitted nectarines
½ cup thinly sliced celery
    Salad greens (optional)
    Nectarine slices (optional)

Combine yogurt, mayonnaise, honey, ginger, salt and curry powder in small bowl. Cover; refrigerate to allow flavors to blend. Combine wild rice, turkey, nectarines and celery in large bowl. Blend in dressing. Serve on bed of salad greens and garnish with nectarine slices, if desired.

Makes 4 servings

Nutrients per Serving:

Calories	344	(16% of calories from fat)			
Total Fat	6 g	Dietary Fiber	3 g	Thiamine	<1 mg
Saturated Fat	1 g	Protein	33 g	Riboflavin	<1 mg
Cholesterol	79 mg	Calcium	128 mg	Niacin	8 mg
Sodium	116 mg	Iron	2 mg	Vitamin A	65 RE
Carbohydrate	40 g	Folate	40 μg	Vitamin C	5 mg

Dietary Exchanges: 1½ Starch/Bread, 3½ Meat, <½ Milk, ½ Fruit

75 Citrus Salad with Bibb Lettuce, Watercress and Balsamic Dressing

All citrus fruits are good sources of vitamin C. Some also contain beta-carotene. Fruits which have a darker orange-red color have a higher level of beta-carotene.

1 medium pink grapefruit, peeled, white pith removed and sectioned
2 large oranges, peeled, white pith removed and sectioned
2 tangerines, peeled and sectioned
1 bunch watercress, rinsed and patted dry
3 tablespoons orange juice
1 tablespoon balsamic vinegar
¼ teaspoon salt
1 tablespoon canola or vegetable oil
1 large head Bibb lettuce, separated, rinsed and patted dry
    Peel from one orange, cut into very fine strips

Combine grapefruit, oranges, tangerines and watercress in medium bowl. Combine orange juice, vinegar and salt in small bowl. Add oil; whisk dressing until combined. Pour over fruit and watercress; gently toss to combine.

Line four serving plates with lettuce. Divide fruit mixture among plates. Garnish each with julienned peel.

Makes 4 servings

Nutrients per Serving:

Calories	113	(28% of calories from fat)			
Total Fat	4 g	Dietary Fiber	4 g	Thiamine	<1 mg
Saturated Fat	<1 mg	Protein	2 g	Riboflavin	<1 mg
Cholesterol	0 mg	Calcium	66 mg	Niacin	1 mg
Sodium	140 mg	Iron	<1 mg	Vitamin A	150 RE
Carbohydrate	20 g	Folate	71 μg	Vitamin C	84 mg

Dietary Exchanges: 1½ Fruit, ½ Fat

Citrus Salad with Bibb Lettuce, Watercress and Balsamic Dressing

76 Pasta and Walnut Fruit Salad

Yogurt is high in calcium which keeps bones healthy and strong.

8 ounces medium pasta shells
1 container (8 ounces) plain nonfat yogurt
¼ cup frozen orange juice concentrate, thawed
1 can (15 ounces) juice-packed mandarin oranges, drained
1 cup seedless red grape halves
1 cup seedless green grape halves
1 apple, cored and chopped
½ cup sliced celery
½ cup walnut halves

Prepare pasta shells according to package directions; drain. In small bowl, blend yogurt and orange juice concentrate. In large bowl, combine pasta shells and remaining ingredients. Add yogurt mixture; toss to coat. Cover and refrigerate thoroughly.

Makes 6 to 8 servings

Nutrients per Serving:					
Calories	231	(21% of calories from fat)			
Total Fat	6 g	Dietary Fiber	3 g	Thiamine	<1 mg
Saturated Fat	1 g	Protein	8 g	Riboflavin	<1 mg
Cholesterol	25 mg	Calcium	86 mg	Niacin	1 mg
Sodium	35 mg	Iron	1 mg	Vitamin A	32 RE
Carbohydrate	38 g	Folate	42 μg	Vitamin C	33 mg

Dietary Exchanges: 1 Starch/Bread, ½ Milk, 1½ Fruit, ½ Fat

FRUITS & VEGETABLES

77 Apple & Carrot Casserole

Carrots are high in sugar, which is why they blend easily into sweet dishes. But don't be fooled—they're just as nutritious as ever.

6 large carrots, sliced
4 large apples, peeled, halved, cored and sliced
5 tablespoons all-purpose flour
1 tablespoon packed brown sugar
½ teaspoon ground nutmeg
1 tablespoon margarine
½ cup orange juice
½ teaspoon salt (optional)

Preheat oven to 350°F. Cook carrots in large saucepan in boiling water for 5 minutes; drain. Layer carrots and apples in large casserole. Mix flour, sugar and nutmeg; sprinkle over top. Dot with margarine; pour orange juice over flour mixture. Bake 30 minutes or until carrots are tender.

Makes 6 servings

Nutrients per Serving:

Calories	144	(15% of calories from fat)			
Total Fat	3 g	Dietary Fiber	5 g	Thiamine	<1 mg
Saturated Fat	1 g	Protein	2 g	Riboflavin	<1 mg
Cholesterol	0 mg	Calcium	32 mg	Niacin	1 mg
Sodium	49 mg	Iron	1 mg	Vitamin A	2,057 RE
Carbohydrate	31 g	Folate	26 µg	Vitamin C	22 mg

Dietary Exchanges: 1 Vegetable, 1½ Fruit, ½ Fat

78 Braised Onions with Tomatoes

Onions enhance the taste of foods by irritating the mouth and nose membranes. In addition to flavor, they also provide fiber and potassium.

¼ cup hot water
1 teaspoon low sodium beef bouillon granules
2 tablespoons white wine
1 teaspoon chopped fresh parsley
¼ teaspoon dry mustard
⅛ teaspoon pepper
2 large onions, sliced and separated into rings
1 small tomato, cut into 8 wedges

Microwave Directions: Combine hot water, bouillon granules, wine, parsley, mustard and pepper in 1-cup measure. Place onion rings in 2-quart microwavable casserole. Pour bouillon mixture over onions. Toss to coat; cover. Microwave at HIGH (100% power) 5 to 7 minutes or until onions are tender, stirring once. Stir in tomato. Microwave at HIGH (100% power) 1 minute.

Makes 4 servings

Nutrients per Serving:

Calories	45	(7% of calories from fat)			
Total Fat	<1 g	Dietary Fiber	2 g	Thiamine	<1 mg
Saturated Fat	<1 g	Protein	1 g	Riboflavin	<1 mg
Cholesterol	0 mg	Calcium	20 mg	Niacin	<1 mg
Sodium	81 mg	Iron	<1 mg	Vitamin A	21 RE
Carbohydrate	9 g	Folate	20 µg	Vitamin C	11 mg

Dietary Exchanges: 1½ Vegetable

Apple & Carrot Casserole

79 Gazpacho

Red peppers rate the highest among peppers when it comes to nutrition. They're all high in vitamin C but red varieties are much higher in vitamin A.

1 cucumber
½ red bell pepper, seeded
2 carrots
1 medium tomato
2 cups spicy tomato juice
½ cup water
½ cup tomato sauce
¼ cup chopped green onions
3 tablespoons vinegar
2 teaspoons sugar
1 clove garlic, minced
1 can (15 ounces) navy beans, drained and rinsed

Chop cucumber, bell pepper, carrots and tomato into large chunks. Add all ingredients except beans to food processor; process until combined but still chunky. Stir in beans. Transfer to large bowl; cover and refrigerate until serving.   Makes 6 servings

Nutrients per Serving:

Calories	130	(4% of calories from fat)		
Total Fat	1 g	Dietary Fiber	3 g	Thiamine	<1 mg
Saturated Fat	<1 g	Protein	7 g	Riboflavin	<1 mg
Cholesterol	0 mg	Calcium	62 mg	Niacin	2 mg
Sodium	737 mg	Iron	2 mg	Vitamin A	775 RE
Carbohydrate	27 g	Folate	77 µg	Vitamin C	24 mg

Dietary Exchanges: 1 Starch/Bread, 2 Vegetable

80 Chinese Sweet and Sour Vegetables

The combination of broccoli and carrots in this recipe packs a giant beta-carotene punch—the substance the body converts to vitamin A.

3 cups broccoli flowerets
2 medium carrots, diagonally sliced
1 large red bell pepper, cut into thin strips
¼ cup water
2 teaspoons cornstarch
1 teaspoon sugar
⅓ cup unsweetened pineapple juice
1 tablespoon soy sauce
1 tablespoon rice vinegar
½ teaspoon Oriental sesame oil
⅛ cup diagonally sliced green onions or chopped cilantro (optional)

Combine broccoli, carrots and bell pepper in large skillet with tight-fitting lid. Add water; bring to a boil over high heat. Reduce heat to medium; cover and steam 4 minutes or until vegetables are crisp-tender.

Meanwhile, combine cornstarch and sugar in small bowl. Blend in pineapple juice, soy sauce and vinegar until smooth.

Transfer vegetables to colander; drain. Stir pineapple mixture and add to skillet. Cook and stir 2 minutes or until sauce boils and thickens.

Return vegetables to skillet; toss with sauce. Stir in sesame oil. Garnish with onions.   Makes 4 servings

Nutrients per Serving:

Calories	67	(11% of calories from fat)		
Total Fat	1 g	Dietary Fiber	3 g	Thiamine	<1 mg
Saturated Fat	<1 g	Protein	3 g	Riboflavin	<1 mg
Cholesterol	0 mg	Calcium	47 mg	Niacin	1 mg
Sodium	288 mg	Iron	1 mg	Vitamin A	1,126 RE
Carbohydrate	14 g	Folate	62 µg	Vitamin C	84 mg

Dietary Exchanges: 2½ Vegetable

81 Crunchy Asparagus

At only 40 calories per cup, asparagus is loaded with nutrition. Not only is it low in fat and calories, it is rich in potassium, niacin and vitamins A and C.

1 package (10 ounces) frozen asparagus cuts
2 tablespoons water
1 teaspoon lemon juice
3 to 4 drops hot pepper sauce
¼ teaspoon salt (optional)
¼ teaspoon dried basil leaves, crushed
⅛ teaspoon pepper
2 teaspoons sunflower kernels
Lemon slices (optional)

Microwave Directions: Place asparagus and water in 1-quart microwavable casserole dish; cover. Microwave at HIGH (100% power) 4½ to 5½ minutes or until asparagus is hot, stirring after half the cooking time to break apart. Drain. Cover; set aside.

In small bowl or 1-cup measure, combine lemon juice, hot pepper sauce, salt, basil and pepper. Pour mixture over asparagus; toss to coat. Sprinkle with sunflower kernels. Garnish with lemon slices, if desired.   Makes 4 servings

Nutrients per Serving:

Calories	29	(27% of calories from fat)			
Total Fat	1 g	Dietary Fiber	1 g	Thiamine	<1 mg
Saturated Fat	<1 g	Protein	2 g	Riboflavin	<1 mg
Cholesterol	0 mg	Calcium	20 mg	Niacin	1 mg
Sodium	4 mg	Iron	1 mg	Vitamin A	59 RE
Carbohydrate	4 g	Folate	99 µg	Vitamin C	18 mg

Dietary Exchanges: 1 Vegetable

82 Orange-Spiked Zucchini and Carrots

Both zucchini and carrots are full of insoluble fiber, which maintains the proper functioning of the digestive system.

1 pound zucchini, cut into ¼-inch slices
1 package (10 ounces) frozen sliced carrots, thawed
1 cup unsweetened orange juice
1 rib celery, finely chopped
2 tablespoons chopped onion
Salt and pepper to taste (optional)

Combine all ingredients in large nonstick saucepan. Simmer, covered, 10 to 12 minutes, or until zucchini is tender. Uncover and continue to simmer, stirring occasionally, until most of the liquid has evaporated.   Makes 7 servings

Nutrients per Serving:

Calories	41	(3% of calories from fat)			
Total Fat	<1 g	Dietary Fiber	3 g	Thiamine	<1 mg
Saturated Fat	<1 g	Protein	1 g	Riboflavin	<1 mg
Cholesterol	0 mg	Calcium	25 mg	Niacin	1 mg
Sodium	31 mg	Iron	<1 mg	Vitamin A	737 RE
Carbohydrate	10 g	Folate	35 µg	Vitamin C	22 mg

Dietary Exchanges: 2 Vegetable

83 Carrot Medley

Carrots are very good for the eyes. They are rich in vitamin A which is a nutrient required for proper functioning of the retina.

4 cups thinly sliced carrots
1 small onion, sliced and separated into rings
1 tablespoon margarine
2 teaspoons chopped fresh parsley
1 teaspoon sugar
1 teaspoon low sodium instant chicken bouillon granules
Paprika

Microwave Directions: Combine carrots, onion, margarine, parsley, sugar and chicken bouillon in 2-quart microwavable casserole; cover. Microwave at HIGH (100% power) 7 to 10 minutes or until carrots are crisp-tender, stirring once. Sprinkle with paprika.   Makes 6 servings

Nutrients per Serving:

Calories	57	(31% of calories from fat)			
Total Fat	2 g	Dietary Fiber	3 g	Thiamine	<1 mg
Saturated Fat	<1 g	Protein	1 g	Riboflavin	<1 mg
Cholesterol	0 mg	Calcium	24 mg	Niacin	1 mg
Sodium	98 mg	Iron	<1 mg	Vitamin A	2,088 RE
Carbohydrate	10 g	Folate	14 µg	Vitamin C	8 mg

Dietary Exchanges: 1½ Vegetable, ½ Fat

Italian Broccoli with Tomatoes

84 | Italian Broccoli with Tomatoes

Broccoli is full of vitamins A and C as well as calcium for healthy bones and teeth.

4 cups broccoli flowerets
½ cup water
½ teaspoon Italian seasoning, crushed
½ teaspoon dried parsley flakes
¼ teaspoon salt (optional)
⅛ teaspoon pepper
2 medium tomatoes, cut into wedges
½ cup grated mozzarella cheese

Microwave Directions: Place broccoli and water in 2-quart microwavable casserole; cover. Microwave at HIGH (100% power) 5 to 8 minutes or until crisp-tender. Drain. Stir in Italian seasoning, parsley, salt, pepper and tomatoes. Microwave, uncovered, at HIGH (100% power) 2 to 4 minutes or until tomatoes are hot. Sprinkle with cheese. Microwave 1 minute or until cheese melts.

Makes 6 servings

Nutrients per Serving:					
Calories	50	(30% of calories from fat)			
Total Fat	2 g	Dietary Fiber	2 g	Thiamine	<1 mg
Saturated Fat	1 g	Protein	4 g	Riboflavin	<1 mg
Cholesterol	5 mg	Calcium	94 mg	Niacin	1 mg
Sodium	64 mg	Iron	1 mg	Vitamin A	136 RE
Carbohydrate	5 g	Folate	49 µg	Vitamin C	63 mg

Dietary Exchanges: ½ Meat, 1 Vegetable

85 Country Bean Soup

Dried beans are full of protein, complex carbohydrates, fiber and B vitamins, which makes them a nutritious addition to any diet.

1¼ cups dried navy beans or lima beans
2½ cups water
4 ounces salt pork or fully cooked ham, chopped
¼ cup chopped onion
½ teaspoon dried oregano leaves, crushed
¼ teaspoon salt
¼ teaspoon ground ginger
¼ teaspoon dried sage, crushed
¼ teaspoon pepper
2 cups milk
2 tablespoons butter

Rinse navy beans. Place in large saucepan; add enough water to cover. Bring to a boil; reduce heat and simmer 2 minutes. Remove from heat; cover and let stand for 1 hour. (Or, cover beans with water and soak overnight.)

Drain; return beans to saucepan. Stir in 2½ cups water, salt pork, onion, oregano, salt, ginger, sage and pepper. Bring to a boil; reduce heat. Cover and simmer 2 to 2½ hours or until beans are tender. (If necessary, add more water during cooking time.) Add milk and butter, stirring until mixture is heated through and butter is melted. Season to taste with additional salt and pepper.

Makes 6 servings

Nutrients per Serving:

Calories	230	(27% of calories from fat)			
Total Fat	7 g	Dietary Fiber	<1 g	Thiamine	<1 mg
Saturated Fat	4 g	Protein	15 g	Riboflavin	<1 mg
Cholesterol	27 mg	Calcium	167 mg	Niacin	2 mg
Sodium	420 mg	Iron	2 mg	Vitamin A	86 RE
Carbohydrate	27 g	Folate	127 μg	Vitamin C	2 mg

Dietary Exchanges: 1½ Starch/Bread, 1 Meat, ½ Milk, 1 Fat

86 Mashed Squash

Winter squash, such as acorn squash, are densely packed with vitamin A. Just ½ cup contains more than a full day's supply.

1 medium acorn squash, halved, seeded
1 tablespoon maple syrup
½ teaspoon pumpkin pie spice
Butter flavored salt to taste (optional)
Pepper to taste

Preheat oven to 400°F. Place squash halves, cut sides down, on baking sheet. Bake 30 minutes or until tender. Scoop out squash into mixing bowl; beat with electric mixer. Stir in syrup, pumpkin pie spice, salt and pepper. Makes 4 servings

Nutrients per Serving:

Calories	70	(2% of calories from fat)			
Total Fat	<1 g	Dietary Fiber	2 g	Thiamine	<1 mg
Saturated Fat	<1 g	Protein	1 g	Riboflavin	<1 mg
Cholesterol	0 mg	Calcium	51 mg	Niacin	1 mg
Sodium	5 mg	Iron	1 mg	Vitamin A	44 RE
Carbohydrate	18 g	Folate	19 μg	Vitamin C	11 mg

Dietary Exchanges: 1 Starch/Bread

87 Broccoli Supreme

Broccoli is not only low in calories, but high in nutrition as well. One cup has all the vitamin A and twice the vitamin C you need each day.

2 packages (10 ounces) frozen chopped broccoli *or* spinach
1 cup ⅓-less-salt chicken broth, defatted
2 tablespoons low fat mayonnaise
2 teaspoons instant minced onion (optional)

Place broccoli in saucepan. Stir in chicken broth, mayonnaise and onion. Simmer, covered, stirring occasionally, until broccoli is tender. Uncover; continue to simmer, stirring occasionally, until most of the liquid has evaporated. Makes 3 servings

Nutrients per Serving:

Calories	76	(30% of calories from fat)			
Total Fat	3 g	Dietary Fiber	5 g	Thiamine	<1 mg
Saturated Fat	<1 g	Protein	5 g	Riboflavin	<1 mg
Cholesterol	3 mg	Calcium	85 mg	Niacin	1 mg
Sodium	60 mg	Iron	1 mg	Vitamin A	308 RE
Carbohydrate	9 g	Folate	92 μg	Vitamin C	65 mg

Dietary Exchanges: 2 Vegetable, ½ Fat

88 Crispy Vegetables with Orange Flavor

Eating tofu is a good way to incorporate protein into your diet without adding lots of fat, cholesterol or sodium.

1 tablespoon vegetable oil
2 cups diagonally sliced celery
1 cup broccoli flowerets
¾ cup red bell pepper, coarsely chopped
¼ cup sliced green onions
4 strips (2 × ½ inch) orange peel
1½ teaspoons ground ginger
1½ cups (about 8 ounces) firm tofu, cut into 1-inch pieces
1 tablespoon low sodium soy sauce
1½ cups water or no-salt-added tomato juice
1 packet low sodium vegetable bouillon
2 tablespoons cornstarch
6 ounces thin spaghetti, cooked
Orange slices (optional)

Heat oil in large nonstick skillet or wok. Add celery, broccoli, bell pepper, onions, orange peel and ginger. Cook until vegetables are crisp-tender, about 4 to 5 minutes, stirring occasionally. Meanwhile, combine tofu with soy sauce in medium bowl; set aside. Combine water, bouillon and cornstarch in measuring cup. Add cornstarch mixture to vegetable mixture; bring to a boil, stirring constantly until mixture is slightly thickened, about 1 minute. Gently stir in tofu mixture; cook until heated through, about 1 minute. Serve over cooked spaghetti. Garnish with quartered orange slices, if desired.

Makes 4 servings

Nutrients per Serving:

Calories	321	(25% of calories from fat)			
Total Fat	9 g	Dietary Fiber	3 g	Thiamine	1 mg
Saturated Fat	1 g	Protein	17 g	Riboflavin	<1 mg
Cholesterol	0 mg	Calcium	169 mg	Niacin	4 mg
Sodium	278 mg	Iron	9 mg	Vitamin A	104 RE
Carbohydrate	46 g	Folate	68 µg	Vitamin C	67 mg

Dietary Exchanges: 2 Starch/Bread, 1½ Meat, 2 Vegetable, 1 Fat

89 Dilled Green Beans

Green beans are a good source of iron, potassium, vitamin A and calcium.

1 package (10 ounces) frozen cut green beans
½ cup plus 2 tablespoons water
2 green onions, finely chopped
2 teaspoons cornstarch
1 teaspoon instant chicken bouillon granules
1 teaspoon cider vinegar
¼ teaspoon grated lime peel
¼ teaspoon dried dill weed
Dash pepper

Microwave Directions: Place beans and 2 tablespoons water in 1-quart microwavable casserole; cover. Microwave at HIGH (100% power) 4 to 7 minutes or until beans are tender, stirring after 3 minutes. Drain. Cover; set aside.

In small microwavable bowl or 2-cup measure, blend remaining ingredients. Microwave at HIGH (100% power) 1½ to 2 minutes or until clear and thickened. Pour over beans. Toss to coat.

Makes 4 servings

Nutrients per Serving:

Calories	40	(23% of calories from fat)			
Total Fat	1 g	Dietary Fiber	1 g	Thiamine	<1 mg
Saturated Fat	<1 g	Protein	2 g	Riboflavin	<1 mg
Cholesterol	0 mg	Calcium	35 mg	Niacin	1 mg
Sodium	365 mg	Iron	1 mg	Vitamin A	50 RE
Carbohydrate	7 g	Folate	7 µg	Vitamin C	7 mg

Dietary Exchanges: 2 Vegetable

Crispy Vegetables with Orange Flavor

Ratatouille

90 **R**atatouille

This Mediterranean dish is full of vitamins and minerals and it tastes great too.

½ **pound eggplant, cut into ½-inch cubes**
1 **small onion, sliced and separated into rings**
1 **small zucchini, thinly sliced**
½ **medium green bell pepper, chopped**
1 **tomato, cut into wedges**
1 **tablespoon grated Parmesan cheese**
1 **stalk celery, chopped**
¼ **teaspoon salt (optional)**
¼ **teaspoon dried chervil, crushed**
¼ **teaspoon dried oregano leaves, crushed**
⅛ **teaspoon instant minced garlic**
⅛ **teaspoon dried thyme, crushed**
  Dash ground pepper

Microwave Directions: Combine all ingredients in 2-quart microwavable casserole; cover. Microwave at HIGH (100% power) 7 to 10 minutes or until eggplant is translucent, stirring every 3 minutes.

Makes 6 servings

Nutrients per Serving:					
Calories	29	(15% of calories from fat)			
Total Fat	1 g	Dietary Fiber	2 g	Thiamine	<1 mg
Saturated Fat	<1 g	Protein	1 g	Riboflavin	<1 mg
Cholesterol	1 mg	Calcium	28 mg	Niacin	<1 mg
Sodium	29 mg	Iron	<1 mg	Vitamin A	29 RE
Carbohydrate	6 g	Folate	18 µg	Vitamin C	13 mg

Dietary Exchanges: 1 Vegetable

91 Broccoli & Cauliflower with Mustard Sauce

Broccoli and cauliflower are both cruciferous vegetables, which research now shows may have cancer-preventing properties.

2 cups broccoli flowerets
2 cups cauliflowerets
⅓ to ½ cup skim milk
1 tablespoon all-purpose flour
1½ teaspoons prepared mustard
¼ teaspoon salt (optional)
Dash garlic powder
Dash white pepper

Microwave Directions: Combine broccoli and cauliflower in microwavable baking dish. Cover. Microwave at HIGH (100% power) 8 to 11 minutes or until tender, stirring once. Drain; set aside.

Combine milk, flour, mustard, salt, garlic powder and pepper in medium microwavable bowl. Microwave at HIGH (100% power) 2 to 3 minutes or until thickened, stirring every minute. Pour over vegetables. Toss to coat.   Makes 4 servings

Nutrients per Serving:

Calories	40	(8% of calories from fat)			
Total Fat	<1 g	Dietary Fiber	2 g	Thiamine	<1 mg
Saturated Fat	<1 g	Protein	3 g	Riboflavin	<1 mg
Cholesterol	<1 mg	Calcium	63 mg	Niacin	1 mg
Sodium	55 mg	Iron	1 mg	Vitamin A	81 RE
Carbohydrate	7 g	Folate	66 µg	Vitamin C	77 mg

Dietary Exchanges: 1½ Vegetable

92 Delicious Apple Compote

Even though watermelon is mostly water, it does have beneficial nutrients, such as vitamins A and C as well as potassium.

2 Red or Golden Delicious Apples
2 cups seeded watermelon cubes
1 cup seedless grapes
1 orange, peeled, sliced and seeded
1 banana, peeled and sliced
2 cups chilled ginger ale
2 tablespoons lime juice

Halve and core apples; cut into bite-sized pieces. Toss with watermelon, grapes, orange and banana. Combine ginger ale and lime juice. Pour over fruit. Serve immediately.   Makes 6 servings

Nutrients per Serving:

Calories	120	(5% of calories from fat)			
Total Fat	1 g	Dietary Fiber	2 g	Thiamine	<1 mg
Saturated Fat	<1 g	Protein	1 g	Riboflavin	<1 mg
Cholesterol	0 mg	Calcium	23 mg	Niacin	<1 mg
Sodium	8 mg	Iron	<1 mg	Vitamin A	30 RE
Carbohydrate	30 g	Folate	14 µg	Vitamin C	25 mg

Dietary Exchanges: 2 Fruit

93 Rosemary Carrots

Carrots have been cultivated for their medicinal purposes as far back as the Greek and Roman empires. We now know it's the vitamin A that makes them so nutritionally valuable.

2 cups thinly sliced carrots
1 teaspoon low sodium instant chicken bouillon granules
2 tablespoons hot water
1 tablespoon packed brown sugar
¼ teaspoon dried rosemary, crushed
1 tablespoon chopped chives
⅛ teaspoon white pepper

Microwave Directions: Place carrots in 2-quart microwavable casserole. In small bowl or 2-cup measure, combine bouillon, water, sugar and seasonings. Pour over carrots. Toss to coat; cover. Microwave at HIGH (100% power) 5 to 8 minutes or until fork-tender, stirring once after half the cooking time.   Makes 4 servings

Nutrients per Serving:

Calories	39	(5% of calories from fat)			
Total Fat	<1 g	Dietary Fiber	2 g	Thiamine	<1 mg
Saturated Fat	<1 g	Protein	1 g	Riboflavin	<1 mg
Cholesterol	0 mg	Calcium	20 mg	Niacin	1 mg
Sodium	95 mg	Iron	<1 mg	Vitamin A	1,552 RE
Carbohydrate	9 g	Folate	8 µg	Vitamin C	6 mg

Dietary Exchanges: 1½ Vegetable

94 Glazed Fruit Kabobs

Fresh pineapple is not only tasty but nutritionally beneficial as well. It contains an enzyme that aids in digestion and is good for arteries and skin.

2 fresh California nectarines, halved, pitted and cut into 6 wedges
3 fresh California plums, halved, pitted and quartered
½ fresh pineapple, peeled and cut into 2-inch cubes
¼ cup packed brown sugar
2 tablespoons water
1½ teaspoons cornstarch
¾ teaspoon rum extract

Alternately thread fruit onto skewers. Combine sugar, water, cornstarch and rum extract in small saucepan. Bring to a boil, stirring constantly, until thickened and clear. Place fruit kabobs in shallow pan. Brush with glaze mixture. (This may be done ahead.) Grill kabobs about 4 to 5 inches from heat 6 to 8 minutes or until hot, turning once, brushing occasionally with glaze.   Makes 4 servings

Nutrients per Serving:

Calories	163	(4% of calories from fat)			
Total Fat	1 g	Dietary Fiber	3 g	Thiamine	<1 mg
Saturated Fat	<1 g	Protein	1 g	Riboflavin	<1 mg
Cholesterol	0 mg	Calcium	26 mg	Niacin	1 mg
Sodium	5 mg	Iron	1 mg	Vitamin A	59 RE
Carbohydrate	41 g	Folate	15 µg	Vitamin C	22 mg

Dietary Exchanges: 2½ Fruit

95 Spiced Pear-Cranberry Soup

If pears are bought while still hard, place them in a paper bag and leave at room temperature to ripen.

2 fresh California Bartlett pears, peeled and chopped
2 thin slices fresh ginger (optional)
¼ teaspoon ground cinnamon
⅛ teaspoon ground cloves
1½ cups low calorie cranberry juice cocktail
Plain low fat yogurt (optional)

Add pears, ginger, cinnamon and cloves to food processor or blender; process until smooth. With machine running, slowly add cranberry juice until

mixture is well blended. Garnish each serving with dollop of yogurt, if desired. Soup may be served warm or cold.   Makes 4 servings

Nutrients per Serving:

Calories	75	(4% of calories from fat)			
Total Fat	<1 g	Dietary Fiber	2 g	Thiamine	<1 mg
Saturated Fat	<1 g	Protein	<1 g	Riboflavin	<1 mg
Cholesterol	0 mg	Calcium	14 mg	Niacin	<1 mg
Sodium	2 mg	Iron	<1 mg	Vitamin A	2 RE
Carbohydrate	19 g	Folate	6 µg	Vitamin C	13 mg

Dietary Exchanges: 1 Fruit

96 Celery and Chickpea Curry with Apple

Chickpeas are higher in calories and fat than other dried beans and peas, but they are also higher in protein.

1 tablespoon vegetable oil
2 cups diagonally sliced celery
1 cup tart apple slices
½ cup chopped onion
2 teaspoons curry powder
1 teaspoon minced garlic
1 can (10½ ounces) chickpeas, rinsed and drained
1 can (8 ounces) stewed tomatoes, broken up
3 cups cooked brown rice

Heat oil in large skillet until hot. Add celery, apple, onion, curry and garlic; cook and stir until vegetables are crisp-tender, about 8 minutes. Stir in chickpeas and tomatoes. Bring to a boil; reduce heat and simmer, uncovered, until flavors are blended, about 5 minutes. Serve over cooked rice.

Makes 4 servings

Nutrients per Serving:

Calories	318	(18% of calories from fat)			
Total Fat	7 g	Dietary Fiber	9 g	Thiamine	<1 mg
Saturated Fat	1 g	Protein	9 g	Riboflavin	<1 mg
Cholesterol	0 mg	Calcium	98 mg	Niacin	3 mg
Sodium	500 mg	Iron	4 mg	Vitamin A	43 RE
Carbohydrate	59 g	Folate	30 µg	Vitamin C	18 mg

Dietary Exchanges: 3 Starch/Bread, 2 Vegetable, 1 Fat

97 Feta Pockets

Sprouts are seeds beginning to grow into plants. They use the carbohydrates in the seed pod for energy, which makes them very low in calories.

2 cups bean sprouts
1 small cucumber, chopped
½ cup (2 ounces) crumbled Wisconsin feta cheese
¼ cup plain low fat yogurt
1 tablespoon sesame seeds, toasted
¼ teaspoon pepper
2 pita bread rounds, cut in half
1 medium tomato, cut into 4 slices

In medium bowl, stir together sprouts, cucumber, cheese, yogurt, sesame seeds and pepper. Spoon mixture into pita bread halves. Place tomato slice on filling in each bread half.   Makes 4 servings

Nutrients per Serving:

Calories	145	(30% of calories from fat)				
Total Fat	5 g	Dietary Fiber	3 g	Thiamine	<1 mg
Saturated Fat	3 g	Protein	7 g	Riboflavin	<1 mg
Cholesterol	14 mg	Calcium	155 mg	Niacin	2 mg
Sodium	289 mg	Iron	2 mg	Vitamin A	46 RE
Carbohydrate	19 g	Folate	66 µg	Vitamin C	17 mg

Dietary Exchanges: 1 Starch/Bread, 1 Vegetable, 1 Fat

98 Sherried Carrots

The beta-carotene content of 1 pound of carrots is 4½ times a full day's supply.

1 package (1 pound) frozen small whole carrots, thawed
½ cup dry sherry
½ cup water
2 teaspoons margarine
Salt and pepper to taste (optional)
1 tablespoon minced fresh parsley or
1 teaspoon parsley flakes

Combine carrots, sherry, water, margarine, salt and pepper in shallow nonstick skillet. Simmer, covered, about 10 minutes or until carrots are crisp-tender.

Uncover and continue to simmer until liquid has reduced to a glaze. Sprinkle with parsley and serve.   Makes 4 servings

Nutrients per Serving:

Calories	98	(18% of calories from fat)				
Total Fat	2 g	Dietary Fiber	4 g	Thiamine	<1 mg
Saturated Fat	<1 g	Protein	1 g	Riboflavin	<1 mg
Cholesterol	0 mg	Calcium	36 mg	Niacin	1 mg
Sodium	90 mg	Iron	<1 mg	Vitamin A	2,035 RE
Carbohydrate	12 g	Folate	14 µg	Vitamin C	4 mg

Dietary Exchanges: 2 Vegetable, 1 Fat

99 Plum Ratatouille

The addition of plums to this classic recipe not only enriches the flavor but adds potassium, fiber and vitamin A as well.

2½ cups diced eggplant
2 cups sliced zucchini
1 onion, cut into wedges
1 tablespoon vegetable oil
2 cups diced tomatoes
2 cups fresh California plum wedges
2 teaspoons minced garlic
1½ teaspoons dried basil leaves, crushed
1 teaspoon dried oregano leaves, crushed
¼ teaspoon pepper
Fresh lemon juice

In large nonstick skillet, cook and stir eggplant, zucchini and onion in oil 15 minutes or until tender. Add remaining ingredients except lemon juice; reduce heat and cover. Cook, stirring occasionally until plums are tender, about 4 minutes. Drizzle with fresh lemon juice just before serving.   Makes 6 servings

Nutrients per Serving:

Calories	69	(30% of calories from fat)				
Total Fat	3 g	Dietary Fiber	3 g	Thiamine	<1 mg
Saturated Fat	<1 g	Protein	1 g	Riboflavin	<1 mg
Cholesterol	0 mg	Calcium	30 mg	Niacin	1 mg
Sodium	4 mg	Iron	1 mg	Vitamin A	29 RE
Carbohydrate	12 g	Folate	24 µg	Vitamin C	7 mg

Dietary Exchanges: 1 Vegetable, ½ Fruit, ½ Fat

Feta Pocket

100 Today's Slim Tuna Stuffed Tomatoes

Tuna contains omega-3 fatty acids, which are special fats that have been shown to lower blood cholesterol.

6 medium tomatoes
1 cup dry curd cottage cheese
½ cup plain low fat yogurt
¼ cup chopped cucumber
¼ cup chopped green bell pepper
¼ cup thinly sliced radishes
¼ cup chopped green onions
½ teaspoon dried basil leaves, crushed
⅛ teaspoon garlic powder
1 can (6½ ounces) tuna, packed in water,
    drained and flaked
    Lettuce leaves

Cut each tomato into 6 wedges, cutting to, but not through, base of each tomato. Refrigerate. In medium bowl, combine cottage cheese and yogurt; mix well. Stir in remaining ingredients except lettuce leaves. Place tomatoes on individual lettuce-lined plates; spread wedges apart. Spoon cottage cheese mixture into center of each tomato.
Makes 6 servings

Nutrients per Serving:

Calories	98	(12% of calories from fat)			
Total Fat	1 g	Dietary Fiber	2 g	Thiamine	<1 mg
Saturated Fat	<1 g	Protein	14 g	Riboflavin	<1 mg
Cholesterol	8 mg	Calcium	59 mg	Niacin	465 mg
Sodium	48 mg	Iron	1 mg	VitaminA	46,113 RE
Carbohydrate	9 g	Folate	29 µg	Vitamin C	4,635 mg

Dietary Exchanges: 1½ Meat, 1 Vegetable

101 Zucchini with Pimiento

For best flavor, buy small- to medium-size zucchini. Avoid large ones which can be stringy and flavorless.

2 cups thinly sliced zucchini
1 small onion, chopped
1 jar (2 ounces) pimiento, drained and
    diced
½ teaspoon salt (optional)
½ teaspoon dried oregano leaves, crushed
⅛ teaspoon garlic powder
⅛ teaspoon ground red pepper

Microwave Directions: In 2-quart microwavable casserole, combine all ingredients; cover. Microwave at HIGH (100% power) 6 to 7 minutes or until fork-tender, stirring after half the cooking time.
Makes 4 servings

Nutrients per Serving:

Calories	22	(8% of calories from fat)			
Total Fat	<1 g	Dietary Fiber	2 g	Thiamine	<1 mg
Saturated Fat	<1 g	Protein	1 g	Riboflavin	<1 mg
Cholesterol	0 mg	Calcium	20 mg	Niacin	<1 mg
Sodium	274 mg	Iron	1 mg	Vitamin A	58 RE
Carbohydrate	5 g	Folate	20 µg	Vitamin C	21 mg

Dietary Exchanges: 1 Vegetable

102 Apricot and Ricotta Stuffed Celery

Dried apricots are a tasty way to get vitamin A, fiber and potassium.

2½ cups (1½-inch) celery pieces
3 tablespoons coarsely chopped dried
    apricots
½ cup part-skim ricotta cheese
1½ teaspoons sugar
¼ teaspoon grated orange peel
⅛ teaspoon salt

Cut a thin lengthwise slice from bottom of each celery piece to prevent tipping; set aside. Add apricots to food processor or blender; process until finely chopped. Set aside 1 tablespoon for garnish. Add cheese, sugar, orange peel and salt to apricots; process until smooth. Fill celery pieces with cheese mixture. Cover and refrigerate up to 3 hours before serving. Just before serving, sprinkle with reserved chopped apricots.
Makes about 25 appetizers

Nutrients per Serving:

Calories	10	(27% of calories from fat)			
Total Fat	<1 g	Dietary Fiber	<1 g	Thiamine	<1 mg
Saturated Fat	<1 g	Protein	1 g	Riboflavin	<1 mg
Cholesterol	2 mg	Calcium	14 mg	Niacin	<1 mg
Sodium	26 mg	Iron	<1 mg	Vitamin A	11 RE
Carbohydrate	1 g	Folate	3 µg	Vitamin C	1 mg

Dietary Exchanges: Free food

Roasted Vegetables with Noodles

103 Honeyed Beets

Beets have more sugar than any other vegetable but are still low in calories at only 60 per cup.

¼ **cup unsweetened apple juice**
2 **tablespoons cider vinegar**
1 **tablespoon honey**
2 **teaspoons cornstarch**
2 **cans (8 ounces each) sliced beets, drained**
   Salt and pepper to taste (optional)

Combine apple juice, vinegar, honey and cornstarch in large nonstick saucepan. Cook, stirring occasionally, over medium heat until simmering. Stir in beets, salt and pepper. Simmer 3 minutes.

Makes 4 servings

Nutrients per Serving:

Calories	63	(2% of calories from fat)			
Total Fat	<1 g	Dietary Fiber	3 g	Thiamine	<1 mg
Saturated Fat	<1 g	Protein	1 g	Riboflavin	<1 mg
Cholesterol	0 mg	Calcium	18 mg	Niacin	<1 mg
Sodium	312 mg	Iron	2 mg	Vitamin A	1 RE
Carbohydrate	16 g	Folate	34 μg	Vitamin C	8 mg

Dietary Exchanges: ½ Fruit, 1½ Vegetable

104 Roasted Vegetables with Noodles

One of the vegetables in this delicious recipe is eggplant, which has almost as much fiber per serving as oat bran.

5 tablespoons soy sauce, divided
3 tablespoons peanut oil
2 tablespoons rice vinegar
2 cloves garlic, minced
1 teaspoon sugar
½ pound large fresh mushrooms
4 ounces shallots
1 medium zucchini, cut into 1-inch slices and halved
1 medium yellow squash, cut into 1-inch slices and halved
1 red bell pepper, cut into 1-inch pieces
1 yellow bell pepper, cut into 1-inch pieces
2 small Oriental eggplants, cut into ½-inch slices
8 ounces Chinese egg noodles or vermicelli, hot cooked and drained
1 tablespoon sesame oil

Preheat oven to 425°F. Combine 2 tablespoons soy sauce, peanut oil, vinegar, garlic and sugar in small bowl; mix well. Combine vegetables in shallow roasting pan (do not line pan with foil). Toss with soy sauce mixture to coat well. Roast vegetables 20 minutes or until browned and tender, stirring well after 10 minutes. Place noodles in large bowl. Toss hot noodles with remaining 3 tablespoons soy sauce and sesame oil. Toss roasted vegetables with noodle mixture; serve warm or at room temperature.

Makes 6 servings

Nutrients per Serving:

Calories	273	(30% of calories from fat)			
Total Fat	10 g	Dietary Fiber	2 g	Thiamine	<1 mg
Saturated Fat	1 g	Protein	6 g	Riboflavin	<1 mg
Cholesterol	0 mg	Calcium	34 mg	Niacin	3 mg
Sodium	867 mg	Iron	2 mg	Vitamin A	272 RE
Carbohydrate	42 g	Folate	38 μg	Vitamin C	35 mg

Dietary Exchanges: 2 Starch/Bread, 2 Vegetable, 2 Fat

105 Lemon Brussels Sprouts

Not only do Brussels sprouts look like miniature cabbages, they have similar nutritional values as well as lots of fiber and vitamin C.

1 package (10 ounces) frozen Brussels sprouts
1 tablespoon water
½ teaspoon lemon juice
¼ teaspoon grated lemon peel
   Dash pepper
   Dash ground thyme

Microwave Directions: Combine Brussels sprouts, water, lemon juice and lemon peel in 1-quart microwavable casserole; cover. Microwave at HIGH (100% power) 3 minutes. Stir to break apart; cover. Microwave at HIGH (100% power) 2 to 3 minutes or until Brussels sprouts are tender. Drain; sprinkle with pepper and thyme.   Makes 4 servings

Nutrients per Serving:

Calories	30	(7% of calories from fat)			
Total Fat	<1 g	Dietary Fiber	2 g	Thiamine	<1 mg
Saturated Fat	<1 g	Protein	3 g	Riboflavin	<1 mg
Cholesterol	0 mg	Calcium	17 mg	Niacin	<1 mg
Sodium	16 mg	Iron	1 mg	Vitamin A	42 RE
Carbohydrate	6 g	Folate	72 μg	Vitamin C	33 mg

Dietary Exchanges: 1 Vegetable

106 Creamy Carrot Soup

Whichever way they're prepared, sliced, steamed or puréed, carrots are one of the beat sources of vitamin A.

**3 cups water
4 cups sliced carrots
½ cup chopped onions
2 tablespoons packed brown sugar
2 teaspoons curry powder
2 cloves garlic, minced
⅛ teaspoon ground ginger
    Dash ground cinnamon
½ chicken flavor bouillon cube
½ cup skim milk**

In large saucepan, bring water to a boil. Add remaining ingredients except milk. Reduce heat to low; simmer 40 minutes or until carrots are tender. Remove from heat; pour mixture in batches into food processor or blender. Process until smooth. Return mixture to saucepan. Over low heat, stir in milk, heating until warm but not boiling. Serve warm.   Makes 6 servings

Nutrients per Serving:

Calories	69	(8% of calories from fat)			
Total Fat	1 g	Dietary Fiber	3 g	Thiamine	<1 mg
Saturated Fat	<1 g	Protein	2 g	Riboflavin	<1 mg
Cholesterol	<1 mg	Calcium	57 mg	Niacin	1 mg
Sodium	157 mg	Iron	1 mg	Vitamin A	2,075 RE
Carbohydrate	15 g	Folate	14 µg	Vitamin C	8 mg

Dietary Exchanges: 3 Vegetable

107 Dilled Brussels Sprouts

Brussels sprouts have as much vitamin C and iron as broccoli but twice the potassium, a regulator of heartbeat and blood pressure.

**1 package (10 ounces) frozen Brussels
    sprouts or 1 pint fresh Brussels
    sprouts
½ cup beef broth, defatted
1 teaspoon dill seed
1 teaspoon instant minced onion
    (optional)
    Salt and pepper to taste (optional)**

Combine all ingredients in saucepan; simmer, covered, 8 to 10 minutes, or until sprouts are nearly tender. Uncover and continue to simmer until most of the liquid has evaporated.   Makes 3 servings

Nutrients per Serving:

Calories	43	(10% of calories from fat)			
Total Fat	1 g	Dietary Fiber	3 g	Thiamine	<1 mg
Saturated Fat	<1 g	Protein	4 g	Riboflavin	<1 mg
Cholesterol	0 mg	Calcium	29 mg	Niacin	1 mg
Sodium	23 mg	Iron	1 mg	Vitamin A	56 RE
Carbohydrate	8 g	Folate	96 µg	Vitamin C	43 mg

Dietary Exchanges: 1½ Vegetable

108 Sesame-Honey Vegetable Casserole

Instead of taking vitamin supplements, get your vitamins the natural way—eat vegetables!

**1 package (16 ounces) frozen mixed
    vegetable medley, such as baby
    carrots, broccoli, onions and red
    peppers, thawed and drained
3 tablespoons honey
1 tablespoon sesame oil
1 tablespoon soy sauce
2 teaspoons sesame seeds**

Preheat oven to 350°F. Place vegetables in shallow, 1½-quart casserole.

Combine remaining ingredients; mix well. Drizzle evenly over vegetables. Bake 20 to 25 minutes or until vegetables are hot, stirring after 15 minutes.

Makes 4 to 6 servings

Nutrients per Serving:

Calories	176	(27% of calories from fat)			
Total Fat	5 g	Dietary Fiber	3 g	Thiamine	<1 mg
Saturated Fat	1 g	Protein	4 g	Riboflavin	<1 mg
Cholesterol	0 mg	Calcium	4 mg	Niacin	<1 mg
Sodium	298 mg	Iron	<1 mg	Vitamin A	<1 mg
Carbohydrate	28 g	Folate	1 µg	Vitamin C	0 mg

Dietary Exchanges: 5 Vegetable, 1 Fat

109 Red Cabbage with Apples

*The combination of cabbage and apples in this recipe
makes a great-tasting way to get lots of fiber.*

**1 small head red cabbage, shredded
2 large apples, peeled and thinly sliced
½ cup medium sliced onion
½ cup unsweetened apple juice
¼ cup lemon juice
2 tablespoons raisins
2 tablespoons brown sugar
Salt and pepper to taste (optional)**

Combine cabbage, apples, onion, apple juice, lemon
juice, raisins and brown sugar in large nonstick
saucepan. Simmer, covered, 30 minutes. Season
with salt and pepper.   Makes 8 servings

Nutrients per Serving:

Calories	68	(3% of calories from fat)			
Total Fat	<1 g	Dietary Fiber	2 g	Thiamine	<1 mg
Saturated Fat	<1 g	Protein	1 g	Riboflavin	<1 mg
Cholesterol	0 mg	Calcium	37 mg	Niacin	<1 mg
Sodium	13 mg	Iron	1 mg	Vitamin A	9 RE
Carbohydrate	17 g	Folate	37 μg	Vitamin C	33 mg

Dietary Exchanges: ½ Fruit, 1½ Vegetable

110 Quick Creamed Cauliflower

*Another cruciferous vegetable with links to cancer
prevention, cauliflower is low in calories, with only
30 calories per cup.*

**1 package (10 ounces) frozen cauliflower
½ cup chicken broth, defatted
½ cup evaporated skim milk
2 tablespoons all-purpose flour
Salt and pepper to taste (optional)
Paprika (optional)**

Combine cauliflower and chicken broth in saucepan.
Simmer, covered, 10 to 12 minutes or until
cauliflower is tender. Combine milk and flour; mix

well. Stir into saucepan. Cook and stir until sauce
simmers and bubbles. Sprinkle with salt, pepper
and paprika before serving.   Makes 3 servings

Nutrients per Serving:

Calories	74	(6% of calories from fat)			
Total Fat	1 g	Dietary Fiber	2 g	Thiamine	<1 mg
Saturated Fat	<1 g	Protein	6 g	Riboflavin	<1 mg
Cholesterol	2 mg	Calcium	140 mg	Niacin	1 mg
Sodium	122 mg	Iron	1 mg	Vitamin A	52 RE
Carbohydrate	13 g	Folate	44 μg	Vitamin C	30 mg

Dietary Exchanges: ½ Milk, 1 Vegetable

111 French Carrot Medley

*The combination of carrots and orange is a classic.
The flavors complement each other and best of all,
it's healthy.*

**2 cups fresh or frozen sliced carrots
¾ cup unsweetened orange juice
1 can (4 ounces) sliced mushrooms,
   undrained
4 ribs celery, sliced
2 tablespoons chopped onion
½ teaspoon dill weed
Salt and pepper to taste (optional)
2 teaspoons cornstarch
¼ cup cold water**

Combine all ingredients except cornstarch and
water in medium saucepan. Simmer, covered, 12 to
15 minutes or until carrots are tender. Combine
cornstarch with water in small bowl. Stir into
vegetable mixture; cook and stir until mixture
thickens and bubbles.   Makes 6 servings

Nutrients per Serving:

Calories	42	(4% of calories from fat)			
Total Fat	<1 g	Dietary Fiber	2 g	Thiamine	<1 mg
Saturated Fat	<1 g	Protein	1 g	Riboflavin	<1 mg
Cholesterol	0 mg	Calcium	27 mg	Niacin	1 mg
Sodium	118 mg	Iron	1 mg	Vitamin A	1,040 RE
Carbohydrate	10 g	Folate	33 μg	Vitamin C	16 mg

Dietary Exchanges: 1 Vegetable, ½ Fruit

[112] **B**russels Sprouts in Orange Sauce

Brussels sprouts are high in fiber and vitamin C. They are also a good source of protein, vitamin A, potassium, iron and calcium.

4 cups fresh Brussels sprouts
1 can (6 ounces) unsweetened orange juice
½ cup water
½ teaspoon cornstarch
¼ teaspoon ground cinnamon
   Salt and pepper to taste (optional)

Combine Brussels sprouts, orange juice, water, cornstarch and cinnamon in saucepan. Simmer, covered, 6 to 7 minutes until sprouts are nearly tender. Uncover and continue to simmer, stirring occasionally, until most of the liquid has evaporated. Season with salt and pepper, if desired.

Makes 4 servings

Nutrients per Serving:

Calories	106	(5% of calories from fat)			
Total Fat	1 g	Dietary Fiber	9 g	Thiamine	<1 mg
Saturated Fat	<1 g	Protein	7 g	Riboflavin	<1 mg
Cholesterol	0 mg	Calcium	90 mg	Niacin	2 mg
Sodium	52 mg	Iron	3 mg	Vitamin A	186 RE
Carbohydrate	23 g	Folate	146 µg	Vitamin C	187 mg

Dietary Exchanges: ½ Fruit, 3 Vegetable

[113] **C**runchy Apple Stir-Fry

Stir-frying, because of its quick cooking and low moisture, is one of the best ways to prepare vegetables to retain their nutritional value.

1 cup thinly sliced carrots
½ cup sliced onion
1 teaspoon dried basil, crushed
1½ teaspoons vegetable oil
1 cup fresh or frozen snow peas
1 tablespoon water
1 medium Washington Golden Delicious or Criterion Apple, halved, cored and thinly sliced

Stir-fry carrots, onion and basil in oil in nonstick skillet until carrots are tender. Stir in snow peas and water; stir-fry 2 minutes. Remove from heat; stir in apple slices. Serve hot.   Makes 4 servings

Nutrients per Serving:

Calories	71	(24% of calories from fat)			
Total Fat	2 g	Dietary Fiber	3 g	Thiamine	<1 mg
Saturated Fat	<1 g	Protein	2 g	Riboflavin	<1 mg
Cholesterol	0 mg	Calcium	37 mg	Niacin	1 mg
Sodium	12 mg	Iron	1 mg	Vitamin A	784 RE
Carbohydrate	13 g	Folate	24 µg	Vitamin C	28 mg

Dietary Exchanges: 1 Vegetable, ½ Fruit, ½ Fat

[114] **H**arvard Beets

Not only are beets low in calories, they're loaded with fiber. One cup of beets has 3.4 grams of fiber, about the same amount found in 1½ cups of cooked oatmeal.

2 teaspoons cornstarch
¼ teaspoon salt (optional)
   Dash pepper
   Dash ground allspice
¼ teaspoon grated orange peel
2 tablespoons cider vinegar
1 can (16 ounces) sliced beets, drained, ⅓ cup liquid reserved
1 tablespoon orange juice

Microwave Directions: Combine cornstarch, salt, pepper, allspice and orange peel in 1-quart microwavable casserole. Blend in vinegar, beet liquid and orange juice.

Microwave at HIGH (100% power) 1¾ to 2½ minutes or until clear and thickened, stirring every minute. Add beets. Microwave at HIGH (100% power) 1 to 4 minutes or until beets are thoroughly heated.   Makes 4 servings

Nutrients per Serving:

Calories	42	(3% of calories from fat)			
Total Fat	<1 g	Dietary Fiber	3 g	Thiamine	<1 mg
Saturated Fat	<1 g	Protein	1 g	Riboflavin	<1 mg
Cholesterol	0 mg	Calcium	18 mg	Niacin	<1 mg
Sodium	312 mg	Iron	2 mg	Vitamin A	2 RE
Carbohydrate	10 g	Folate	36 µg	Vitamin C	10 mg

Dietary Exchanges: 2 Vegetable

Harvard Beets

115 Fruit Soup

Nectarines are a member of the peach family but are not, as commonly believed, a cross between a peach and a plum.

5 fresh California nectarines, peeled, halved, pitted and diced
1 cup plain low fat yogurt
½ cup low fat milk
1 tablespoon sugar
1 teaspoon almond extract
¼ teaspoon curry powder
½ cup diced strawberries
Mint leaves (optional)

Reserve ½ cup nectarines. Add remaining nectarines, yogurt, milk, sugar, almond extract and curry to blender; blend until smooth. Stir in reserved nectarines and strawberries. Refrigerate; garnish with mint.   Makes 6 servings

Nutrients per Serving:

Calories	103	(13% of calories from fat)			
Total Fat	2 g	Dietary Fiber	2 g	Thiamine	<1 mg
Saturated Fat	1 g	Protein	4 g	Riboflavin	<1 mg
Cholesterol	4 mg	Calcium	102 mg	Niacin	1 mg
Sodium	37 mg	Iron	<1 mg	Vitamin A	104 RE
Carbohydrate	20 g	Folate	12 µg	Vitamin C	14 mg

Dietary Exchanges: ½ Milk, 1 Fruit

[116] Apple Slices with Citrus-Yogurt Dip

The colored peel of citrus is where a lot of flavor is; it is also a good source of vitamins.

2 to 3 Empire apples, cored and sliced
¼ cup lemon juice
1 cup plain low fat yogurt
2 tablespoons honey
1 tablespoon frozen orange juice
    concentrate, thawed
1 teaspoon grated orange peel
½ teaspoon grated lemon peel

Dip apple slices in lemon juice to prevent browning; set aside. Combine remaining ingredients in small bowl. Cover; refrigerate thoroughly. Arrange apple slices on platter; serve with dip.   Makes 1¼ cups

Nutrients per Serving:					
Calories	24	(8% of calories from fat)			
Total Fat	<1 g	Dietary Fiber	<1 g	Thiamine	<1 mg
Saturated Fat	<1 g	Protein	1 g	Riboflavin	<1 mg
Cholesterol	1 mg	Calcium	23 mg	Niacin	<1 mg
Sodium	8 mg	Iron	<1 mg	Vitamin A	3 RE
Carbohydrate	5 g	Folate	3 μg	Vitamin C	4 mg

Dietary Exchanges: ½ Fruit

[117] Mint-Glazed Carrots & Snow Peas

Snow peas, unlike regular English peas, can be eaten pod and all, which makes them higher in fiber than regular peas.

1 tablespoon margarine
3 medium carrots, thinly sliced diagonally
½ pound fresh snow peas, trimmed
2 tablespoons sugar
1 tablespoon fresh lemon juice
1 tablespoon chopped fresh mint leaves
    or 1 teaspoon dried mint, crushed

In large, nonstick skillet, melt margarine over medium heat. Cook and stir carrots 3 to 4 minutes. Add peas, sugar, lemon juice and mint. Cook and stir 1 to 2 minutes until vegetables are glazed and crisp-tender.   Makes 4 servings

Nutrients per Serving:					
Calories	94	(28% of calories from fat)			
Total Fat	3 g	Dietary Fiber	3 g	Thiamine	<1 mg
Saturated Fat	1 g	Protein	2 g	Riboflavin	<1 mg
Cholesterol	0 mg	Calcium	38 mg	Niacin	1 mg
Sodium	54 mg	Iron	1 mg	Vitamin A	1,561 RE
Carbohydrate	16 g	Folate	24 μg	Vitamin C	33 mg

Dietary Exchanges: 3 Vegetables, ½ Fat

[118] Oriental Stir-Fried Vegetables

The fresh vegetables in this recipe make it not only pleasing to the palate, but it's also loaded with vitamin C, fiber and potassium.

1 pound broccoli, asparagus spears,
    green beans or sliced zucchini
2 cups sliced carrots
1 onion, thinly sliced
1 can (2 ounces) sliced mushrooms,
    undrained
2 tablespoons low sodium soy sauce,
    white wine or water (optional)
2 teaspoons safflower oil

Chop broccoli into 1½-inch pieces. Combine broccoli, carrots, onion, mushrooms, soy sauce and oil in nonstick skillet. Cook and stir, uncovered, until liquid has evaporated and broccoli is crisp-tender.   Makes 4 servings

Nutrients per Serving:					
Calories	92	(24% of calories from fat)			
Total Fat	3 g	Dietary Fiber	6 g	Thiamine	<1 mg
Saturated Fat	<1 g	Protein	5 g	Riboflavin	<1 mg
Cholesterol	0 mg	Calcium	78 mg	Niacin	1 mg
Sodium	81 mg	Iron	1 mg	Vitamin A	1,722 RE
Carbohydrate	15 g	Folate	97 μg	Vitamin C	113 mg

Dietary Exchanges: 3 Vegetable, ½ Fat

Apple Slices with Citrus-Yogurt Dip

MEATS

119 Pork Tenderloin with Sherry-Mushroom Sauce

A serving of cooked pork tenderloin (3 ounces) has only about 140 calories and 4 grams of fat. The leanest cuts of pork are tenderloin, loin roast and loin chops.

1 pork tenderloin (1 to 1½ pounds)
1½ cups chopped fresh mushrooms or shiitake mushroom caps
2 tablespoons sliced green onion
1 clove garlic, minced
1 tablespoon reduced calorie margarine
1 tablespoon cornstarch
1 tablespoon chopped fresh parsley
½ teaspoon dried thyme leaves, crushed Dash ground black pepper
⅓ cup water
1 tablespoon dry sherry
½ teaspoon beef bouillon granules

Preheat oven to 375°F. Place pork on rack in shallow baking pan. Insert meat thermometer into thickest part of tenderloin. Roast, uncovered, 25 to 35 minutes or until pork is 155°F. Let stand, covered, 5 to 10 minutes. Slice pork.

Cook and stir mushrooms, green onion and garlic in margarine in small saucepan over medium heat until tender. Stir in cornstarch, parsley, thyme and pepper. Stir in water, sherry and bouillon granules. Cook and stir until sauce boils and thickens. Cook and stir 2 minutes more. Serve with pork.

Makes 4 servings

Nutrients per Serving:

Calories	179	(30% of calories from fat)		
Total Fat	6 g	Dietary Fiber	<1 g	Thiamine	1 mg
Saturated Fat	2 g	Protein	26 g	Riboflavin	<1 mg
Cholesterol	81 mg	Calcium	16 mg	Niacin	5 mg
Sodium	205 mg	Iron	2 mg	Vitamin A	53 RE
Carbohydrate	4 g	Folate	13 µg	Vitamin C	3 mg

Dietary Exchanges: 3 Meat, 1 Vegetable

120 Fragrant Beef with Garlic Sauce

Beef is an excellent source of complete protein, which means it supplies all of the essential amino acids necessary for growth.

1 boneless beef top sirloin steak, cut 1 inch thick (about 1¼ pounds)
⅓ cup low sodium teriyaki sauce
10 large cloves garlic, peeled
½ cup ⅓-less-salt beef broth

Place beef in large resealable plastic food storage bag. Pour teriyaki sauce over beef. Close bag securely; turn to coat. Marinate in refrigerator 30 minutes or up to 4 hours.

Combine garlic and broth in small saucepan. Bring to a boil over high heat. Reduce heat to medium. Simmer, uncovered, 5 minutes. Cover and simmer 8 to 9 minutes until garlic is softened. Transfer to food processor or blender; process until smooth.

Meanwhile, drain beef; reserve marinade. Place beef on rack of broiler pan. Brush with half reserved marinade. Broil 5 to 6 inches from heat 5 minutes. Turn beef over; brush with remaining marinade. Broil 5 minutes.

Slice beef thinly; serve with garlic sauce.

Makes 4 servings

Nutrients per Serving:

Calories	212	(24% of calories from fat)		
Total Fat	6 g	Dietary Fiber	<1 g	Thiamine	<1 mg
Saturated Fat	2 g	Protein	33 g	Riboflavin	<1 mg
Cholesterol	67 mg	Calcium	47 mg	Niacin	6 mg
Sodium	1106 mg	Iron	4 mg	Vitamin A	0 RE
Carbohydrate	6 g	Folate	17 µg	Vitamin C	2 mg

Dietary Exchanges: 4 Meat

Pork Tenderloin with Sherry-Mushroom Sauce

121 Peppercorn Beef Kabobs

Sirloin steaks are cut from the beef loin, which is where the most tender cuts of meat are from.

1 pound boneless beef sirloin steak, cut 1 inch thick
1½ teaspoons black peppercorns, crushed
½ teaspoon salt
½ teaspoon paprika
1 clove garlic, minced
1 medium onion, cut into 12 wedges
Cherry tomato halves (optional)

Cut beef steak into 1-inch pieces. Combine peppercorns, salt, paprika and garlic in shallow dish. Add beef; toss to coat. Thread an equal number of beef pieces onto each of four 12-inch skewers along with 3 onion wedges. Place kabobs on rack in broiler pan. Broil 3 to 4 inches from heat source. Broil 9 to 12 minutes, turning occasionally. Garnish with tomatoes, if desired.

Makes 4 servings

Nutrients per Serving:

Calories	158	(26% of calories from fat)			
Total Fat	4 g	Dietary Fiber	1 g	Thiamine	<1 mg
Saturated Fat	2 g	Protein	25 g	Riboflavin	<1 mg
Cholesterol	54 mg	Calcium	33 mg	Niacin	4 mg
Sodium	339 mg	Iron	3 mg	Vitamin A	16 RE
Carbohydrate	3 g	Folate	15 μg	Vitamin C	3 mg

Dietary Exchanges: 3 Meat

122 Honey-Glazed Pork

Pork is much leaner today than it was 30 years ago. The pork industry, through selective breeding, has been able to produce meat that is lower in calories and cholesterol.

1 large or 2 small pork tenderloins (about 1¼ pounds total weight)
¼ cup low sodium soy sauce
2 cloves garlic, minced
3 tablespoons honey
2 tablespoons packed brown sugar
1 teaspoon minced fresh ginger
1 tablespoon toasted sesame seeds*

Place pork in large resealable plastic food storage bag. Combine soy sauce and garlic in small cup; pour over pork. Close bag securely; turn to coat. Marinate in refrigerator up to 2 hours.

Preheat oven to 400°F. Drain pork; reserve 1 tablespoon marinade. Combine honey, brown sugar, ginger and reserved marinade in small bowl.

Place pork in shallow, foil-lined roasting pan. Brush with half the honey mixture. Roast 10 minutes. Turn pork over; brush with remaining honey mixture and sprinkle with sesame seeds. Roast 10 minutes for small or 15 minutes for large tenderloin or until internal temperature reaches 155°F when tested with meat thermometer inserted in thickest part of pork.

Let pork stand, tented with foil, on cutting board 5 minutes. (Temperature will rise to 160°F.) Pour pan juices into gravy boat. Cut pork across the grain into ½-inch slices. Serve with pan juices.

Makes 4 servings

*To toast sesame seeds, spread seeds in small skillet. Shake skillet over medium heat 2 minutes or until seeds begin to pop and turn golden.

Nutrients per Serving:

Calories	203	(21% of calories from fat)			
Total Fat	5 g	Dietary Fiber	<1 g	Thiamine	1 mg
Saturated Fat	1 g	Protein	31 g	Riboflavin	<1 mg
Cholesterol	80 mg	Calcium	21 mg	Niacin	7 mg
Sodium	380 mg	Iron	2 mg	Vitamin A	3 RE
Carbohydrate	8 g	Folate	9 μg	Vitamin C	1 mg

Dietary Exchanges: 3½ Meat

Peppercorn Beef Kabobs

123 Ground Beef, Spinach and Barley Soup

This recipe contains less sodium because it uses a small amount of beef bouillon granules and a little salt instead of regular beef broth. If you are closely watching your sodium intake, omit the salt.

12 ounces 95% lean ground beef
4 cups water
1 can (14½ ounces) no-salt-added stewed tomatoes, undrained
1½ cups thinly sliced carrots
1 cup chopped onion
½ cup quick-cooking barley
1½ teaspoons beef bouillon granules
1½ teaspoons dried thyme leaves, crushed
1 teaspoon dried oregano leaves, crushed
½ teaspoon garlic powder
¼ teaspoon pepper
⅛ teaspoon salt
3 cups torn stemmed washed spinach leaves

Cook beef in large saucepan over medium heat until no longer pink, stirring to separate. Rinse beef under warm water; drain. Return beef to saucepan; add water, stewed tomatoes with liquid, carrots, onion, barley, bouillon granules, thyme, oregano, garlic powder, pepper and salt.

Bring to a boil over high heat. Reduce heat to medium-low. Cover and simmer 12 to 15 minutes or until barley and vegetables are tender, stirring occasionally. Stir in spinach; cook until spinach starts to wilt.   Makes 4 servings

Nutrients per Serving:

Calories	265	(19% of calories from fat)			
Total Fat	6 g	Dietary Fiber	8 g	Thiamine	<1 mg
Saturated Fat	2 g	Protein	22 g	Riboflavin	<1 mg
Cholesterol	22 mg	Calcium	96 mg	Niacin	6 mg
Sodium	512 mg	Iron	5 mg	Vitamin A	1,523 RE
Carbohydrate	33 g	Folate	118 μg	Vitamin C	42 mg

Dietary Exchanges: 1 Starch/Bread, 2 Meat

124 Oriental Lamb-Lentil Stew

Unlike most dried beans, lentils don't require pre-soaking so they're a snap to use when you need something quick.

2 tablespoons vegetable oil
1 pound boneless fresh American lamb (leg or shoulder), trimmed and cut into ¾-inch cubes
4 cups reduced sodium beef broth or lamb stock
1 cup chopped onion
2 tablespoons tomato paste
3 cloves garlic, minced
2 bay leaves
1 teaspoon dried oregano leaves, crushed
⅛ teaspoon ground pepper
1 cup dried lentils
½ cup sliced celery
2 medium carrots, cut into 1-inch pieces
3 cups hot cooked rice

Heat oil in large skillet or wok until hot. Add lamb cubes and stir-fry until slightly brown; remove from skillet. Drain; return lamb to skillet. Stir in broth, onion, tomato paste, garlic, bay leaves, oregano and pepper. Bring to a boil; reduce heat and simmer, covered 15 minutes. Rinse lentils; add to lamb mixture. Stir in celery and carrots. Cover; simmer about 45 minutes more or until lamb and vegetables are tender. Remove and discard bay leaves. Serve over rice.   Makes 6 servings

Nutrients per Serving:

Calories	427	(20% of calories from fat)			
Total Fat	9 g	Dietary Fiber	4 g	Thiamine	<1 mg
Saturated Fat	2 g	Protein	27 g	Riboflavin	<1 mg
Cholesterol	38 mg	Calcium	73 mg	Niacin	7 mg
Sodium	398 mg	Iron	7 mg	Vitamin A	694 RE
Carbohydrate	59 g	Folate	224 μg	Vitamin C	9 mg

Dietary Exchanges: 1½ Starch/Bread, 3½ Meat, 1 Vegetable, ½ Fat

Ground Beef, Spinach and Barley Soup

125 Margarita Pork Kabobs

In the U.S., cilantro is the name used to describe the fresh leaves of the coriander plant, but the dried seeds are called coriander.

1 cup margarita drink mix *or* 1 cup lime juice, 4 teaspoons sugar and ½ teaspoon salt
1 teaspoon ground coriander
1 clove garlic, minced
1 pound pork tenderloin, cut into 1-inch cubes
2 tablespoons margarine, softened
2 teaspoons lime juice
⅛ teaspoon sugar
1 tablespoon minced fresh parsley
1 large green or red bell pepper, cut into 1-inch cubes
2 ears corn, cut into 8 pieces

Combine margarita mix, coriander and garlic in small bowl. Place pork cubes in large resealable plastic food storage bag; pour marinade over pork. Close bag securely; turn to coat. Marinate for at least 30 minutes. Combine margarine, lime juice, sugar and parsley in small bowl; set aside. Thread pork cubes onto skewers, alternating with pieces of bell pepper and corn. (If using bamboo skewers, soak in water 20 to 30 minutes before using to prevent them from burning). Grill over hot coals, basting with margarine mixture, for 15 to 20 minutes, turning frequently.   Makes 4 servings

Nutrients per Serving:

Calories	298	(27% of calories from fat)			
Total Fat	9 g	Dietary Fiber	2 g	Thiamine	1 mg
Saturated Fat	2 g	Protein	26 g	Riboflavin	<1 mg
Cholesterol	64 mg	Calcium	18 mg	Niacin	6 mg
Sodium	309 mg	Iron	2 mg	Vitamin A	102 RE
Carbohydrate	28 g	Folate	31 µg	Vitamin C	23 mg

Dietary Exchanges: 1 Starch/Bread, 3 Meat, 1 Fruit

126 Wild Rice, Snow Peas and Pork Stir-Fry

The variety of sliced vegetables in this recipe lend crunch, color and vitamin C.

2 tablespoons canola oil
½ pound pork tenderloin, sliced ¼ inch thick
1 cup sliced celery
1 cup sliced green onions
1 cup sliced fresh mushrooms
1 can (8 ounces) sliced water chestnuts
½ pound fresh or frozen thawed snow peas or sugar snap peas
1 tablespoon grated fresh ginger
2 cups cooked wild rice
1 tablespoon cornstarch
1 tablespoon dry sherry
3 tablespoons low sodium soy sauce
½ teaspoon salt
  Cashews, sunflower kernels or carrots (optional)

Heat oil in heavy skillet over high heat. Add pork; cook and stir 2 minutes until meat is no longer pink. Add celery, green onions, mushrooms, water chestnuts, snowpeas and ginger. Cook and stir 5 minutes over high heat until vegetables are crisp-tender. Stir in wild rice until evenly blended. Combine cornstarch, sherry, soy sauce and salt in small saucepan; cook and stir about 1 minute or until thickened. Add to skillet. Toss mixture together to coat evenly with glaze. Garnish with cashews, sunflower kernels or carrots.

Makes 6 servings

Nutrients per Serving:

Calories	201	(28% of calories from fat)			
Total Fat	7 g	Dietary Fiber	3 g	Thiamine	<1 mg
Saturated Fat	1 g	Protein	13 g	Riboflavin	<1 mg
Cholesterol	27 mg	Calcium	42 mg	Niacin	3 mg
Sodium	523 mg	Iron	3 mg	Vitamin A	75 RE
Carbohydrate	24 g	Folate	46 µg	Vitamin C	31 mg

Dietary Exchanges: 1 Starch/Bread, 1 Meat, 1 Vegetable, 1 Fat

Vegetable Spaghetti Sauce with Meatballs

127 Orange-Pepper Steaks

Beef is an excellent source of zinc, a mineral which is important for proper growth and metabolism.

2 teaspoons coarsely ground black pepper
4 beef tenderloin steaks, cut 1 inch thick
½ cup orange marmalade
4 teaspoons cider vinegar
½ teaspoon ground ginger
4 cups hot cooked rice

Press pepper evenly onto both sides of beef steaks. Place steaks on rack in broiler pan. Combine marmalade, vinegar and ginger in small bowl. Brush tops of steaks with half the marmalade mixture. Broil steaks 2 to 3 inches from heat, 10 to 15 minutes, turning once and brushing with remaining marmalade mixture. Serve over rice.

Makes 4 servings

Nutrients per Serving:

Calories	508	(16% of calories from fat)			
Total Fat	9 g	Dietary Fiber	2 g	Thiamine	<1 mg
Saturated Fat	3 g	Protein	33 g	Riboflavin	<1 mg
Cholesterol	83 mg	Calcium	42 mg	Niacin	6 mg
Sodium	70 mg	Iron	6 mg	Vitamin A	2 RE
Carbohydrate	74 g	Folate	27 μg	Vitamin C	4 mg

Dietary Exchanges: 3 Starch/Bread, 3 Meat, 2 Fruit

128 Vegetable Spaghetti Sauce with Meatballs

Herbs are a good way to add flavor to foods without adding calories, sodium or fat. This recipe uses Italian seasoning, which is a blend of herbs and spices including oregano, basil, red pepper, rosemary and garlic powder.

1½ cups sliced fresh mushrooms
½ cup chopped onion plus 2 tablespoons finely chopped onion
½ cup chopped carrot
½ cup chopped green bell pepper
2 cloves garlic, minced
2 cans (14½ ounces *each*) no-salt-added stewed tomatoes, undrained
1 can (6 ounces) no-salt-added tomato paste
2½ teaspoons dried Italian seasoning, divided
½ teaspoon salt
¼ teaspoon black pepper
1 egg white
2 tablespoons fine dry bread crumbs
8 ounces 95% lean ground beef
4 cups hot cooked spaghetti

Preheat oven to 375°F. Coat large saucepan with nonstick cooking spray; heat over medium heat. Add mushrooms, ½ cup onion, carrot, bell pepper and garlic. Cook and stir 4 to 5 minutes or until vegetables are crisp-tender. Stir in stewed tomatoes with liquid, tomato paste, 2 teaspoons Italian seasoning, salt and black pepper. Bring to a boil over medium-high heat. Reduce heat to medium-low. Cover and simmer 20 minutes, stirring occasionally.

Combine egg white, bread crumbs, remaining 2 tablespoons onion and remaining ½ teaspoon Italian seasoning in medium bowl. Add beef; mix until well blended. Shape to form 16 meatballs. Place in 11 × 7-inch baking pan. Bake 18 to 20 minutes or until beef is no longer pink. Drain on paper towels.

Stir meatballs into sauce. Return sauce to a boil; reduce heat. Simmer, uncovered, about 10 minutes more or until sauce slightly thickens, stirring occasionally. Serve over spaghetti.

Makes 4 servings

Nutrients per Serving:

Calories	341	(13% of calories from fat)			
Total Fat	5 g	Dietary Fiber	7 g	Thiamine	<1 mg
Saturated Fat	2 g	Protein	21 g	Riboflavin	1 mg
Cholesterol	25 mg	Calcium	74 mg	Niacin	7 mg
Sodium	381 mg	Iron	5 mg	Vitamin A	593 RE
Carbohydrate	56 g	Folate	62 μg	Vitamin C	71 mg

Dietary Exchanges: 3½ Starch/Bread, 1½ Meat, 3 Vegetable

129 Beef Steaks with Peppercorn Wine Sauce

This recipe is a snap to make and is very low in calories.

4 beef eye round steaks, cut 1 inch thick
1½ teaspoons cornstarch
1 cup beef broth
⅛ teaspoon dried thyme leaves, crushed
1 small bay leaf
2 tablespoons dry red wine
¼ teaspoon black peppercorns, crushed

Heat large heavy skillet over medium heat 5 minutes. Place beef steaks in skillet; cook 8 to 10 minutes, turning once. Dissolve cornstarch in broth in small saucepan. Bring to a boil; cook until slightly thickened, about 1 minute. Stir in thyme and bay leaf. Reduce heat to medium and cook until mixture reduces to ½ cup, about 5 minutes. Stir in wine and peppercorns; cook 3 minutes, stirring occasionally. Remove and discard bay leaf. Spoon sauce over steaks.   Makes 4 servings

Nutrients per Serving:

Calories	155	(25% of calories from fat)			
Total Fat	4 g	Dietary Fiber	<1 g	Thiamine	<1 mg
Saturated Fat	2 g	Protein	25 g	Riboflavin	<1 mg
Cholesterol	59 mg	Calcium	10 mg	Niacin	4 mg
Sodium	253 mg	Iron	2 mg	Vitamin A	1 RE
Carbohydrate	1 g	Folate	7 μg	Vitamin C	<1 mg

Dietary Exchanges: 3 Meat

130 Apple-icious Lamb Kabobs

Lamb is a great meat for the grill, and combined with the flavor of apple makes a perfect barbecue meal.

1 cup apple juice or cider
2 tablespoons Worcestershire sauce
½ teaspoon lemon pepper
2 cloves garlic, peeled and sliced
1½ pounds fresh American lamb (leg or shoulder), cut into 1¼-inch cubes
    Apple Barbecue Sauce (recipe follows)
1 large apple, cut into 12 wedges
    Assorted vegetables, such as green or red bell pepper, onion or summer squash, cut into wedges

Combine apple juice, Worcestershire sauce, lemon pepper and garlic in large resealable plastic food storage bag or nonmetal container. Add lamb cubes and coat well. To marinate, place in refrigerator for 2 to 24 hours.

Prepare Apple Barbecue Sauce. Preheat grill or broiler. Remove meat from marinade and thread onto skewers, alternating meat, apple and vegetables.

To grill, place kabobs 4 inches from medium coals. Cook about 10 to 12 minutes, turning occasionally and brushing with Apple Barbecue Sauce. To broil, place kabobs on broiler pan which has been sprayed with nonstick cooking spray. Broil lamb 4 inches from heat. Cook about 10 to 12 minutes for

medium-rare, turning occasionally and brushing with Apple Barbecue Sauce.   Makes 6 servings

Nutrients per Serving (not including sauce):					
Calories	165	(29% of calories from fat)			
Total Fat	5 g	Dietary Fiber	2 g	Thiamine	<1 mg
Saturated Fat	2 g	Protein	19 g	Riboflavin	<1 mg
Cholesterol	57 mg	Calcium	25 mg	Niacin	4 mg
Sodium	62 mg	Iron	2 mg	Vitamin A	18 RE
Carbohydrate	10 g	Folate	29 μg	Vitamin C	25 mg

Dietary Exchanges: 2 Meat, 1 Vegetable, 1 Fruit

Apple Barbecue Sauce

½ cup apple juice or cider
½ cup finely chopped onion
1 cup chili sauce
½ cup unsweetened applesauce
2 tablespoons packed brown sugar
1 tablespoon Worcestershire sauce
1 teaspoon dry mustard
5 drops hot pepper sauce

Combine apple juice and onion in 1-quart saucepan; simmer 2 minutes. Stir in chili sauce, applesauce, brown sugar, Worcestershire sauce, dry mustard and hot pepper sauce. Simmer 10 minutes, stirring occasionally. Remove from heat.

Makes about 2 cups

Nutrients per Serving:					
Calories	90	(1% of calories from fat)			
Total Fat	<1 g	Dietary Fiber	3 g	Thiamine	<1 mg
Saturated Fat	<1 g	Protein	1 g	Riboflavin	<1 mg
Cholesterol	0 mg	Calcium	19 mg	Niacin	1 mg
Sodium	36 mg	Iron	1 mg	Vitamin A	51 RE
Carbohydrate	22 g	Folate	21 μg	Vitamin C	22 mg

Dietary Exchanges: 1½ Fruit

Apple-icious Lamb Kabob

131 Honey-Citrus Glazed Veal Chops

Veal is almost as nutrient dense as beef, but it has about ⅓ less fat.

3 tablespoons fresh lime juice
2 tablespoons honey
2 teaspoons grated fresh ginger
½ teaspoon grated lime peel
4 veal rib chops, cut 1 inch thick (about 8 ounces each)

Combine lime juice, honey, ginger and lime peel in small bowl. Place veal rib chops in dish large enough to hold chops. Brush lime mixture liberally over both sides of chops. Refrigerate, covered, 30 minutes while preparing coals. Remove chops from dish; brush with remaining lime mixture. Place chops on grid over medium coals and grill 12 to 14 minutes, turning once. Or, broil 4 to 5 inches from heat 5 to 6 minutes per side, turning once.

Makes 4 servings

Nutrients per Serving:

Calories	479	(29% of calories from fat)		
Total Fat	15 g	Dietary Fiber	<1 g	Thiamine	<1 mg
Saturated Fat	4 g	Protein	72 g	Riboflavin	1 mg
Cholesterol	267 mg	Calcium	55 mg	Niacin	19 mg
Sodium	204 mg	Iron	3 mg	Vitamin A	<1 RE
Carbohydrate	10 g	Folate	36 µg	Vitamin C	4 mg

Dietary Exchanges: 1 Meat, ½ Fruit

132 Microwavable Savory Lamb Potatoes

Lamb is becoming more popular in the U.S. because of its leanness and wonderful flavor.

4 large baking potatoes (about 2 pounds)
½ cup sliced celery
½ cup sliced carrot
¼ cup chopped onion
¾ pound ground lean American lamb
1 cup tomato sauce
2 teaspoons Worcestershire sauce

Microwave Directions: Pierce potatoes with fork. Place in circle on paper towel in microwave oven. Microwave at HIGH (100% power) 11 to 13 minutes or until tender turning over and rearranging once. Wrap each potato in foil and set aside.

Combine celery, carrot and onion in 2-quart microwavable casserole. Cover with glass lid. Microwave at HIGH (100% power) 1 minute. Stir in lamb; cover. Microwave at HIGH (100% power) 4 to 5 minutes or until meat is no longer pink, stirring once.

Drain drippings. Stir in tomato sauce and Worcestershire sauce. Microwave covered at HIGH (100% power) 2 minutes. Slit baked potatoes down center, press open and top with lamb mixture.

Makes 4 servings

Nutrients per Serving:

Calories	349	(10% of calories from fat)		
Total Fat	4 g	Dietary Fiber	2 g	Thiamine	<1 mg
Saturated Fat	1 g	Protein	20 g	Riboflavin	<1 mg
Cholesterol	43 mg	Calcium	38 mg	Niacin	8 mg
Sodium	462 mg	Iron	3 mg	Vitamin A	450 RE
Carbohydrate	60 g	Folate	53 µg	Vitamin C	45 mg

Dietary Exchanges: 3½ Starch/Bread, 1½ Meat, 1 Vegetable

Honey-Citrus Glazed Veal Chop

133 Tandoori Pork Sauté

Plums add a fruity flavor to this traditional Indian dish.

Nutty Rice (recipe follows)
8 ounces lean pork, cut into 2 × ½-inch strips
½ cup sliced onion
1 clove garlic, minced
4 fresh California plums, halved, pitted and cut into thick wedges
1 cup plain low fat yogurt
1 tablespoon all-purpose flour
1½ teaspoons grated fresh ginger
½ teaspoon ground turmeric
⅛ teaspoon ground black pepper
Additional plum wedges, orange sections and sliced green onions

Prepare Nutty Rice. Cook pork in nonstick skillet 2 minutes or until browned, turning occasionally. Transfer to platter. Add onion and garlic to skillet; cook 1 minute. Add plums; cook and stir 1 minute. Remove from heat. Return pork to pan. Combine yogurt and flour. Add to skillet. Stir in ginger, turmeric and pepper. Bring to a boil; reduce heat and simmer 10 minutes, stirring occasionally. Serve over Nutty Rice and surround with plum wedges, orange sections and green onions.

Makes 4 servings

Nutty Rice: Bring 2 cups water to a boil in medium saucepan. Add ¾ cup brown rice and ¼ cup wheat berries. (Or, omit wheat berries and use 1 cup brown rice.) Return to a boil; cover. Reduce heat to low and simmer 40 to 45 minutes or until rice is tender and liquid is absorbed.

Makes about 2 cups

Nutrients per Serving:

Calories	287	(13% of calories from fat)			
Total Fat	4 g	Dietary Fiber	3 g	Thiamine	1 mg
Saturated Fat	2 g	Protein	19 g	Riboflavin	<1 mg
Cholesterol	44 mg	Calcium	127 mg	Niacin	4 mg
Sodium	73 mg	Iron	2 mg	Vitamin A	20 RE
Carbohydrate	43 g	Folate	23 µg	Vitamin C	3 mg

Dietary Exchanges: 2 Starch/Bread, 2 Meat, 1 Vegetable

134 Mexican Barbecued Lamb Steaks

Lamb meat is very tender; its flavor is at its peak when there's still pink in the center.

1 teaspoon vegetable oil
¼ cup finely chopped onion
½ cup finely chopped red bell pepper
¼ cup packed brown sugar
1 can (15 ounces) tomato sauce
1 can (4 ounces) diced green chilies
1 teaspoon Worcestershire sauce
½ teaspoon chili powder
¼ teaspoon garlic powder
¼ teaspoon black pepper
¼ teaspoon hot pepper sauce
3 American lamb sirloin steaks *or* 6 shoulder chops (2 pounds), cut ¾ to 1 inch thick

Heat oil over medium-high heat in large nonstick skillet. Add onion and bell pepper; cook and stir until onion is transparent. Add brown sugar; stir until melted. Add tomato sauce, green chilies, Worcestershire sauce, chili powder, garlic powder, black pepper and hot pepper sauce; heat thoroughly. Brush on steaks or chops. Grill over moderate coals, 8 to 10 minutes, basting chops frequently with sauce.

Makes 6 servings

Nutrients per Serving:

Calories	241	(28% of calories from fat)			
Total Fat	8 g	Dietary Fiber	2 g	Thiamine	<1 mg
Saturated Fat	2 g	Protein	26 g	Riboflavin	1 mg
Cholesterol	76 mg	Calcium	31 mg	Niacin	7 mg
Sodium	724 mg	Iron	3 mg	Vitamin A	101 RE
Carbohydrate	17 g	Folate	34 µg	Vitamin C	36 mg

Dietary Exchanges: 3 Meat, 3 Vegetable

[135] **P**ronto Pizza

Ground lamb is probably not available in the meat section of the grocery store. However, you should be able to find prepackaged cuts of lamb that the butcher could grind for you.

6 ounces lean fresh ground American lamb
½ teaspoon onion salt
½ teaspoon fennel seeds
¼ teaspoon dried oregano leaves, crushed
¼ teaspoon dried basil leaves, crushed
⅛ teaspoon crushed red pepper flakes
½ cup chopped bell pepper
½ cup chopped Italian plum tomatoes
1 (10- to 12-inch) prebaked pizza shell
½ cup pizza sauce
1 tablespoon grated Parmesan cheese
¼ cup thinly sliced fresh basil leaves, optional
½ cup (2 ounces) grated part-skim mozzarella cheese

Preheat oven to 450°F.

Combine lamb, onion salt, fennel, oregano, dried basil and red pepper flakes in small bowl; knead until well blended.

Spray nonstick skillet with nonstick cooking spray. Cook and stir lamb over medium-high heat, stirring to separate lamb, until lightly browned. Drain on paper towel. In same skillet cook and stir bell pepper for 3 to 4 minutes, stirring occasionally. Add tomatoes; cook and stir 1 minute. Place pizza shell on cookie sheet or pizza pan; top with pizza sauce and vegetables. Sprinkle with Parmesan cheese, fresh basil, cooked lamb and mozzarella cheese. Bake 8 to 10 minutes. Cool for 5 minutes and slice into wedges.   Makes 6 to 8 servings

Microwave Directions: In 2-quart microwavable dish cook lamb mixture at HIGH (100% power) 3 minutes; stirring several times to crumble lamb. Add bell pepper and tomatoes, microwave at HIGH (100% power) 2 minutes, stirring once. Drain well. Assemble pizza as directed.

Nutrients per Serving:

Calories	218	(22% of calories from fat)			
Total Fat	5 g	Dietary Fiber	1 g	Thiamine	<1 mg
Saturated Fat	2 g	Protein	12 g	Riboflavin	<1 mg
Cholesterol	20 mg	Calcium	96 mg	Niacin	4 mg
Sodium	360 mg	Iron	2 mg	Vitamin A	83 RE
Carbohydrate	31 g	Folate	11 μg	Vitamin C	26 mg

Dietary Exchanges: 1½ Starch/Bread, 1 Meat, 1 Vegetable, ½ Fat

[136] **B**eef and Pineapple Kabobs

These tasty teriyaki kabobs are reminiscent of a Hawaiian luau.

1 pound boneless beef top sirloin steak,* cut 1 inch thick
1 small onion, finely chopped
½ cup bottled teriyaki sauce
16 fresh pineapple cubes
1 can (8 ounces) water chestnuts, drained

Prepare grill for medium coals. Cut beef steak into ¼-inch-thick strips. For marinade, combine onion and teriyaki sauce. Place beef strips in small bowl; add marinade, stirring to coat. Alternately thread beef strips (weaving back and forth), pineapple cubes and water chestnuts on bamboo** or thin metal skewers. Place kabobs on grid over medium coals. Grill 4 minutes, turning once.

Makes 4 servings

**You may substitute beef top round steak, cut 1 inch thick.*

***Soak bamboo skewers in water 20 minutes before using to prevent them from burning.*

Nutrients per Serving:

Calories	308	(20% of calories from fat)			
Total Fat	7 g	Dietary Fiber	1 g	Thiamine	<1 mg
Saturated Fat	3 g	Protein	38 g	Riboflavin	<1 mg
Cholesterol	101 mg	Calcium	33 mg	Niacin	6 mg
Sodium	1460 mg	Iron	5 mg	Vitamin A	2 RE
Carbohydrate	24 g	Folate	33 μg	Vitamin C	14 mg

Dietary Exchanges: 4 Meat, 1 Vegetable, 1 Fruit

137 Thai Beef with Noodles

The spicy ingredients in this recipe give it lots of flavor without a lot of fat.

¼ cup dry sherry
1½ tablespoons reduced sodium soy sauce
1 teaspoon *each* grated fresh ginger, minced garlic and Oriental dark roasted sesame oil*
¼ to ½ teaspoon crushed red pepper flakes
1 pound boneless beef top sirloin, cut 1 inch thick
2 teaspoons cornstarch
¼ cup water
2 cups cooked ramen noodles or linguine
¼ cup chopped green onion tops or fresh cilantro

Combine sherry, soy sauce, ginger, garlic, sesame oil and red pepper flakes. Place beef steak in resealable plastic food storage bag; add marinade. Close bag securely and marinate 15 minutes. Pour off marinade; reserve. Heat nonstick skillet over medium heat 5 minutes. Add steak and cook 12 to 15 minutes, turning once. Remove steak; keep warm. Dissolve cornstarch in reserved marinade and ¼ cup water; add to skillet. Bring to a boil, stirring constantly. Stir in noodles. Carve steak into thin slices and serve over noodles. Sprinkle with green onions.   Makes 4 servings

*Available in the Oriental section of large supermarkets or in specialty food shops.

Nutrients per Serving:

Calories	310	(30% of calories from fat)		
Total Fat	11 g	Dietary Fiber	1 g	Thiamine	<1 mg
Saturated Fat	2 g	Protein	31 g	Riboflavin	<1 mg
Cholesterol	99 mg	Calcium	25 mg	Niacin	5 mg
Sodium	673 mg	Iron	4 mg	Vitamin A	136 RE
Carbohydrate	19 g	Folate	14 μg	Vitamin C	2 mg

Dietary Exchanges: 1 Starch/Bread, 4 Meat, ½ Fat

138 Zesty Lamb Taco Skillet

By using lamb instead of the traditional beef or chicken in this recipe you create a new version of this tasty Mexican dish.

1 tablespoon vegetable or olive oil
1 clove garlic, minced
1 pound boneless lamb, cut into ⅛-inch strips (leg or shoulder)
1½ cans (21 ounces) reduced sodium beef broth
1½ cans (12 ounces) tomato sauce
1 package taco seasoning mix (about 1.25 ounces)
1½ cups corn, fresh or frozen
2 cups green or red bell pepper strips
2 cups quick-cooking rice, white or brown
Grated cheese (optional)
Sliced ripe olives (optional)
Crushed tortilla chips (optional)

Heat oil over medium-high heat in large skillet. Add garlic and lamb strips. Cook and stir until lamb is no longer pink. Add broth, tomato sauce and seasoning mix. Bring to a boil; reduce heat. Cover and simmer 5 minutes. Add corn and bell peppers. Bring to a boil; stir in rice. Remove from heat. Cover and let stand 5 minutes or until moisture is absorbed. Fluff with fork. May be topped with grated cheese, sliced ripe olives and crushed tortilla chips for serving.   Makes 6 servings

Nutrients per Serving:

Calories	331	(27% of calories from fat)		
Total Fat	10 g	Dietary Fiber	2 g	Thiamine	<1 mg
Saturated Fat	3 g	Protein	26 g	Riboflavin	<1 mg
Cholesterol	69 mg	Calcium	28 mg	Niacin	7 mg
Sodium	539 mg	Iron	3 mg	Vitamin A	68 RE
Carbohydrate	34 g	Folate	36 μg	Vitamin C	37 mg

Dietary Exchanges: 2 Starch/Bread, 3 Meat, 1 Vegetable

Zesty Lamb Taco Skillet

139 Creole Pepper Steak

Beef has high levels of nutrients compared to the amount of calories, which is why it is considered a nutrient-dense food.

2 cloves garlic, minced
1 teaspoon dried thyme leaves, crushed
1 teaspoon paprika
½ teaspoon ground white pepper
½ teaspoon ground red pepper
½ teaspoon ground black pepper
1 pound beef top round steak, cut 1 inch thick
Salt (optional)

Combine garlic, thyme, paprika, white pepper, red pepper and black pepper; press evenly onto both sides of steak. Place steak on grid over medium coals. Grill steak 12 to 14 minutes, turning once. Season with salt, if desired. Carve steak diagonally into thin slices.   Makes 4 servings

Nutrients per Serving:

Calories	239	(25% of calories from fat)		
Total Fat	7 g	Dietary Fiber	<1 g	Thiamine	<1 mg
Saturated Fat	2 g	Protein	41 g	Riboflavin	<1 mg
Cholesterol	101 mg	Calcium	16 mg	Niacin	4 mg
Sodium	52 mg	Iron	4 mg	Vitamin A	42 RE
Carbohydrate	2 g	Folate	11 μg	Vitamin C	1 mg

Dietary Exchanges: 4½ Meat

140 Pork Chops with Red Pepper and Sweet Potato

Pork is one of the best sources of niacin (vitamin B₁).
This vitamin works to help maintain the skin, nerves
and digestive system as well as working with thiamin
and riboflavin to release energy from foods.

4 pork loin chops (about 1 pound), cut
** ½ inch thick**
1 teaspoon lemon pepper
½ cup water
1 tablespoon lemon juice
1 teaspoon dried fines herbes, crushed
½ teaspoon beef bouillon granules
1¼ cups red or yellow bell pepper strips
1 cup sliced sweet potato, cut into 1-inch
** pieces**
¾ cup sliced onion
4 cups hot cooked rice

Trim fat from chops; rub both sides with lemon
pepper. Coat large skillet with nonstick cooking
spray; heat skillet over medium-high heat. Add
chops. Cook on both sides until browned. Combine
water, lemon juice, fines herbes and bouillon
granules in small bowl; pour over chops. Reduce
heat to medium-low. Cover; simmer 5 minutes.

Add bell pepper, sweet potato and onion. Return to
a boil; reduce heat. Cover; simmer 10 to 15 minutes
more or until chops are slightly pink in center and
vegetables are crisp-tender. Remove chops and
vegetables; keep warm. Bring mixture in skillet to a
boil over high heat. Reduce heat to medium. Cook
and stir until mixture slightly thickens, stirring
occasionally. Arrange chops and vegetables over
rice; spoon sauce over chops and vegetables.

Makes 4 servings

Nutrients per Serving:

Calories	443	(21% of calories from fat)		
Total Fat	10 g	Dietary Fiber	2 g	Thiamine	1 mg
Saturated Fat	3 g	Protein	23 g	Riboflavin	<1 mg
Cholesterol	59 mg	Calcium	59 mg	Niacin	7 mg
Sodium	286 mg	Iron	3 mg	Vitamin A	772 RE
Carbohydrate	63 g	Folate	40 μg	Vitamin C	72 mg

Dietary Exchanges: 3½ Starch/Bread, 2 Meat, 2 Vegetable, ½ Fat

141 Beef Chili

Cubed meat and no beans make this recipe a more
traditional Texas-style chili.

2 teaspoons vegetable oil
1 pound lean beef cubed steaks
4½ teaspoons Spicy Seasoning Mix
** (recipe follows), divided**
1 medium onion, chopped
** Salt (optional)**
1 can (28 ounces) plum tomatoes,
** undrained**
2 cups frozen whole kernel corn

Heat oil in deep large skillet or wok over medium
heat 5 minutes. Meanwhile, cut each beef steak
lengthwise into 1-inch-wide strips; cut crosswise
into 1-inch pieces. Sprinkle beef with 2 teaspoons
Spicy Seasoning Mix. Stir-fry beef and onion in hot
oil 2 to 3 minutes. Season with salt, if desired. Add
tomatoes with juice, breaking up with back of
spoon; stir in corn and remaining 2½ teaspoons
Spicy Seasoning Mix. Bring to a boil; reduce heat to
medium-low and simmer, uncovered, 18 to 20
minutes until beef is tender.   Makes 4 servings

Spicy Seasoning Mix

3 tablespoons chili powder
2 teaspoons ground cumin
1½ teaspoons garlic powder
¾ teaspoon dried oregano leaves, crushed
½ teaspoon ground red pepper

Combine all ingredients. Cover; store in airtight
container. Shake before using.   Makes about ⅓ cup

Nutrients per Serving:

Calories	301	(29% of calories from fat)		
Total Fat	10 g	Dietary Fiber	4 g	Thiamine	<1 mg
Saturated Fat	3 g	Protein	27 g	Riboflavin	<1 mg
Cholesterol	64 mg	Calcium	74 mg	Niacin	6 mg
Sodium	393 mg	Iron	5 mg	Vitamin A	201 RE
Carbohydrate	29 g	Folate	43 μg	Vitamin C	35 mg

Dietary Exchanges: 1 Starch/Bread, 3 Meat, 2 Vegetable, ½ Fat

Pork Chops with Red Pepper and
Sweet Potato

142 Beef Burgers with Corn Salsa

Corn, an excellent source of complex carbohydrates, provides vitamins, minerals, protein and fiber, in addition to energy.

½ cup frozen corn
½ cup peeled, seeded and chopped tomato
1 can (4 ounces) diced green chilies, divided
1 tablespoon chopped fresh cilantro *or* 1 teaspoon dried cilantro leaves, crushed
1 tablespoon vinegar
1 teaspoon olive oil
¼ cup fine dry bread crumbs
3 tablespoons skim milk
¼ teaspoon garlic powder
12 ounces 95% lean ground beef

Prepare corn according to package directions, omitting salt; drain. Combine corn, tomato, 2 tablespoons green chilies, cilantro, vinegar and oil in small bowl. Cover and refrigerate.

Preheat broiler. Combine bread crumbs, remaining green chilies, skim milk and garlic powder in medium bowl. Add beef; blend well to combine. Shape to form four ¾-inch-thick patties. Place on broiler pan. Broil 4 inches from heat 6 minutes. Turn and broil 6 to 8 minutes or until beef is no longer pink in center. Spoon salsa over patties.

Makes 4 servings

Nutrients per Serving:

Calories	180	(30% of calories from fat)			
Total Fat	6 g	Dietary Fiber	2 g	Thiamine	<1 mg
Saturated Fat	2 g	Protein	19 g	Riboflavin	<1 mg
Cholesterol	33 mg	Calcium	35 mg	Niacin	4 mg
Sodium	101 mg	Iron	2 mg	Vitamin A	43 RE
Carbohydrate	13 g	Folate	16 μg	Vitamin C	52 mg

Dietary Exchanges: ½ Starch/Bread, 2½ Meat, 1 Vegetable, 1 Fat

143 Pork Chops with Pineapple-Raisin Chutney

The pineapple in this zesty main dish provides you with vitamins A and C.

4 pork loin chops (about 1 pound), cut ½ inch thick
1 can (8 ounces) crushed pineapple in juice, drained, juice reserved
½ teaspoon ground cumin
¼ teaspoon ground cinnamon
⅛ teaspoon crushed red pepper flakes
3 tablespoons sliced green onions
2 tablespoons raisins
1 tablespoon packed brown sugar
1 tablespoon vinegar
4 cups hot cooked rice

Trim fat from chops. Coat large skillet with nonstick cooking spray; heat over medium-high heat. Add chops. Cook on both sides until browned. Combine pineapple juice, cumin, cinnamon and red pepper flakes in small bowl; pour over chops. Reduce heat to medium-low. Cover; simmer 20 to 25 minutes or until chops are slightly pink in center. Remove chops; keep warm.

Stir pineapple, green onions, raisins, brown sugar and vinegar into juice in skillet. Cook, uncovered, over medium heat 2 to 3 minutes or until mixture boils and slightly thickens, stirring occasionally. Spoon over chops and rice.   Makes 4 servings

Nutrients per Serving:

Calories	427	(21% of calories from fat)			
Total Fat	10 g	Dietary Fiber	1 g	Thiamine	1 mg
Saturated Fat	3 g	Protein	22 g	Riboflavin	<1 mg
Cholesterol	59 mg	Calcium	40 mg	Niacin	6 mg
Sodium	50 mg	Iron	3 mg	Vitamin A	25 RE
Carbohydrate	61 g	Folate	12 μg	Vitamin C	8 mg

Dietary Exchanges: 3 Starch/Bread, 2 Meat, 1 Fruit, ½ Fat

Beef Burgers with Corn Salsa

POULTRY

144 Crunchy Apple Salsa with Grilled Chicken

Chili peppers can charge the clot-dissolving system in the blood, open sinuses and air passages and also act as a decongestant.

2 cups Washington Gala apples, halved, cored and chopped
¾ cup (1 large) Anaheim chile pepper, seeded and chopped
½ cup chopped onion
¼ cup lime juice
   Salt and pepper to taste
   Grilled Chicken (recipe follows)

Combine all ingredients except chicken and mix well; allow flavors to blend about ¾ hour. Prepare Grilled Chicken. Serve over or alongside Grilled Chicken.   **Makes 3 cups salsa**

Grilled Chicken: Marinate 2 whole boneless, skinless chicken breasts in a mixture of ¼ cup dry white wine, ¼ cup apple juice, ½ teaspoon grated lime peel, ½ teaspoon salt and dash pepper for 20 to 30 minutes. Drain and grill over medium-hot coals, turning once, until chicken is no longer pink in center.   **Makes 4 servings**

Nutrients per Serving:

Calories	211	(14% of calories from fat)			
Total Fat	3 g	Dietary Fiber	3 g	Thiamine	<1 mg
Saturated Fat	1 g	Protein	28 g	Riboflavin	<1 mg
Cholesterol	73 mg	Calcium	30 mg	Niacin	12 mg
Sodium	155 mg	Iron	1 mg	Vitamin A	31 RE
Carbohydrate	17 g	Folate	17 μg	Vitamin C	80 mg

Dietary Exchanges: 3 Meat, ½ Fruit, 1 Vegetable

145 White Turkey Wild Rice Chili

Canola oil is made from rape seeds and has the highest levels of unsaturated fat compared to other oils. It is only 6% saturated fat.

1 tablespoon canola oil
1 medium onion, chopped
1 clove garlic, minced
1¼ pounds turkey breast slices, cut into ½-inch pieces
2 cups cooked wild rice
1 can (15 ounces) Great Northern white beans, drained
1 can (11 ounces) white corn (optional)
2 cans (4 ounces) diced green chilies
1 can (14½ ounces) low sodium chicken broth
1 teaspoon ground cumin
   Hot pepper sauce (optional)
4 ounces low fat Monterey Jack Cheese, shredded
   Parsley (optional)

Heat oil in large pan over medium heat; add onion and garlic. Cook until tender. Add turkey, wild rice, beans, corn, chilies, broth and cumin. Cover and simmer over low heat 30 minutes or until turkey is tender. Stir hot pepper sauce into chili to taste. Serve with shredded cheese. Garnish with parsley.   **Makes 8 servings**

Nutrients per Serving:

Calories	272	(19% of calories from fat)			
Total Fat	6 g	Dietary Fiber	2 g	Thiamine	<1 mg
Saturated Fat	1 g	Protein	26 g	Riboflavin	<1 mg
Cholesterol	36 mg	Calcium	202 mg	Niacin	5 mg
Sodium	199 mg	Iron	3 mg	Vitamin A	41 RE
Carbohydrate	31 g	Folate	81 μg	Vitamin C	28 mg

Dietary Exchanges: 1½ Starch/Bread, 2½ Meat, 1 Vegetable

Crunchy Apple Salsa with Grilled Chicken

146 Dad's Turkey Dagwood

It looks like guacamole, it's served like guacamole, but voilà there's no avocado—and virtually no fat. Enjoy it without guilt and get your vitamin C for the day to boot.

Mock Guacamole (recipe follows)
16 slices low calorie whole wheat bread
2 tomatoes, sliced
8 cups shredded iceberg lettuce
2 packages (6 ounces) smoked turkey breast slices
8 slices (1 ounce each) reduced fat Cheddar cheese
8 tablespoons sweet hot mustard

Prepare Mock Guacamole. Spread 3 tablespoons Mock Guacamole on 8 slices of bread. Arrange 2 tomato slices, 1 cup lettuce, 2 slices turkey and 1 slice of cheese over top of guacamole on each bread slice.

Spread 1 tablespoon mustard over each remaining slice of bread and place on top of each sandwich.

Makes 8 servings

Mock Guacamole

2 large cloves garlic
2 cups frozen peas, cooked and drained
½ cup fresh cilantro
¼ cup chopped onion
1 tablespoon lemon juice
¼ teaspoon ground black pepper
⅛ teaspoon hot pepper sauce

In food processor or blender, process garlic cloves 10 seconds. Add peas, cilantro, onion, lemon juice, black pepper and hot pepper sauce; process until smooth. Refrigerate at least 1 hour.

Nutrients per Serving:

Calories	255	(28% of calories from fat)			
Total Fat	9 g	Dietary Fiber	6 g	Thiamine	<1 mg
Saturated Fat	4 g	Protein	24 g	Riboflavin	<1 mg
Cholesterol	35 mg	Calcium	270 mg	Niacin	6 mg
Sodium	1,044 mg	Iron	3 mg	Vitamin A	103 RE
Carbohydrate	23 g	Folate	89 μg	Vitamin C	17 mg

Dietary Exchanges: 1 Starch/Bread, 2½ Meat, 1½ Vegetable

147 Chicken Wild Rice Soup

There is as much nutrition in nonfat dried milk as there is in regular skim milk. It is virtually fat and cholesterol free and contains vitamins A and D.

⅓ cup instant nonfat dry milk
2 tablespoons cornstarch
2 teaspoons low sodium instant chicken bouillon
¼ teaspoon dried onion flakes
¼ teaspoon dried basil leaves, crushed
¼ teaspoon dried thyme leaves, crushed
⅛ teaspoon ground pepper
4 cups low sodium chicken broth
½ cup sliced celery
½ cup sliced carrots
½ cup chopped onion
2 cups cooked wild rice
1 cup cooked cubed chicken breasts

In small bowl, combine dry milk, cornstarch, bouillon, onion flakes, basil, thyme and pepper. Stir in small amount of chicken broth; set aside. In large saucepan, combine remaining broth, celery, carrots and onion. Cook until vegetables are crisp-tender. Gradually add dry milk mixture. Stir in wild rice and chicken. Simmer 5 to 10 minutes.

Makes 8 servings

Nutrients per Serving:

Calories	103	(10% of calories from fat)			
Total Fat	1 g	Dietary Fiber	1 g	Thiamine	<1 mg
Saturated Fat	<1 g	Protein	8 g	Riboflavin	<1 mg
Cholesterol	13 mg	Calcium	55 mg	Niacin	4 mg
Sodium	70 mg	Iron	1 g	Vitamin A	216 RE
Carbohydrate	15 g	Folate	18 μg	Vitamin C	2 mg

Dietary Exchanges: 1 Meat, 2 Vegetable

Dad's Turkey Dagwood

148 California Apricot Mixed Grill

Four cloves of garlic may seem high but recent studies have shown that garlic may play a role in the protection against heart disease.

4 chicken breast halves, skinned
4 cloves garlic, coarsely chopped
¼ teaspoon salt
¼ teaspoon pepper
2 tablespoons California Apricot Nectar
2 tablespoons balsamic vinegar
1 teaspoon olive oil
Additional salt and pepper
1 tablespoon olive oil
2 small red onions, sliced ⅓ inch thick
6 fresh California apricots, halved and pitted
4 cups mixed salad greens

Up to 12 hours ahead, combine chicken and garlic; season with ¼ teaspoon salt, ¼ teaspoon pepper and refrigerate until ready to prepare dish. Combine nectar and vinegar in small bowl; whisk in 1 teaspoon olive oil. Season with additional salt and pepper to taste; set aside. Heat grill to medium-high. Brush grill lightly with 1 tablespoon oil and grill chicken about 4 minutes on each side or just until firm. Brush onions lightly with oil and grill about 2 minutes on each side or just until tender. Brush apricots lightly with oil and grill about 1 minute on each side or just until tender. Serve mixed grill with salad greens dressed with apricot nectar vinaigrette. **Makes 4 servings**

Nutrients per Serving:

Calories	249	(29% of calories from fat)			
Total Fat	8 g	Dietary Fiber	3 g	Thiamine	<1 mg
Saturated Fat	2 g	Protein	29 g	Riboflavin	<1 mg
Cholesterol	73 mg	Calcium	73 mg	Niacin	13 mg
Sodium	215 mg	Iron	3 mg	Vitamin A	337 RE
Carbohydrate	15 g	Folate	75 μg	Vitamin C	25 mg

Dietary Exchanges: 3 Meat, 1 Fruit, 1 Vegetable

149 Washington Apple Turkey Gyros

Pita is a flat bread from the Middle East which is served as an accompaniment to meals, stuffed to form sandwiches or cut into wedges for dipping. Using whole-wheat pitas provides an extra boost of vitamins, minerals and fiber.

1 cup vertically sliced onion
1 cup thinly sliced red bell pepper
1 cup thinly sliced green bell pepper
2 tablespoons lemon juice
1 tablespoon vegetable oil
½ pound cooked turkey breast, cut into thin strips
1 medium Washington Golden Delicious or Winesap apple, cored and thinly sliced
8 pita rounds, lightly toasted
½ cup plain low fat yogurt

Cook and stir onion, bell peppers and lemon juice in oil in nonstick skillet until crisp-tender; stir in turkey and cook until heated through. Remove from heat; stir in apple. Fold pita in half and fill with apple mixture; drizzle with yogurt. Repeat with remaining ingredients. Serve warm.

Makes 6 servings

Nutrients per Serving:

Calories	268	(13% of calories from fat)			
Total Fat	4 g	Dietary Fiber	3 g	Thiamine	<1 mg
Saturated Fat	1 g	Protein	19 g	Riboflavin	<1 mg
Cholesterol	33 mg	Calcium	95 mg	Niacin	5 mg
Sodium	322 mg	Iron	2 mg	Vitamin A	53 RE
Carbohydrate	40 g	Folate	56 μg	Vitamin C	73 mg

Dietary Exchanges: 2 Bread/Starch, 2 Meat, 1 Vegetable

Washington Apple Turkey Gyro

150 Cherry Glazed Turkey Breast

The sweet cherry glaze complements the taste of the roasted turkey without adding additional fat or cholesterol.

1 bone-in (2½-pound) turkey breast half
½ cup cherry preserves
1 tablespoon red wine vinegar

Prepare grill for indirect-heat cooking. Place turkey, skin side up, on rack over drip pan. Cover and grill turkey breast 1 to 1¼ hours or until meat thermometer inserted in thickest portion of breast registers 170°F.

Combine preserves and vinegar in small bowl. Brush glaze on breast ½ hour before end of grilling time. Remove turkey breast from grill and let stand 15 minutes.

To serve, slice breast and arrange on platter.

Makes 6 servings

Nutrients per Serving:					
Calories	335	(28% of calories from fat)			
Total Fat	10 g	Dietary Fiber	<1 g	Thiamine	<1 mg
Saturated Fat	3 g	Protein	40 g	Riboflavin	<1 mg
Cholesterol	103 mg	Calcium	35 mg	Niacin	9 mg
Sodium	89 mg	Iron	2 mg	Vitamin A	0 RE
Carbohydrate	19 g	Folate	10 µg	Vitamin C	0 mg

Dietary Exchanges: 5 Meat, 1 Fruit

151 Chicken with Mandarin Orange and Water Chestnut Sauce

Even though they're called water chestnuts, they're really tubers—not nuts. But they are low in calories, about 14 per ounce, and virtually fat free.

1 can (11 ounces) mandarin oranges, drained
1 can (8 ounces) sliced water chestnuts, drained
4 teaspoons packed brown sugar
2 tablespoons white vinegar
1 tablespoon low sodium soy sauce
2 teaspoons cornstarch
¼ cup water
1½ cups chicken broth or stock
4 split chicken breast halves, skinned and boned

In small saucepan, combine mandarin oranges, water chestnuts, brown sugar, vinegar, soy sauce and cornstarch dissolved in ¼ cup water. Cook until clear and mixture thickens, about 4 to 5 minutes, stirring occasionally. Remove from heat. In large skillet, bring broth to a simmer. Pound chicken breasts with meat mallet to ½-inch thickness. Place chicken in skillet, cover and simmer over medium-low heat about 8 to 10 minutes or until chicken is no longer pink in center. Remove chicken from poaching liquid. Place on serving platter. Heat sauce if needed; spoon sauce over chicken.

Makes 4 servings

Nutrients per Serving:

Calories	253	(18% of calories from fat)		
Total Fat	5 g	Dietary Fiber	<1 g	Thiamine	<1 mg
Saturated Fat	1 g	Protein	20 g	Riboflavin	<1 mg
Cholesterol	73 mg	Calcium	35 mg	Niacin	13 mg
Sodium	755 mg	Iron	2 mg	Vitamin A	31 RE
Carbohydrate	22 g	Folate	25 µg	Vitamin C	23 mg

Dietary Exchanges: 3 Meat, 1 Fruit, 1 Vegetable

152 Lemon Turkey Stir-Fry and Pasta

This delicious recipe contains spinach, a leafy vegetable high in antioxidants, including beta-carotene and folate.

1 pound linguine or other long pasta
1½ pounds turkey cutlets, cut into ½-inch strips
1 tablespoon soy sauce
1 tablespoon white wine vinegar
2 teaspoons cornstarch
1 teaspoon lemon pepper
2 tablespoons olive oil
6 medium green onions, sliced
1 medium fresh lemon, cut into 10 thin slices and slivered
1 clove garlic, finely minced
1 bag (10 ounces) fresh spinach, washed, stemmed, drained and chopped
Fresh parsley and additional lemon slices (optional)

Prepare linguine according to package directions; drain. In resealable plastic food storage bag, combine turkey, soy sauce, vinegar, cornstarch and lemon pepper. Shake bag to coat turkey thoroughly. Refrigerate 30 minutes to allow flavors to blend.

In large skillet, over medium heat, cook and stir turkey and marinade in oil 2 to 3 minutes, or until turkey is no longer pink. Add onions, lemon slivers and garlic; continue to cook until onions are soft. Stir in spinach and cook until just wilted. Spoon over hot linguine and garnish with parsley and lemon slices, if desired.

Makes 6 servings

Nutrients per Serving:

Calories	433	(19% of calories from fat)		
Total Fat	9 g	Dietary Fiber	5 g	Thiamine	1 mg
Saturated Fat	2 g	Protein	33 g	Riboflavin	1 mg
Cholesterol	115 mg	Calcium	89 mg	Niacin	7 mg
Sodium	267 mg	Iron	5 mg	Vitamin A	355 RE
Carbohydrate	55 g	Folate	112 µg	Vitamin C	30 mg

Dietary Exchanges: 3 Starch/Bread, 2 Meat, 2 Vegetable, 1 Fat

Chicken with Mandarin Orange and Water Chestnut Sauce

153 Shotgun Billy's Turkey Chili with Black Beans

Capsaicin, the substance in peppers that makes them hot is also credited with medicinal properties like painkilling and headache relief.

1 cup coarsely chopped onions
1 red bell pepper, cut into ¼-inch cubes
2 cloves garlic, minced
2 jalapeño peppers, seeded and minced
1 can (28 ounces) tomatoes, coarsely chopped, with juice
1 tablespoon chili powder
1½ teaspoons ground cumin
1½ teaspoons ground coriander
½ teaspoon dried oregano leaves, crushed
½ teaspoon dried marjoram leaves, crushed
¼ teaspoon crushed red pepper flakes
¼ teaspoon ground cinnamon
1 can (16 ounces) black beans, drained and rinsed
2 cups cooked turkey, cut into ½-inch cubes
½ cup coarsely chopped fresh cilantro
4 tablespoons shredded reduced-fat Cheddar cheese

In 3-quart microwavable dish combine onions, bell pepper, garlic, jalapeño peppers and tomatoes with juice. Stir in chili powder, cumin, coriander, oregano, marjoram, red pepper flakes and cinnamon; cover dish. Microwave at HIGH (100% power) 10 minutes; stir half way through. Stir in beans and turkey; cover dish. Microwave at HIGH (100% power) 4 minutes; stir in cilantro. To serve, ladle into bowls and garnish with cheese.

Makes 4 servings

Nutrients per Serving:

Calories	323	(9% calories from fat)			
Total Fat	3 g	Dietary Fiber	9 g	Thiamine	<1 mg
Saturated Fat	1 g	Protein	32 g	Riboflavin	<1 mg
Cholesterol	52 mg	Calcium	180 mg	Niacin	7 mg
Sodium	621 mg	Iron	6 mg	Vitamin A	264 RE
Carbohydrate	43 g	Folate	219 µg	Vitamin C	61 mg

Dietary Exchanges: 1½ Starch/Bread, 3 Meat, 2 Vegetable

154 Peppered Turkey Medallions with Chutney Sauce

Turkey tenderloin comes from the underside of the turkey breast and is one of the leanest meat cuts available. One 3½-ounce portion has less than 1 gram of fat.

½ to 1 tablespoon mixed peppercorns
1 pound turkey tenderloins, cut into ¾-inch medallions
1 teaspoon margarine
2 teaspoons olive oil, divided
2 tablespoons finely chopped green onion
¼ cup reduced sodium chicken bouillon
2 tablespoons brandy
¼ cup prepared chutney

Crush peppercorns in spice grinder, food processor or mortar with pestle. Press peppercorns onto both sides of turkey medallions. Refrigerate 30 minutes.

Heat margarine and 1 teaspoon oil over medium heat in large nonstick skillet. Add medallions; cook and stir 5 minutes per side or until no longer pink in center. Remove medallions from pan and keep warm.

Add remaining 1 teaspoon oil to skillet; add onion. Cook and stir 30 seconds. Add bouillon and cook 45 seconds to reduce liquid. Stir in brandy and cook 1 to 2 minutes. Reduce heat to low; blend in chutney.

To serve, pour chutney sauce over medallions.

Makes 4 servings

Nutrients per Serving:

Calories	266	(24% of calories from fat)			
Total Fat	7 g	Dietary Fiber	1 g	Thiamine	<1 mg
Saturated Fat	2 g	Protein	34 g	Riboflavin	<1 mg
Cholesterol	79 mg	Calcium	29 mg	Niacin	8 mg
Sodium	89 mg	Iron	2 mg	Vitamin A	34 RE
Carbohydrate	11 g	Folate	8 µg	Vitamin C	3 mg

Dietary Exchanges: 4 Meat, 1 Fruit

Shotgun Billy's Turkey Chili with Black Beans

Chicken Breast with Orange Basil Pesto

155 Chicken Breasts with Orange Basil Pesto

Use fresh herbs to add a lot of flavor to your dishes without adding fat or calories.

½ **cup fresh basil leaves**
2 **tablespoons grated orange peel**
2 **cloves garlic**
2 **teaspoons olive oil**
3 **tablespoons Florida orange juice**
1 **tablespoon Dijon-style mustard**
　 Salt and pepper to taste
6 **chicken breast halves**

Preheat broiler. Add basil, orange peel and garlic to food processor; process until finely chopped. Add oil, orange juice, mustard, salt and pepper; process a few seconds or until paste forms. Spread equal amounts mixture under skin and on bone side of each chicken breast. Place chicken skin-side down on broiler pan and place 4 inches from heat. Broil 10 minutes. Turn chicken over and broil 10 to 12 minutes or until chicken is no longer pink in center. If chicken browns too quickly, cover with foil. Remove skin from chicken before serving.

Makes 6 servings

Nutrients per Serving:

Calories	206	(25% of calories from fat)			
Total Fat	6 g	Dietary Fiber	<1 g	Thiamine	<1 mg
Saturated Fat	1 g	Protein	34 g	Riboflavin	<1 mg
Cholesterol	91 mg	Calcium	65 mg	Niacin	15 mg
Sodium	113 mg	Iron	2 mg	Vitamin A	27 RE
Carbohydrate	3 g	Folate	9 μg	Vitamin C	8 mg

Dietary Exchanges: 3½ Meat, ½ Vegetable

156 **A**pricot-Stuffed Turkey Thighs

Fruit is dried either in the sun or by hot air. Dried fruit is a compact package of nutrition, full of iron, copper, potassium and fiber.

⅓ **cup chopped dried apricots**
2 **tablespoons chopped raisins**
⅔ **cup plain dry bread cubes**
½ **cup finely chopped celery**
¼ **cup finely chopped green onions**
1 **small clove garlic, minced**
1½ **pounds boneless turkey thighs, skin removed**

Creamy Mustard Sauce
1 **teaspoon cornstarch**
⅓ **cup reduced sodium chicken bouillon**
1½ **teaspoons whole grain country-style mustard**
1½ **teaspoons honey**
1 **teaspoon lemon juice**
3 **tablespoons reduced calorie mayonnaise**

Preheat oven to 325°F. In medium microwavable bowl, combine apricots and raisins. Cover with hot water. Microwave at HIGH (100% power) 1½ to 2 minutes or until fruit is soft; drain well. Add bread cubes, celery, green onions and garlic. Cover bowl with vented plastic wrap. Microwave at HIGH (100% power) 1½ minutes or until onion and celery are soft. Set aside.

Place turkey thighs between 2 pieces of waxed paper; flatten with meat mallet to ¾-inch thickness. Divide stuffing evenly among thighs. Place stuffing on edge of flattened thigh. Fold opposite end over stuffing and secure with string or metal skewers.

Arrange thighs, seam side down, on lightly greased rack in shallow roasting pan. Roast 1½ to 1¾ hours or until meat thermometer placed in thigh registers 180°F.

For Creamy Mustard Sauce, combine cornstarch, bouillon, mustard, honey and lemon juice in small saucepan over medium heat. Cook and stir until sauce thickens. Remove from heat and fold in mayonnaise.

To serve, remove string or skewers from thighs. Slice into rolls and top with Creamy Mustard Sauce.

Makes 4 servings

Nutrients per Serving:

Calories	333	(28% of calories from fat)				
Total Fat	10 g	Dietary Fiber	2 g	Thiamine	<1 mg
Saturated Fat	3 g	Protein	41 g	Riboflavin	<1 mg
Cholesterol	108 mg	Calcium	62 mg	Niacin	8 mg
Sodium	180 mg	Iron	3 mg	Vitamin A	106 RE
Carbohydrate	18 g	Folate	18 µg	Vitamin C	5 mg

Dietary Exchanges: 5 Meat, 1 Fruit

157 **S**weet 'n' Sour with Rice

Chicken is a good choice for low sodium diets. One three-ounce serving contains only 63 milligrams of sodium.

4 **(3-ounce) boneless, skinless chicken breasts**
1½ **cups water**
¼ **cup vinegar**
1 **cup uncooked converted rice**
2 **tablespoons packed brown sugar**
8 **ounces canned chunk pineapple, drained, reserving 2 tablespoons juice**

Broil chicken for 10 to 15 minutes or until cooked through, turning once. Meanwhile, in medium saucepan bring water and vinegar to a boil. Add rice and brown sugar. Cover; cook 20 minutes or until water is absorbed and rice is fluffy. Stir in pineapple and 2 tablespoons of reserved juice. Serve chicken over rice.

Makes 4 servings

Nutrients per Serving:

Calories	284	(6% of calories from fat)				
Total Fat	2 g	Dietary Fiber	1 g	Thiamine	<1 mg
Saturated Fat	<1 g	Protein	16 g	Riboflavin	<1 mg
Cholesterol	34 mg	Calcium	49 mg	Niacin	7 mg
Sodium	25 mg	Iron	3 mg	Vitamin A	3 RE
Carbohydrate	50 g	Folate	12 µg	Vitamin C	4 mg

Dietary Exchanges: 2 Starch/Bread, 2 Meat, ½ Fruit

158 Chicken and Vegetable Couscous

A staple of North African cuisine, couscous is a quick-cooking food with many uses. It can be served with milk as a cereal, in casseroles or as a side dish.

    1 tablespoon vegetable oil
    3 (3-ounce) boneless chicken breasts, cut
        into 3-inch cubes
    ½ cup chopped green onions
    3 cloves garlic, minced
    1¼ cups tomato sauce
    ¼ cup water
    1¼ cups chopped carrots
    1 cup canned Great Northern beans,
        rinsed and drained
    ¼ cup chopped red bell pepper
    ¼ cup raisins
    1 large potato, cubed
    1 yellow squash, chopped
    1 medium tomato, chopped
    2 tablespoons packed brown sugar
    2 teaspoons ground cumin
    ¾ teaspoon ground cinnamon
    3 to 4 drops hot sauce
    1½ cups water
    1 cup dry couscous

Add oil to medium skillet; brown chicken over medium heat. Add onions and garlic; cook and stir 1 minute. Stir in tomato sauce and ¼ cup water. Add remaining ingredients except 1½ cups water and couscous. Bring to a simmer and cook 15 minutes. Meanwhile, bring remaining water to a boil, add couscous, cover and remove from heat. Let stand 5 minutes. Serve chicken and vegetables over couscous.

Makes 6 servings

Nutrients per Serving:

Calories	322	(11% of calories from fat)			
Total Fat	4 g	Dietary Fiber	9 g	Thiamine	<1 mg
Saturated Fat	1 g	Protein	17 g	Riboflavin	<1 mg
Cholesterol	22 mg	Calcium	80 mg	Niacin	6 mg
Sodium	348 mg	Iron	3 mg	Vitamin A	759 RE
Carbohydrate	56 g	Folate	71 µg	Vitamin C	26 mg

Dietary Exchanges: 2½ Starch/Bread, 1 Meat, ½ Fruit, 2 Vegetable

159 Light 'n' Lean Chicken Breasts

Boneless chicken breasts are a favorite choice for today's cook because they're quick to cook, low in fat and high in protein.

    4 broiler-fryer chicken breast halves,
        skinned and fat removed
    ½ teaspoon pepper, divided
    2 cloves garlic, halved
    1 cup low sodium chicken broth
    ½ cup dry white wine
    ⅔ cup skim milk
    2 teaspoons arrowroot
    1 teaspoon finely chopped chives
    1 cup cooked rice

Spray nonstick skillet with nonstick cooking spray. Heat to medium-hot; add chicken and sprinkle with ¼ teaspoon pepper. Cook, turning, after 20 minutes or until brown on both sides. Reduce temperature to low. Add garlic; continue cooking until chicken is tender, about 10 minutes. Remove chicken to warm plate, leaving garlic in pan. Add chicken broth and wine; bring to a boil. Boil 5 minutes; reduce temperature to low. Combine skim milk and arrowroot; slowly add to pan liquids. Sprinkle with remaining ¼ teaspoon pepper and stir until thickened, about 2 minutes. Return chicken to pan and sprinkle with chives, spooning sauce over chicken. Simmer until heated through, about 5 minutes. Serve over rice.　　　　Makes 4 servings

Nutrients per Serving:

Calories	253	(13% of calories from fat)			
Total Fat	3 g	Dietary Fiber	1 g	Thiamine	<1 mg
Saturated Fat	1 g	Protein	30 g	Riboflavin	<1 mg
Cholesterol	74 mg	Calcium	78 mg	Niacin	13 mg
Sodium	95 mg	Iron	2 mg	Vitamin A	32 RE
Carbohydrate	19 g	Folate	7 µg	Vitamin C	1 mg

Dietary Exchanges: 1 Starch/Bread, 3 Meat, ½ Vegetable

Chicken and Vegetable Couscous

160 Persian Chicken

Cracked wheat, also called bulgur or tabbouleh, are wheat kernels that have been steamed, dried and crushed. This process makes the wheat easy to cook and retains the nutrients of the wheat bran.

2 cups ⅓-less-salt chicken broth
1 cup cracked wheat
½ teaspoon dried basil leaves, crushed
½ teaspoon grated lemon peel
¼ teaspoon dried mint leaves, crushed
¼ cup whole natural California Almonds
1 tablespoon almond or olive oil
½ cup sliced green onions
⅓ cup raisins
2 tablespoons chopped parsley
1 tablespoon lemon juice
1 cup diced cooked chicken or turkey

Combine broth, cracked wheat, basil, lemon peel and mint; bring to a boil over medium-high heat. Cover, reduce heat to low and cook 15 minutes. Meanwhile, chop almonds and brown lightly in oil, stirring constantly, over moderate heat. Add onions, raisins, parsley and lemon juice to almonds; toss lightly to mix. Add chicken and heat 1 minute. Serve over cracked wheat.   Makes 3 servings

Nutrients per Serving:

Calories	370	(27% of calories from fat)		
Total Fat	11 g	Dietary Fiber	3 g	Thiamine	<1 mg
Saturated Fat	1 g	Protein	22 g	Riboflavin	<1 mg
Cholesterol	32 mg	Calcium	96 mg	Niacin	7 mg
Sodium	70 mg	Iron	4 mg	Vitamin A	84 RE
Carbohydrate	48 g	Folate	10 μg	Vitamin C	12 mg

Dietary Exchanges: 2 Starch/Bread, 2 Meat, 1 Fruit, 1½ Fat

161 Turkey Medallions with Marsala Mustard Sauce

Not only does it add tang to sauces, mustard can help to relieve congestion and sinus problems.

¼ cup all-purpose flour
¼ teaspoon salt
¼ teaspoon pepper
1 pound turkey tenderloins, cut into ¾-inch medallions
½ cup marsala wine
¼ cup reduced sodium chicken bouillon
2 teaspoons Dijon-style mustard
1 tablespoon olive oil
1 clove garlic, minced

Combine flour, salt and pepper in 9-inch pie plate. Dredge turkey medallions in flour mixture. Reserve 2 teaspoons remaining flour mixture and combine with wine, bouillon and mustard.

Heat oil over medium heat in large nonstick skillet. Add medallions. Cook and stir 4 to 5 minutes per side or until turkey is no longer pink in center. Remove medallions from pan and keep warm.

Over medium heat cook and stir garlic until lightly browned. Add wine mixture, stirring constantly 1 minute or until mixture thickens.

To serve, pour sauce over medallions.

Makes 4 servings

Nutrients per Serving:

Calories	261	(26% of calories from fat)		
Total Fat	7 g	Dietary Fiber	<1 g	Thiamine	<1 mg
Saturated Fat	2 g	Protein	35 g	Riboflavin	<1 mg
Cholesterol	79 mg	Calcium	31 mg	Niacin	8 mg
Sodium	260 mg	Iron	2 mg	Vitamin A	<1 RE
Carbohydrate	7 g	Folate	9 μg	Vitamin C	<1 mg

Dietary Exchanges: ½ Starch/Bread, 4 Meat

Persian Chicken

162 Turkey Split Pea Soup

Peas are a good source of fiber with moderate amounts of potassium and iron.

7 cups Turkey Broth (recipe follows) or low sodium chicken bouillon
1 pound dried split peas, washed and drained
2 cups chopped onions
1 cup chopped carrots
½ cup chopped celery
1 clove garlic, minced
3 tablespoons dried parsley
1 bay leaf
1 pound turkey ham, cut into ½-inch cubes

Prepare Turkey Broth. In 5-quart saucepan, over high heat, combine broth, peas, onions, carrots, celery, garlic, parsley and bay leaf; bring to a boil. Reduce heat to simmer, cover and cook one hour. Remove saucepan from heat and discard bay leaf.

With wire whisk, gently whisk soup to blend peas. If desired, soup can be processed in food processor or blender for smoother texture.

Return soup to medium-high heat, add turkey ham and bring to a boil. Reduce heat to simmer and cook, uncovered, 10 to 15 minutes.

Makes 8 servings

Turkey Broth

4 cups water
Turkey giblets
1 rib celery, sliced
1 carrot, sliced
1 onion, sliced
1 bay leaf
3 sprigs parsley
4 black peppercorns

In large saucepan, over high heat, bring water, giblets, celery, carrot, onion, bay leaf, parsley and peppercorns to a boil. Reduce heat to low, cover and simmer 1 hour.

Strain broth and refrigerate until needed. Store giblets in refrigerator until ready to make gravy or dressing.   Makes about 5 cups

Nutrients per Serving:

Calories	243	(14% of calories from fat)			
Total Fat	4 g	Dietary Fiber	7 g	Thiamine	<1 mg
Saturated Fat	1 g	Protein	23 g	Riboflavin	<1 mg
Cholesterol	34 mg	Calcium	52 mg	Niacin	5 mg
Sodium	754 mg	Iron	5 mg	Vitamin A	401 RE
Carbohydrate	31 g	Folate	89 µg	Vitamin C	5 mg

Dietary Exchanges: 1½ Starch/Bread, 2 Meat, 1 Vegetable

163 Peach Lemon Sauce for Chicken

To get more juice from a lemon, roll it firmly between the palm of your hand and countertop before squeezing.

2 lemons
3 fresh California peaches, peeled, halved, pitted and quartered
3 tablespoons ⅓-less-salt chicken broth
Pepper
Grilled chicken

Thinly peel one lemon; reserve peel. Squeeze both lemons to measure ¼ cup juice. Combine juice and peaches in saucepan. Cover and cook 20 minutes or until peaches are tender. Meanwhile, cut reserved lemon peel into fine julienne strips; cut strips in half. Boil strips in water 7 or 8 minutes. Drain; set aside. Add cooked peaches and chicken broth to food processor or blender. Process until smooth. Stir in julienned lemon strips and pepper to taste. Serve hot over grilled chicken.   Makes 2½ cups

Nutrients per Serving:

Calories	16	(4% of calories from fat)			
Total Fat	<1 g	Dietary Fiber	1 g	Thiamine	<1 mg
Saturated Fat	<1 g	Protein	<1 g	Riboflavin	<1 mg
Cholesterol	0 mg	Calcium	15 mg	Niacin	<1 mg
Sodium	1 mg	Iron	<1 mg	Vitamin A	15 RE
Carbohydrate	5 g	Folate	2 µg	Vitamin C	18 mg

Dietary Exchanges: ½ Fruit

Turkey Split Pea Soup

164 **Turkey Pistachio Sandwich**

Eating yogurt regularly can help in the functioning of the immune system by stimulating the production of proteins that attack viruses.

½ cup plain low fat yogurt
¼ cup chopped salted pistachio nuts
1 teaspoon dried dill weed
4 lettuce leaves
8 slices whole wheat bread
8 ounces cooked turkey breast, sliced

In small bowl, combine yogurt, pistachios and dill. Cover and refrigerate at least 1 hour or overnight to allow flavors to blend.

To serve, arrange 1 lettuce leaf on bread slice and top leaf with 2 ounces turkey. Spoon 2 tablespoons yogurt mixture over turkey and top with bread slice. Repeat with remaining ingredients.

Makes 4 servings

Nutrients per Serving:					
Calories	284	(21% calories from fat)			
Total Fat	7 g	Dietary Fiber	4 g	Thiamine	<1 mg
Saturated Fat	1 g	Protein	26 g	Riboflavin	<1 mg
Cholesterol	51 mg	Calcium	129 mg	Niacin	<1 mg
Sodium	350 mg	Iron	3 mg	Vitamin A	14 RE
Carbohydrate	32 g	Folate	53 μg	Vitamin C	2 mg

Dietary Exchanges: 2 Bread/Starch, 2½ Meat

165 Chicken Chop Suey

Chop suey was first concocted by Chinese cooks in the mid-nineteenth century to feed the workers on the Pacific railroad lines. It literally means "chopped up" leftovers.

1 package (1 ounce) dried black Chinese mushrooms
3 tablespoons reduced sodium soy sauce
1 tablespoon cornstarch
1 pound boneless, skinless chicken breasts or thighs
2 cloves garlic, minced
1 tablespoon peanut or vegetable oil
½ cup thinly sliced celery
½ cup sliced water chestnuts
½ cup bamboo shoots
1 cup chicken broth
  Hot cooked white rice or chow mein noodles
  Thinly sliced green onions (optional)

Place mushrooms in small bowl; cover with warm water. Soak 20 minutes to soften. Drain; squeeze out excess water. Discard stems; quarter caps.

Blend soy sauce with cornstarch in cup until smooth.

Cut chicken into 1-inch pieces; toss with garlic in small bowl. Heat wok or large skillet over medium-high heat; add oil. Add chicken mixture and celery; stir-fry 2 minutes. Add water chestnuts and bamboo shoots; stir-fry 1 minute. Add broth and mushrooms; cook 3 minutes or until chicken is no longer pink in center, stirring frequently.

Stir soy sauce mixture and add to wok. Cook and stir 1 to 2 minutes until sauce boils and thickens. Serve over rice. Garnish with onions.

Makes 4 servings

Nutrients per Serving:

Calories	208	(28% of calories from fat)			
Total Fat	6 g	Dietary Fiber	1 g	Thiamine	<1 mg
Saturated Fat	1 g	Protein	25 g	Riboflavin	<1 mg
Cholesterol	58 mg	Calcium	27 mg	Niacin	12 mg
Sodium	657 mg	Iron	2 mg	Vitamin A	7 RE
Carbohydrate	11 g	Folate	24 µg	Vitamin C	3 mg

Dietary Exchanges: 3 Meat, 2 Vegetable

166 Turkey, Potato and Corn Casserole

Corn is high in cancer fighting compounds and also has substances that fight viruses.

½ cup chopped green bell pepper
½ cup sliced green onions
3 tablespoons margarine
1 can (15 ounces) cream-style corn
2 cups skim milk
½ teaspoon salt
⅛ teaspoon ground black pepper
2 cups cooked turkey, cut into ½-inch cubes
2 cups instant potato flakes
¼ cup grated Parmesan cheese
2 tablespoons green onion tops, sliced

Preheat oven to 375°F. In 3-quart saucepan, over medium-high heat, cook and stir bell pepper and ½ cup onions in margarine 4 to 5 minutes or until crisp-tender. Add corn, milk, salt and black pepper. Reduce heat to medium and cook until mixture begins to bubble; remove from heat. Fold in turkey and potato flakes.

Pour turkey mixture into lightly greased 9-inch square casserole dish. Sprinkle with cheese and 2 tablespoons onion. Bake 25 minutes or until top is lightly browned.   Makes 6 servings

Nutrients per Serving:

Calories	300	(23% of calories from fat)			
Total Fat	8 g	Dietary Fiber	1 g	Thiamine	<1 mg
Saturated Fat	2 g	Protein	19 g	Riboflavin	<1 mg
Cholesterol	36 mg	Calcium	175 mg	Niacin	4 mg
Sodium	619 mg	Iron	1 mg	Vitamin A	189 RE
Carbohydrate	40 g	Folate	44 µg	Vitamin C	25 mg

Dietary Exchanges: 2 Starch/Bread, 2 Meat, 1 Fruit, 1½ Fat

Chicken Chop Suey

167 Turkey Waldorf Sandwich

When choosing lettuce, pick heads that are dark green. Avoid wilted, brown or rust-spotted leaves. The darker the color of the lettuce, the more nutritious it is.

6 ounces cooked turkey breast, cubed
½ cup diced celery
1 small Red Delicious apple, cored and cut into small cubes
2 tablespoons chopped walnuts
1 tablespoon reduced calorie mayonnaise
1 tablespoon nonfat yogurt
⅛ teaspoon ground nutmeg
⅛ teaspoon ground cinnamon
4 lettuce leaves
8 slices reduced calorie raisin bread

In medium bowl, combine turkey, celery, apple, walnuts, mayonnaise, yogurt, nutmeg and cinnamon. Cover and refrigerate at least 1 hour or overnight to allow flavors to blend.

To serve, arrange 1 lettuce leaf on bread slice. Spoon ¾ cup turkey mixture over lettuce and top with bread slice. Repeat with remaining ingredients. Turkey mixture will keep up to four days in refrigerator.　　　　　　　　**Makes 4 servings**

Nutrients per Serving:

Calories	188	(22% of calories from fat)			
Total Fat	5 g	Dietary Fiber	2 g	Thiamine	<1 mg
Saturated Fat	1 g	Protein	16 g	Riboflavin	<1 mg
Cholesterol	37 mg	Calcium	54 mg	Niacin	4 mg
Sodium	137 mg	Iron	2 mg	Vitamin A	20 RE
Carbohydrate	20 g	Folate	31 μg	Vitamin C	4 mg

Dietary Exchanges: ½ Starch/Bread, 2 Meat, ½ Fruit

168 Stuffed Turkey Tenderloins

One ½-cup serving of wild rice has about 10 times the amount of folic acid as white rice, a nutrient important for the formation and growth of red blood cells.

1¼ pounds boneless turkey tenderloins
2 cups frozen spinach, thawed
3 cups cooked wild rice
¼ cup reduced calorie margarine, softened
¼ cup raisins
¼ cup chopped almonds (optional)
¼ cup chopped onion
1 teaspoon grated orange peel
1 teaspoon lemon pepper
¼ teaspoon dried thyme
1 tablespoon sherry (optional)
2 tablespoons reduced calorie margarine, melted

Preheat oven to 325°F. Butterfly the turkey tenderloins by starting at curved edge, slicing horizontally almost cutting all the way through. Lay each cut open. Drain spinach and press out excess liquid. Spoon half of spinach evenly over each butterflied piece of turkey. In large bowl, mix wild rice, softened margarine, raisins, almonds, onion, orange peel, lemon pepper, thyme and sherry. Spoon ½ cup wild rice mixture evenly over spinach layer.

Roll up tenderloins, starting at pointed short edge. Secure with string or toothpicks. Set aside. Grease 2½-quart square baking dish. Spoon remaining wild rice stuffing into dish. Place turkey rolls over stuffing. Cover; bake 45 minutes. Remove cover; brush with melted margarine and bake 15 minutes. Slice turkey rolls and serve over stuffing.

　　　　　　　　Makes 6 servings

Nutrients per Serving:

Calories	249	(29% of calories from fat)			
Total Fat	8 g	Dietary Fiber	3 g	Thiamine	<1 mg
Saturated Fat	2 g	Protein	23 g	Riboflavin	<1 mg
Cholesterol	41 mg	Calcium	118 mg	Niacin	5 mg
Sodium	230 mg	Iron	3 mg	Vitamin A	663 RE
Carbohydrate	22 g	Folate	100 μg	Vitamin C	10 mg

Dietary Exchanges: 1 Starch/Bread, 2 Meat, 1 Vegetable, 1 Fat

Turkey Waldorf Sandwich

Chunky Sweet 'n' Sour Sauce

169 Chunky Sweet 'n' Sour Sauce

The colorful sauce in this recipe adds lots of nutrients and flavor without adding much fat.

- **1 tablespoon vegetable oil**
- **1 clove garlic, minced**
- **½ cup packed light brown sugar**
- **⅓ cup cider vinegar**
- **4 teaspoons reduced sodium soy sauce**
- **1 tablespoon paprika**
- **1 cup water**
- **2 tablespoons cornstarch**
- **1 cup diced fresh pineapple**
- **1 cup peeled, seeded and chopped tomato**
- **½ cup diced green bell pepper**
- **½ cup diced onion**

Heat oil over medium heat in medium saucepan. Add garlic and cook for 1 minute. Add brown sugar, vinegar, soy sauce, paprika and water. Cook over medium heat for 1 minute. Combine cornstarch with about 3 tablespoons of sauce in cup. Gradually stir cornstarch mixture back into sauce. Add pineapple, tomato, bell pepper and onion. Cook, uncovered, 5 to 7 minutes or until sauce thickens and vegetables are crisp-tender. Serve hot over broiled chicken breasts.

Makes 12 (⅓-cup) servings

Nutrients per Serving:					
Calories	68	(16% of calories from fat)			
Total Fat	1 g	Dietary Fiber	1 g	Thiamine	<1 mg
Saturated Fat	<1 g	Protein	1 g	Riboflavin	<1 mg
Cholesterol	0 mg	Calcium	14 mg	Niacin	<1 mg
Sodium	64 mg	Iron	1 mg	Vitamin A	49 RE
Carbohydrate	15 g	Folate	8 μg	Vitamin C	15 mg

Dietary Exchanges: 1 Fruit

170 Broccoli Cheese Casserole

Chicken is an excellent source of high-quality protein and B vitamins, yet low in saturated fat.

   3 whole chicken breasts, skinned and halved
1½ pounds fresh broccoli
   2 tablespoons margarine
   ½ cup chopped onion
   1 clove garlic, minced
   3 tablespoons all-purpose flour
1¼ cups skim milk
   2 tablespoons fresh parsley
   ½ teaspoon salt
   ½ teaspoon dried oregano leaves, crushed
1½ cups 1% low fat cream-style small curd cottage cheese
1½ cups shredded reduced fat Wisconsin Cheddar cheese
   ¼ cup grated Wisconsin Romano cheese
   1 jar (4½ ounces) sliced mushrooms, drained
   6 ounces noodles, cooked and drained

Microwave Directions: Place chicken breasts in microwavable glass baking dish. Microwave at HIGH (100% power) 7 minutes. Cool slightly and cube. Set aside. Remove flowerets from broccoli and cut larger ones in half. Cut stems into 1-inch pieces. Place broccoli in 3-quart microwavable baking dish with ½ cup water. Cover and microwave at HIGH (100% power) 7 minutes, stirring once. Let stand, covered, 2 minutes. Drain well; set aside.

Place margarine, onion and garlic in same baking dish. Cover and microwave at HIGH (100% power) 3 minutes. Stir in flour. Gradually add milk. Add parsley, salt and oregano. Microwave at HIGH (100% power) 1 minute. Stir well; microwave 1 minute. Stir in cottage cheese. Microwave at HIGH (100% power) 2 minutes. Stir; microwave 2 minutes. Add Cheddar and Romano cheeses, stirring well.

Microwave at MEDIUM-HIGH (70% power) 2 minutes. Stir in chicken, broccoli, mushrooms and noodles. Cover and microwave at MEDIUM (50% power) 5 minutes or until heated through.

Makes 6 to 8 servings

Nutrients per Serving:

Calories	462	(24% of calories from fat)			
Total Fat	12 g	Dietary Fiber	6 g	Thiamine	<1 mg
Saturated Fat	5 g	Protein	51 g	Riboflavin	1 mg
Cholesterol	96 mg	Calcium	432 mg	Niacin	14 mg
Sodium	1,085 mg	Iron	3 mg	Vitamin A	304 RE
Carbohydrate	36 g	Folate	83 µg	Vitamin C	88 mg

Dietary Exchanges: 2 Starch/Bread, 5 Meat, 1½ Vegetable

171 Celery-Chicken Gumbo

Celery is nearly calorie-free because it contains so much water, but its flavor is irreplaceable in the foundations of soups and stews.

1 tablespoon vegetable oil
3 cups thinly sliced celery
1 cup chopped onion
1 teaspoon crushed garlic
8 ounces boneless, skinless chicken breasts, cut into ½-inch chunks
1 can (16 ounces) tomatoes packed in juice
2 cans (13¾ ounces each) ⅓-less-salt chicken broth
½ cup long-grain rice

Heat oil until hot in large saucepan. Add celery, onion and garlic; cook and stir vegetables until crisp-tender, about 5 minutes. Add chicken; cook, stirring occasionally until chicken is no longer pink in center, about 2 minutes. Cut up tomatoes in can; add to chicken mixture. Stir in chicken broth and rice; bring to a boil; reduce heat and simmer, covered, until rice is tender, 10 to 12 minutes. Serve immediately.

Makes 4 servings

Nutrients per Serving:

Calories	234	(21% of calories from fat)			
Total Fat	6 g	Dietary Fiber	3 g	Thiamine	<1 mg
Saturated Fat	1 g	Protein	16 g	Riboflavin	<1 mg
Cholesterol	29 mg	Calcium	92 mg	Niacin	8 mg
Sodium	318 mg	Iron	3 mg	Vitamin A	82 RE
Carbohydrate	31 g	Folate	45 µg	Vitamin C	26 mg

Dietary Exchanges: 1½ Starch/Bread, 1½ Meat, 2 Vegetable

172 Oriental Chicken Kabobs

Poultry is a good source of niacin (vitamin B₃). One serving of this recipe fulfills over half the daily requirement of niacin, which is crucial in the conversion of food into energy.

1 pound boneless, skinless chicken breasts
2 small zucchini or yellow squash, cut into 1-inch slices
8 large fresh mushrooms
1 large red, yellow or green bell pepper, cut into 1-inch pieces
¼ cup low sodium soy sauce
2 tablespoons dry sherry
2 teaspoons sesame oil
2 cloves garlic, minced
2 large green onions, cut into 1-inch pieces

Cut chicken into 1½-inch pieces; place in large freezer food storage bag. Add zucchini, mushrooms and bell pepper to bag. Combine soy sauce, sherry, oil and garlic in cup; pour over chicken and vegetables. Close bag securely; turn to coat. Marinate in refrigerator 30 minutes or up to 4 hours.

Drain chicken and vegetables; reserve marinade. Alternately thread chicken and vegetables with onions onto metal skewers.

Place kabobs on rack of broiler pan. Brush with half the reserved marinade. Broil 5 to 6 inches from heat 5 minutes. Turn kabobs over; brush with remaining marinade. Discard remaining marinade. Broil 5 minutes or until chicken is no longer pink in center. *Makes 4 servings*

Nutrients per Serving:

Calories	176	(25% of calories from fat)			
Total Fat	5 g	Dietary Fiber	2 g	Thiamine	<1 mg
Saturated Fat	1 g	Protein	24 g	Riboflavin	<1 mg
Cholesterol	58 mg	Calcium	31 mg	Niacin	11 mg
Sodium	582 mg	Iron	2 mg	Vitamin A	51 RE
Carbohydrate	7 g	Folate	28 μg	Vitamin C	25 mg

Dietary Exchanges: 3 Meat, 1 Vegetable

173 Celery with Sausage and Peppers

New information on celery has shown that it may lower blood pressure and act as a mild diuretic.

8 ounces sweet Italian turkey sausage, sliced ½ inch thick
3 cups sliced celery
1 cup diced onion
1 cup diced green bell pepper
2 cans (14½ ounces *each*) no-salt-added stewed tomatoes
¼ teaspoon black pepper
3 cups cooked rotelle pasta

Spray large skillet with nonstick cooking spray; heat over medium-high heat. Add turkey sausage; cook, stirring occasionally, until brown, 5 to 6 minutes. Add celery, onion and bell pepper; cook, stirring occasionally, until vegetables are crisp-tender, about 5 minutes. Break up tomatoes and add with black pepper to sausage mixture; simmer, uncovered, until mixture thickens, about 5 minutes. Stir in rotelle; cook until heated through, about 2 minutes. Serve hot. *Makes 4 servings*

Nutrients per Serving:

Calories	333	(30% of calories from fat)			
Total Fat	11 g	Dietary Fiber	5 g	Thiamine	<1 mg
Saturated Fat	2 g	Protein	16 g	Riboflavin	<1 mg
Cholesterol	46 mg	Calcium	92 mg	Niacin	6 mg
Sodium	484 mg	Iron	4 mg	Vitamin A	109 RE
Carbohydrate	44 g	Folate	58 μg	Vitamin C	75 mg

Dietary Exchanges: 2 Starch/Bread, 1½ Meat, 3 Vegetable, 2 Fat

Oriental Chicken Kabobs

174 Turkey, Corn and Sweet Potato Soup

Since there is about five times the amount of the Recommended Daily Allowance of vitamin A in a medium sweet potato, they are high on the list of foods that may reduce the risk of cancer.

½ **cup chopped onion**
1 **small jalapeño pepper, minced**
1 **teaspoon margarine**
5 **cups turkey broth or reduced sodium chicken bouillon**
1½ **pounds sweet potatoes, peeled and cut into 1-inch cubes**
2 **cups cooked turkey, cut into ½-inch cubes**
½ **teaspoon salt**
1½ **cups frozen corn**
Fresh cilantro (optional)

In 5-quart saucepan, over medium-high heat, cook and stir onion and jalapeño pepper in margarine 5 minutes or until onion is soft. Add broth, potatoes, turkey and salt; bring to a boil. Reduce heat to low, cover and simmer 20 to 25 minutes or until potatoes are tender. Stir in corn. Increase heat to medium and cook 5 to 6 minutes.

To serve, spoon 1 cup soup in bowl and garnish with cilantro, if desired.   Makes 8 servings

Nutrients per Serving:

Calories	155	(7% of calories from fat)			
Total Fat	1 g	Dietary Fiber	3 g	Thiamine	<1 mg
Saturated Fat	<1 g	Protein	12 g	Riboflavin	<1 mg
Cholesterol	24 mg	Calcium	36 mg	Niacin	4 mg
Sodium	254 mg	Iron	1 mg	Vitamin A	1,462 RE
Carbohydrate	24 g	Folate	26 µg	Vitamin C	18 mg

Dietary Exchanges: 1½ Starch/Bread, 1 Meat

175 Peruvian Chicken with Plums

Some compounds in plums may combat bacteria and viruses in the body. They are also high in fiber and taste delicious.

1 **chicken (3½ pounds), skinned and cut up**
1 **teaspoon vegetable oil**
1 **cup chopped onion**
1 **cup diced green bell pepper**
2 **teaspoons minced garlic**
1 **tomato, chopped**
1 **fresh jalapeño pepper, seeded and diced**
¼ **teaspoon powdered saffron (optional)**
3½ **cups ⅓-less-salt chicken broth**
1 **bay leaf**
4 **fresh California plums, halved, pitted and quartered**
4 **cups cooked brown rice**
Additional plum wedges (optional)

Cook and stir chicken in oil in large nonstick skillet, turning often until golden brown on all sides, about 12 minutes. Add onion, bell pepper and garlic; cook and stir 2 minutes longer. Add tomato, jalapeño pepper, saffron, broth and bay leaf. Bring to a boil; cover and simmer 10 minutes. Add quartered plums and rice; heat through. Remove and discard bay leaf. Serve with plum wedges, if desired.

Makes 8 servings

Nutrients per Serving:

Calories	344	(25% of calories from fat)			
Total Fat	9 g	Dietary Fiber	3 g	Thiamine	<1 mg
Saturated Fat	2 g	Protein	33 g	Riboflavin	<1 mg
Cholesterol	90 mg	Calcium	43 mg	Niacin	12 mg
Sodium	174 mg	Iron	2 mg	Vitamin A	51 RE
Carbohydrate	31 g	Folate	24 µg	Vitamin C	31 mg

Dietary Exchanges: 1½ Starch/Bread, 4 Meat

Turkey, Corn and Sweet Potato Soup

SEAFOOD

176 Red Clam Sauce with Vegetables

This recipe is loaded with nutrients. The tomatoes, bell pepper and squash provide vitamins A and C, the clams provide protein and iron and the spaghetti contributes carbohydrates and B vitamins.

2 cups sliced fresh mushrooms
1 can (14½ ounces) no-salt-added stewed tomatoes, undrained
1 cup chopped green bell pepper
1 can (8 ounces) no-salt-added tomato sauce
½ cup chopped onion
1½ teaspoons dried basil leaves, crushed
¾ teaspoon dried savory leaves, crushed
½ teaspoon black pepper
1 small yellow squash, sliced and halved
2 cans (6½ ounces each) minced clams, drained, reserving liquid
2 tablespoons cornstarch
3 cups hot cooked spaghetti

Combine mushrooms, tomatoes with liquid, bell pepper, tomato sauce, onion, basil, savory and black pepper in large saucepan. Bring to a boil over medium-high heat. Reduce heat to medium. Cover and cook 5 to 6 minutes or until vegetables are tender.

Stir in squash and clams. Combine ½ cup clam liquid and cornstarch in small bowl. Stir into mixture in saucepan. Cook and stir over medium heat until mixture boils and thickens. Cook and stir 2 minutes more. Serve over spaghetti.

Makes 4 servings

Nutrients per Serving:

Calories	393	(8% of calories from fat)			
Total Fat	3 g	Dietary Fiber	7 g	Thiamine	1 mg
Saturated Fat	<1 g	Protein	33 g	Riboflavin	1 mg
Cholesterol	62 mg	Calcium	148 mg	Niacin	8 mg
Sodium	136 mg	Iron	30 mg	Vitamin A	344 RE
Carbohydrate	58 g	Folate	72 μg	Vitamin C	99 mg

Dietary Exchanges: 3 Starch/Bread, 3 Meat, 1 Vegetable

177 Beijing Fillet of Sole

These rolled, stuffed fillets are easy to bake in just 30 minutes.

2 tablespoons low sodium soy sauce
2 teaspoons Oriental sesame oil
4 sole fillets (6 ounces each)
1¼ cups preshredded coleslaw mix or shredded cabbage
½ cup crushed chow mein noodles
1 egg white, slightly beaten
2 teaspoons toasted sesame seeds*
1 package (10 ounces) frozen snow peas, cooked and drained

Preheat oven to 350°F. Combine soy sauce and sesame oil in small bowl. Place sole in shallow dish. Lightly brush both sides of sole with soy sauce mixture.

Combine coleslaw mix, noodles, egg white and remaining soy sauce mixture in small bowl. Spoon evenly over sole. Roll up each fillet and place, seam side down, in shallow, foil-lined roasting pan. Sprinkle rolls with sesame seeds. Bake 25 to 30 minutes until fish flakes easily when tested with fork. Serve with snow peas.   Makes 4 servings

*To toast sesame seeds, spread seeds in small skillet. Shake skillet over medium heat 2 minutes or until seeds begin to pop and turn golden.

Nutrients per Serving:

Calories	252	(29% of calories from fat)			
Total Fat	8 g	Dietary Fiber	<1 g	Thiamine	<1 mg
Saturated Fat	1 g	Protein	34 g	Riboflavin	<1 mg
Cholesterol	80 mg	Calcium	86 mg	Niacin	4 mg
Sodium	435 mg	Iron	2 mg	Vitamin A	237 RE
Carbohydrate	6 g	Folate	29 μg	Vitamin C	32 mg

Dietary Exchanges: 4 Meat, 1½ Vegetable

Red Clam Sauce with Vegetables

178 Lemon Poached Halibut with Carrots

Halibut's low fat content makes it ideal for poaching. It is also lower in cholesterol and sodium than many other kinds of fish.

3 medium carrots, cut into julienne strips
¾ cup water
¼ cup dry white wine
2 tablespoons lemon juice
1 teaspoon dried rosemary leaves, crushed
1 teaspoon dried marjoram leaves, crushed
1 teaspoon chicken or fish bouillon granules
¼ teaspoon pepper
4 fresh or frozen halibut steaks, cut 1 inch thick (about 1½ pounds)
½ cup sliced green onions
Lemon slices for garnish

Combine carrots, water, wine, lemon juice, rosemary, marjoram, bouillon granules and pepper in large skillet. Bring to a boil over high heat. Carefully place fish and onions in skillet. Return just to boiling. Reduce heat to medium-low. Cover; simmer 8 to 10 minutes or until fish flakes easily when tested with fork.

Carefully transfer fish to serving platter with slotted spatula. Spoon vegetables over fish. Garnish with lemon slices, if desired.   Makes 4 servings

Nutrients per Serving:

Calories	224	(17% of calories from fat)			
Total Fat	4 g	Dietary Fiber	2 g	Thiamine	<1 mg
Saturated Fat	1 g	Protein	36 g	Riboflavin	<1 mg
Cholesterol	55 mg	Calcium	110 mg	Niacin	10 mg
Sodium	338 mg	Iron	2 mg	Vitamin A	1,670 RE
Carbohydrate	8 g	Folate	10 μg	Vitamin C	14 mg

Dietary Exchanges: 4 Meat, 1½ Vegetable

179 Chinese Steamed Fish

When buying peaches for use in cooking, try to find "freestone" variety peaches. These are peaches in which the pit separates easily from the flesh for easy halving and slicing.

12 ounces firm white fish fillets, such as swordfish
Ground pepper
2 teaspoons cornstarch
2 teaspoons low sodium soy sauce
2 teaspoons dry sherry
1 tablespoon finely chopped green onion
¼ teaspoon minced fresh ginger
1 clove garlic, minced
1½ cups sliced fresh California peaches

Cut fish lengthwise into 2-inch-wide strips. Sprinkle with pepper to taste. Combine cornstarch, soy sauce and sherry in bowl.

Add fish strips; coat with cornstarch mixture. Lay fish strips in spirals in shallow baking dish; sprinkle with onion, ginger, garlic and peaches. Place rack in bottom of large wok. Pour hot water into bottom of wok, under rack, and bring to a boil. Place dish on rack; cover. Steam 10 to 15 minutes or just until fish flakes easily when tested with fork. Transfer fish strips and peaches to serving dish using wide spatula. Spoon sauce from wok over fish, if desired.

Makes 4 servings

Nutrients per Serving:

Calories	129	(25% of calories from fat)			
Total Fat	3 g	Dietary Fiber	1 g	Thiamine	<1 mg
Saturated Fat	1 g	Protein	17 g	Riboflavin	<1 mg
Cholesterol	34 mg	Calcium	8 mg	Niacin	8 mg
Sodium	177 mg	Iron	1 mg	Vitamin A	51 RE
Carbohydrate	6 g	Folate	4 μg	Vitamin C	4 mg

Dietary Exchanges: 2 Meat, ½ Fruit

180 Shrimp and Fish Gumbo

Although shrimp are high in cholesterol (about 150 mg for one 3-ounce serving), this recipe combines them with lower cholesterol orange roughy (about 25 mg for one 3-ounce serving) to provide a great-tasting gumbo with no cholesterol worries.

**8 ounces fresh or frozen orange roughy or
   other fish fillets
6 ounces deveined shelled raw shrimp
3¾ cups water, divided
1 cup chopped onion
½ cup chopped green bell pepper
2 cloves garlic, minced
½ teaspoon chicken or fish bouillon
   granules
2 cans (14½ ounces each) no-salt-added
   stewed tomatoes, undrained
1½ cups frozen okra, thawed
1 teaspoon dried thyme leaves, crushed
1 teaspoon dried savory leaves, crushed
¼ teaspoon ground red pepper
⅛ teaspoon black pepper
2 tablespoons cornstarch
2 tablespoons finely chopped low
   sodium ham
2 cups hot cooked brown rice**

Remove and discard skin from fish; cut fish into 1-inch pieces. Bring 3 cups water to a boil over high heat in medium saucepan. Add fish and shrimp. Cook 3 to 4 minutes or until fish flakes easily when tested with fork and shrimp are opaque; drain. Combine onion, bell pepper, additional ½ cup water, garlic and bouillon granules in large saucepan. Bring to a boil over medium-high heat; reduce to medium-low. Cover and simmer 2 to 3 minutes or until vegetables are crisp-tender.

Stir in stewed tomatoes with liquid, okra, thyme, savory, red pepper and black pepper. Return to a boil; reduce heat. Simmer, uncovered, 3 to 5

minutes or until okra is tender. Combine remaining ¼ cup water and cornstarch in small bowl. Stir into mixture in saucepan. Cook and stir over medium heat until mixture boils and thickens. Cook and stir 2 minutes more. Add fish, shrimp and ham; heat through. Serve over rice. Makes 4 servings

Nutrients per Serving:

Calories	338	(17% of calories from fat)			
Total Fat	7 g	Dietary Fiber	7 g	Thiamine	<1 mg
Saturated Fat	1 g	Protein	22 g	Riboflavin	<1 mg
Cholesterol	77 mg	Calcium	112 mg	Niacin	6 mg
Sodium	274 mg	Iron	4 mg	Vitamin A	258 RE
Carbohydrate	49 g	Folate	77 µg	Vitamin C	86 mg

Dietary Exchanges: 2 Starch/Bread, 2 Meat, 3 Vegetable

181 Shanghai Steamed Fish

By steaming the fish in this recipe, not only is the chance of it drying out reduced but there is also no added fat.

**1 cleaned whole small sea bass, red
   snapper, carp or a small grouper
   (about 1½ pounds)
¼ cup teriyaki sauce
2 teaspoons shredded fresh ginger
2 green onions, cut into 4-inch pieces**

Sprinkle cavity of fish with teriyaki sauce and ginger. Place onions in cavity in single layer.

Pour enough water into wok to reach level just below steaming rack. Bring water to a boil over high heat. Reduce heat to medium-low; simmer. Place fish on steaming rack. Cover; steam fish 10 minutes per inch of thickness measured at thickest part of fish. Fish is done when it flakes easily when tested with fork.

Carefully remove fish; discard onions. Cut fish into four serving-size portions. Makes 4 servings

Nutrients per Serving:

Calories	181	(18% of calories from fat)			
Total Fat	3 g	Dietary Fiber	<1 g	Thiamine	<1 mg
Saturated Fat	1 g	Protein	33 g	Riboflavin	<1 mg
Cholesterol	71 mg	Calcium	24 mg	Niacin	3 mg
Sodium	806 mg	Iron	1 mg	Vitamin A	98 RE
Carbohydrate	3 g	Folate	14 µg	Vitamin C	5 mg

Dietary Exchanges: 3½ Meat

Shrimp and Fish Gumbo

182 Fish Fillets with Yogurt Sauce

Scientific studies have shown that Acidophilus yogurt cultures may neutralize cancer-causing agents in the intestinal tract.

1 pound frozen fish fillets, thawed and drained
⅓ cup plain yogurt
1 tablespoon lemon juice
1 tablespoon Dijon-style mustard

Microwave Directions: Place fillets in shallow glass baking dish. Blend together yogurt, lemon juice and mustard. Spread mixture over fish. Cover; microwave at HIGH (100% power) 4 minutes. Allow to stand, covered, 3 minutes before serving.

Makes 4 servings

Nutrients per Serving:

Calories	108	(15% of calories from fat)			
Total Fat	2 g	Dietary Fiber	<1 g	Thiamine	<1 mg
Saturated Fat	1 g	Protein	20 g	Riboflavin	<1 mg
Cholesterol	54 mg	Calcium	54 mg	Niacin	2 mg
Sodium	146 mg	Iron	<1 mg	Vitamin A	12 RE
Carbohydrate	2 g	Folate	10 μg	Vitamin C	2 mg

Dietary Exchanges: 2½ Meat

[183] Red Snapper with Brown Rice and Tomato Stuffing

Red snapper is considered a lean fish because it is less than 5% fat by weight and less than 9% of its calories come from fat.

1 can (14½ ounces) low sodium chicken broth, defatted
⅓ cup water
1 cup brown rice
1½ tablespoons chopped fresh savory or
  1½ teaspoons dried savory leaves, crushed
1 tablespoon chopped fresh oregano or
  ¾ teaspoon dried oregano leaves, crushed
⅛ teaspoon ground red pepper
¾ cup coarsely chopped yellow summer squash
⅓ cup sliced green onions
¼ cup chopped fresh parsley
1 cup chopped tomatoes
3 to 4 lime slices
  Fresh savory sprigs (optional)
  Fresh oregano sprigs (optional)
2 to 2½ pounds fresh or frozen red or yellow tail snapper, scaled and head removed
  Diagonally sliced green onions or green onion fans for garnish

Bring broth and water to a boil over high heat in medium saucepan. Stir in rice, 1½ tablespoons savory, 1 tablespoon oregano and red pepper. Return to a boil. Reduce heat to medium-low. Cover and simmer 20 minutes. Stir in squash, ⅓ cup green onions and parsley. Cover; simmer 15 minutes more until rice is almost tender and liquid is absorbed. Stir in tomatoes. Spoon into ungreased 1½-quart covered casserole.

Preheat oven to 400°F. Spray shallow baking pan with nonstick cooking spray. Arrange lime slices, savory and/or oregano sprigs in fish cavity. Place

fish in pan. Place fish and stuffing in oven at same time. Bake 25 to 30 minutes or until fish flakes easily when tested with fork and stuffing is heated through. Spoon stuffing onto platter; arrange fish on top. Garnish fish with green onions.

Makes 4 servings

Nutrients per Serving:

Calories	430	(11% of calories from fat)			
Total Fat	5 g	Dietary Fiber	4 g	Thiamine	<1 mg
Saturated Fat	1 g	Protein	52 g	Riboflavin	<1 mg
Cholesterol	83 mg	Calcium	130 mg	Niacin	4 mg
Sodium	130 mg	Iron	2 mg	Vitamin A	101 RE
Carbohydrate	42 g	Folate	33 μg	Vitamin C	21 mg

Dietary Exchanges: 2½ Starch/Bread, 4 Meat, 1 Vegetable

[184] Broiled Hunan Fish Fillets

When cooking fish be careful not to overcook it. Fish cooks quickly, so it doesn't take much to dry it out. The fish is done when it turns opaque and flakes easily when tested with a fork.

3 tablespoons low sodium soy sauce
1 tablespoon finely chopped green onion
2 teaspoons sesame oil
1 teaspoon minced fresh ginger
1 clove garlic, minced
¼ teaspoon crushed red pepper flakes
1 pound red snapper, scrod or cod fillets

Combine soy sauce, onion, sesame oil, ginger, garlic and red pepper flakes in cup.

Spray rack of broiler pan with nonstick cooking spray. Place fish on rack; brush with soy sauce mixture.

Broil 4 to 5 inches from heat 10 minutes or until fish flakes easily when tested with fork.

Makes 4 servings

Nutrients per Serving:

Calories	143	(24% of calories from fat)			
Total Fat	4 g	Dietary Fiber	<1 g	Thiamine	<1 mg
Saturated Fat	1 g	Protein	24 g	Riboflavin	<1 mg
Cholesterol	42 mg	Calcium	40 mg	Niacin	1 mg
Sodium	446 mg	Iron	1 mg	Vitamin A	11 RE
Carbohydrate	1 g	Folate	2 μg	Vitamin C	1 mg

Dietary Exchanges: 2½ Meat

Red Snapper with Brown Rice and Tomato Stuffing

185 Broccoli, Scallop and Linguine Toss

Scallops are ideal for a healthy diet. They are low in calories (about 100 calories for one 3-ounce serving), low in fat (about 1 g) and moderate in cholesterol (about 40 mg).

12 ounces fresh or frozen scallops
2 medium onions, halved lengthwise and sliced
1 cup apple juice
2 tablespoons dry white wine
2 cloves garlic, minced
2 teaspoons dried marjoram leaves, crushed
1 teaspoon dried basil leaves, crushed
¼ teaspoon pepper
3 cups broccoli flowerets
¼ cup water
4 teaspoons cornstarch
1½ cups chopped seeded tomatoes
¼ cup grated Parmesan cheese
4 cups cooked linguine

Cut large scallops into 1-inch pieces. Combine onions, apple juice, wine, garlic, marjoram, basil and pepper in large skillet. Bring to a boil over high heat. Add broccoli. Return to a boil. Reduce heat to medium-low. Cover and simmer 7 minutes; add scallops. Return to a boil; reduce heat. Cover and simmer 1 to 2 minutes or until scallops are opaque. Remove scallops and vegetables.

Combine water and cornstarch in small bowl. Stir into mixture in skillet. Cook and stir over medium heat until mixture boils and thickens. Cook and stir 2 minutes more. Stir in tomatoes and cheese; heat through. Return scallops and vegetables to skillet; heat through. Toss mixture with linguine.

Makes 4 servings

Nutrients per Serving:

Calories	248	(13% of calories from fat)			
Total Fat	4 g	Dietary Fiber	4 g	Thiamine	<1 mg
Saturated Fat	1 g	Protein	22 g	Riboflavin	<1 mg
Cholesterol	33 mg	Calcium	174 mg	Niacin	3 mg
Sodium	309 mg	Iron	2 mg	Vitamin A	185 RE
Carbohydrate	33 g	Folate	87 µg	Vitamin C	109 mg

Dietary Exchanges: 1 Starch/Bread, 2 Meat, ½ Fruit, 1½ Vegetable

186 Baked Sole Pacifica

Not only do red pepper strips add color to this recipe, they add nutritional value as well. Red peppers add over twice the amount of vitamin C and six times the amount of vitamin A and beta-carotene as green peppers.

1 can (16 ounces) California cling peach slices in juice or extra light syrup
4 sole fillets (about 1 pound)
½ teaspoon dill weed
1 tablespoon olive oil
2 onions, cut into wedges
4 cups julienned zucchini strips
2 cups red bell pepper strips
½ teaspoon herb pepper seasoning
Lemon wedges

Preheat broiler. Drain peaches, reserving liquid. Place fish on broiler pan. Brush both sides of fillets with reserved liquid and sprinkle with dill weed. Broil about 4 inches from heat 10 minutes or until fish flakes easily when tested with fork. Turn halfway through cooking. Heat oil over medium-high heat in 10-inch skillet. Add onions; cook and stir until crisp-tender. Stir in zucchini; cook and stir 2 minutes. Add bell peppers and peach slices. Cook until heated through. Stir in herb pepper seasoning. To serve, place vegetable-peach mixture onto serving plate and top with fish. Serve with lemon wedges.

Makes 4 servings

Nutrients per Serving:

Calories	241	(18% of calories from fat)			
Total Fat	5 g	Dietary Fiber	6 g	Thiamine	<1 mg
Saturated Fat	1 g	Protein	23 g	Riboflavin	<1 mg
Cholesterol	53 mg	Calcium	61 mg	Niacin	4 mg
Sodium	96 mg	Iron	2 mg	Vitamin A	155 RE
Carbohydrate	29 g	Folate	76 µg	Vitamin C	120 mg

Dietary Exchanges: 2½ Meat, 1 Fruit, 2 Vegetable

Broccoli, Scallop and Linguine Toss

Ragoût of Tuna

187 Dilled Tuna Sandwiches

Capers are pickled unopened flower buds of a Mediterranean shrub. They are used for flavoring and garnish.

1 can (12½ ounces) chunk light tuna in water, drained
¼ cup thinly sliced green onions
¼ cup chopped, seeded cucumber
3 tablespoons reduced calorie mayonnaise
1½ teaspoons drained capers
1 teaspoon Dijon-style mustard
½ to 1 teaspoon lemon juice
¾ teaspoon dried dill weed
Ground white pepper
4 slices multigrain bread, toasted
8 slices cucumber
2 slices tomato, cut into halves

Break tuna into chunks in small bowl; add green onions and chopped cucumber. Stir in mayonnaise, capers, mustard, lemon juice and dill weed; season with pepper to taste. Spread tuna mixture on toasted bread slices (open-faced); garnish with cucumber and tomato slices.   Makes 4 servings

Nutrients per Serving:				
Calories	200	(24% of calories from fat)		
Total Fat	6 g	Dietary Fiber	1 g	Thiamine	<1 mg
Saturated Fat	1 g	Protein	25 g	Riboflavin	<1 mg
Cholesterol	20 mg	Calcium	42 mg	Niacin	12 mg
Sodium	180 mg	Iron	2 mg	Vitamin A	46 RE
Carbohydrate	15 g	Folate	23 µg	Vitamin C	3 mg

Dietary Exchanges: 1 Starch/Bread, 2½ Meat

188 Ragoût of Tuna

Tuna is considered a fatty fish and contains the omega-3 fatty acid which has been shown to lower blood cholesterol.

2 cloves garlic, minced, divided
1 or 2 sprigs fresh mint, chopped or
  1 teaspoon dried mint
½ to 1 teaspoon salt, divided
  Pepper to taste
2 to 2½ pounds fresh tuna or swordfish
2 teaspoons olive oil
½ cup dry white wine
2 medium onions, thinly sliced
1 teaspoon sugar
1 pound ripe tomatoes, coarsely chopped
1 cup hot water
4 cups hot cooked noodles or rice
  (optional)

Combine half of garlic, mint, half of salt and pepper in small bowl. Make about 12 slices into sides of fish. Into each cut insert garlic mixture. Heat oil over medium-high heat in large nonstick skillet; add fish and brown on both sides. Pour wine over fish; continue cooking, basting with liquid, until wine has completely evaporated, about 5 minutes. Remove fish to warm casserole.

Add remaining garlic and onions to skillet; sprinkle with sugar and remaining salt; cook over low heat, about 5 minutes. Return fish to skillet. Add tomatoes and hot water; simmer until fish is cooked through and sauce thickens. To serve, pour sauce over fish and serve remaining sauce with noodles or rice, if desired.

Makes 6 servings

Nutrients per Serving:

Calories	224	(13% of calories from fat)			
Total Fat	3 g	Dietary Fiber	2 g	Thiamine	1 mg
Saturated Fat	1 g	Protein	37 g	Riboflavin	<1 mg
Cholesterol	69 mg	Calcium	40 mg	Niacin	15 mg
Sodium	243 mg	Iron	2 mg	Vitamin A	76 RE
Carbohydrate	8 g	Folate	22 µg	Vitamin C	19 mg

Dietary Exchanges: 4 Meat, 1 Vegetable

189 Lobster Wild Rice Bisque

Imitation lobster is made from a fish paste known as surimi. Surimi was invented by the Japanese who flavored and shaped it into other forms of seafood, such as crab legs and lobster tails. Rich in protein and low in cholesterol, surimi is great in salads, soups and casseroles.

2 tablespoons reduced calorie margarine
1 cup chopped onion
1 can (4 ounces) sliced mushrooms,
  drained
1 tablespoon all-purpose flour
2 teaspoons rosemary leaves, crushed
½ teaspoon salt
½ teaspoon pepper
4 cups low sodium chicken broth
1 cup skim milk
¼ cup dry sherry
2 cups cooked wild rice
1 cup chopped, canned tomatoes
6 ounces imitation lobster, cut in 1-inch
  chunks
1 cup shredded low fat Cheddar cheese

Heat margarine in large skillet until melted and bubbly. Add onion and mushrooms; cook and stir until tender. Stir in flour, rosemary, salt and pepper. Cook until bubbly. Gradually stir in chicken broth; bring to a boil, stirring often. Stir in milk and sherry. Add wild rice, tomatoes and lobster. Cook until heated through. Fold in cheese.

Makes 10 servings

Nutrients per Serving:

Calories	135	(26% of calories from fat)			
Total Fat	4 g	Dietary Fiber	1 g	Thiamine	<1 mg
Saturated Fat	1 g	Protein	9 g	Riboflavin	<1 mg
Cholesterol	15 mg	Calcium	132 mg	Niacin	2 mg
Sodium	36 mg	Iron	1 mg	Vitamin A	62 RE
Carbohydrate	15 g	Folate	19 µg	Vitamin C	5 mg

Dietary Exchanges: 1 Starch/Bread, 1 Meat, ½ Vegetable

190 Oriental Baked Seafood

Whereas oysters and clams are eaten whole, only the white adductor muscle of a scallop is used in cooking.

¼ cup chopped California Almonds
2 cups water
½ teaspoon salt
1 cup long-grain white rice
1 tablespoon sesame oil
1 tablespoon grated fresh ginger
1 teaspoon grated lemon peel
1 pound halibut
½ pound large scallops
¼ pound medium shrimp, shelled and deveined
1 clove garlic, minced
1 tablespoon light soy sauce
½ cup slivered green onions

Preheat oven to 350°F. Spread almonds in shallow baking pan. Toast in oven 5 to 8 minutes until lightly browned, stirring occasionally; cool. Bring water and salt to a boil in medium saucepan. Stir in rice, sesame oil, ginger and lemon peel. Bring to a boil; cover and reduce heat to low. Simmer 20 to 25 minutes until water is absorbed. Meanwhile, preheat oven to 400°F or preheat broiler or grill. Remove skin and bones from halibut; cut into large pieces. Cut 4 (12-inch) squares of foil. Divide halibut, scallops and shrimp among foil. Sprinkle seafood with garlic and soy sauce; seal squares tightly. Bake 12 minutes or broil or grill 4 inches from heat 15 minutes, turning once. Stir almonds into rice. Pour seafood mixture and juices over rice. Sprinkle with green onions. *Makes 4 servings*

Microwave Directions: Spread almonds in shallow pan. Cook at HIGH (100% power) 2 minutes, stirring often; cool. Combine water, salt, rice, sesame oil, ginger and lemon peel in 3-quart microwave-safe dish. Cover with plastic wrap. Cook at HIGH (100% power) 12 minutes, stirring halfway through. Let stand 10 minutes. Prepare fish packets as above on parchment paper, not foil. Bring edges up and seal with rubber band. Place packets in microwave-safe baking dish. Cook at HIGH (100% power) 5 minutes, rotating dish. Serve as directed.

Nutrients per Serving:

Calories	412	(17% of calories from fat)			
Total Fat	8 g	Dietary Fiber	1 g	Thiamine	<1 mg
Saturated Fat	1 g	Protein	43 g	Riboflavin	<1 mg
Cholesterol	99 mg	Calcium	122 mg	Niacin	10 mg
Sodium	629 mg	Iron	4 mg	Vitamin A	124 RE
Carbohydrate	41 g	Folate	21 μg	Vitamin C	8 mg

Dietary Exchanges: 2 Starch/Bread, ½ Meat

191 Fish Steaks with Pear Jardiniére

Bass contains a moderately high amount of omega-3 fatty acids. These fatty acids have been shown to protect against heart disease by reducing the chance of blood clots that can lead to heart attacks.

2 teaspoons vegetable oil
1 cup thinly sliced onion
1 cup julienne carrot strips
½ teaspoon dry mustard
¼ teaspoon *each* dried basil leaves and dill weed, crushed
2 fresh California Bartlett pears, cored and quartered
1½ pounds firm fish fillets such as sea bass, haddock or salmon
2 tomatoes, sliced
1 lemon, thinly sliced

Heat oil in large nonstick skillet. Add onion and carrot; stir to mix well. Cover and cook over medium heat 5 to 10 minutes. Mix mustard, basil and dill weed in large bowl. Add pears; toss lightly. Add fish, tomatoes and lemon slices to skillet. Cover; simmer 10 minutes or until fish flakes easily when tested with fork. Serve immediately with mustard-pear mixture. *Makes 4 servings*

Nutrients per Serving:

Calories	278	(20% of calories from fat)			
Total Fat	6 g	Dietary Fiber	5 g	Thiamine	<1 mg
Saturated Fat	1 g	Protein	33 g	Riboflavin	<1 mg
Cholesterol	71 mg	Calcium	49 mg	Niacin	4 mg
Sodium	132 g	Iron	1 mg	Vitamin A	899 RE
Carbohydrate	23 g	Folate	39 μg	Vitamin C	32 mg

Dietary Exchanges: 3½ Meat, 1 Fruit, 1 Vegetable

192 Crab Spinach Salad with Tarragon Dressing

Scientists urge us to eat more spinach because it's such a rich source of beta-carotene.

12 ounces coarsely flaked cooked crabmeat *or* 2 packages (6 ounces each) frozen crabmeat, thawed and drained
1 cup chopped tomato
1 cup sliced cucumber
⅓ cup sliced red onion
¼ cup nonfat salad dressing or mayonnaise
¼ cup low fat sour cream
¼ cup chopped fresh parsley
2 tablespoons skim milk
2 teaspoons chopped fresh tarragon *or* ½ teaspoon dried tarragon leaves, crushed
1 clove garlic, minced
¼ teaspoon hot pepper sauce
8 cups torn washed stemmed spinach

Combine crabmeat, tomato, cucumber and onion in medium bowl. Combine salad dressing, sour cream, parsley, milk, tarragon, garlic and hot pepper sauce in small bowl. Line four salad plates with spinach. Place crabmeat mixture on spinach; drizzle with dressing.   *Makes 4 servings*

Nutrients per Serving:

Calories	170	(18% of calories from fat)			
Total Fat	4 g	Dietary Fiber	4 g	Thiamine	<1 mg
Saturated Fat	<1 g	Protein	22 g	Riboflavin	<1 mg
Cholesterol	91 mg	Calcium	226 mg	Niacin	4 mg
Sodium	481 mg	Iron	4 mg	Vitamin A	816 RE
Carbohydrate	14 g	Folate	281 µg	Vitamin C	51 mg

Dietary Exchanges: 2½ Meat, 2 Vegetable

193 Fruitful Sole and Nectarines Rémoulade

Nectarines used to be available in the U.S. only during the summer months. Since it's summer in the southern hemisphere when it's winter here, we now can import them from Chile and buy them at the supermarket all winter long.

Rémoulade Sauce (recipe follows)
4 sole fillets (1 pound)
Ground pepper
Dill weed
2 tablespoons water
2 cups sliced halved pitted fresh California nectarines or peaches

Prepare Rémoulade Sauce. Refrigerate until needed. Roll up sole fillets and fasten with wooden toothpicks. (If fillets are large, cut in half lengthwise before rolling.) Stand on end, turban-fashion, in microwavable dish. Season with pepper and dill weed to taste. Add water to dish. Cover and microwave at HIGH (100% power) 3 to 4 minutes or until fish flakes easily when tested with fork. Add nectarine slices to dish and microwave, covered, 1 minute more or until hot. Transfer fish and fruit to warm serving platter and remove picks. Serve with Rémoulade Sauce.   *Makes 4 servings*

Rémoulade Sauce: Combine 1 cup plain low fat yogurt, ¼ cup chopped dill pickle or capers, 2 tablespoons chopped green onion, 2 teaspoons Dijon-style mustard and 1 teaspoon tarragon leaves, crushed.   *Makes about 1¼ cups*

Nutrients per Serving:

Calories	165	(14% of calories from fat)			
Total Fat	3 g	Dietary Fiber	1 g	Thiamine	<1 mg
Saturated Fat	1 g	Protein	23 g	Riboflavin	<1 mg
Cholesterol	57 mg	Calcium	126 mg	Niacin	2 mg
Sodium	208 mg	Iron	1 mg	Vitamin A	82 RE
Carbohydrate	13 g	Folate	17 µg	Vitamin C	5 mg

Dietary Exchanges: 2½ Meat, ½ Fruit

Crab Spinach Salad with Tarragon Dressing

194 Baked Fish with Honey-Mustard Sauce

Although most fish are low in fat, white fish, like those used in this recipe, have the least amount of fat.

1¼ pounds firm white fish fillets (cod, haddock, snapper, halibut, orange roughy, trout or catfish)
1 teaspoon vegetable oil
1 teaspoon lemon juice
⅛ teaspoon salt
⅛ teaspoon pepper
Honey-Mustard Sauce (recipe follows)

Cut fish into serving pieces. Place single layer in shallow baking dish coated with oil. Tuck under any thin edges. Combine oil and lemon juice in cup; brush on fish. Sprinkle with salt and pepper.

Preheat oven to 450°F. Prepare Honey-Mustard Sauce. Bake fish until it flakes easily when tested with fork at its thickest part, about 4 to 6 minutes per ½-inch thickness. Transfer to plates using slotted spatula. Serve hot with Honey-Mustard Sauce. *Makes 4 servings*

Honey-Mustard Sauce

3 tablespoons coarse-grain mustard
2 tablespoons reduced calorie mayonnaise
1 tablespoon *plus* 1 teaspoon honey
1½ teaspoons yellow mustard

Combine coarse grained mustard, mayonnaise, honey and yellow mustard. Stir well; reserve. *Makes about ½ cup*

Nutrients per Serving:

Calories	171	(26% of calories from fat)			
Total Fat	5 g	Dietary Fiber	<1 g	Thiamine	<1 mg
Saturated Fat	1 g	Protein	24 g	Riboflavin	<1 mg
Cholesterol	59 mg	Calcium	31 mg	Niacin	3 mg
Sodium	329 mg	Iron	1 mg	Vitamin A	14 RE
Carbohydrate	7 g	Folate	9 μg	Vitamin C	2 mg

Dietary Exchanges: 3 Meat

195 Chilled Poached Salmon with Cucumber Sauce

This recipe calls for pink or Humpback salmon, which is lowest in fat and calories among all varieties of salmon.

1 cup water
½ teaspoon chicken or fish bouillon granules
⅛ teaspoon pepper
4 fresh or frozen pink salmon fillets, thawed (about 6 ounces each)
½ cup chopped peeled seeded cucumber
⅓ cup plain low fat yogurt
2 tablespoons sliced green onion
2 tablespoons nonfat salad dressing or mayonnaise
1 tablespoon chopped fresh cilantro *or* 1 teaspoon dried cilantro leaves, crushed
1 teaspoon Dijon-style mustard
2 cups shredded lettuce

Combine water, bouillon granules and pepper in large skillet. Bring to a boil over high heat. Carefully place salmon in skillet. Return just to a boil. Reduce heat to medium-low. Cover; simmer 8 to 10 minutes or until salmon flakes easily when tested with fork. Remove salmon. Cover and refrigerate.

Meanwhile, combine cucumber, yogurt, onion, salad dressing, cilantro and mustard in small bowl. Cover and refrigerate. Place chilled salmon fillets on lettuce-lined plates. Spoon sauce over salmon. *Makes 4 servings*

Nutrients per Serving:

Calories	223	(26% of calories from fat)			
Total Fat	6 g	Dietary Fiber	1 g	Thiamine	<1 mg
Saturated Fat	1 g	Protein	36 g	Riboflavin	<1 mg
Cholesterol	89 mg	Calcium	57 mg	Niacin	10 mg
Sodium	322 mg	Iron	2 mg	Vitamin A	91 RE
Carbohydrate	4 g	Folate	29 μg	Vitamin C	4 mg

Dietary Exchanges: 4 Meat, 1 Vegetable

Chilled Poached Salmon with Cucumber Sauce

196 Today's Slim Stuffed Trout Steaks

If all that's on hand are underripe winter tomatoes, they can be ripened by placing them in a paper bag with an apple at room temperature for a few days.

1 cup 1% low fat cottage cheese
½ cup chopped tomato
½ cup chopped celery
1 teaspoon dried dill weed
½ teaspoon salt
¼ teaspoon dry mustard
1 pound fresh or frozen trout steaks
1 teaspoon margarine

Combine cottage cheese, tomato, celery, dill, salt and mustard in small bowl; stir until well blended. Fill trout cavity with cottage cheese mixture. Secure pocket in trout steak with toothpick. Melt margarine in large skillet. Fry trout steaks, turning once, 10 to 15 minutes or until fish flakes easily when tested with fork.   *Makes 4 servings*

Nutrients per Serving:

Calories	194	(27% of calories from fat)			
Total Fat	6 g	Dietary Fiber	1 g	Thiamine	<1 mg
Saturated Fat	1 g	Protein	31 g	Riboflavin	<1 mg
Cholesterol	67 mg	Calcium	126 mg	Niacin	7 mg
Sodium	553 mg	Iron	3 mg	Vitamin A	57 RE
Carbohydrate	4 g	Folate	34 μg	Vitamin C	10 mg

Dietary Exchanges: 3½ Meat, ½ Vegetable

197 Florida Grapefruit Marinated Shrimp

Shrimp are crustaceans which have segmented bodies covered by a thin shell. They are low in calories and are an excellent source of protein, zinc and copper.

1 cup frozen Florida grapefruit juice concentrate, thawed
2 cloves garlic, minced
3 tablespoons chopped cilantro or parsley
2 teaspoons ketchup
1 tablespoon honey
¼ teaspoon crushed red pepper flakes
½ teaspoon salt
1 pound medium raw shrimp, shelled and deveined
2 teaspoons cornstarch
1 cup long-grain white rice
1 tablespoon olive oil
1 large red bell pepper, cut into strips
2 ribs celery, sliced diagonally into ¼-inch-thick slices
2 Florida grapefruit, peeled and sectioned
Fresh cilantro sprigs
Hot cooked rice (optional)

Combine grapefruit juice concentrate, garlic, cilantro, ketchup, honey, red pepper flakes and salt in medium bowl. Stir in shrimp. Marinate 20 minutes, turning shrimp once. Drain shrimp, reserving marinade. Combine marinade with cornstarch. Meanwhile, prepare rice according to package directions. Heat oil over medium-high heat in large nonstick skillet; add shrimp. Cook and stir 2 to 3 minutes until shrimp turn pink and opaque. Add red bell pepper, celery and reserved marinade. Bring to a boil over high heat; boil until mixture thickens slightly, stirring constantly. Add grapefruit and heat 30 seconds. Garnish with fresh sprigs of cilantro. Serve over rice, if desired.

Makes 4 servings

Nutrients per Serving:

Calories	442	(10% of calories from fat)			
Total Fat	5 g	Dietary Fiber	3 g	Thiamine	<1 mg
Saturated Fat	1 g	Protein	24 g	Riboflavin	<1 mg
Cholesterol	174 mg	Calcium	100 mg	Niacin	5 mg
Sodium	519 mg	Iron	6 mg	Vitamin A	139 RE
Carbohydrate	75 g	Folate	41 µg	Vitamin C	137 mg

Dietary Exchanges: 2½ Starch/Bread, 2 Meat, 2 Fruit

Florida Grapefruit Marinated Shrimp

198 Snapper Fillets with Orange-Shallot Sauce

Although freshly squeezed orange juice might be more flavorful than juice made from concentrate, juice from the concentrate may have more vitamin C. Oranges used in juice concentrate are left to ripen on the tree longer and this extended exposure to the sun produces more vitamin C as a result.

2 Florida oranges
6 fish fillets (red snapper, flounder, grouper or scrod)
1 tablespoon olive oil
1 cup finely chopped shallots
2 cloves garlic, minced
3 tablespoons all-purpose flour
1 cup chicken broth
1 cup Florida orange juice
1 tablespoon grated orange peel
2 tablespoons cooking sherry
1½ teaspoons dried oregano leaves, crushed
Salt and ground pepper to taste
2 tablespoons chopped fresh parsley for garnish

Preheat broiler. Thinly slice oranges; set aside. Place fillets, skin side down, on nonstick jelly-roll pan. Broil about 4 inches from heat, 5 to 8 minutes until fish flakes easily with fork. Remove from broiler; set aside. Meanwhile, in large, nonstick skillet, heat oil over medium-high heat until hot. Add shallots and garlic; cook and stir 3 to 4 minutes until shallots begin to brown. Add flour; cook and stir about 30 seconds, until well blended. Stir in broth, orange juice, orange peel, sherry, oregano, salt and pepper. Bring to a boil, stirring constantly, until slightly thickened. Add orange slices and fish fillets, skin side up. Cook 1 to 2 minutes until fish is heated through and orange slices are slightly softened. Garnish with parsley, if desired. Serve immediately.

Makes 6 servings

Nutrients per Serving:

Calories	282	(15% of calories from fat)			
Total Fat	5 g	Dietary Fiber	2 g	Thiamine	<1 mg
Saturated Fat	1 g	Protein	37 g	Riboflavin	<1 mg
Cholesterol	62 mg	Calcium	97 mg	Niacin	2 mg
Sodium	316 mg	Iron	1 mg	Vitamin A	353 RE
Carbohydrate	19 g	Folate	42 µg	Vitamin C	44 mg

Dietary Exchanges: 4 Meat, ½ Fruit, 1 Vegetable

PASTA

199 | Radiatore Salad with Salmon and Papaya

Radiatore is a small rolled ruffled pasta that got its name because of its resemblance to a radiator.

- 1 pound radiatore or other medium-size pasta
- 2 tablespoons vegetable oil
  Freshly ground black pepper to taste
- 1 pound boneless, skinless, fresh or frozen salmon fillets, cooked and chopped, *or* 2 cans (7.5 ounces) salmon, drained and flaked
- 1 papaya *or* mango, peeled, seeded and chopped
- 1 cup cherry tomatoes
- 1 bunch green onions, finely sliced
- 1 yellow bell pepper, seeded and chopped
- 1 medium cucumber, quartered lengthwise and sliced
- 1 small jalapeño pepper, seeded and finely minced
- 3 tablespoons rice wine vinegar
- 3 tablespoons white wine vinegar
- 2 tablespoons chopped fresh cilantro
- 3 drops hot pepper sauce

Prepare radiatore according to package directions; drain and transfer to medium bowl. Toss warm pasta with oil; season with black pepper. Set aside until cool. Add salmon, papaya, tomatoes, onions, bell pepper and cucumber; toss until mixed.

In small bowl, combine jalapeño, vinegars, cilantro and hot pepper sauce. Pour over pasta mixture; toss until well coated. Cover; refrigerate until chilled.

Makes 6 to 8 servings

Nutrients per Serving:

Calories	343	(23% of calories from fat)			
Total Fat	9 g	Dietary Fiber	4 g	Thiamin	<1 mg
Saturated Fat	1 g	Protein	21 g	Riboflavin	<1 mg
Cholesterol	71 mg	Calcium	55 mg	Niacin	6 mg
Sodium	93 mg	Iron	3 mg	Vitamin A	215 RE
Carbohydrate	45 g	Folate	28 µg	Vitamin C	41 mg

Dietary Exchanges: 2 Starch/Bread, 2 Meat, ½ Fruit, 1 Vegetable, ½ Fat

200 | Sesame Noodle Cake

This side dish may be used in place of rice as a base for entrées.

- 4 ounces vermicelli or Chinese egg noodles
- 1 tablespoon low sodium soy sauce
- 1 tablespoon peanut or vegetable oil
- ½ teaspoon sesame oil

Prepare vermicelli according to package directions; drain. Place in large bowl; toss with soy sauce.

Heat 10- or 11-inch nonstick skillet over medium heat; add peanut oil. Add vermicelli mixture; press into even layer with spatula.

Cook, uncovered, 6 minutes or until bottom is lightly browned. Invert onto plate; slide back into skillet, browned side up. Cook 4 minutes or until bottom is well browned. Drizzle with sesame oil. Transfer to serving platter and cut into quarters.

Makes 4 servings

Nutrients per Serving:

Calories	139	(26% of calories from fat)			
Total Fat	4 g	Dietary Fiber	0 g	Thiamin	<1 mg
Saturated Fat	1 g	Protein	3 g	Riboflavin	<1 mg
Cholesterol	<1 mg	Calcium	9 mg	Niacin	1 mg
Sodium	686 mg	Iron	1 mg	Vitamin A	1 RE
Carbohydrate	22 g	Folate	2 µg	Vitamin C	0 mg

Dietary Exchanges: 1½ Starch/Bread, ½ Fat

Radiatore Salad with Salmon and Papaya

201 Saucy Broccoli and Spaghetti

Leeks, which look like giant green onions, have a milder and sweeter flavor than other members of the onion family. Along with the oregano and pepper sauce, the leek adds enough flavor to the spaghetti and broccoli that there is no need to add salt.

3 ounces spaghetti
1 package (10 ounces) frozen chopped broccoli
½ cup thinly sliced leek, white part only
½ cup skim milk
2 teaspoons cornstarch
2 teaspoons chopped fresh oregano *or* ½ teaspoon dried oregano leaves, crushed
⅛ teaspoon hot pepper sauce
3 tablespoons reduced calorie soft cream cheese
1 tablespoon grated Romano or Parmesan cheese
1 tablespoon chopped fresh parsley

Prepare spaghetti according to package directions, omitting salt; drain and keep warm. Meanwhile, cook broccoli and leek together according to package directions for broccoli, omitting salt. Drain; reserve ¼ cup liquid. Add additional water if needed.

Combine milk, cornstarch, oregano and pepper sauce in medium saucepan. Stir in reserved liquid. Cook and stir over medium heat until mixture boils and thickens. Stir in cream cheese. Cook and stir until cheese melts. Stir in vegetables; heat through.

Serve vegetable mixture over pasta. Sprinkle with Romano cheese and parsley. Makes 4 servings

Nutrients per Serving:

Calories	162	(16% of calories from fat)			
Total Fat	3 g	Dietary Fiber	3 g	Thiamin	<1 mg
Saturated Fat	2 g	Protein	8 g	Riboflavin	<1 mg
Cholesterol	9 mg	Calcium	120 mg	Niacin	1 mg
Sodium	133 mg	Iron	2 mg	Vitamin A	176 RE
Carbohydrate	26 g	Folate	59 μg	Vitamin C	32 mg

Dietary Exchanges: 1½ Starch/Bread, 1 Vegetable, ½ Fat

202 Creamed Vegetables and Pasta

When it comes to adding flavor and body to a sauce, a little low fat process American cheese goes a long way. This shell macaroni and vegetable combination is rich and creamy, yet uses only 1½ ounces of cheese.

1 cup shell macaroni
1 cup frozen mixed vegetables
¼ cup chopped onion
1 cup skim milk, divided
2 tablespoons all-purpose flour
1 teaspoon dried fines herbes* *or* dried basil leaves, crushed
Dash ground red pepper
⅓ cup shredded low fat process American cheese
1 tablespoon grated Parmesan cheese

Prepare macaroni according to package directions, omitting salt. During last 5 minutes of cooking add frozen vegetables and onion; drain pasta and vegetables.

Combine ¼ cup milk and flour in medium saucepan until smooth. Stir in remaining ¾ cup milk, fines herbes and red pepper. Cook and stir over medium heat until mixture boils and thickens. Cook and stir 1 minute. Stir in American cheese. Cook and stir until cheese melts. Stir in pasta and vegetables; heat through. Sprinkle each serving with Parmesan cheese. Makes 4 servings

*Fines herbes is a blend of dried French herbs usually containing chervil, chives, parsley and tarragon. It can be found in the spice section of large supermarkets.

Nutrients per Serving:

Calories	198	(13% of calories from fat)			
Total Fat	3 g	Dietary Fiber	3 g	Thiamin	<1 mg
Saturated Fat	1 g	Protein	11 g	Riboflavin	<1 mg
Cholesterol	6 mg	Calcium	217 mg	Niacin	1 mg
Sodium	135 mg	Iron	2 mg	Vitamin A	266 RE
Carbohydrate	32 g	Folate	21 μg	Vitamin C	3 mg

Dietary Exchanges: 2 Starch/Bread, 1 Vegetable, ½ Fat

203 Today's Slim Ricotta Spinach Rolls

Spinach is an excellent source of antioxidants, including beta-carotene.

8 lasagna noodles, cooked and drained

Sauce:
  1 medium onion, finely chopped
  2 cloves garlic, minced
  1 tablespoon butter
  3 cups no-salt-added tomato sauce
  1 teaspoon dried oregano leaves, crushed
  ½ teaspoon dried thyme leaves, crushed
  ½ teaspoon dried basil leaves, crushed
  ¼ teaspoon dried marjoram leaves, crushed

Filling:
  1 package (10 ounces) frozen chopped spinach
  1 cup (8 ounces) Wisconsin part-skim ricotta cheese
  2 tablespoons Wisconsin Parmesan cheese
  ⅛ teaspoon ground nutmeg
  Dash ground black pepper

Cook and stir onion and garlic in butter in large skillet over medium heat until tender. Add tomato sauce and seasonings. Reduce heat; simmer 30 minutes, stirring occasionally. Prepare spinach according to package directions. Drain and squeeze out excess water. In medium bowl, combine spinach, cheeses, nutmeg and pepper until thoroughly mixed.

Preheat oven to 350°F. Spread mixture evenly along entire length of each noodle. Roll up each noodle lengthwise and place on its side in a buttered shallow baking dish. Pour sauce over rolls. Bake 20 to 30 minutes or until heated through.

Makes 4 servings

Nutrients per Serving:

Calories	499	(18% of calories from fat)			
Total Fat	10 g	Dietary Fiber	8 g	Thiamin	1 mg
Saturated Fat	3 g	Protein	24 g	Riboflavin	1 mg
Cholesterol	104 mg	Calcium	309 mg	Niacin	5 mg
Sodium	266 mg	Iron	6 mg	Vitamin A	796 RE
Carbohydrate	79 g	Folate	113 µg	Vitamin C	33 mg

Dietary Exchanges: 4 Starch/Bread, 1 Meat, 4 Vegetable, 1 Fat

204 Cavatelli and Vegetable Stir-Fry

Although soy sauce is high in sodium, it can boost the flavor of dishes, such as this one, without adding a lot of calories and fat. It is sold in both regular and low sodium versions.

¾ cup cavatelli or elbow macaroni
6 ounces fresh snow peas, cut lengthwise into halves
½ cup thinly sliced carrot
1 teaspoon minced fresh ginger
½ cup chopped yellow or green bell pepper
½ cup chopped onion
¼ cup chopped fresh parsley
1 tablespoon chopped fresh oregano *or* 1 teaspoon dried oregano leaves, crushed
1 tablespoon reduced calorie margarine
2 tablespoons water
1 tablespoon low sodium soy sauce

Prepare cavatelli according to package directions, omitting salt; drain.

Coat wok or large skillet with nonstick cooking spray. Add snow peas, carrot and ginger; stir-fry 2 minutes over medium-high heat. Add bell pepper, onion, parsley, oregano and margarine. Stir-fry 2 to 3 minutes or until vegetables are crisp-tender. Stir in water and soy sauce. Stir in pasta; heat through.

Makes 4 servings

Nutrients per Serving:

Calories	130	(14% of calories from fat)			
Total Fat	2 g	Dietary Fiber	3 g	Thiamin	<1 mg
Saturated Fat	<1 g	Protein	5 g	Riboflavin	<1 mg
Cholesterol	0 mg	Calcium	44 mg	Niacin	1 mg
Sodium	175 mg	Iron	2 mg	Vitamin A	470 RE
Carbohydrate	23 g	Folate	42 µg	Vitamin C	57 mg

Dietary Exchanges: 1 Starch/Bread, 1½ Vegetable, ½ Fat

Cavatelli and Vegetable Stir-Fry

205 Not Fried Asian Rice

This rice dish comes alive with the vibrant colors of green onion and red pepper. The vegetables also boost the amount of vitamins and minerals in this not-so-traditional Chinese favorite.

2 teaspoons sesame oil
¾ cup chopped green onions
½ cup chopped red bell pepper
2 cloves garlic, minced
2 cups water
1 cup uncooked converted rice
2 egg whites
1 tablespoon lite soy sauce
2 teaspoons sugar

In large nonstick skillet, heat oil over medium-high heat. Add onions, bell pepper and garlic; cook and stir 1 minute. Add water; bring to a boil. Reduce heat to low; stir in rice and egg whites. Simmer, stirring frequently, 20 minutes or until rice is tender. Stir in soy sauce and sugar. Cook and stir for 3 to 5 minutes or until sugar caramelizes.

Makes 6 servings

Nutrients per Serving:

Calories	147	(11% of calories from fat)			
Total Fat	2 g	Dietary Fiber	1 g	Thiamin	<1 mg
Saturated Fat	<1 g	Protein	4 g	Riboflavin	<1 mg
Cholesterol	0 mg	Calcium	30 mg	Niacin	1 mg
Sodium	125 mg	Iron	1 mg	Vitamin A	62 RE
Carbohydrate	29 g	Folate	11 μg	Vitamin C	22 mg

Dietary Exchanges: 1½ Starch/Bread, ½ Vegetable, ½ Fat

206 Couscous and Apricots

This colorful pilaf is packed with nutrition. The couscous supplies protein, thiamin, niacin and iron. The brown rice adds fiber, protein and niacin. The apricots contribute vitamin A and potassium.

1 can (5½ ounces) apricot nectar or apple juice
½ cup thinly sliced celery
½ cup water
¼ cup chopped dried apricots or apples
¼ teaspoon ground allspice
⅛ teaspoon salt
⅓ cup couscous
⅓ cup quick-cooking brown rice
¼ cup coarsely chopped walnuts

Combine apricot nectar, celery, water, apricots, allspice and salt in large saucepan. Bring to a boil over high heat. Remove from heat. Stir in couscous, brown rice and walnuts. Cover; let stand 5 minutes until liquid is absorbed. Fluff couscous mixture with fork.   Makes 4 servings

Nutrients per Serving:

Calories	206	(22% of calories from fat)			
Total Fat	5 g	Dietary Fiber	5 g	Thiamin	<1 mg
Saturated Fat	<1 g	Protein	6 g	Riboflavin	<1 mg
Cholesterol	0 mg	Calcium	25 mg	Niacin	2 mg
Sodium	84 mg	Iron	1 mg	Vitamin A	115 RE
Carbohydrate	36 g	Folate	17 µg	Vitamin C	15 mg

Dietary Exchanges: 2 Starch/Bread, ½ Fruit, 1 Fat

207 Creamy Cheese and Macaroni

The bell pepper and celery in this recipe are both good sources of fiber and potassium. Bell pepper also adds substantial amounts of vitamins A and C.

1½ cups elbow macaroni
1 cup chopped onion
1 cup chopped red or green bell pepper
¾ cup chopped celery
3 egg whites
1 cup 1% low fat cottage cheese
1 cup shredded low fat Swiss cheese
½ cup shredded low fat processed American cheese
½ cup skim milk
3 tablespoons all-purpose flour
1 tablespoon reduced calorie margarine
¼ teaspoon black pepper
¼ teaspoon hot pepper sauce

Preheat oven to 350°F. Coat 2-quart casserole with nonstick cooking spray; set aside. Prepare macaroni according to package directions, omitting salt. During last 5 minutes of cooking add onion, bell pepper and celery. Drain pasta and vegetables.

Add egg whites, cottage cheese, Swiss cheese, American cheese, milk, flour, margarine, black pepper and pepper sauce to food processor or blender. Process until smooth. Stir cheese mixture into pasta and vegetables.

Pour mixture into prepared casserole. Bake at 350°F, uncovered, 35 to 40 minutes or until golden brown. Let stand 10 minutes before serving.

Makes 4 servings

Nutrients per Serving:

Calories	410	(22% of calories from fat)			
Total Fat	10 g	Dietary Fiber	2 g	Thiamin	1 mg
Saturated Fat	1 g	Protein	30 g	Riboflavin	1 mg
Cholesterol	23 mg	Calcium	234 mg	Niacin	4 mg
Sodium	567 mg	Iron	2 mg	Vitamin A	127 RE
Carbohydrate	50 g	Folate	47 µg	Vitamin C	55 mg

Dietary Exchanges: 3 Starch/Bread, 2 Meat, 1½ Vegetable, ½ Fat

208 Tabbouleh Salad

Bulgur wheat, a good source of fiber, is made from the whole wheat kernel that has been soaked, steamed and dried. Then, part of the bran layer is removed and the kernel is cracked into pieces.

¾ **cup bulgur wheat, cooked**
¾ **cup chopped green bell pepper**
½ **cup chopped fresh parsley**
2 **tablespoons thinly sliced green onion**
¼ **cup lemon juice**
2 **tablespoons water**
4 **teaspoons vegetable oil**
2 **teaspoons chopped fresh dill** *or*
    ½ **teaspoon dried dill weed**
1 **teaspoon sugar**
¼ **teaspoon salt**
    Lettuce leaves
½ **cup coarsely chopped seeded tomato**

Place bulgur in colander. Rinse under cold water; drain. Combine bulgur, bell pepper, parsley and green onion in medium bowl.

Combine lemon juice, water, oil, dill, sugar and salt in jar with tight-fitting lid. Cover; shake well. Add to bulgur mixture; toss to combine. Cover and refrigerate at least 4 hours or up to 24 hours.

Line salad bowl with lettuce. Add bulgur mixture. Arrange tomato on top.   **Makes 4 servings**

Nutrients per Serving:

Calories	158	(27% of calories from fat)			
Total Fat	5 g	Dietary Fiber	8 g	Thiamin	<1 mg
Saturated Fat	<1 g	Protein	4 g	Riboflavin	<1 mg
Cholesterol	0 mg	Calcium	30 mg	Niacin	2 mg
Sodium	145 mg	Iron	2 mg	Vitamin A	98 RE
Carbohydrate	27 g	Folate	37 µg	Vitamin C	58 mg

Dietary Exchanges: 1½ Starch/Bread, ½ Vegetable, 1 Fat

209 Macaroni Italiano

Walnuts, like other nuts, contain a large quantity of vitamin E which has been linked to cancer prevention and reduced rates of heart disease.

8 **ounces elbow macaroni, cooked and**
    drained
1 **can (16 ounces) whole tomatoes with**
    juice, coarsely chopped
1 **can (8 ounces) tomato sauce**
1¼ **cups 1% low fat cottage cheese, at**
    room temperature
1 **package (10 ounces) frozen chopped**
    spinach, thawed and squeezed dry
1½ **cups frozen peas, thawed**
¼ **cup grated Parmesan cheese**
1 **teaspoon dried basil leaves, crushed**
½ **teaspoon low sodium baking soda**
½ **teaspoon ground black pepper**
¾ **cup chopped toasted California walnuts**
2 **tablespoons chopped fresh parsley**

Preheat oven to 350°F. Prepare macaroni according to package directions, omitting salt; drain and set aside. In large bowl, combine tomatoes with juice, tomato sauce, cottage cheese, spinach, peas, Parmesan cheese, basil, baking soda and pepper; mix well. Add pasta to tomato mixture, tossing to mix thoroughly. Transfer mixture to greased 2½-quart baking dish. Cover; bake 20 minutes. Uncover; bake an additional 10 minutes. Stir in walnuts; sprinkle with parsley.   **Makes 6 servings**

Nutrients per Serving:

Calories	366	(28% of calories from fat)			
Total Fat	12 g	Dietary Fiber	5 g	Thiamin	<1 mg
Saturated Fat	2 g	Protein	21 g	Riboflavin	<1 mg
Cholesterol	5 mg	Calcium	213 mg	Niacin	4 mg
Sodium	770 mg	Iron	4 mg	Vitamin A	504 RE
Carbohydrate	47 g	Folate	109 µg	Vitamin C	29 mg

Dietary Exchanges: 2½ Starch/Bread, 1½ Meat, 1½ Vegetable, 1½ Fat

Spinach Lasagna

210 Today's Slim Noodles Romanov

Save yourself some calories by using the best aged Parmesan cheese possible. It is more flavorful than processed Parmesan cheese so you'll need less of it for your recipes.

8 ounces uncooked noodles
1 cup low fat yogurt
1 cup 1% low fat cottage cheese
¼ cup finely chopped onion
¼ cup chopped fresh parsley
2 tablespoons Worcestershire sauce
½ teaspoon salt
3 drops hot pepper sauce
2 tablespoons grated Wisconsin
**   Parmesan cheese**

Prepare noodles according to package directions; drain. Preheat oven to 350°F. In medium bowl, combine remaining ingredients except Parmesan cheese. Fold into cooked noodles. Spoon into 1½-quart buttered casserole; sprinkle with Parmesan cheese. Bake 30 minutes or until heated through.

Makes 6 to 8 servings

Nutrients per Serving:					
Calories	150	(14% of calories from fat)			
Total Fat	2 g	Dietary Fiber	<1 g	Thiamin	<1 mg
Saturated Fat	1 g	Protein	9 g	Riboflavin	<1 mg
Cholesterol	29 mg	Calcium	108 mg	Niacin	1 mg
Sodium	340 mg	Iron	2 mg	Vitamin A	28 RE
Carbohydrate	22 g	Folate	17 µg	Vitamin C	9 mg

Dietary Exchanges: 1½ Starch/Bread, 1 Meat

[211] Spinach Lasagna

Ricotta cheese is available in regular, light and nonfat varieties. This recipe calls for 1% cottage cheese or light ricotta. If you are really watching the fat in your diet, try using the nonfat ricotta.

5 lasagna noodles
2 cups sliced fresh mushrooms
1 cup chopped onion
1 cup chopped green bell pepper
2 cloves garlic, minced
2 cans (8 ounces *each*) no-salt-added tomato sauce
1 teaspoon chopped fresh basil *or* ¼ teaspoon dried basil leaves, crushed
1 teaspoon chopped fresh oregano *or* ¼ teaspoon dried oregano leaves, crushed
¼ teaspoon ground red pepper
2 egg whites
1½ cups 1% low fat cottage cheese or light ricotta cheese
¼ cup grated Romano or Parmesan cheese
3 tablespoons fine dry bread crumbs
1 package (10 ounces) frozen chopped spinach, thawed and well drained
¾ cup (3 ounces) shredded part-skim mozzarella cheese
¼ cup chopped fresh parsley

Prepare noodles according to package directions, omitting salt; drain. Rinse under cold water; drain.

Coat large skillet with nonstick cooking spray. Add mushrooms, onion, bell pepper and garlic; cook and stir over medium heat until vegetables are tender. Stir in tomato sauce, basil, oregano and red pepper. Bring to a boil over medium-high heat. Reduce heat to medium-low. Simmer, uncovered, 10 minutes, stirring occasionally.

Preheat oven to 350°F. Combine egg whites, cottage cheese, Romano cheese and bread crumbs in medium bowl. Stir spinach into cottage cheese mixture. Cut noodles in half crosswise. Spread ½ cup sauce in ungreased 8- or 9-inch square baking dish. Top with half the noodles, half the spinach mixture and half the remaining sauce. Repeat layers.

Cover and bake 45 minutes or until heated through. Sprinkle with mozzarella cheese. Bake, uncovered, 2 to 3 minutes more or until cheese melts. Sprinkle with parsley. Let stand 10 minutes before serving.

Makes 4 servings

Nutrients per Serving:

Calories	350	(21% of calories from fat)				
Total Fat	8 g	Dietary Fiber	7 g	Thiamin	<1 mg
Saturated Fat	4 g	Protein	30 g	Riboflavin	1 mg
Cholesterol	23 mg	Calcium	422 mg	Niacin	5 mg
Sodium	746 mg	Iron	4 mg	Vitamin A	796 RE
Carbohydrate	40 g	Folate	138 μg	Vitamin C	82 mg

Dietary Exchanges: 1 Starch/Bread, 2½ Meat, 5 Vegetable, ½ Fat

[212] Tomato Zucchini Pesto

Tomatoes are a good source of antioxidants. They have also been linked to lowering the rates of certain cancers.

6 ounces uncooked pasta
1 cup chopped fresh basil leaves
1 teaspoon sugar
1 teaspoon vegetable oil
2 cloves garlic, minced
1 tablespoon grated Parmesan cheese
¼ cup part-skim ricotta cheese
1 medium zucchini, sliced
2 teaspoons water
1 cup quartered cherry tomatoes
½ teaspoon salt (optional)

Prepare pasta according to package directions. Rinse and drain; cover. In food processor or blender, process basil, sugar, oil and garlic. Blend in Parmesan and ricotta cheeses. Set aside. Place zucchini in large casserole dish; add water. Cover; microwave at HIGH (100% power) 4 minutes. Drain. Stir in pasta and cheese mixture. Garnish with tomatoes. Sprinkle with salt, if desired.

Makes 4 servings

Nutrients per Serving:

Calories	212	(18% of calories from fat)				
Total Fat	4 g	Dietary Fiber	4 g	Thiamin	<1 mg
Saturated Fat	1 g	Protein	9 g	Riboflavin	<1 mg
Cholesterol	43 mg	Calcium	101 mg	Niacin	2 mg
Sodium	67 mg	Iron	3 mg	Vitamin A	158 RE
Carbohydrate	35 g	Folate	55 μg	Vitamin C	28 mg

Dietary Exchanges: 2 Starch/Bread, 1½ Vegetable, ½ Fat

213 Vegetable-Barley Pilaf

Besides adding a nutty, chewy quality to this pilaf, the quick-cooking barley supplies fiber, potassium and phosphorus.

¾ cup chopped onion
¾ cup chopped celery
¾ cup sliced fresh mushrooms
1 cup water
¾ cup sliced yellow summer squash
½ cup quick-cooking barley
½ cup sliced carrot
¼ cup chopped fresh parsley
2 teaspoons chopped fresh basil *or*
  ½ teaspoon dried basil leaves, crushed
½ teaspoon chicken bouillon granules
⅛ teaspoon pepper

Coat large skillet with nonstick cooking spray. Add onion, celery and mushrooms; cook and stir over medium heat until vegetables are tender.

Stir in water, squash, barley, carrot, parsley, basil, bouillon granules and pepper. Bring to a boil over high heat. Reduce heat to medium-low. Cover; simmer 10 to 12 minutes or until barley and vegetables are tender.   Makes 4 servings

Nutrients per Serving:

Calories	111	(10% of calories from fat)			
Total Fat	1 g	Dietary Fiber	5 g	Thiamin	<1 mg
Saturated Fat	<1 g	Protein	4 g	Riboflavin	<1 mg
Cholesterol	0 mg	Calcium	37 mg	Niacin	2 mg
Sodium	147 mg	Iron	2 mg	Vitamin A	429 RE
Carbohydrate	22 g	Folate	28 μg	Vitamin C	9 mg

Dietary Exchanges: 1 Starch/Bread, 1½ Vegetable

214 Bryani

Contrary of popular belief, curry is not a single spice but a combination of spices. Some common ingredients used in curry are cardamom, hot chilies, cinnamon, cloves, coriander and turmeric.

Curry Rice (recipe follows)
1 onion, chopped
1 clove garlic, minced
2½ cups chopped pitted halved peeled fresh California peaches
½ cup roasted cashews, chopped (optional)
1 package (9 ounces) frozen cut green beans, thawed
Plain low fat yogurt, additional sliced peaches and raisins (optional)

Prepare Curry Rice. In large bowl, combine onion, garlic and Curry Rice. Spoon half of Curry Rice mixture into 1½-quart casserole. Top with peaches, cashews and green beans. Spoon remaining Curry Rice mixture over top. Microwave at HIGH (100% power) 5 minutes or until heated through or cover with foil and bake in 375°F oven 50 minutes. Serve with yogurt, additional sliced peaches and raisins, if desired.   Makes 6 servings

Curry Rice: Combine 2 cups water, 2 teaspoons curry powder, ½ teaspoon ground turmeric and ¼ teaspoon ground cinnamon in large saucepan. Cover; bring to a boil. Add 1 cup long-grain white rice. Cover; return to a boil. Reduce heat; simmer 20 minutes or until liquid is absorbed.

Nutrients per Serving:

Calories	150	(3% of calories from fat)			
Total Fat	<1 g	Dietary Fiber	2 g	Thiamin	<1 mg
Saturated Fat	<1 g	Protein	3 g	Riboflavin	<1 mg
Cholesterol	0 mg	Calcium	40 mg	Niacin	2 mg
Sodium	8 mg	Iron	2 mg	Vitamin A	39 RE
Carbohydrate	34 g	Folate	12 μg	Vitamin C	7 mg

Dietary Exchanges: 1½ Starch/Bread, ½ Fruit, ½ Vegetable

215 Creamy Spinach and Brown Rice

Because brown rice is rich in complex carbohydrates, it is considered a nutrient-dense food. What does that mean? It's loaded with vitamins, minerals, protein and fiber without a lot of calories.

1½ cups sliced fresh mushrooms
½ cup thinly sliced leek, white part only
2 teaspoons reduced calorie margarine
2 cups skim milk
½ cup brown rice
⅓ cup shredded low fat Swiss cheese
1 tablespoon chopped fresh thyme or
**   1 teaspoon dried thyme leaves,**
**   crushed**
⅛ teaspoon pepper
2 cups chopped stemmed washed
**   spinach**

Cook and stir mushrooms and leek in margarine in medium saucepan, over medium-high heat, until leek is tender. Add milk and brown rice. Bring to a boil over medium-high heat. Reduce heat to medium-low. Cover; simmer 45 to 50 minutes or until rice is tender, stirring frequently. Remove from heat.

Add cheese, thyme and pepper. Cook and stir until cheese melts. Stir in spinach. Cover; let stand 5 minutes.   Makes 4 servings

Nutrients per Serving:

Calories	190	(19% of calories from fat)			
Total Fat	4 g	Dietary Fiber	3 g	Thiamin	<1 mg
Saturated Fat	<1 g	Protein	11 g	Riboflavin	<1 mg
Cholesterol	8 mg	Calcium	201 mg	Niacin	3 mg
Sodium	158 mg	Iron	2 mg	Vitamin A	288 RE
Carbohydrate	29 g	Folate	81 μg	Vitamin C	12 mg

Dietary Exchanges: 1½ Starch/Bread, ½ Milk, 1 Vegetable, ½ Fat

216 Linguine and Fresh Fruit Cooler

Melons like cantaloupe and honeydew have been shown to aid in the prevention of blood clots. Cantaloupe also has high levels of beta-carotene.

1 cup fresh berries
1 cup honeydew or cantaloupe cut into
**   1-inch chunks**
1 cup kiwi slices or plum slices
¼ cup lemon juice
1 teaspoon finely grated orange peel
2 tablespoons cornstarch
1½ cups apricot nectar
1 stick cinnamon
4 whole cloves
4 whole allspice berries
¼ cup dry white wine
½ pound linguine, vermicelli or angel hair
**   pasta, cooked and drained**
½ cup fresh mint leaves

In large bowl, combine fruit, lemon juice and orange peel. Place cornstarch in 2-quart saucepan. Slowly add apricot nectar, over high heat, stirring until well blended. Add cinnamon, cloves and allspice. Bring to a boil, stirring frequently. Reduce heat; simmer uncovered 15 minutes or until thick. Remove spices. Stir into fruit mixture. Add wine and linguine; garnish with mint leaves.

Makes 4 lunch or 8 dessert servings

Nutrients per Serving:

Calories	346	(7% of calories from fat)			
Total Fat	3 g	Dietary Fiber	4 g	Thiamin	<1 mg
Saturated Fat	<1 g	Protein	9 g	Riboflavin	<1 mg
Cholesterol	49 mg	Calcium	81 mg	Niacin	3 mg
Sodium	23 mg	Iron	4 mg	Vitamin A	226 RE
Carbohydrate	71 g	Folate	42 μg	Vitamin C	144 mg

Dietary Exchanges: 2½ Starch/Bread, 2½ Fruit, ½ Fat

Creamy Spinach and Brown Rice

217 Cheese-Sauced Manicotti

This hearty pasta dish gets much of its wonderful flavor from Italian seasoning. A nonfat, no-salt blend of herbs and seasonings.

**8 manicotti shells
1 cup chopped onion
¼ cup water
2 cloves garlic, minced
1⅔ cups skim milk, divided
3 tablespoons all-purpose flour
¾ cup shredded part-skim mozzarella
    cheese
1 teaspoon dried Italian seasoning,
    crushed
¼ teaspoon pepper
1 package (10 ounces) frozen chopped
    spinach, thawed and well drained
1 cup nonfat ricotta cheese
½ cup 1% low fat cottage cheese
½ teaspoon dried marjoram leaves,
    crushed
1 medium tomato, sliced**

Prepare manicotti according to package directions, omitting salt; drain. Rinse under cold water; drain.

Meanwhile, preheat oven to 350°F. Coat 13 × 9-inch baking dish with nonstick cooking spray.

To make sauce, combine onion, water and garlic in medium saucepan. Bring to a boil over high heat. Reduce heat to medium-low. Cover; simmer 3 to 4 minutes or until onion is tender. Combine ⅓ cup milk and flour in small bowl until smooth. Stir into onion mixture. Stir in remaining 1⅓ cups milk. Cook and stir over medium heat until mixture boils and thickens. Cook and stir 1 minute. Add mozzarella cheese, Italian seasoning and pepper. Cook and stir until cheese melts.

Combine spinach, ricotta cheese, cottage cheese, marjoram and ⅓ cup sauce in medium bowl. Spoon ⅓ cup spinach mixture into each manicotti shell. Place in prepared baking dish. Pour remaining sauce over top. Cover; bake 30 to 35 minutes or until heated through. Arrange tomato slices on top.

Bake, uncovered, 4 to 5 minutes or until tomato is heated through.   Makes 4 servings

Nutrients per Serving:

Calories	317	(13% of calories from fat)			
Total Fat	5 g	Dietary Fiber	4 g	Thiamin	<1 mg
Saturated Fat	3 g	Protein	28 g	Riboflavin	1 mg
Cholesterol	21 mg	Calcium	412 mg	Niacin	2 mg
Sodium	377 mg	Iron	3 mg	Vitamin A	682 RE
Carbohydrate	47 g	Folate	106 μg	Vitamin C	19 mg

Dietary Exchanges: 2 Starch/Bread, 2 Meat, ½ Milk, 1 Vegetable

218 Swiss Orzo Chowder

Orzo is a rice-shaped pasta made from semolina and durham wheat. You may find it in your supermarket under the name rosamarina.

**1¼ cups canned low sodium chicken broth,
    defatted
1 cup frozen cut green beans
½ cup shredded carrot
⅓ cup (2 ounces) orzo or rosamarina
1 teaspoon dried basil leaves, crushed
¼ teaspoon pepper
½ cup sliced yellow summer squash or
    zucchini
2½ cups skim milk, divided
3 tablespoons all-purpose flour
¼ cup shredded low fat Swiss cheese**

Combine broth, green beans, carrot, orzo, basil and pepper in medium saucepan. Bring to a boil over high heat; reduce heat to medium-low. Cover; simmer 10 minutes. Add squash. Cover; simmer about 2 minutes or until vegetables are tender.

Mix ½ cup milk and flour together in small bowl until smooth. Stir into vegetable mixture. Stir in remaining 2 cups milk. Cook and stir over medium heat until mixture boils and thickens. Cook and stir 1 minute more. Stir in Swiss cheese; heat until melted.   Makes 4 servings

Nutrients per Serving:

Calories	167	(11% of calories from fat)			
Total Fat	2 g	Dietary Fiber	2 g	Thiamin	<1 mg
Saturated Fat	<1 g	Protein	11 g	Riboflavin	<1 mg
Cholesterol	6 mg	Calcium	226 mg	Niacin	2 mg
Sodium	130 mg	Iron	1 mg	Vitamin A	509 RE
Carbohydrate	26 g	Folate	20 μg	Vitamin C	7 mg

Dietary Exchanges: 1 Starch/Bread, ½ Milk, 1 Vegetable, ½ Fat

Swiss Orzo Chowder

219 **P**asta Primavera

Fresh broccoli, cauliflower, carrots and peppers are
loaded with vitamins and minerals. They make this
Italian dish an excellent choice for lighter eating.

- ⅓ **cup broccoli flowerettes**
- ⅓ **cup cauliflower flowerettes**
- **1 baby carrot, peeled and cut into**
  julienne strips
- **1 tablespoon olive oil**
- ⅓ **cup *each* red and yellow bell pepper,**
  peeled and cut into julienne strips
- ⅓ **cup snow peas**
- ⅛ **cup shiitaki, morel or chanterelle**
  mushrooms
- **1 clove garlic, minced**
- **1 package (16 ounces) linguini or other**
  long pasta, cooked and drained
- **4 leaves minced fresh basil *or***
  2 teaspoons minced fresh chervil

Steam broccoli, cauliflower and carrot until
crisp-tender, about 3 minutes. Heat olive oil in large
skillet over medium heat. Add steamed vegetables,
peppers, snow peas, mushrooms and garlic. Cook and
stir for 3 minutes. Toss with hot linguini. Sprinkle
with basil; serve immediately.   Makes 4 servings

Nutrients per Serving:					
Calories	439	(14% of calories from fat)			
Total Fat	7 g	Dietary Fiber	6 g	Thiamin	1 mg
Saturated Fat	1 g	Protein	16 g	Riboflavin	<1 mg
Cholesterol	98 mg	Calcium	33 mg	Niacin	3 mg
Sodium	24 mg	Iron	4 mg	Vitamin A	288 RE
Carbohydrate	79 g	Folate	36 μg	Vitamin C	28 mg

Dietary Exchanges: ½ Starch/Bread, 1 Vegetable, 1 Fat

220 Rigatoni with Fresh Tomatoes

Roma tomatoes are small and plum-shaped. They are also called Italian tomatoes. Romas are thick and meaty with less juice than regular tomatoes. They have about the same nutritional content as a regular tomato, which means they are high in vitamins A and C.

1 cup rigatoni or mostaccioli
¼ cup sliced green onions
2 cloves garlic, minced
1 cup sliced zucchini
1 teaspoon chopped fresh basil *or*
  ¼ teaspoon dried basil leaves, crushed
1 teaspoon chopped fresh marjoram *or*
  ¼ teaspoon dried marjoram leaves, crushed
⅛ teaspoon salt
⅛ teaspoon pepper
1 cup coarsely chopped seeded Roma tomatoes
¼ cup (1 ounce) crumbled feta cheese or shredded part-skim mozzarella cheese

Prepare rigatoni according to package directions, omitting salt; drain.

Coat wok or large skillet with nonstick cooking spray; heat over medium-high heat. Add onions and garlic. Stir-fry 1 minute. Add zucchini, basil, marjoram, salt and pepper. Stir-fry 2 to 3 minutes or until zucchini is tender. Stir in tomatoes and pasta; heat through.

Divide pasta mixture onto four plates; sprinkle with cheese. Makes 4 servings

Nutrients per Serving:

Calories	112	(17% of calories from fat)			
Total Fat	2 g	Dietary Fiber	2 g	Thiamin	<1 mg
Saturated Fat	1 g	Protein	5 g	Riboflavin	<1 mg
Cholesterol	6 mg	Calcium	55 mg	Niacin	1 mg
Sodium	154 mg	Iron	1 mg	Vitamin A	84 RE
Carbohydrate	19 g	Folate	22 μg	Vitamin C	16 mg

Dietary Exchanges: 1 Starch/Bread, 1 Vegetable, ½ Fat

221 Ginger Noodles with Sesame Egg Strips

Even though this recipe gets most of its protein from eggs, it's virtually cholesterol free. Only the egg whites are used, thus eliminating the fat and cholesterol contained in the yolks.

2 egg whites
1 egg
3 tablespoons low sodium soy sauce, divided
3 teaspoons toasted sesame seeds,* divided
1 tablespoon peanut or vegetable oil
½ cup low sodium chicken broth
1 teaspoon minced fresh ginger
1 teaspoon sesame oil
6 ounces Chinese egg noodles or vermicelli, hot cooked and drained
⅓ cup sliced green onions

Beat together egg whites, egg, 1 tablespoon soy sauce and 1 teaspoon sesame seeds in small bowl.

Heat large nonstick skillet over medium-high heat; add peanut oil. For omelet, pour egg mixture into skillet; cook 1½ to 2 minutes or until bottom of omelet is set. Turn omelet over; cook 30 seconds to 1 minute. Slide out onto plate; cool and cut into ½-inch strips.

Add broth, remaining 2 tablespoons soy sauce, ginger and sesame oil to skillet. Bring to a boil; reduce heat. Add noodles; heat through. Add omelet strips and onions; heat through. Sprinkle with remaining 2 teaspoons sesame seeds.

Makes 4 servings

*To toast sesame seeds, spread seeds in small skillet. Shake skillet over medium heat 2 minutes or until seeds begin to pop and turn golden.

Nutrients per Serving:

Calories	238	(26% of calories from fat)			
Total Fat	7 g	Dietary Fiber	<1 g	Thiamin	<1 mg
Saturated Fat	1 g	Protein	9 g	Riboflavin	<1 mg
Cholesterol	53 mg	Calcium	21 mg	Niacin	1 mg
Sodium	445 mg	Iron	2 mg	Vitamin A	57 RE
Carbohydrate	35 g	Folate	9 μg	Vitamin C	3 mg

Dietary Exchanges: 2 Starch/Bread, 1 Meat, 1 Fat

Rigatoni with Fresh Tomatoes

222 Baked Spanish Rice and Barley

When it comes to good nutrition, this two-grain combo stacks up pretty well: 72% of its calories come from carbohydrate, 9% from protein and 19% from fat. There are even 2.2 grams of fiber per serving.

½ cup chopped onion
½ cup chopped green bell pepper
2 cloves garlic, minced
2 teaspoons vegetable oil
1 cup coarsely chopped seeded tomatoes
1 cup low sodium chicken broth, defatted
½ cup long-grain white rice
½ cup water
3 tablespoons quick-cooking barley
¼ teaspoon black pepper
⅛ teaspoon salt

Preheat oven to 350°F. Coat 1½-quart casserole with nonstick cooking spray. Cook and stir onion, bell pepper and garlic in oil in medium saucepan over medium heat until vegetables are tender. Stir in tomatoes, broth, rice, water, barley, black pepper and salt. Bring to a boil over high heat.

Pour mixture into prepared casserole. Cover; bake 25 to 30 minutes or until rice and barley are tender and liquid is absorbed. Fluff rice mixture with fork.

Makes 4 servings

Nutrients per Serving:

Calories	167	(16% of calories from fat)			
Total Fat	3 g	Dietary Fiber	3 g	Thiamin	<1 mg
Saturated Fat	<1 g	Protein	4 g	Riboflavin	<1 mg
Cholesterol	0 mg	Calcium	24 mg	Niacin	2 mg
Sodium	83 mg	Iron	2 mg	Vitamin A	52 RE
Carbohydrate	32 g	Folate	22 μg	Vitamin C	38 mg

Dietary Exchanges: 1½ Starch/Bread, 1½ Vegetable, ½ Fat

223 Herbed Rotini and Vegetables

Peas are a real nutritional powerhouse. They are good sources of protein, niacin, iron and phosphorus. They also provide some calcium, thiamin and vitamin C.

1 cup low sodium chicken broth, defatted
¾ cup (2 ounces) rotini
¼ cup chopped red or green bell pepper
2 cups sliced fresh mushrooms
1 cup frozen peas
¼ cup chopped fresh parsley
2 teaspoons chopped fresh tarragon *or*
    ½ teaspoon dried tarragon leaves,
    crushed
1 teaspoon grated lemon peel
⅛ teaspoon black pepper

Bring broth to a boil over high heat in medium saucepan. Add rotini and bell pepper; return to a boil. Reduce heat to medium-low. Cover; simmer 8 to 10 minutes or until pasta is tender.

Stir in mushrooms, peas, parsley, tarragon, lemon peel and black pepper. Return to a boil; reduce heat. Cover; simmer 2 to 3 minutes more or until heated through.

Makes 4 servings

Nutrients per Serving:

Calories	98	(6% of calories from fat)			
Total Fat	1 g	Dietary Fiber	3 g	Thiamin	<1 mg
Saturated Fat	<1 g	Protein	5 g	Riboflavin	<1 mg
Cholesterol	0 mg	Calcium	25 mg	Niacin	3 mg
Sodium	47 mg	Iron	2 mg	Vitamin A	60 RE
Carbohydrate	18 g	Folate	44 μg	Vitamin C	22 mg

Dietary Exchanges: 1 Starch/Bread, 1 Vegetable

MEATLESS

224 Two Beans and Rice

For protein and fiber, beans are hard to beat. There are about 5 grams of protein and almost 6 grams of fiber in one ⅓-cup portion of canned kidney beans.

1½ cups chopped onion
1 cup chopped green bell pepper
1 cup thinly sliced celery
2 cloves garlic, minced
1 teaspoon olive oil
2 cups chopped seeded tomatoes
1 can (15½ ounces) low sodium kidney beans, rinsed, drained and slightly mashed
1 can (15 ounces) black beans, rinsed, drained and slightly mashed
¼ cup water
1 bay leaf
½ teaspoon chicken bouillon granules
¼ teaspoon ground red pepper
4 cups hot cooked brown or white rice
¼ cup low fat sour cream
¼ cup chopped fresh cilantro or parsley

Spray 3-quart saucepan with nonstick cooking spray; heat saucepan over medium heat. Cook and stir onion, bell pepper, celery and garlic in oil until vegetables are tender.

Stir in tomatoes, kidney beans, black beans, water, bay leaf, bouillon and red pepper. Bring to a boil over high heat. Reduce heat to medium-low. Simmer 15 minutes, stirring occasionally. Remove bay leaf. Serve bean mixture over rice. Top with sour cream and sprinkle with cilantro.

Makes 4 servings

Nutrients per Serving:

Calories	507	(11% of calories from fat)			
Total Fat	6 g	Dietary Fiber	19 g	Thiamine	<1 mg
Saturated Fat	1 g	Protein	23 g	Riboflavin	<1 mg
Cholesterol	6 mg	Calcium	96 mg	Niacin	5 mg
Sodium	517 mg	Iron	4 mg	Vitamin A	135 RE
Carbohydrate	98 g	Folate	80 μg	Vitamin C	85 mg

Dietary Exchanges: 5½ Starch/Bread, 3 Vegetable, 1 Fat

225 Sprouts and Bulgur Sandwiches

The mung bean sprouts in these sandwiches are high in potassium. If you like, substitute alfalfa sprouts, they are high in vitamin A.

½ cup bulgur wheat
1 cup water
1 carton (8 ounces) plain low fat yogurt
¼ cup nonfat salad dressing or mayonnaise
1½ teaspoons curry powder
1 cup shredded carrots
½ cup chopped apple
⅓ cup coarsely chopped peanuts
2 cups fresh bean sprouts
8 very thin slices wheat bread, toasted

Rinse bulgur under cold water; drain. Bring 1 cup water to a boil in small saucepan over high heat. Stir in bulgur. Remove from heat. Let stand, uncovered, 20 minutes. Drain well; squeeze out excess liquid.

Combine yogurt, salad dressing and curry in medium bowl. Stir in bulgur, carrots, apple and peanuts. Cover and refrigerate.

Arrange sprouts on 4 slices wheat toast. Spread with bulgur mixture. Top with remaining bread slices.

Makes 4 servings

Nutrients per Serving:

Calories	274	(26% of calories from fat)			
Total Fat	9 g	Dietary Fiber	10 g	Thiamine	<1 mg
Saturated Fat	2 g	Protein	12 g	Riboflavin	<1 mg
Cholesterol	3 mg	Calcium	153 mg	Niacin	4 mg
Sodium	439 mg	Iron	2 mg	Vitamin A	787 RE
Carbohydrate	43 g	Folate	78 μg	Vitamin C	11 mg

Dietary Exchanges: 2 Starch/Bread, ½ Milk, 1 Vegetable, 1½ Fat

Two Beans and Rice

226 Spicy Mexican Frittata

Jalapeño peppers pack a mighty flavor wallop without adding many calories or much fat. One pepper has only about 7 calories and just half a gram of fat. The hotness of jalapeño peppers varies by the way they're used. For milder flavor, seed peppers before adding them to a dish. For a really hot dish, use the seeds too.

1 fresh jalapeño pepper*
1 clove garlic
1 medium tomato, peeled, halved, seeded and quartered
½ teaspoon ground coriander
½ teaspoon chili powder
½ cup chopped onion
1 cup frozen corn
6 egg whites
2 eggs
¼ cup skim milk
¼ teaspoon salt
¼ teaspoon black pepper
¼ cup (1 ounce) shredded part-skim farmer or mozzarella cheese

Add jalapeño pepper and garlic to food processor or blender. Process until finely chopped. Add tomato, coriander and chili powder. Cover; process until tomato is almost smooth.

Spray large skillet with nonstick cooking spray; heat skillet over medium heat. Cook and stir onion in hot skillet until tender. Stir in tomato mixture and corn. Cook 3 to 4 minutes or until liquid is almost evaporated, stirring occasionally.

Combine egg whites, eggs, milk, salt and black pepper in medium bowl. Add egg mixture all at once to skillet. Cook, without stirring, 2 minutes until eggs begin to set. Run large spoon around edge of skillet, lifting eggs for even cooking. Remove skillet from heat when eggs are almost set but surface is still moist.

Sprinkle with cheese. Cover; let stand 3 to 4 minutes or until surface is set and cheese melts. Cut into wedges.　　　Makes 4 servings

Chili peppers can sting and irritate the skin; wear rubber gloves when handling peppers and do not touch eyes. Wash your hands after handling chili peppers.

Nutrients per Serving:

Calories	129	(22% of calories from fat)			
Total Fat	3 g	Dietary Fiber	2 g	Thiamine	<1 mg
Saturated Fat	1 g	Protein	12 g	Riboflavin	<1 mg
Cholesterol	108 mg	Calcium	47 mg	Niacin	1 mg
Sodium	371 mg	Iron	1 mg	Vitamin A	104 RE
Carbohydrate	14 g	Folate	32 μg	Vitamin C	10 mg

Dietary Exchanges: ½ Starch/Bread, 1 Meat, 1½ Vegetable

227 Open-Faced Garbanzo Melts

The reduced calorie cream cheese in this recipe saves about half the fat and one third the calories of regular cream cheese.

1 can (15 ounces) garbanzo beans, rinsed and drained
¼ cup chopped fresh parsley
¼ cup reduced calorie soft cream cheese
**1 tablespoon chopped fresh dill *or*
    1 teaspoon dried dill weed**
1 tablespoon skim milk
⅛ teaspoon pepper
8 very thin slices wheat bread, toasted
¼ cup (1 ounce) shredded part-skim mozzarella cheese

Preheat broiler. Place beans, parsley, cream cheese, dill, milk and pepper in small bowl. Beat with electric mixer on medium-low speed about 2 minutes or until almost smooth.

Spread bean mixture on wheat toast. Sprinkle with mozzarella cheese. Place on ungreased baking sheet. Broil 4 inches below heat 2 to 3 minutes or until cheese melts and sandwiches are heated through.

Makes 4 servings

Nutrients per Serving:

Calories	217	(27% of calories from fat)			
Total Fat	7 g	Dietary Fiber	8 g	Thiamine	<1 mg
Saturated Fat	4 g	Protein	11 g	Riboflavin	<1 mg
Cholesterol	9 mg	Calcium	140 mg	Niacin	1 mg
Sodium	654 mg	Iron	4 mg	Vitamin A	100 RE
Carbohydrate	31 g	Folate	24 μg	Vitamin C	9 mg

Dietary Exchanges: 2 Starch/Bread, ½ Meat, 1 Fat

Spicy Mexican Frittata

228 Hot and Spicy Spuds

The flavorful seasonings in this sauce spice up the potatoes so well there is no need to add the usual calorie-, fat- and sodium-laden toppers you find at potato bars.

4 medium baking potatoes
1 cup chopped onion
½ cup chopped green bell pepper
2 cloves garlic, minced
1 teaspoon olive oil
1 can (15½ ounces) low sodium kidney beans, rinsed and drained
1 can (14½ ounces) no-salt-added tomatoes, cut up and undrained
1 can (4 ounces) diced green chilies
¼ cup chopped fresh cilantro or parsley
1 teaspoon ground cumin
1 teaspoon chili powder
¼ teaspoon ground red pepper
¼ cup low fat sour cream
¼ cup (1 ounce) shredded low fat Cheddar cheese

Preheat oven 350°F. Scrub potatoes; pierce with fork. Bake 1¼ to 1½ hours or until tender.

Meanwhile, spray 2-quart saucepan with nonstick cooking spray; heat saucepan over medium heat. Cook and stir onion, bell pepper and garlic in oil until vegetables are tender. Stir in beans, tomatoes with liquid, chilies, cilantro, cumin, chili powder and red pepper. Bring to a boil over high heat. Reduce heat to medium-low. Cover; simmer 8 minutes, stirring occasionally.

Gently roll potatoes under your hand using hot pad to loosen pulp. Cut crisscross slit in each potato. Place potatoes on four plates. Press potato ends to open slits. Spoon bean mixture over potatoes. Top with sour cream and sprinkle with cheese.

Makes 4 servings

Nutrients per Serving:

Calories	384	(12% of calories from fat)			
Total Fat	5 g	Dietary Fiber	8 g	Thiamine	<1 mg
Saturated Fat	1 g	Protein	15 g	Riboflavin	<1 mg
Cholesterol	11 mg	Calcium	149 mg	Niacin	5 mg
Sodium	88 mg	Iron	5 mg	Vitamin A	119 RE
Carbohydrate	72 g	Folate	67 µg	Vitamin C	121 mg

Dietary Exchanges: 4 Starch/Bread, 2½ Vegetable, 1 Fat

229 Hearty White Bean Soup

Bacteria in the intestines work hard at breaking down the large quantities of complex carbohydrates found in beans. A side effect of this digestion is gas. One rumored anti-gas remedy is to add a dash of ginger to a recipe with beans.

2⅔ cups water, divided
1 can (15 ounces) Great Northern beans or navy beans, rinsed and drained
1 cup chopped carrots
1 cup chopped green bell pepper
1 cup low sodium chicken broth, defatted
½ cup chopped celery
2 tablespoons chopped fresh thyme *or* 2 teaspoons dried thyme leaves, crushed
2 tablespoons chopped fresh marjoram *or* 2 teaspoons dried marjoram leaves, crushed
½ teaspoon ground cumin
¼ teaspoon black pepper
3 tablespoons all-purpose flour
⅔ cup (about 3 ounces) shredded low fat Swiss or Cheddar cheese

Combine 2⅓ cups water, beans, carrots, bell pepper, broth, celery, thyme, marjoram, cumin and black pepper in 3-quart saucepan. Bring to a boil over high heat. Reduce heat to medium-low. Cover; simmer 20 to 25 minutes or until vegetables are tender, stirring occasionally.

Combine remaining ⅓ cup water and flour in small bowl. Stir into mixture in saucepan. Cook and stir over medium heat until mixture boils and thickens. Cook and stir 1 minute more. Ladle soup into four bowls. Sprinkle with cheese. Makes 4 servings

Nutrients per Serving:

Calories	240	(17% of calories from fat)			
Total Fat	5 g	Dietary Fiber	2 g	Thiamine	<1 mg
Saturated Fat	<1 g	Protein	16 g	Riboflavin	<1 mg
Cholesterol	11 mg	Calcium	100 mg	Niacin	2 mg
Sodium	127 mg	Iron	4 mg	Vitamin A	817 RE
Carbohydrate	36 g	Folate	109 µg	Vitamin C	56 mg

Dietary Exchanges: 2 Starch/Bread, 1 Meat, 1½ Vegetable, ½ Fat

Hot and Spicy Spud

230 Garbanzo Sandwich Bundles

Garbanzo beans or chickpeas are a staple in Italian, Spanish, Mexican and Middle Eastern cooking. They provide protein, fiber and complex carbohydrates while being low in fat and having no cholesterol.

¼ **cup reduced calorie ketchup**
1 **tablespoon red wine vinegar**
1 **teaspoon dried fines herbes**
1 **teaspoon Dijon-style mustard**
⅛ **teaspoon pepper**
1 **can (15 ounces) low sodium garbanzo beans, rinsed and drained**
1 **cup sliced fresh mushrooms**
8 **cherry tomatoes, quartered**
½ **cup shredded carrot**
½ **cup (2 ounces) shredded low fat Swiss cheese**
8 **lettuce leaves**
4 **(10-inch) flour tortillas**

Combine ketchup, vinegar, fines herbes, mustard and pepper in medium bowl. Stir in beans, mushrooms, tomatoes, carrot and cheese. Cover and refrigerate.

Place lettuce on tortillas. Spoon bean mixture on top. Fold in ends of tortillas; roll up tortillas.

Makes 4 servings

Nutrients per Serving:

Calories	277	(21% of calories from fat)			
Total Fat	7 g	Dietary Fiber	8 g	Thiamine	<1 mg
Saturated Fat	1 g	Protein	14 g	Riboflavin	<1 mg
Cholesterol	7 mg	Calcium	110 mg	Niacin	3 mg
Sodium	660 mg	Iron	5 mg	Vitamin A	461 RE
Carbohydrate	43 g	Folate	41 μg	Vitamin C	22 mg

Dietary Exchanges: 2½ Starch/Bread, ½ Meat, 1 Vegetable, 1 Fat

231 Zesty Lentil Stew

Dried legumes, such as lentils, beans and black-eyed peas are good sources of iron, thiamine, riboflavin, niacin, potassium and phosphorus.

1 cup dried lentils
2 cups chopped peeled potatoes
1 can (14½ ounces) low sodium chicken broth, defatted
1⅔ cups water
1½ cups chopped seeded tomatoes
1 can (11½ ounces) no-salt-added spicy vegetable juice cocktail
1 cup chopped onion
½ cup chopped carrot
½ cup chopped celery
2 tablespoons chopped fresh basil or 2 teaspoons dried basil leaves, crushed
2 tablespoons chopped fresh oregano or 2 teaspoons dried oregano leaves, crushed
1 to 2 tablespoons finely chopped jalapeño pepper*
¼ teaspoon salt

Rinse lentils under cold water; drain. Combine lentils, potatoes, broth, water, tomatoes, vegetable juice cocktail, onion, carrot, celery, basil, oregano, jalapeño pepper and salt in 3-quart saucepan.

Bring to a boil over high heat. Reduce heat to medium-low. Cover; simmer 45 to 50 minutes or until lentils are tender, stirring occasionally.

Makes 4 servings

*Chili peppers can sting and irritate the skin; wear rubber gloves when handling peppers and do not touch eyes. Wash your hands after handling chili peppers.

Nutrients per Serving:

Calories	369	(3% of calories from fat)			
Total Fat	1 g	Dietary Fiber	7 g	Thiamine	1 mg
Saturated Fat	<1 g	Protein	19 g	Riboflavin	<1 mg
Cholesterol	0 mg	Calcium	104 mg	Niacin	6 mg
Sodium	620 mg	Iron	8 mg	Vitamin A	604 RE
Carbohydrate	72 g	Folate	335 μg	Vitamin C	58 mg

Dietary Exchanges: 4 Starch/Bread, 3 Vegetable

232 Garbanzo-Vegetable Soup

The no-salt-added tomatoes have only about 20 milligrams of sodium per serving, while regular canned tomatoes have about ten times that amount.

1 cup chopped onion
½ cup chopped green bell pepper
2 cloves garlic, minced
1 teaspoon olive oil
2 cans (14½ ounces each) no-salt-added tomatoes, cut up and undrained
3 cups water
2 cups broccoli flowerets
1 can (15 ounces) garbanzo beans, rinsed, drained and slightly mashed
½ cup (3 ounces) orzo or rosamarina pasta
1 bay leaf
1 tablespoon chopped fresh thyme or 1 teaspoon dried thyme leaves, crushed
1 tablespoon chopped fresh rosemary or 1 teaspoon dried rosemary leaves, crushed
1 tablespoon lime juice or lemon juice
½ teaspoon ground turmeric
¼ teaspoon salt
¼ teaspoon ground red pepper
¼ cup toasted pumpkin seeds or sunflower kernels

Spray 3-quart saucepan with nonstick cooking spray; heat saucepan over medium heat. Cook and stir onion, bell pepper and garlic in oil until vegetables are tender. Add tomatoes with liquid, water, broccoli, beans, orzo, bay leaf, thyme, rosemary, lime juice, turmeric, salt and red pepper. Bring to a boil over high heat. Reduce heat to medium-low. Cover; simmer 10 to 12 minutes or until orzo is tender. Remove bay leaf. Ladle soup into four bowls. Sprinkle with pumpkin seeds.

Makes 4 servings

Nutrients per Serving:

Calories	268	(16% of calories from fat)			
Total Fat	5 g	Dietary Fiber	11 g	Thiamine	<1 mg
Saturated Fat	1 g	Protein	12 g	Riboflavin	<1 mg
Cholesterol	0 mg	Calcium	122 mg	Niacin	2 mg
Sodium	541 mg	Iron	5 mg	Vitamin A	161 RE
Carbohydrate	47 g	Folate	58 μg	Vitamin C	92 mg

Dietary Exchanges: 2 Starch/Bread, 3 Vegetable, 1 Fat

233 Pea and Spinach Frittata

Tablespoon for tablespoon, grated Romano or Parmesan cheese goes a lot farther than other cheeses toward boosting the flavor of recipes.

1 cup chopped onion
¼ cup water
1 cup frozen peas
1 cup torn stemmed washed spinach
6 egg whites
2 eggs
½ cup cooked brown rice
¼ cup skim milk
2 tablespoons grated Romano or
        Parmesan cheese
1 tablespoon chopped fresh mint *or*
        1 teaspoon dried mint leaves, crushed
¼ teaspoon pepper
⅛ teaspoon salt
    Additional grated Romano or Parmesan
        cheese for garnish

Coat large skillet with nonstick cooking spray. Combine onion and water in skillet. Bring to a boil over high heat. Reduce heat to medium. Cover; cook 2 to 3 minutes or until onion is tender. Stir in peas. Cook until peas are heated through; drain. Stir in spinach. Cook and stir about 1 minute or until spinach just starts to wilt.

Meanwhile, combine egg whites, eggs, rice, milk, 2 tablespoons Romano cheese, mint, pepper and salt in medium bowl. Add egg mixture to skillet. Cook, without stirring, 2 minutes until eggs begin to set. Run large spoon around edge of skillet, lifting eggs for even cooking. Remove skillet from heat when eggs are almost set but surface is still moist.

Cover; let stand 3 to 4 minutes or until surface is set. Garnish top with additional Romano cheese. Cut into wedges.   Makes 4 servings

Nutrients per Serving:

Calories	162	(22% of calories from fat)			
Total Fat	4 g	Dietary Fiber	4 g	Thiamine	<1 mg
Saturated Fat	1 g	Protein	14 g	Riboflavin	<1 mg
Cholesterol	110 mg	Calcium	112 mg	Niacin	1 mg
Sodium	246 mg	Iron	2 mg	Vitamin A	190 RE
Carbohydrate	18 g	Folate	75 µg	Vitamin C	14 mg

Dietary Exchanges: 1 Starch/Bread, 1 Meat, 1½ Vegetable

234 Pinto Bean Soup

Although high in total fat, walnuts are a good source of protein, phosphorus, iron and potassium. Used in moderation, they can be a good addition to a healthy diet.

1 cup chopped onion
2 cloves garlic, minced
1 teaspoon canola oil
4½ cups water
2 cups broccoli flowerets
1 can (15 ounces) pinto beans, rinsed and
        drained
1½ cups frozen corn
1 cup chopped carrots
1 cup chopped plum tomatoes
2 tablespoons low sodium Worcestershire
        sauce
1 tablespoon chili powder
1 teaspoon ground cumin
½ teaspoon chicken bouillon granules
¼ teaspoon pepper
¼ cup low fat sour cream
¼ cup chopped walnuts

Spray 3-quart saucepan with nonstick cooking spray; heat saucepan over medium heat. Cook and stir onion and garlic in oil until onion is tender.

Add water, broccoli, beans, corn, carrots, tomatoes, Worcestershire sauce, chili powder, cumin, bouillon granules and pepper. Bring to a boil over high heat. Reduce heat to medium-low. Cover; simmer about 15 minutes or until vegetables are tender. Ladle soup into four bowls. Top with sour cream and sprinkle with walnuts.   Makes 4 servings

Nutrients per Serving:

Calories	283	(25% of calories from fat)			
Total Fat	8 g	Dietary Fiber	6 g	Thiamine	<1 mg
Saturated Fat	1 g	Protein	13 g	Riboflavin	<1 mg
Cholesterol	6 mg	Calcium	106 mg	Niacin	2 mg
Sodium	673 mg	Iron	4 mg	Vitamin A	965 RE
Carbohydrate	45 g	Folate	133 µg	Vitamin C	75 mg

Dietary Exchanges: 2 Starch/Bread, 3 Vegetable, 1½ Fat

Vegetable-Tofu Stir-Fry

235 Potato-Corn Chowder

*If you would like to increase the nutritional value of
the potatoes in this soup, leave their skins on.
Potatoes, especially with skins, are good sources of
vitamin C, phosphorus and potassium.*

- **1 cup chopped onion**
- **½ cup chopped green bell pepper**
- **1 teaspoon canola oil**
- **2 cups chopped peeled potatoes**
- **1 can (14½ ounces) low sodium chicken
    broth, defatted**
- **1 cup frozen corn**
- **1 cup frozen lima beans**
- **1 tablespoon chopped fresh dill *or*
    1 teaspoon dried dill weed**
- **¼ teaspoon black pepper**
- **1⅔ cups skim milk, divided**
- **3 tablespoons all-purpose flour**
- **⅓ cup nonfat dry milk**
- **¼ cup chopped fresh parsley**

Coat 3-quart saucepan with nonstick cooking spray;
heat saucepan over medium heat. Cook and stir
onion and bell pepper in oil until vegetables are
tender.

Add potatoes, broth, corn, lima beans, dill and
black pepper. Bring to a boil over high heat. Reduce
heat to medium-low. Cover; simmer 10 to 12
minutes or until potatoes are tender.

Combine ⅓ cup skim milk and flour in small bowl.
Stir into potato mixture. Stir in remaining 1⅓ cups
skim milk and dry milk. Cook and stir over
medium heat until mixture boils and thickens. Cook
and stir 1 minute more. Ladle chowder into four
bowls. Sprinkle with parsley.　　Makes 4 servings

Nutrients per Serving:

Calories	304	(6% of calories from fat)			
Total Fat	2 g	Dietary Fiber	6 g	Thiamine	<1 mg
Saturated Fat	<1 g	Protein	14 g	Riboflavin	<1 mg
Cholesterol	3 mg	Calcium	238 mg	Niacin	4 mg
Sodium	132 mg	Iron	2 mg	Vitamin A	160 RE
Carbohydrate	60 g	Folate	80 μg	Vitamin C	56 mg

Dietary Exchanges: 3 Starch/Bread, 1½ Vegetable

236 Vegetable-Tofu Stir-Fry

Tofu is sold in soft, firm and extra-firm varieties. Extra-firm tofu is best for stir-frying because it holds its shape and does not crumble. Although the nutritional content of tofu varies by manufacturer, generally one ½-cup serving of tofu has about 95 calories, 10 grams of protein, 6 grams of fat and no cholesterol. Usually, soft tofu is lower in calories and protein than firm tofu.

- ⅓ cup water
- 4 teaspoons low sodium soy sauce
- 1 tablespoon rice wine or dry white wine
- 2 teaspoons cornstarch
- 1½ teaspoons sugar
- ¼ teaspoon chicken bouillon granules
- 1 package (10½ ounces) extra-firm tofu, drained
- 3 teaspoons vegetable oil, divided
- 3 cups sliced fresh mushrooms
- 1 cup sliced leek
- 2 cloves garlic, minced
- 2 teaspoons minced fresh ginger
- 2 cups diagonally sliced carrots
- 3 cups torn stemmed washed spinach
- 4 cups hot cooked rice

Combine water, soy sauce, rice wine, cornstarch, sugar and bouillon granules in small bowl. Press tofu lightly between paper towels; cut into ¾-inch squares or triangles.

Spray wok or large skillet with nonstick cooking spray; heat over medium-high heat. Add 1 teaspoon oil. Add mushrooms, leek, garlic and ginger. Stir-fry 2 to 3 minutes or until vegetables are tender. Remove from wok.

Add remaining 2 teaspoons oil to wok; add carrots. Stir-fry 5 to 6 minutes or until crisp-tender. Add cornstarch mixture; stir-fry about 1 minute or until mixture boils and thickens. Stir in mushroom mixture, tofu and spinach. Cover; cook about 1 minute or until heated through. Serve over rice.

Makes 4 servings

Nutrients per Serving:

Calories	487	(20% of calories from fat)			
Total Fat	11 g	Dietary Fiber	7 g	Thiamine	1 mg
Saturated Fat	1 g	Protein	21 g	Riboflavin	<1 mg
Cholesterol	0 mg	Calcium	257 mg	Niacin	7 mg
Sodium	308 mg	Iron	13 mg	Vitamin A	1,844 RE
Carbohydrate	78 g	Folate	150 µg	Vitamin C	23 mg

Dietary Exchanges: 4 Starch/Bread, ½ Meat, 3 Vegetable, 2 Fat

237 Leek Cheese Pie

Canola oil is lower in saturated fat than other vegetable oils. It has only 6 percent saturated fat as compared to 18 percent in peanut oil. It also is second highest in monounsaturated fat behind olive oil.

- ⅔ cup thinly sliced leek
- ¼ cup water
- 1 clove garlic, minced
- 1 cup all-purpose flour
- 2 teaspoons baking powder
- 4 egg whites, divided
- ¼ cup skim milk
- 1½ tablespoons canola oil
- ¼ cup reduced calorie soft cream cheese
- 1 carton (12 ounces) dry curd cottage cheese
- ¾ cup shredded carrot
- 2 tablespoons fine dry bread crumbs
- 2 tablespoons chopped fresh basil or 2 teaspoons dried basil leaves, crushed
- ¼ teaspoon pepper

Preheat oven to 325°F. Coat 9-inch pie plate with nonstick cooking spray. Combine leek, water and garlic in small saucepan. Bring to a boil over high heat. Reduce heat to medium-low. Cover; simmer 3 to 4 minutes or until leek is tender. Drain.

Combine flour and baking powder in medium bowl. Stir in leek mixture, 2 egg whites, milk and oil until nearly smooth. Spread half of batter into prepared pie plate. Bake 20 to 22 minutes or until crust starts to brown.

Meanwhile, combine remaining 2 egg whites and cream cheese in medium bowl. Stir in cottage cheese, carrot, bread crumbs, basil and pepper. Spread over crust in pie plate. Spoon remaining batter on top. Bake 40 to 45 minutes more or until golden brown. Let stand 10 minutes before serving.

Makes 6 servings

Nutrients per Serving:

Calories	215	(24% of calories from fat)			
Total Fat	6 g	Dietary Fiber	1 g	Thiamine	<1 mg
Saturated Fat	3 g	Protein	16 g	Riboflavin	<1 mg
Cholesterol	7 mg	Calcium	93 mg	Niacin	2 mg
Sodium	236 mg	Iron	2 mg	Vitamin A	445 RE
Carbohydrate	24 g	Folate	27 µg	Vitamin C	4 mg

Dietary Exchanges: 1½ Starch/Bread, 1½ Meat, ½ Fat

238 Vegetable-Cheese Pizzas

If you are closely watching the fat in your diet, be sure to use pita bread rather than tortillas. You will save about 5 grams of fat per serving.

2½ cups chopped tomatoes
1 cup thinly sliced onion
1 cup chopped green bell pepper
6 tablespoons water, divided
2 cloves garlic, minced
1½ teaspoons dried Italian seasoning, crushed
1 teaspoon sugar
2 tablespoons cornstarch
4 large pita bread rounds, split horizontally, *or* 8 (7-inch) flour tortillas
½ cup (2 ounces) shredded part-skim mozzarella cheese
⅓ cup (1½ ounces) shredded low fat sharp Cheddar or colby cheese
2 tablespoons grated Parmesan or Romano cheese

Preheat oven to 375°F. Combine tomatoes, onion, bell pepper, 2 tablespoons water, garlic, Italian seasoning and sugar in 2-quart saucepan. Bring to a boil over medium-high heat. Reduce heat to medium-low. Cover; simmer 8 to 10 minutes or until onion is tender.

Combine remaining 4 tablespoons water and cornstarch in small bowl; add to tomato mixture. Cook and stir until mixture boils and thickens. Cook and stir 2 minutes more.

Meanwhile, place pita bread halves on ungreased baking sheets. Bake 8 to 10 minutes or until edges just start to brown.

Spread vegetable mixture over pita bread halves. Sprinkle with mozzarella, Cheddar and Parmesan cheeses. Bake about 5 minutes more or until cheeses melt and pizzas are heated through.

Makes 4 servings

Nutrients per Serving:

Calories	268	(21% of calories from fat)			
Total Fat	6 g	Dietary Fiber	4 g	Thiamine	<1 mg
Saturated Fat	3 g	Protein	14 g	Riboflavin	<1 mg
Cholesterol	18 mg	Calcium	273 mg	Niacin	3 mg
Sodium	407 mg	Iron	2 mg	Vitamin A	164 RE
Carbohydrate	40 g	Folate	66 µg	Vitamin C	80 mg

Dietary Exchanges: 1½ Starch/Bread, 1 Meat, 3 Vegetable, ½ Fat

239 Barley Stew with Cornmeal-Cheese Dumplings

The parsnip in this stew provides calcium and potassium, while zucchini adds vitamins A and C.

2 cans (11½ ounces each) no-salt-added spicy vegetable juice cocktail
1 can (15½ ounces) butter beans, drained
1 can (14½ ounces) no-salt-added stewed tomatoes, undrained
1 cup sliced zucchini
1 cup sliced carrots
1 cup water
½ cup chopped peeled parsnip
⅓ cup quick pearl barley
1 bay leaf
2 tablespoons chopped fresh thyme
1½ tablespoons chopped fresh rosemary
⅓ cup all-purpose flour
⅓ cup cornmeal
1 teaspoon baking powder
¼ cup skim milk
1 tablespoon canola oil
⅓ cup (1½ ounces) shredded low fat Cheddar cheese

Add vegetable juice, beans, tomatoes with liquid, zucchini, carrots, water, parsnip, barley, bay leaf, thyme and rosemary to 3-quart saucepan. Bring to a boil over high heat. Reduce heat to medium-low. Cover; simmer 20 to 25 minutes or until tender, stirring occasionally. Remove and discard bay leaf.

Combine flour, cornmeal and baking powder in small bowl. Combine milk and oil in separate small bowl; stir into flour mixture. Stir in cheese. Drop dough by spoonfuls to make 4 mounds onto boiling stew. Cover; simmer 10 to 12 minutes or until wooden toothpick inserted near center of dumpling comes out clean.

Make 4 servings

Nutrients per Serving:

Calories	366	(16% of calories from fat)			
Total Fat	7 g	Dietary Fiber	13 g	Thiamine	<1 mg
Saturated Fat	2 g	Protein	14 g	Riboflavin	<1 mg
Cholesterol	8 mg	Calcium	204 mg	Niacin	5 mg
Sodium	454 mg	Iron	6 mg	Vitamin A	1,051 RE
Carbohydrate	64 g	Folate	68 µg	Vitamin C	59 mg

Dietary Exchanges: 3 Starch/Bread, 4 Vegetable, 1 Fat

BREADS

240 Soda Bread

Although it sounds as if buttermilk should be high in fat, it is usually made from low fat or skim milk.

1½ cups whole wheat flour
1 cup all-purpose flour
½ cup rolled oats
¼ cup sugar
1½ teaspoons baking powder
½ teaspoon baking soda
¼ teaspoon ground cinnamon
⅓ cup raisins (optional)
¼ cup walnuts (optional)
1¼ cups low fat buttermilk
1 tablespoon vegetable oil

Preheat oven to 375°F. Combine whole wheat flour, all-purpose flour, oats, sugar, baking powder, baking soda and cinnamon in large bowl. Stir in raisins and walnuts, if desired. Gradually stir in buttermilk and oil until dough forms. Knead in bowl for 30 seconds. Spray loaf pan with nonstick cooking spray; place dough in pan. Bake 40 to 50 minutes until wooden toothpick inserted in center comes out clean. Makes 16 slices

Nutrients per Serving:

Calories	103	(12% of calories from fat)			
Total Fat	1 g	Dietary Fiber	2 g	Thiamine	<1 mg
Saturated Fat	<1 g	Protein	3 g	Riboflavin	<1 mg
Cholesterol	1 mg	Calcium	34 mg	Niacin	1 mg
Sodium	77 mg	Iron	1 mg	Vitamin A	3 RE
Carbohydrate	20 g	Folate	9 µg	Vitamin C	<1 mg

Dietary Exchanges: 1½ Starch/Bread

241 Granola-Bran Muffins

Bran is the edible outer layer of a grain kernel which contains most of the nutritional value of the plant.

1 cup boiling water
2½ cups whole bran cereal
1 egg, lightly beaten
1 egg white
2 cups buttermilk
¼ cup vegetable oil
½ cup finely chopped apple
2 cups all-purpose flour
1 cup sugar
½ cup quick-cooking rolled oats
½ cup wheat germ
2 teaspoons baking soda
½ teaspoon salt
1 cup raisins
½ cup chopped almonds, walnuts or pecans

Spray nonstick cooking spray in muffin cups or use paper liners. Preheat oven to 400°F. Pour boiling water over cereal in large bowl; cool. Stir in egg, egg white, buttermilk, oil and apple. Combine flour, sugar, oats, wheat germ, baking soda and salt in separate bowl. Stir in bran mixture. Stir in raisins and nuts. Fill prepared muffin cups ⅔ full. Bake 20 to 22 minutes or until wooden toothpick inserted in center comes out clean.

Makes 36 muffins

Nutrients per Serving:

Calories	108	(24% of calories from fat)			
Total Fat	3 g	Dietary Fiber	2 g	Thiamine	<1 mg
Saturated Fat	<1 g	Protein	3 g	Riboflavin	<1 mg
Cholesterol	6 mg	Calcium	29 mg	Niacin	2 mg
Sodium	150 mg	Iron	1 mg	Vitamin A	4 RE
Carbohydrate	20 g	Folate	14 µg	Vitamin C	5 mg

Dietary Exchanges: 1½ Starch/Bread, ½ Fat

242 Bran and Honey Rye Breadsticks

There is more than one way to get your fiber and these breadsticks are a delightfully delicious way. The rye flour and whole bran cereal raise the fiber tally to 3.4 grams for each serving of two breadsticks.

1 package (¼ ounce) active dry yeast
1 teaspoon sugar
1½ cups warm water (110°F)
3¾ cups all-purpose flour, divided
1 tablespoon honey
1 tablespoon vegetable oil
½ teaspoon salt
1 cup rye flour
½ cup whole bran cereal
Skim milk

Dissolve yeast and sugar in warm water in large mixer bowl. Let stand 10 minutes. Add 1 cup all-purpose flour, honey, oil and salt. Beat with electric mixer at medium speed 3 minutes. Stir in rye flour, bran cereal and enough additional 2 cups all-purpose flour to make moderately stiff dough.

Knead dough on lightly floured surface 10 minutes or until smooth and elastic, adding remaining ¾ cup all-purpose flour as necessary to prevent sticking. Place in greased bowl; turn greased side up. Cover with damp cloth; let rise in warm place 40 to 45 minutes or until doubled in bulk.

Spray 2 baking sheets with nonstick cooking spray. Punch dough down. Divide into 24 equal pieces on lightly floured surface. Roll each piece into an 8-inch rope. Place on prepared baking sheets. Cover with damp cloth; let rise in warm place 30 to 35 or until doubled in bulk.

Preheat oven to 375°F. Brush breadsticks with milk. Bake 18 to 20 minutes or until breadsticks are golden brown. Remove from baking sheets. Cool on wire racks.   Makes 24 breadsticks (2 per serving)

Nutrients per Serving:

Calories	198	(8% of calories from fat)			
Total Fat	2 g	Dietary Fiber	3 g	Thiamine	<1 mg
Saturated Fat	<1 g	Protein	5 g	Riboflavin	<1 mg
Cholesterol	0 mg	Calcium	10 mg	Niacin	4 mg
Sodium	109 mg	Iron	2 mg	Vitamin A	0 RE
Carbohydrate	40 g	Folate	38 μg	Vitamin C	3 mg

Dietary Exchanges: 2½ Starch/Bread

243 Bubbling Wisconsin Cheese Bread

Adding cheese to your diet adds calcium and protein but should be eaten sparingly because it is also high in fat.

½ cup (2 ounces) shredded Wisconsin mozzarella cheese
⅓ cup mayonnaise or salad dressing
⅛ teaspoon garlic powder
⅛ teaspoon onion powder
1 loaf (16 ounces) French bread, halved lengthwise
⅓ cup (1 ounce) grated Wisconsin Parmesan cheese

Preheat oven to 350°F. Combine mozzarella cheese, mayonnaise, garlic powder and onion powder in mixing bowl; mix well (mixture will be very thick). Spread half the mixture over each bread half. Sprinkle half the Parmesan cheese over each half. Bake 20 to 25 minutes or until bubbly and lightly browned.* Cut each half into 8 slices.

Makes 16 servings

*To broil, position on rack 4 inches from heat for 3 to 5 minutes.

Nutrients per Serving:

Calories	117	(30% of calories from fat)			
Total Fat	4 g	Dietary Fiber	1 g	Thiamine	<1 mg
Saturated Fat	1 g	Protein	4 g	Riboflavin	<1 mg
Cholesterol	5 mg	Calcium	75 mg	Niacin	1 mg
Sodium	237 mg	Iron	1 mg	Vitamin A	15 RE
Carbohydrate	16 g	Folate	11 μg	Vitamin C	<1 mg

Dietary Exchanges: 1 Starch/Bread, 1 Fat

Bran and Honey Rye Breadsticks

244 Wild Rice Three-Grain Bread

Whole rye contains more protein, phosphorus, iron, potassium and B vitamins than whole wheat.

1 package active dry yeast
⅓ cup warm water (105° to 115°F)
2 cups skim milk, scalded and cooled (105° to 115°F)
½ cup honey
2 tablespoons shortening, melted
1½ teaspoons salt
4 to 4½ cups all-purpose flour or bread flour, divided
2 cups whole wheat flour
½ cup rye flour
½ cup rolled oats
1 cup cooked wild rice
1 egg white, beaten with 1 tablespoon water
½ cup sunflower kernels

Dissolve yeast in water in large bowl. Add milk, honey, shortening and salt. Stir in 2 cups all-purpose flour, whole wheat flour, rye flour and oats to make soft dough. Add wild rice. Cover; let rest 15 minutes. Stir in enough remaining all-purpose flour to make stiff dough. Transfer dough to flat surface; knead 10 minutes. Add more flour as necessary to keep dough from sticking. Transfer dough to lightly greased bowl; turn over. Cover; let rise until doubled in bulk, about 2 hours.

Preheat oven to 375°F. Punch down dough; knead briefly on lightly oiled surface. Divide dough into 3 equal parts and shape into strands; braid and place on greased baking sheet to make wreath, or divide into two parts and place into two 9½ × 5½-inch greased bread pans. Let rise until doubled, about 45 minutes. Brush tops of loaves with egg white mixed with water; sprinkle with sunflower kernels. Bake 45 minutes or until loaves sound hollow when tapped.

Makes 20 servings

Nutrients per Serving:

Calories	226	(15% of calories from fat)			
Total Fat	4 g	Dietary Fiber	4 g	Thiamine	<1 mg
Saturated Fat	1 g	Protein	8 g	Riboflavin	<1 mg
Cholesterol	<1 mg	Calcium	46 mg	Niacin	3 mg
Sodium	177 mg	Iron	2 mg	Vitamin A	16 RE
Carbohydrate	42 g	Folate	38 µg	Vitamin C	<1 mg

Dietary Exchanges: 3 Starch/Bread

245 Plum Oatmeal Muffins

Oats, unlike wheat, are not refined during processing. This is why they retain most of their nutritional integrity.

5 fresh California plums, halved and pitted, divided
2 cups all-purpose flour
1¾ cups rolled oats
¾ cup packed brown sugar
⅓ cup vegetable oil
1 egg
3 teaspoons baking powder
1 teaspoon salt
1 teaspoon vanilla
1 teaspoon grated orange peel

Spray nonstick cooking spray in muffin cups or use paper liners. Preheat oven to 350°F. Cut up 3 plums to measure 1 cup. Add to food processor or blender; process until smooth. Coarsely chop remaining 2 plums; set aside. Combine puréed plums, flour, oats, brown sugar, oil, egg, baking powder, salt, vanilla and orange peel. Stir until just blended. Stir in chopped plums. Fill prepared muffin cups ⅔ full. Bake 30 to 35 minutes or until wooden toothpick inserted in center comes out clean.

Makes 18 muffins

Nutrients per Serving:

Calories	166	(27% of calories from fat)			
Total Fat	5 g	Dietary Fiber	1 g	Thiamine	<1 mg
Saturated Fat	1 g	Protein	3 g	Riboflavin	<1 mg
Cholesterol	12 mg	Calcium	27 mg	Niacin	1 mg
Sodium	180 mg	Iron	1 mg	Vitamin A	13 RE
Carbohydrate	27 g	Folate	8 µg	Vitamin C	2 mg

Dietary Exchanges: 1½ Starch/Bread, ½ Fruit, 1 Fat

Banana Nut Bread

246 Banana Nut Bread

Green bananas can be ripened uncovered or in a brown paper bag at room temperature. After they're ripe, further ripening can be delayed by placing them in the refrigerator. The skin may turn dark, but the fruit will be fine.

½ cup granulated sugar
2 tablespoons packed brown sugar
5 tablespoons margarine
1 egg
2 egg whites
1⅓ cups mashed ripe bananas
2½ cups all-purpose flour
1 teaspoon baking soda
½ teaspoon salt
⅓ cup walnuts

Preheat oven to 375°F. Cream sugars and margarine with electric mixer at medium speed in large bowl. Add egg, egg whites and bananas. Sift together flour, baking soda and salt in separate bowl; add to banana mixture. Stir in walnuts. Pour into large loaf pan sprayed with nonstick cooking spray. Bake 1 hour or until wooden toothpick inserted in center comes out clean. Cool. To serve, slice thinly.

Makes 16 servings

Nutrients per Serving:					
Calories	174	(28% of calories from fat)			
Total Fat	6 g	Dietary Fiber	1 g	Thiamine	<1 mg
Saturated Fat	1 g	Protein	4 g	Riboflavin	<1 mg
Cholesterol	13 mg	Calcium	11 mg	Niacin	1 mg
Sodium	171 mg	Iron	1 mg	Vitamin A	52 RE
Carbohydrate	28 g	Folate	13 μg	Vitamin C	2 mg

Dietary Exchanges: 1½ Starch/Bread, ½ Fruit, 1 Fat

247 Raspberry-Applesauce Coffee Cake

Notice, this fruity coffee cake has just a touch of margarine and no egg yolks. That is why it's perfect for a low fat diet.

1½ **cups fresh or frozen raspberries**
¼ **cup water**
7 **tablespoons sugar, divided**
2 **tablespoons cornstarch**
½ **teaspoon ground nutmeg, divided**
1¾ **cups all-purpose flour, divided**
3 **tablespoons margarine**
1 **tablespoon finely chopped walnuts**
1½ **teaspoons baking powder**
½ **teaspoon baking soda**
⅛ **teaspoon ground cloves**
2 **egg whites**
1 **cup unsweetened applesauce**

Preheat oven to 350°F. Spray 8-inch square baking pan with nonstick cooking spray. Combine raspberries and water in small saucepan. Bring to a boil over high heat. Reduce heat to medium. Combine 2 tablespoons sugar, cornstarch and ¼ teaspoon nutmeg in small bowl. Stir into raspberry mixture. Cook and stir until mixture boils and thickens. Cook and stir 2 minutes more; set aside.

Combine ¾ cup flour and remaining 5 tablespoons sugar in medium bowl. Cut in margarine with pastry blender until mixture resembles coarse meal. Set aside ½ cup mixture for topping; stir walnuts into remaining crumb mixture.

To remaining mixture add remaining 1 cup flour, baking powder, baking soda, remaining ¼ teaspoon nutmeg and cloves. Add egg whites and applesauce; beat until well combined. Spread half of batter into prepared baking pan. Spread raspberry mixture over batter. Drop remaining batter in small mounds on top. Sprinkle with reserved topping. Bake 40 to 45 minutes or until edges start to pull away from sides of pan. Serve warm or cool.   Makes 9 servings

Nutrients per Serving:					
Calories	196	(21% of calories from fat)			
Total Fat	5 g	Dietary Fiber	2 g	Thiamine	<1 mg
Saturated Fat	1 g	Protein	4 g	Riboflavin	<1 mg
Cholesterol	0 mg	Calcium	21 mg	Niacin	2 mg
Sodium	158 mg	Iron	1 mg	Vitamin A	50 RE
Carbohydrate	35 g	Folate	13 μg	Vitamin C	6 mg

Dietary Exchanges: 1 Starch/Bread, 1½ Fruit, 1 Fat

248 French Toast

By using 4 egg whites instead of whole eggs, the cholesterol in this recipe is cut by more than 75%.

1 **egg**
4 **egg whites**
¼ **cup skim milk**
3 **tablespoons packed brown sugar, divided**
½ **teaspoon almond extract**
¼ **teaspoon ground cinnamon**
1 **teaspoon vegetable oil**
6 **slices bread**
1 **ripe banana, sliced**

Combine egg and egg whites in large bowl; beat with wire whisk until frothy. Add milk, 2 tablespoons sugar, almond extract and cinnamon. Heat oil over medium-high heat in nonstick skillet. Dip each bread slice in egg mixture. Place bread in skillet; cook each side 2 to 3 minutes until browned. If necessary, spray pan with nonstick cooking spray and continue to cook remaining bread slices. Top each piece with banana slices, sprinkle with remaining 1 tablespoon sugar and serve immediately.
    Makes 6 servings

Nutrients per Serving:					
Calories	140	(17% of calories from fat)			
Total Fat	3 g	Dietary Fiber	1 g	Thiamine	<1 mg
Saturated Fat	1 g	Protein	6 g	Riboflavin	<1 mg
Cholesterol	36 mg	Calcium	55 mg	Niacin	1 mg
Sodium	173 mg	Iron	1 mg	Vitamin A	24 RE
Carbohydrate	24 g	Folate	17 μg	Vitamin C	2 mg

Dietary Exchanges: 1 Starch/Bread, ½ Meat, ½ Fruit

Raspberry-Applesauce Coffee Cake

249 Chive Whole Wheat Drop Biscuits

Wheat germ is the embryo of the wheat plant. It contains most of the nutrient content of the wheat kernel and is especially high in vitamin E.

1¼ cups whole wheat flour
¾ cup all-purpose flour
3 tablespoons toasted wheat germ, divided
1 tablespoon baking powder
1 tablespoon chopped fresh chives *or*
   1 teaspoon dried chives
2 teaspoons sugar
3 tablespoons margarine
1 cup skim milk
½ cup shredded low fat process American cheese

Preheat oven to 450°F. Spray baking sheet with nonstick cooking spray. Combine whole wheat flour, all-purpose flour, 2 tablespoons wheat germ, baking powder, chives and sugar in medium bowl. Cut in margarine with pastry blender until mixture resembles coarse meal. Add milk and American cheese; stir until just combined.

Drop dough by rounded teaspoonfuls onto prepared baking sheet about 1 inch apart. Sprinkle with remaining 1 tablespoon wheat germ. Bake 10 to 12 minutes or until golden brown. Remove immediately from baking sheet. Serve warm.

Makes 12 servings

Nutrients per Serving:

Calories	125	(28% of calories from fat)			
Total Fat	4 g	Dietary Fiber	2 g	Thiamine	<1 mg
Saturated Fat	1 g	Protein	5 g	Riboflavint	<1 mg
Cholesterol	2 mg	Calcium	88 mg	Niacin	1 mg
Sodium	152 mg	Iron	1 mg	Vitamin A	59 RE
Carbohydrate	18 g	Folate	14 μg	Vitamin C	<1 mg

Dietary Exchanges: 1 Starch/Bread, 1 Fat

250 Wild Rice Blueberry Muffins

Blueberries contain iron plus potassium, fiber and vitamins A and C.

1½ cups all-purpose flour
½ cup sugar
2 teaspoons baking powder
1 teaspoon ground cinnamon
½ teaspoon salt
¼ cup applesauce
4 egg whites
½ cup skim milk
1 cup fresh blueberries
1 cup cooked wild rice

Spray nonstick cooking spray in muffin cups or use paper liners. Preheat oven to 400°F. Combine flour, sugar, baking powder, cinnamon and salt in large bowl. Combine applesauce, egg whites and milk in separate bowl. Sprinkle 1 tablespoon dry ingredients over blueberries. Fold liquid ingredients into dry ingredients. Coat blueberries with flour mixture; fold, with wild rice, into batter. Batter will be stiff. Fill prepared muffin cups ⅔ full. Bake 15 to 20 minutes or until wooden toothpick inserted in center comes out clean. Makes 12 muffins

Nutrients per Serving:

Calories	120	(2% of calories from fat)			
Total Fat	<1 g	Dietary Fiber	1 g	Thiamine	<1 mg
Saturated Fat	<1 g	Protein	4 g	Riboflavin	<1 mg
Cholesterol	<1 mg	Calcium	29 mg	Niacin	1 mg
Sodium	169 mg	Iron	1 mg	Vitamin A	8 RE
Carbohydrate	26 g	Folate	9 μg	Vitamin C	2 mg

Dietary Exchanges: 1 Starch/Bread, ½ Fruit

Chive Whole Wheat Drop Biscuits

251 Sesame Crunch Banana Muffins

One ounce of sesame seeds contains about four milligrams of iron—three times the amount found in one ounce of beef liver.

Sesame Crunch Topping (recipe follows)
2 ripe, medium bananas, mashed
1 cup low fat milk
2 egg whites
2 tablespoons vegetable oil
1 teaspoon vanilla
1½ cups quick-cooking rolled oats
½ cup all-purpose flour
½ cup whole wheat flour
2 tablespoons granulated sugar
1 tablespoon baking powder
½ teaspoon salt

Prepare Sesame Crunch Topping. Spray nonstick cooking spray in muffin cups or use paper liners. Preheat oven to 400°F. Combine bananas, milk, egg whites, oil and vanilla in large bowl; set aside. In medium bowl, combine oats, all-purpose flour, whole wheat flour, sugar, baking powder and salt. Stir in banana mixture until just moistened (batter will be lumpy). Fill prepared muffin cups about ¾ full. Sprinkle 2 teaspoons Sesame Crunch over batter in each cup and bake 20 to 25 minutes or until golden on top and wooden toothpick inserted in center comes out clean. Cool slightly in pan before transferring to wire rack. Serve warm.

Makes 17 muffins

Sesame Crunch Topping

4 tablespoons packed brown sugar
2 tablespoons chopped walnuts
2 tablespoons whole wheat flour
1 tablespoon sesame seeds
1 tablespoon margarine
¼ tablespoon ground nutmeg
¼ teaspoon ground cinnamon

Combine all ingredients; mix well.

Makes about ¾ cup

Nutrients per Serving:

Calories	124	(28% of calories from fat)			
Total Fat	4 g	Dietary Fiber	1 g	Thiamine	<1 mg
Saturated Fat	1 g	Protein	4 g	Riboflavin	<1 mg
Cholesterol	1 mg	Calcium	33 mg	Niacin	1 mg
Sodium	105 mg	Iron	1 mg	Vitamin A	20 RE
Carbohydrate	20 g	Folate	10 µg	Vitamin C	1 mg

Dietary Exchanges: 1 Starch/Bread, ½ Fruit, ½ Fat

252 Spiced Apple Toast

Some good cooking apple varieties to try in this recipe are Rome, Cortland, Granny Smith or Rhode Island Greening.

1 tablespoon margarine
2 all-purpose apples, unpeeled, cored and thinly sliced
⅓ cup orange juice
4 teaspoons packed brown sugar
½ teaspoon ground cinnamon
4 slices whole wheat bread, toasted
2 teaspoons granulated sugar

Preheat oven to 450°F. Melt margarine in medium nonstick skillet. Add apples, orange juice, brown sugar and cinnamon; cook over medium-high heat about 4 minutes or until apples are tender, stirring occasionally. Drain; reserve cooking liquid. Cool apples 2 to 3 minutes. Place toast on lightly buttered baking sheet. Arrange apples, overlapping slices, in spiral design. Sprinkle ½ teaspoon granulated sugar over each slice. Bake 4 to 5 minutes or until bread is crisp. Drizzle reserved liquid over slices; serve immediately.

Makes 4 servings

Nutrients per Serving:

Calories	159	(22% of calories from fat)			
Total Fat	4 g	Dietary Fiber	4 g	Thiamine	<1 mg
Saturated Fat	1 g	Protein	3 g	Riboflavin	<1 mg
Cholesterol	0 mg	Calcium	33 mg	Niacin	1 mg
Sodium	188 mg	Iron	1 mg	Vitamin A	43 RE
Carbohydrate	30 g	Folate	27 µg	Vitamin C	14 mg

Dietary Exchanges: 1 Starch/Bread, 1 Fruit, ½ Fat

Sesame Crunch Banana Muffins

253 Spice-Prune Loaf

Generally, prunes have the same nutritional content as fresh plums of the same variety. That means prunes have lots of vitamin A, iron and fiber.

1 cup chopped pitted prunes
½ cup prune juice
1 cup all-purpose flour
1 cup whole wheat flour
1 teaspoon baking powder
¾ teaspoon ground cinnamon
½ teaspoon baking soda
¼ teaspoon ground ginger
⅛ teaspoon salt
2 egg whites
⅓ cup molasses
3 tablespoons vegetable oil
¼ teaspoon vanilla

Preheat oven to 350°F. Spray 8×4-inch loaf pan with nonstick cooking spray. Combine prunes and prune juice in small saucepan. Bring to a boil over medium-high heat. Remove from heat; let stand 5 minutes.

Combine all-purpose flour, whole wheat flour, baking powder, cinnamon, baking soda, ginger and salt in medium bowl. Combine egg whites, molasses, oil and vanilla in small bowl. Add to flour mixture and stir until just combined. Add prune mixture; stir until just combined.

Pour mixture into prepared loaf pan. Bake 55 to 60 minutes or until wooden toothpick inserted in center comes out clean. Cool in pan on wire rack 10 minutes. Remove bread from pan; cool thoroughly on rack. Wrap and store overnight at room temperature before slicing.

Makes 16 servings (1 loaf)

Nutrients per Serving:

Calories	124	(20% of calories from fat)			
Total Fat	3 g	Dietary Fiber	2 g	Thiamine	<1 mg
Saturated Fat	<1 g	Protein	3 g	Riboflavin	<1 mg
Cholesterol	0 mg	Calcium	62 mg	Niacin	1 mg
Sodium	78 mg	Iron	2 mg	Vitamin A	20 RE
Carbohydrate	23 g	Folate	6 µg	Vitamin C	1 mg

Dietary Exchanges: 1 Starch/Bread, ½ Fruit, ½ Fat

254 Quick Nectarine Oat Muffins

Bran contains the insoluble dietary fibers cellulose and hemicellulose which absorb many times their weight in water, which is why you feel full after eating whole grain foods.

2 cups whole wheat flour
1 cup rolled oats
½ cup unprocessed bran
½ cup packed brown sugar
1½ teaspoons baking soda
1 teaspoon salt
2 eggs
1½ cups buttermilk
¼ cup vegetable oil
3 fresh California nectarines, halved, pitted and chopped
3 teaspoons grated orange peel
1½ teaspoons ground cinnamon

Spray nonstick cooking spray in muffin cups or use paper liners. Preheat oven to 400°F. Combine all ingredients in mixing bowl. Stir until blended. Fill prepared muffin cups ⅔ full. Bake 20 minutes or until wooden toothpick inserted in center comes out clean. Serve warm.　　　　Makes about 20 muffins

Nutrients per Serving:

Calories	130	(26% of calories from fat)			
Total Fat	4 g	Dietary Fiber	2 g	Thiamine	<1 mg
Saturated Fat	1 g	Protein	4 g	Riboflavin	<1 mg
Cholesterol	22 mg	Calcium	40 mg	Niacin	1 mg
Sodium	196 mg	Iron	1 mg	Vitamin A	28 RE
Carbohydrate	21 g	Folate	12 µg	Vitamin C	2 mg

Dietary Exchanges: 1 Starch/Bread, ½ Fruit, ½ Fat

DESERTS

255 Northwoods Buttermilk Cake

Wild rice is fairly difficult to cultivate and until recently was grown mostly in the northern Great Lakes region. Today it is grown in California as well as in the Midwest.

- 2 cups all-purpose flour
- 1 cup whole wheat flour
- 2 teaspoons baking soda
- 1 teaspoon ground cinnamon
- ½ teaspoon salt
- ½ teaspoon ground nutmeg
- ½ cup reduced calorie margarine
- 1 cup packed brown sugar
- 1 teaspoon vanilla
- 5 egg whites
- ⅔ cup applesauce
- 1 cup buttermilk
- 2 cups cooked wild rice
- Powdered sugar (optional)

Preheat oven to 350°F. Spray 13 × 9-inch pan with nonstick cooking spray; lightly flour. Combine flours, baking soda, cinnamon, salt and nutmeg in medium bowl. Beat margarine with electric mixer on medium speed for 30 seconds in large mixing bowl. Add brown sugar and vanilla; beat until fluffy. Add egg whites; beat well. Add applesauce, blending well. Add dry ingredients and buttermilk alternately to mixture, blending well. Stir in wild rice. Pour into prepared pan. Bake 45 to 50 minutes or until wooden pick inserted in center comes out clean. *Do not overbake.* Cool. Sprinkle with powdered sugar, if desired.   Makes 16 servings

Nutrients per Serving:

Calories	197	(16% of calories from fat)			
Total Fat	4 g	Dietary Fiber	2 g	Thiamin	<1 mg
Saturated Fat	1 g	Protein	5 g	Riboflavin	<1 mg
Cholesterol	1 mg	Calcium	39 mg	Niacin	2 mg
Sodium	233 mg	Iron	2 mg	Vitamin A	77 RE
Carbohydrate	37 g	Folate	14 μg	Vitamin C	<1 mg

Dietary Exchanges: 2 Starch/Bread, ½ Fruit, ½ Fat

256 Applesauce Cookies

The rolled oats in these cookies provide lots of fiber while contributing just a few calories. They also have selenium, potassium, iron and B vitamins.

- ⅓ cup reduced calorie margarine, softened
- ¾ cup sugar
- 2 egg whites
- 1 cup unsweetened applesauce
- 1½ cups all-purpose flour
- 2 tablespoons baking powder
- 1 teaspoon ground cinnamon
- ½ teaspoon baking soda
- ½ teaspoon ground nutmeg
- ½ teaspoon ground cloves
- 1½ cups rolled oats
- ½ cup diced apple
- ½ cup raisins
- ¼ cup chopped walnuts

Preheat oven to 375°F. Spray baking sheet with nonstick cooking spray. Mix margarine and sugar until creamy in large bowl. Beat in egg whites; add applesauce. Combine flour, baking powder, cinnamon, baking soda, nutmeg and cloves in separate bowl. Stir into applesauce mixture. Add oats, apple, raisins and walnuts. Drop by level tablespoonfuls onto prepared baking sheet. Bake 12 minutes or until edges are lightly browned. Remove from baking sheet; cool on wire rack before serving.

Makes 3 dozen cookies

Nutrients per Serving:

Calories	73	(20% of calories from fat)			
Total Fat	2 g	Dietary Fiber	<1 g	Thiamine	<1 mg
Saturated Fat	<1 g	Protein	2 g	Riboflavin	<1 mg
Cholesterol	0 mg	Calcium	15 mg	Niacin	<1 mg
Sodium	95 mg	Iron	1 mg	Vitamin A	33 RE
Carbohydrate	13 g	Folate	4 μg	Vitamin C	<1 mg

Dietary Exchanges: 1 Starch/Bread

[257] Cranberry Apple Pie with Soft Gingersnap Crust

Cranberries are tart little fruits full of potassium and vitamin C.

20 gingersnaps
1 tablespoon reduced calorie margarine
2 McIntosh apples, cored
1 cup fresh cranberries
5 tablespoons packed dark brown sugar
¼ teaspoon vanilla
¼ teaspoon ground cinnamon
1 teaspoon granulated sugar

Preheat oven to 375°F. Add gingersnaps and margarine to food processor or blender; process until crumbs form. Press gingersnap mixture into 8-inch pie plate. Use slightly smaller pie plate to press down uniformly. Bake 5 to 8 minutes. Remove and cool crust. In food processor slice apples. Add cranberries, brown sugar, vanilla and cinnamon; process just until combined. Spoon apple-cranberry filling into separate pie plate or casserole. Top with granulated sugar. Bake 35 minutes or until tender. Spoon over gingersnap crust and serve immediately.   Makes 8 servings

Nutrients per Serving:

Calories	141	(16% of calories from fat)			
Total Fat	3 g	Dietary Fiber	1 g	Thiamine	<1 mg
Saturated Fat	<1 g	Protein	1 g	Riboflavin	<1 mg
Cholesterol	0 mg	Calcium	24 mg	Niacin	1 mg
Sodium	135 mg	Iron	1 mg	Vitamin A	19 RE
Carbohydrate	30 g	Folate	1 μg	Vitamin C	4 mg

Dietary Exchanges: 1 Starch/Bread, 1 Fruit, ½ Fat

[258] Florida Grapefruit Mousse

Both pink and white grapefruit are high in vitamin C and potassium, but pink grapefruit is higher in vitamin A.

¼ cup plus 1 tablespoon frozen Florida grapefruit juice concentrate, thawed, divided
1 teaspoon gelatin
1 tablespoon granulated sugar
2 Florida grapefruit
¾ cup evaporated whole or skim milk, chilled
3 tablespoons powdered sugar

Combine 2 tablespoons grapefruit juice concentrate and gelatin in small saucepan; stir until gelatin softens. Add granulated sugar and additional 2 tablespoons concentrate. Place saucepan over medium heat, stirring constantly until just dissolved, about 3 to 5 minutes. Remove from heat; cool.

Peel grapefruit and remove white pith. Section grapefruits, removing membrane that separates segments. Cut fruit into bite-size pieces. Beat evaporated milk until frothy. Add remaining 1 tablespoon grapefruit juice concentrate and continue beating until mixture becomes stiff. Add powdered sugar and beat 10 seconds until combined. Fold mixture into gelatin until combined. Fold fruit into mousse mixture and spoon into parfait glasses. Serve immediately or refrigerate until ready to serve.

Note: Mousse should be prepared the same day it is to be served.   Makes 6 servings

Nutrients per Serving:

Calories	105	(21% of calories from fat)			
Total Fat	3 g	Dietary Fiber	1 g	Thiamin	<1 mg
Saturated Fat	1 g	Protein	3 g	Riboflavin	<1 mg
Cholesterol	9 mg	Calcium	98 mg	Niacin	<1 mg
Sodium	34 mg	Iron	<1 mg	Vitamin A	45 RE
Carbohydrate	19 g	Folate	12 μg	Vitamin C	45 mg

Dietary Exchanges: ½ Milk, ½ Fruit, ½ Fat

Cranberry Apple Pie with
Soft Gingersnap Crust

259 Apple-Cheddar Turnovers

Apples and Cheddar are a traditional flavor combination; the apples provide the fiber while the cheese provides protein.

2 packages active dry yeast
¼ cup warm water (110° to 115°F)
⅓ cup reduced calorie margarine
⅓ cup granulated sugar
1 teaspoon salt
1 container (8 ounces) low fat sour cream
1 egg, slightly beaten
3½ to 4 cups all-purpose flour
⅓ cup (2 ounces) shredded aged
**   Wisconsin Cheddar cheese**
1¼ cups apple pie filling
1 cup powdered sugar
½ teaspoon vanilla
1 to 2 teaspoons milk

Sprinkle yeast over warm water in small bowl. Heat margarine in large saucepan over medium heat; add sugar and salt. Heat until just warm (115° to 120°F) and margarine is almost melted, stirring constantly. Pour into large bowl. Add sour cream and egg; mix well. Stir in 1½ cups flour and cheese; beat well. Add yeast mixture; stir until smooth. Stir in enough remaining flour to make soft dough. Place on floured surface; knead 2 minutes. Cover; let rest 10 minutes.

Roll half of dough into 12-inch square. Cut into nine 4-inch squares. Place about 1 tablespoon apple pie filling in center of each square. Fold dough over to form triangle; seal edges well. Repeat with remaining half of dough. Preheat oven to 350°F. Spray baking sheet with nonstick cooking spray. Place pastries on prepared baking sheets; cover and let rise in warm place until doubled in bulk (about 20 minutes). Bake 10 to 15 minutes or until lightly browned. Remove from baking sheets to wire rack.

For frosting, combine powdered sugar and vanilla in small bowl. Stir in enough milk for spreading consistency. Spread on top of warm pastries. Serve warm or cooled.   Makes 18 pastries

Nutrients per Serving:

Calories	189	(20% of calories from fat)				
Total Fat	4 g	Dietary Fiber	1 g	Thiamine	<1 mg	
Saturated Fat	1 g	Protein	4 g	Riboflavin	<1 mg	
Cholesterol	19 mg	Calcium	46 mg	Niacin	2 mg	
Sodium	196 mg	Iron	1 mg	Vitamin A	121 RE	
Carbohydrate	33 g	Folate	40 μg	Vitamin C	2 mg	

Dietary Exchanges: 1 Starch/Bread, 1 Fruit, ½ Fat

260 Hot Butter Rum Sauce

Heating the rum evaporates its alcohol; all that's left is its delicious flavor.

1 cup sugar
2 tablespoons cornstarch
⅛ teaspoon salt
¾ cup water
¼ cup dark rum
2 tablespoons margarine

Combine sugar, cornstarch and salt in medium saucepan. Stir in water. Heat slowly until mixture comes to a boil. Boil 1 minute until thickened. Remove from heat. Stir in rum and margarine.

Makes 1⅔ cups

Nutrients per Serving:

Calories	43	(18% of calories from fat)				
Total Fat	1 g	Dietary Fiber	<1 g	Thiamin	0 mg	
Saturated Fat	<1 g	Protein	<1 g	Riboflavin	0 mg	
Cholesterol	0 mg	Calcium	<1 mg	Niacin	0 mg	
Sodium	21 mg	Iron	<1 mg	Vitamin A	11 RE	
Carbohydrate	8 g	Folate	<1 μg	Vitamin C	<1 mg	

Dietary Exchanges: ½ Fruit

261 Angel Food Cake with Blueberry Yogurt Sauce

Not only are blueberries light and flavorful, they're low in calories, high in vitamin C, potassium and fiber.

Small angel food cake
½ cup vanilla nonfat yogurt
3 teaspoons sugar
1 teaspoon lemon juice
½ cup frozen blueberries, thawed

Slice angel food cake into twelfths; reserve 4 slices and save remaining cake for another use. Combine yogurt, sugar and lemon juice in medium bowl. To serve, top each cake slice with 2 tablespoons sauce and 2 tablespoons blueberries.   Makes 4 servings

Nutrients per Serving:

Calories	252	(0% of calories from fat)				
Total Fat	<1 g	Dietary Fiber	1 g	Thiamine	<1 mg	
Saturated Fat	0 g	Protein	6 g	Riboflavin	<1 mg	
Cholesterol	1 mg	Calcium	116 mg	Niacin	<1 mg	
Sodium	290 mg	Iron	<1 mg	Vitamin A	2 RE	
Carbohydrate	58 g	Folate	8 μg	Vitamin C	1 mg	

Dietary Exchanges: 2½ Starch/Bread, ½ Milk, ½ Fruit

Mocha Cookies

262 Mocha Cookies

These delicious cookies have a taste reminiscent of mocha cappuccino.

2½ tablespoons instant coffee granules
1½ tablespoons skim milk
⅓ cup packed light brown sugar
¼ cup granulated sugar
¼ cup margarine
1 egg
½ teaspoon almond extract
2 cups all-purpose flour, sifted
¼ cup wheat flakes
½ teaspoon ground cinnamon
¼ teaspoon baking powder

Preheat oven to 350°F. Spray cookie sheet with nonstick cooking spray. Dissolve coffee granules in milk. In large bowl, cream together sugars and margarine. Beat in egg, almond extract and coffee mixture. Stir together dry ingredients and gradually beat into egg mixture. Drop by teaspoonfuls onto cookie sheet. Flatten with back of fork. Bake 8 to 10 minutes.   Makes about 40 cookies

Nutrients per Serving:					
Calories	48	(25% of calories from fat)			
Total Fat	1 g	Dietary Fiber	<1 g	Thiamin	<1 mg
Saturated Fat	<1 g	Protein	1 g	Riboflavin	<1 mg
Cholesterol	5 mg	Calcium	6 mg	Niacin	1 mg
Sodium	20 mg	Iron	<1 mg	Vitamin A	19 RE
Carbohydrate	8 g	Folate	2 µg	Vitamin C	<1 mg

Dietary Exchanges: ½ Starch/Bread, ½ Fat

263 Raspberry Shortcake

Raspberries are similar in nutritional content to oranges and lemons, but they're higher in dietary fiber.

1½ cups whole raspberries, frozen, divided
6 tablespoons granulated sugar, divided
1 cup all-purpose flour
1 teaspoon baking powder
¼ teaspoon baking soda
1 tablespoon margarine
1 egg white
⅓ cup skim evaporated milk
¼ teaspoon almond extract
¾ cup 1% low fat cottage cheese
1 teaspoon lemon juice

Preheat oven to 450°F. Spray baking sheet with nonstick cooking spray. Toss 1¼ cup raspberries with 2½ tablespoons sugar; refrigerate. Combine flour, additional 2 tablespoons sugar, baking powder and baking soda in medium bowl. Cut in margarine; set aside. In separate bowl, beat egg white, milk and almond extract. Add to dry ingredients. Mix lightly. Knead slightly on lightly floured board. Roll out to ½-inch thickness. Use 2½-inch biscuit cutter to cut out 8 biscuits. Place biscuits on baking sheet. Bake 10 minutes until slightly brown on top.

Add cottage cheese, remaining 1½ tablespoons sugar and lemon juice to food processor or blender; process until smooth. Transfer mixture to medium bowl. Fold in remaining ¼ cup raspberries. When biscuits are done, split in half and place bottom half on each serving dish. Top each with 2 tablespoons raspberries and 1 tablespoon cottage cheese whipped topping; cover with biscuit top. Add remaining raspberries and whipped cottage cheese topping. Makes 8 servings

Nutrients per Serving:

Calories	140	(14% of calories from fat)			
Total Fat	2 g	Dietary Fiber	1 g	Thiamin	<1 mg
Saturated Fat	1 g	Protein	6 g	Riboflavin	<1 mg
Cholesterol	2 mg	Calcium	61 mg	Niacin	1 mg
Sodium	189 mg	Iron	1 mg	Vitamin A	37 RE
Carbohydrate	24 g	Folate	14 µg	Vitamin C	6 mg

Dietary Exchanges: 1 Starch/Bread, ½ Meat, ½ Fruit, ½ Fat

264 California Apricot-Cherry Cornmeal Cobbler

Sweet, delicious cherries are low in calories, fat and sodium and even provide potassium for good blood maintenance.

2 cups sliced pitted halved fresh California apricots
⅓ cup sugar
2 cups pitted fresh California cherries
1 cup plus 1 tablespoon all-purpose flour, divided
½ cup yellow cornmeal
¼ teaspoon salt
1½ tablespoons plus 1 teaspoon sugar
2 teaspoons baking powder
5 tablespoons margarine
½ teaspoon grated orange peel
¾ cup low fat milk

Preheat oven to 375°F. Combine apricots and ⅓ cup sugar in small bowl. Combine cherries and 1 tablespoon flour in separate bowl; set aside. Combine remaining 1 cup flour, cornmeal, salt, 1½ tablespoons sugar and baking powder in large bowl. Cut in margarine until mixture resembles coarse meal; mix in orange peel. Add milk and combine to evenly moisten dry ingredients. Place fruit in 1½-quart baking dish; top with batter and sprinkle with remaining 1 teaspoon sugar. Bake 25 to 30 minutes or until golden brown. Let cool slightly and serve. Makes 8 servings

Nutrients per Serving:

Calories	252	(29% of calories from fat)			
Total Fat	8 g	Dietary Fiber	3 g	Thiamin	<1 mg
Saturated Fat	2 g	Protein	4 g	Riboflavin	<1 mg
Cholesterol	2 mg	Calcium	61 mg	Niacin	2 mg
Sodium	246 mg	Iron	1 mg	Vitamin A	259 RE
Carbohydrate	42 g	Folate	14 µg	Vitamin C	8 mg

Dietary Exchanges: 2 Starch/Bread, 1 Fruit, 1 Fat

Raspberry Shortcake

265 Wild Rice Applesauce Bars

Wild rice is very nutritious. It is full of fiber, protein, B vitamins, minerals and is very low in fat.

2 cups cooked wild rice
1 cup buttermilk, divided
1⅓ cup applesauce
⅓ cup shortening
1 cup packed brown sugar
6 egg whites
2 teaspoons vanilla
2½ cups all-purpose flour
1 teaspoon baking soda
1 teaspoon salt
1 teaspoon ground cinnamon
1 cup chopped nuts (optional)
Powdered sugar (optional)

Preheat oven to 350°F. Spray bottom of 15×10×1-inch jelly-roll pan with nonstick cooking spray. Combine wild rice, ½ cup buttermilk and applesauce in medium bowl; set aside. Combine shortening, brown sugar, egg whites and vanilla in large bowl; beat at high speed 5 minutes or until smooth and creamy. Add remaining ½ cup buttermilk; beat at low speed until well blended. Add flour, baking soda, salt and cinnamon; beat at low speed until well blended. Stir in wild rice mixture and nuts. Spread in prepared pan. Bake 20 to 25 minutes or until toothpick inserted in center comes out clean. Sprinkle with powdered sugar. Cool completely. *Makes 48 bars*

Nutrients per Serving:

Calories	68	(20% of calories from fat)			
Total Fat	2 g	Dietary Fiber	<1 g	Thiamin	<1 mg
Saturated Fat	<1 g	Protein	2 g	Riboflavin	<1 mg
Cholesterol	<1 mg	Calcium	12 mg	Niacin	1 mg
Sodium	76 mg	Iron	1 mg	Vitamin A	1 RE
Carbohydrate	12 g	Folate	4 mg	Vitamin C	<1 mg

Dietary Exchanges: ½ Starch/Bread, ½ Fruit

266 Peach Sorbet

Sorbet is a cool refreshing dessert without the fat of traditional ice cream.

7 fresh California peaches, peeled, halved, pitted and quartered
¾ cup sugar
3 tablespoons light corn syrup
1 teaspoon lemon juice

Add peaches to food processor or blender; process to measure 3½ cups purée. Combine peach purée, sugar, corn syrup and lemon juice in saucepan. Cook and stir over low heat until sugar dissolves; cool. Prepare in ice cream maker according to manufacturer's directions. Pack into freezing containers. Freeze until firm.

Makes 8 servings

Nutrients per Serving:

Calories	160	(0% of calories from fat)			
Total Fat	0 g	Dietary Fiber	2 g	Thiamin	<1 mg
Saturated Fat	0 g	Protein	<1 g	Riboflavin	<1 mg
Cholesterol	0 mg	Calcium	10 mg	Niacin	1 mg
Sodium	13 mg	Iron	1 mg	Vitamin A	17 RE
Carbohydrate	43 g	Folate	4 μg	Vitamin C	31 mg

Dietary Exchanges: 2½ Fruit

267 Citrus Sauced Pears

The combination of fresh citrus peel, juice and fresh pears packs this recipe with lots of vitamin C and fiber.

2 tablespoons reduced calorie margarine
⅓ cup sugar
¾ cup freshly squeezed orange juice
⅓ cup freshly squeezed lemon juice
½ teaspoon grated orange peel
½ teaspoon grated lemon peel
3 fresh California Bartlett pears, cored and sliced

Melt margarine with sugar in medium saucepan over medium heat. Add orange juice, lemon juice, orange peel and lemon peel. Bring to a boil and reduce liquid slightly. Reduce heat to low. Add pear slices; cook to heat through. Spoon topping over waffles, pancakes or cereal. *Makes 6 servings*

Nutrients per Serving:

Calories	123	(15% of calories from fat)			
Total Fat	2 g	Dietary Fiber	2 g	Thiamin	<1 mg
Saturated Fat	<1 g	Protein	1 g	Riboflavin	<1 mg
Cholesterol	0 mg	Calcium	14 mg	Niacin	<1 mg
Sodium	44 mg	Iron	<1 mg	Vitamin A	52 RE
Carbohydrate	28 g	Folate	25 μg	Vitamin C	25 mg

Dietary Exchanges: 2 Fruit, ½ Fat

Wild Rice Applesauce Bars

Almond-Pumpkin Chiffon Pudding

268 California Plum Sorbet

This delightful recipe has little fat and no cholesterol but has lots of fresh fruit flavor.

12 fresh California plums, halved, pitted and sliced
3 tablespoons sugar
1 cup orange juice
1 tablespoon grated orange peel

Add plums, sugar, orange juice and orange peel to food processor or blender; process until smooth.

Pour into loaf pan and freeze, about 4 hours. Process again 30 minutes before serving. Return to freezer until ready to serve.   Makes 6 servings

Nutrients per Serving:

Calories	115	(7% of calories from fat)			
Total Fat	1 g	Dietary Fiber	3 g	Thiamin	<1 mg
Saturated Fat	<1 g	Protein	1 g	Riboflavin	<1 mg
Cholesterol	0 mg	Calcium	11 mg	Niacin	1 mg
Sodium	<1 mg	Iron	<1 mg	Vitamin A	51 RE
Carbohydrate	28 g	Folate	26 µg	Vitamin C	35 mg

Dietary Exchanges: 2 Fruit

269 Almond-Pumpkin Chiffon Pudding

Five times a full day's supply of vitamin A, which is good for vision and helps boost immunity, is packed into only ½ cup pumpkin.

1 envelope gelatin
1 cup low fat milk
1 cup solid pack pumpkin
½ teaspoon pumpkin pie spice
1 container (8 ounces) plain low fat yogurt
3 egg whites
Dash salt
⅔ cup packed brown sugar
½ cup chopped toasted California Almonds, divided

Sprinkle gelatin over milk in small saucepan; let stand 5 minutes to soften. Cook and stir constantly over low heat until gelatin dissolves; remove from heat. Stir in pumpkin and pumpkin pie spice. Cool to room temperature; stir in yogurt. Refrigerate until mixture begins to thicken and gel. Beat egg whites with salt to form soft peaks. Gradually beat in brown sugar, beating to form stiff peaks; fold into pumpkin mixture. Sprinkle 1 tablespoon almonds over bottom of greased 6-cup mold. Fold remaining almonds into pumpkin mixture; spoon into mold. Refrigerate until firm. Unmold to serve.

Makes 8 servings

Nutrients per Serving:

Calories	170	(27% of calories from fat)			
Total Fat	5 g	Dietary Fiber	1 g	Thiamine	<1 mg
Saturated Fat	1 g	Protein	7 g	Riboflavin	<1 mg
Cholesterol	4 mg	Calcium	136 g	Niacin	<1 mg
Sodium	65 mg	Iron	1 mg	Vitamin A	700 RE
Carbohydrate	25 g	Folate	14 μg	Vitamin C	2 mg

Dietary Exchanges: 1½ Starch/Bread, ½ Milk, ½ Fat

270 Fresh Pear Topping

Pears may be one of the oldest cultivated fruits and go back as far as 35 to 40 centuries.

4 fresh cored California Bartlett pears, sliced or cubed
1 cup low calorie maple syrup
⅓ cup low fat milk
¾ teaspoon vanilla

Heat pears over medium heat in large nonstick skillet. Add syrup, milk and vanilla; heat until bubbly. Spoon topping over waffles, French toast, pancakes or cereal.

Makes about 5 cups

Nutrients per Serving:

Calories	101	(4% of calories from fat)			
Total Fat	1 g	Dietary Fiber	2 g	Thiamin	<1 mg
Saturated Fat	<1 g	Protein	1 g	Riboflavin	<1 mg
Cholesterol	1 mg	Calcium	22 mg	Niacin	<1 mg
Sodium	62 mg	Iron	<1 mg	Vitamin A	8 RE
Carbohydrate	26 g	Folate	7 μg	Vitamin C	3 mg

Dietary Exchanges: 1½ Fruit

271 Fruitful Frozen Yogurt

Use dark fruits like strawberries, raspberries or cherries to make this recipe as pleasing to the eye as it is to the palate.

1 envelope gelatin
¼ cup cold water
1½ cups puréed fresh fruit
1 carton (16 ounces) vanilla low fat yogurt
¼ to ½ cup sugar

Sprinkle gelatin over cold water in small saucepan; allow to stand 5 minutes to soften. Stir over low heat until gelatin dissolves. Combine with fruit purée; stir into yogurt. Add sugar to taste. Pour into 9-inch square pan; freeze until almost firm. Coarsely chop mixture; spoon into chilled bowl. Beat with electric mixer until smooth; freeze.

Makes 5 servings

Nutrients per Serving:

Calories	185	(8% of calories from fat)			
Total Fat	2 g	Dietary Fiber	2 g	Thiamin	<1 mg
Saturated Fat	1 g	Protein	6 g	Riboflavin	<1 mg
Cholesterol	5 mg	Calcium	138 mg	Niacin	<1 mg
Sodium	71 mg	Iron	<1 mg	Vitamin A	12 RE
Carbohydrate	38 g	Folate	12 μg	Vitamin C	22 mg

Dietary Exchanges: 1 Milk, 1½ Fruit

272 Calorie Watchers "Cheesecake"

By substituting low fat cottage cheese and low fat yogurt for the traditional cream cheese used in cheesecakes, the fat content in this recipe is cut by more than half.

1 envelope gelatin
¼ cup skim milk
1 container (16 ounces) 1% low fat cottage cheese with pineapple
1 container (8 ounces) vanilla low fat yogurt, divided
¼ cup sugar
¼ teaspoon salt
4 tablespoons graham cracker crumbs, divided
Strawberries for garnish

Sprinkle gelatin over milk in small saucepan; let stand 1 minute to soften. Cook and stir constantly over low heat until gelatin dissolves, about 3 to 5 minutes. Remove from heat; cool slightly. Add cottage cheese, ½ cup yogurt, sugar and salt to food processor or blender; process until smooth. With motor running, slowly add gelatin mixture; process until combined. Spoon ½ tablespoon crumbs into each of 4 large dessert or wine glasses. Spoon an equal amount of cottage cheese mixture into each glass; sprinkle with another ½ tablespoon crumbs. Cover and refrigerate, until firm, about 2 hours. Just before serving, top each cheesecake with spoonful of remaining vanilla yogurt. Garnish with strawberries, if desired.   Makes 4 servings

Nutrients per Serving:

Calories	251	(15% of calories from fat)			
Total Fat	4 g	Dietary Fiber	0 g	Thiamin	<1 mg
Saturated Fat	2 g	Protein	21 g	Riboflavin	<1 mg
Cholesterol	13 mg	Calcium	182 mg	Niacin	<1 mg
Sodium	683 mg	Iron	1 mg	Vitamin A	33 RE
Carbohydrate	32 g	Folate	22 µg	Vitamin C	1 mg

Dietary Exchanges: 2 Starch/Bread, 2 Meat, 1 Milk

273 Butterscotch Crispies

Even though walnuts are high in fat, it is primarily polyunsaturated fat, which has been shown to lower "bad" cholesterol levels in the blood.

2 cups sifted all-purpose flour
1 teaspoon baking soda
1 teaspoon salt
½ cup margarine
2½ cups packed light brown sugar
2 eggs
1 teaspoon vanilla
2 cups quick-cooking rolled oats
2 cups puffed rice cereal
½ cup chopped walnuts

Preheat oven to 350°F. Sift flour, baking soda and salt onto waxed paper. Cream margarine and brown sugar with electric mixer at medium speed in large bowl until fluffy. Beat in eggs, 1 at a time, until fluffy. Stir in vanilla.

Add flour mixture, ⅓ at a time, until well blended; stir in rolled oats, rice cereal and walnuts. Drop by teaspoonfuls, about 1-inch apart, onto large cookie sheets lightly sprayed with nonstick cooking spray. Bake 10 minutes or until cookies are firm and lightly golden. Remove to wire racks; cool.

Makes 8½ dozen cookies

Nutrients per Serving:

Calories	50	(26% of calories from fat)			
Total Fat	1 g	Dietary Fiber	<1 g	Thiamin	<1 mg
Saturated Fat	<1 g	Protein	1 g	Riboflavin	<1 mg
Cholesterol	4 mg	Calcium	7 mg	Niacin	<1 mg
Sodium	48 mg	Iron	<1 mg	Vitamin A	13 RE
Carbohydrate	9 g	Folate	2 µg	Vitamin C	<1 mg

Dietary Exchanges: ½ Starch/Bread, ¼ Fat

Calorie Watchers "Cheesecakes"

274 No-Bake Fruit Crisp

Read the label when purchasing granola cereal. Even though it is considered a "healthy" food, it can be loaded with fat.

2 cans (16 ounces each) California chunky mixed fruit in juice or extra light syrup
1 cup cinnamon granola cereal
¼ cup toasted sliced almonds
1 tablespoon reduced calorie margarine
2 tablespoons packed brown sugar
1 teaspoon ground cinnamon
½ cup vanilla nonfat yogurt
¼ teaspoon ground nutmeg

Drain fruit, reserving liquid for other uses. Combine granola and almonds in small bowl. Melt margarine in small saucepan. Blend in brown sugar and cinnamon; simmer until sugar dissolves, about 2 minutes. Toss with granola and almonds; cool. Combine yogurt and nutmeg in small bowl. To serve, spoon approximately ½ cup chunky mixed fruit onto each serving plate. Top with yogurt mixture and sprinkle with granola mixture.

Makes 6 servings

Nutrients per Serving:					
Calories	224	(26% of calories from fat)			
Total Fat	7 g	Dietary Fiber	2 g	Thiamin	<1 mg
Saturated Fat	3 g	Protein	5 g	Riboflavin	<1 mg
Cholesterol	<1 mg	Calcium	79 mg	Niacin	1 mg
Sodium	80 mg	Iron	1 mg	Vitamin A	69 RE
Carbohydrate	39 g	Folate	23 μg	Vitamin C	4 mg

Dietary Exchanges: 1 Starch/Bread, 2 Fruit, 1 Fat

275 Plum Good Topping

Currants have been grown in Italy for at least 400 years where they were knows as "grapes of the monks."

8 fresh California plums, halved, pitted and sliced
½ cup currants *or* raisins
⅓ cup orange juice
2 tablespoons sugar
1 stick cinnamon *or* ½ teaspoon ground cinnamon
¼ cup almonds, coarsely chopped

Combine plums, currants, orange juice, sugar and cinnamon in saucepan; simmer over medium-high heat 20 minutes. Stir in almonds. Use to top waffles, pancakes, cereal, yogurt, granola or cottage cheese.

Makes about 6 cups

Nutrients per Serving:					
Calories	107	(26% of calories from fat)			
Total Fat	4 g	Dietary Fiber	3 g	Thiamin	<1 mg
Saturated Fat	<1 g	Protein	2 g	Riboflavin	<1 mg
Cholesterol	0 mg	Calcium	25 mg	Niacin	<1 mg
Sodium	<1 mg	Iron	1 mg	Vitamin A	32 RE
Carbohydrate	20 g	Folate	13 μg	Vitamin C	19 mg

Dietary Exchanges: 1 Fruit, 1 Fat

276 Orange-Almond Angel Food Cake

Nuts and seeds are equal to beans and peas in the amount of protein they contain, but they are higher in fat.

1 cup whole natural California Almonds, divided
1 package (14.5 ounces) angel food cake mix
1⅓ cups orange juice
2 tablespoons grated orange peel
Sorbet (optional)
Fresh fruit (optional)

Preheat oven to 350°F. Spread almonds in single layer on baking sheet. Toast 12 to 15 minutes, stirring occasionally, until lightly browned; cool and chop. Prepare cake mix according to package directions, substituting orange juice for water in package directions. Fold in grated orange peel and ½ cup chopped almonds. Spoon batter into 10-inch tube pan. Sprinkle with remaining ½ cup chopped almonds. Bake and cool as directed. Serve with sorbet and fresh fruit, if desired.

Makes 10 servings

Nutrients per Serving:					
Calories	247	(23% of calories from fat)			
Total Fat	7 g	Dietary Fiber	2 g	Thiamin	<1 mg
Saturated Fat	1 g	Protein	7 g	Riboflavin	<1 mg
Cholesterol	0 mg	Calcium	104 mg	Niacin	1 mg
Sodium	204 mg	Iron	1 mg	Vitamin A	7 RE
Carbohydrate	42 g	Folate	21 μg	Vitamin C	18 mg

Dietary Exchanges: 2½ Starch/Bread, ½ Fruit, 1 Fat

No-Bake Fruit Crisp

277 Wisconsin Cheese Pinwheel Danish

Whole wheat flour is more nutritious than white flour. Even among whole wheat flours, some are more nutritious than others.

1½ cups all-purpose flour
¾ cup whole wheat flour
3 tablespoons granulated sugar
2 teaspoons baking powder
½ teaspoon baking soda
⅛ teaspoon salt
¼ teaspoon ground cinnamon
1 cup plain low fat yogurt
2 tablespoons margarine, melted

Cheese Filling:
½ cup Wisconsin part-skim Ricotta cheese
2 teaspoons sugar
Grated peel of 1 lemon

Glaze:
¼ cup powdered sugar
1¾ teaspoons milk
¼ teaspoon vanilla

Combine flours, granulated sugar, baking powder, baking soda, salt and cinnamon in large bowl; set aside. Combine yogurt and margarine in small bowl. Add yogurt mixture to dry mixture. Turn out onto floured board and knead several times to make soft dough.

Divide dough in half. Roll half the dough into an 8-inch square. Cut square into 4-inch squares. Form pinwheel with each square by cutting slit 1 inch from center to each corner diagonally. Place dough on baking sheet with spatula.

Preheat oven to 400°F. Combine Cheese Filling ingredients and place a heaping spoonful in center of each dough square. Lift and fold every other point over filling. Press center to hold points in

place. Repeat with remaining dough. Bake 10 to 12 minutes or until golden brown. Prepare Glaze. Remove pinwheels to cooling rack; drizzle immediately with Glaze. Serve warm.

Makes 8 pinwheels

Nutrients per Serving:					
Calories	223	(20% of calories from fat)			
Total Fat	5 g	Dietary Fiber	2 g	Thiamin	<1 mg
Saturated Fat	2 g	Protein	7 g	Riboflavin	<1 mg
Cholesterol	7 mg	Calcium	119 mg	Niacin	2 mg
Sodium	241 mg	Iron	2 mg	Vitamin A	61 RE
Carbohydrate	38 g	Folate	16 μg	Vitamin C	<1 mg

Dietary Exchanges: 2½ Starch/Bread, 1 Fat

278 Meringue-Filled Pears

The Bartlett pear is the most popular variety in the U.S.

1 can (29 ounces) Bartlett pear halves
2 tablespoons packed brown sugar
1 teaspoon grated lemon peel
½ teaspoon ground nutmeg
2 egg whites
Dash salt
2 tablespoons granulated sugar
2 tablespoons slivered almonds (optional)

Preheat oven to 325°F. Drain pears; reserve ⅓ cup liquid. Place pears, cut side up, in 8-inch baking pan. Pour reserved pear liquid into pan. Combine brown sugar, lemon peel and nutmeg in small bowl; mix well. Sprinkle mixture evenly over pears. For meringue, beat egg whites and salt, in small bowl, until soft peaks form. Gradually add granulated sugar; beat until stiff peaks form. Spoon meringue evenly over pear halves. Sprinkle meringue with almonds. Bake 15 to 20 minutes or until thoroughly heated and golden brown on top. Serve warm.

Makes 4 to 6 servings

Nutrients per Serving:					
Calories	176	(1% of calories from fat)			
Total Fat	<1 g	Dietary Fiber	4 g	Thiamin	<1 mg
Saturated Fat	<1 g	Protein	2 g	Riboflavin	<1 mg
Cholesterol	0 mg	Calcium	18 mg	Niacin	<1 mg
Sodium	40 mg	Iron	1 mg	Vitamin A	<1 RE
Carbohydrate	44 g	Folate	3 μg	Vitamin C	3 mg

Dietary Exchanges: 3 Fruit

Meringue-Filled Pear

279 Sweet Potato-Apple Bake

The sweet potato is not related in any way to the white potato. The only similarity between them is their high starch content.

3 cups mashed sweet potatoes
2 to 3 medium apples, peeled and sliced
Cinnamon
½ cup apple jelly

Preheat oven to 350°F. Spray 9-inch glass pie plate with nonstick cooking spray. Fill dish evenly with mashed sweet potatoes. Arrange apple slices on top. Sprinkle apples with cinnamon. Melt apple jelly over low heat in small saucepan. Brush over apples. Bake 30 minutes or until apples are tender.

Makes 6 servings

Nutrients per Serving:					
Calories	278	(2% of calories from fat)			
Total Fat	1 g	Dietary Fiber	6 g	Thiamin	<1 mg
Saturated Fat	<1 g	Protein	3 g	Riboflavin	<1 mg
Cholesterol	0 mg	Calcium	39 mg	Niacin	1 mg
Sodium	29 mg	Iron	1 mg	Vitamin A	2,800 RE
Carbohydrate	67 g	Folate	19 μg	Vitamin C	31 mg

Dietary Exchanges: 1½ Starch/Bread, 3 Fruit

280 Scrumptious Apple Cake

Apples produce ethylene, a gas, which accelerates the ripening of fruit. Place an apple with unripe fruit in a paper bag; it should be ripe within a few days.

3 egg whites
1½ cups sugar
1 cup unsweetened applesauce
1 teaspoon vanilla
2 cups all-purpose flour
2 teaspoons ground cinnamon
1 teaspoon baking soda
½ teaspoon salt
4 cups cored peeled tart apple slices (McIntosh or Crispin)
Yogurt Glaze (recipe follows)

Preheat oven to 350°F. Beat egg whites until slightly foamy; add sugar, applesauce and vanilla. Combine flour, cinnamon, baking soda and salt in separate bowl; add to applesauce mixture. Spread apples in 13 × 9-inch pan or 9-inch round springform pan sprayed with nonstick cooking spray. Spread batter over apples. Bake 35 to 40 minutes or until wooden toothpick inserted in center comes out clean; cool on wire rack. Prepare Yogurt Glaze; spread over cooled cake.   Makes 15 to 20 servings

Yogurt Glaze: Combine 1½ cups plain nonfat or vanilla yogurt, 3 tablespoons brown sugar (or to taste) and 1 teaspoon vanilla or 1 teaspoon lemon juice. Stir together until smooth.

Makes about 2 cups

Nutrients per Serving:

Calories	186	(2% of calories from fat)			
Total Fat	<1 g	Dietary Fiber	1 g	Thiamin	<1 mg
Saturated Fat	<1 g	Protein	4 g	Riboflavin	<1 mg
Cholesterol	<1 mg	Calcium	57 mg	Niacin	1 mg
Sodium	156 mg	Iron	1 mg	Vitamin A	3 RE
Carbohydrate	43 g	Folate	8 µg	Vitamin C	2 mg

Dietary Exchanges: 1 Starch/Bread, 2 Fruit

281 Fresh Nectarine Ovenbake

When purchasing nectarines, avoid those that are hard with greenish skin because they may never ripen properly. Choose plump fully colored fruits with an aromatic fragrance.

2 tablespoons margarine
2 eggs
1 egg white
¾ cup skim milk
¾ cup all-purpose flour
6 fresh California nectarines, halved, pitted and sliced
1 tablespoon packed brown sugar
¾ cup plain low fat yogurt
2 tablespoons low calorie maple syrup

Place margarine in 10- or 12-inch skillet with ovenproof handle. Place in 450°F oven. In medium bowl, beat eggs and egg white with wire whisk until light and lemon colored; beat in milk. Gradually stir in flour; beat until smooth. Remove skillet from oven. Pour batter into skillet. Bake 15 minutes. Reduce oven heat to 350°F and continue baking 10 minutes until pancake is puffed and browned.

Meanwhile, toss nectarines with sugar in serving bowl; set aside. Mix yogurt with syrup in separate bowl. Serve hot. Top with nectarines and yogurt mixture.   Makes 6 servings

Nutrients per Serving:

Calories	244	(29% of calories from fat)			
Total Fat	8 g	Dietary Fiber	3 g	Thiamin	<1 mg
Saturated Fat	2 g	Protein	9 g	Riboflavin	<1 mg
Cholesterol	111 mg	Calcium	114 mg	Niacin	2 mg
Sodium	121 mg	Iron	1 mg	Vitamin A	218 RE
Carbohydrate	36 g	Folate	25 µg	Vitamin C	8 mg

Dietary Exchanges: 1 Starch/Bread, ½ Milk, 1 Fruit, 1½ Fat

282 Peach Oatmeal Cookies

The whole wheat flour used in this recipe not only provides more fiber but more nutrition than white flour.

¾ cup granulated sugar
¾ cup packed brown sugar
⅔ cup margarine
2 eggs
1½ teaspoons vanilla
1½ cups whole wheat flour
2 teaspoons baking powder
1 teaspoon salt
2½ cups rolled oats
1½ cups diced pitted halved peeled fresh California peaches
1 cup raisins

Preheat oven to 350°F. Beat sugars, margarine, eggs and vanilla in large mixing bowl with electric mixer at medium speed. Combine flour, baking powder and salt in separate bowl. Add to egg mixture and beat at low speed 2 to 3 minutes or until smooth. Stir in oats, peaches and raisins. Drop by tablespoonfuls onto nonstick baking sheet. Bake 10 to 15 minutes or until golden.

Makes 3 dozen cookies

Nutrients per Serving:

Calories	121	(29% of calories from fat)				
Total Fat	4 g	Dietary Fiber	1 g	Thiamin	<1 mg	
Saturated Fat	1 g	Protein	2 g	Riboflavin	<1 mg	
Cholesterol	12 mg	Calcium	17 mg	Niacin	<1 mg	
Sodium	123 mg	Iron	1 mg	Vitamin A	52 RE	
Carbohydrate	20 g	Folate	6 µg	Vitamin C	1 mg	

Dietary Exchanges: ½ Starch/Bread, ½ Fruit, 1 Fat

283 Lemony Light Vineyard Cups

Grapes are one of the oldest foods still eaten today and have been cultivated for over 6,000 years.

1 envelope gelatin
¼ cup cold water
1¼ cups plain low fat yogurt
½ cup orange juice
¼ cup honey
1 tablespoon grated lemon peel
1 tablespoon lemon juice
3 cups seedless Chilean grapes
Additional lemon peel for garnish

In small saucepan, soften gelatin in cold water; warm over low heat until gelatin is completely dissolved. Stir in yogurt, orange juice, honey, lemon peel and lemon juice, whisking gently to blend. Divide grapes between six 6-ounce custard cups or individual dessert dishes. Pour yogurt mixture over each, dividing equally. Refrigerate until firm. Garnish with additional lemon peel before serving.

Makes 6 servings

Nutrients per Serving:

Calories	117	(7% of calories from fat)				
Total Fat	1 g	Dietary Fiber	1 g	Thiamin	<1 mg	
Saturated Fat	1 g	Protein	4 g	Riboflavin	<1 mg	
Cholesterol	3 mg	Calcium	97 mg	Niacin	<1 mg	
Sodium	36 mg	Iron	<1 mg	Vitamin A	18 RE	
Carbohydrate	25 g	Folate	19 µg	Vitamin C	16 mg	

Dietary Exchanges: ½ Milk, 1½ Fruit

284 Plums and Bavarian Cream

Using only egg whites and low fat yogurt not only cuts the fat but also the cholesterol in this recipe.

9 fresh California plums, halved, pitted and sliced, divided
3 egg whites
⅓ cup sugar
¼ cup plain low fat yogurt
Mint sprigs and additional plum slices for garnish

Add 4 plums to food processor or blender; process to measure 1 cup purée. Beat egg whites with sugar in medium bowl until stiff peaks form. Fold in puréed plums and yogurt. Place remaining plums in serving bowl. Spoon plum cream on top. Garnish with fresh mint and plum slices, if desired.

Makes 6 servings

Nutrients per Serving:

Calories	109	(6% of calories from fat)				
Total Fat	1 g	Dietary Fiber	2 g	Thiamin	<1 mg	
Saturated Fat	<1 g	Protein	3 g	Riboflavin	<1 mg	
Cholesterol	1 mg	Calcium	22 mg	Niacin	1 mg	
Sodium	34 mg	Iron	<1 mg	Vitamin A	34 RE	
Carbohydrate	24 g	Folate	4 mg	Vitamin C	9 mg	

Dietary Exchanges: ½ Meat, 1½ Fruit

Baked Banana Doughnuts

285 Lemon Banana Yogurt Pops

Americans consume over 12 billion bananas per year.

2 egg whites
2 tablespoons sugar
1 ripe banana
2 cartons (8 ounces each) lemon low fat yogurt
6 popsicle molds *or* 6 (5-ounce) paper cups
6 wooden sticks

In small bowl, beat egg whites until soft peaks form. Gradually add sugar, beating until stiff peaks form. Add banana and yogurt to food processor or blender; process until smooth. Fold egg white mixture into lemon yogurt. Divide mixture among molds or paper cups; insert wooden sticks in centers. Freeze pops until solid. At serving time, peel away paper from cups and serve.

Makes 6 servings

Nutrients per Serving:					
Calories	123	(10% of calories from fat)			
Total Fat	1 g	Dietary Fiber	<1 g	Thiamin	<1 mg
Saturated Fat	<1 g	Protein	5 g	Riboflavin	<1 mg
Cholesterol	4 mg	Calcium	113 mg	Niacin	<1 mg
Sodium	67 mg	Iron	<1 mg	Vitamin A	2 RE
Carbohydrate	23 g	Folate	4 μg	Vitamin C	2 mg

Dietary Exchanges: 1 Milk, ½ Fruit

286 Baked Banana Doughnuts

Bananas are the most popular fruit sold in the U.S. They are a good source of potassium and fiber.

2 ripe bananas, mashed
2 egg whites
1 tablespoon vegetable oil
1 cup packed brown sugar
1½ cups all-purpose flour
¾ cup whole wheat flour
2 teaspoons baking powder
½ teaspoon baking soda
¼ teaspoon pumpkin pie spice
1 tablespoon granulated sugar
2 tablespoons chopped walnuts (optional)

Preheat oven to 425°F. Spray baking sheet with nonstick cooking spray. Beat bananas, egg whites, oil and brown sugar in large bowl or food processor. Add flours, baking powder, baking soda and pumpkin pie spice. Mix until well blended. Let stand for five minutes for dough to rise. Scoop out heaping tablespoonfuls of dough onto prepared baking sheet. Using thin rubber spatula or butter knife round out doughnut hole in center of dough (if dough sticks to knife or spatula spray with cooking spray). With spatula, smooth outside edges of dough into round doughnut shape. Repeat until all dough is used. Sprinkle with granulated sugar and walnuts, if desired. Bake 6 to 10 minutes or until tops are golden.   Makes about 22 doughnuts

Variation: Use 8 ounces solid pack pumpkin instead of bananas to make pumpkin doughnuts.

Nutrients per Serving:

Calories	101	(7% of calories from fat)				
Total Fat	1 g	Dietary Fiber	1 g	Thiamin	<1 mg
Saturated Fat	<1 g	Protein	2 g	Riboflavin	<1 mg
Cholesterol	0 mg	Calcium	17 mg	Niacin	1 mg
Sodium	57 mg	Iron	1 mg	Vitamin A	1 RE
Carbohydrate	22 g	Folate	6 µg	Vitamin C	1 mg

Dietary Exchanges: 1 Starch/Bread, ½ Fruit

287 Strawberries with Honeyed Yogurt Sauce

Strawberries are an excellent source of vitamin C, the production of which is stimulated by sunlight.

1 quart fresh strawberries
1 cup plain low fat yogurt
1 tablespoon orange juice
1 to 2 teaspoons honey
Ground cinnamon to taste

Rinse and hull strawberries. Combine yogurt, orange juice, honey and cinnamon in small bowl; mix well. Serve sauce over berries.

Makes 4 servings

Nutrients per Serving:

Calories	88	(14% of calories from fat)				
Total Fat	1 g	Dietary Fiber	4 g	Thiamin	<1 mg
Saturated Fat	1 g	Protein	4 g	Riboflavin	<1 mg
Cholesterol	4 mg	Calcium	125 mg	Niacin	<1 mg
Sodium	41 mg	Iron	1 mg	Vitamin A	16 RE
Carbohydrate	16 g	Folate	35 µg	Vitamin C	87 mg

Dietary Exchanges: ½ Milk, 1 Fruit

288 Ginger Snap Sandwiches

Apples are great for quenching thirst because they're 85% water.

¼ cup 1% low fat cottage cheese
¼ cup vanilla nonfat yogurt
1 McIntosh apple, peeled, cored and grated
2 tablespoons sugar
30 ginger snaps

Add cottage cheese and yogurt to food processor or blender; process until smooth. Blend in apple and sugar. Using rubber spatula spread apple filling onto flat side of ginger snap; top with another ginger snap to make sandwich. Repeat with remaining ingredients.   Makes 15 servings

Nutrients per Serving:

Calories	76	(17% of calories from fat)				
Total Fat	1 g	Dietary Fiber	<1 g	Thiamin	<1 mg
Saturated Fat	<1 g	Protein	1 g	Riboflavin	<1 mg
Cholesterol	<1 mg	Calcium	20 mg	Niacin	<1 mg
Sodium	110 mg	Iron	1 mg	Vitamin A	1 RE
Carbohydrate	15 g	Folate	1 µg	Vitamin C	1 mg

Dietary Exchanges: 1 Starch/Bread

[289] **N**ectarine Meringue Crowns

Cranberry juice has been used to help fight urinary tract infections.

2 egg whites
⅛ teaspoon *each* cream of tartar and
   nutmeg
⅔ cup sugar
1 can (6 ounces) frozen cranberry juice
   concentrate, thawed
½ cup water
1½ tablespoons cornstarch
5 fresh California nectarines, halved,
   pitted and sliced

Preheat oven to 250°F. Place egg whites, cream of tartar and nutmeg in mixing bowl; beat until foamy. Gradually add sugar, beating constantly, until stiff and glossy. Divide egg white mixture into 6 equal mounds on baking sheet. With back of spoon, shape into round tarts. Bake 1 hour; cool.

Pour cranberry juice concentrate into saucepan. Stir in water and cornstarch. Cook, stirring constantly, until sauce thickens and clears; cool. Fill each meringue tart with ½ cup nectarine slices. Spoon sauce over fruit.   Makes 6 servings

Nutrients per Serving:

Calories	203	(2% of calories from fat)			
Total Fat	1 g	Dietary Fiber	2 g	Thiamin	<1 mg
Saturated Fat	<1 g	Protein	2 g	Riboflavin	<1 mg
Cholesterol	0 mg	Calcium	10 mg	Niacin	1 mg
Sodium	20 mg	Iron	<1 mg	Vitamin A	84 RE
Carbohydrate	50 g	Folate	5 µg	Vitamin C	28 mg

Dietary Exchanges: 3½ Fruit

[290] **L**ime Sorbet

British sailors ate limes to prevent scurvy during long sea voyages, which is how they got the nickname "limeys."

4 large limes
1 tablespoon grated lime peel
1½ cups hot water
6 tablespoons sugar
1 egg white, slightly beaten
1 drop *each* green and yellow food color
   Mint leaves or citrus leaves for garnish

Juice limes to measure ½ cup juice; place in medium mixing bowl with lime peel. Combine hot water and sugar; stir to dissolve. Add sugar mixture, egg white and food color to lime juice. Pour mixture into shallow pan. Cover and freeze, stirring once an hour to break up ice crystals, until firm. Remove sorbet from freezer about 20 minutes before serving. Garnish with mint leaves if desired.

Makes 6 servings

Nutrients per Serving:

Calories	54	(0% of calories from fat)			
Total Fat	<1 g	Dietary Fiber	0 g	Thiamin	<1 mg
Saturated Fat	<1 g	Protein	1 g	Riboflavin	<1 mg
Cholesterol	0 mg	Calcium	4 mg	Niacin	<1 mg
Sodium	9 mg	Iron	<1 mg	Vitamin A	<1 RE
Carbohydrate	14 g	Folate	2 µg	Vitamin C	7 mg

Dietary Exchanges: 1 Fruit

[291] **B**erries Good

Not only are raspberries and blackberries pleasing to the palate as well as the eye, they're also good sources of vitamin C, fiber and potassium.

1 package (10 ounces) frozen
   unsweetened raspberries, thawed
1 tablespoon sugar
2 teaspoons cornstarch
1 cup fresh or frozen blackberries or
   boysenberries, thawed
2 fresh California Bartlett pears, halved
   and cored
   Plain low fat yogurt (optional)

Combine raspberries, sugar and cornstarch in large saucepan. Cook over medium-high heat, stirring constantly, until mixture comes to a boil and thickens; cool. Spoon blackberries into pear halves. Spoon raspberry sauce over. Dollop with yogurt, if desired.   Makes 4 servings

Nutrients per Serving:

Calories	119	(6% of calories from fat)			
Total Fat	1 g	Dietary Fiber	8 g	Thiamin	<1 mg
Saturated Fat	<1 g	Protein	1 g	Riboflavin	<1 mg
Cholesterol	0 mg	Calcium	36 mg	Niacin	1 mg
Sodium	<1 mg	Iron	1 mg	Vitamin A	17 RE
Carbohydrate	30 g	Folate	37 µg	Vitamin C	29 mg

Dietary Exchanges: 2 Fruit

Nectarine Meringue Crown

292 Peach-Walnut Praline Sauce

This sauce adds a splash of spicy sweetness to what could otherwise be a plain dessert.

¼ cup packed brown sugar
1½ teaspoons cornstarch
½ cup water
1 tablespoon brandy (optional)
1 teaspoon margarine
½ teaspoon vanilla
1 can (16 ounces) sliced peaches in juice, drained
2 tablespoons coarsely chopped walnuts
Frozen vanilla yogurt or angel food cake slices

Mix sugar and cornstarch in small saucepan; stir in water. Bring to a boil; boil, stirring constantly, until thickened, about 1 minute. Stir in brandy, margarine and vanilla. Gently stir in peaches and walnuts; simmer until peaches are warm, 1 to 2 minutes. Serve over vanilla or peach frozen yogurt or angel food cake. Makes 4 servings

Nutrients per Serving:

Calories	139	(19% of calories from fat)			
Total Fat	3 g	Dietary Fiber	1 g	Thiamin	<1 mg
Saturated Fat	<1 g	Protein	2 g	Riboflavin	<1 mg
Cholesterol	0 mg	Calcium	21 mg	Niacin	1 mg
Sodium	20 mg	Iron	1 mg	Vitamin A	56 RE
Carbohydrate	28 g	Folate	6 μg	Vitamin C	4 mg

Dietary Exchanges: 2 Fruit, ½ Fat

293 Peach Ice Cream

By using low fat milk and low fat yogurt in this recipe you get the creamy texture and delicious flavor of ice cream without most of the fat.

7 fresh California peaches, peeled, halved and pitted
2 cups 2% low fat milk
1 envelope gelatin
1 cup plain low fat yogurt
½ cup sugar
1 tablespoon vanilla

Chop enough peaches to measure 1 cup. Add remaining peaches to food processor or blender; process to measure 2½ cups purée. Combine milk and gelatin in medium saucepan. Heat, stirring, until gelatin dissolves; remove from heat. Add

chopped peaches, peach purée, yogurt, sugar and vanilla to gelatin mixture; mix well. Prepare in ice cream maker according to manufacturer's directions. Transfer to freezing containers and freeze until firm. Makes 7 servings

Nutrients per Serving:

Calories	184	(9% of calories from fat)			
Total Fat	2 g	Dietary Fiber	2 g	Thiamin	<1 mg
Saturated Fat	1 g	Protein	5 g	Riboflavin	<1 mg
Cholesterol	7 mg	Calcium	151 mg	Niacin	1 mg
Sodium	65 mg	Iron	<1 mg	Vitamin A	77 RE
Carbohydrate	38 g	Folate	11 μg	Vitamin C	28 mg

Dietary Exchanges: ½ Milk, 2½ Fruit

294 Spiced Oranges

Oranges are native to the Far East where they've been cultivated for at least 4,000 years. Oranges have been popular in the U.S. only for the last century.

4 oranges
¾ cup water
¼ cup lemon juice
3 tablespoons packed brown sugar
¼ teaspoon ground cinnamon
¼ teaspoon ground cloves
Dash ground ginger

Peel and section oranges, reserving 2-inch peel piece to add to syrup. Cut orange sections into thirds; set aside. Combine ¼ cup orange sections, 2-inch piece orange peel, water, lemon juice, brown sugar, cinnamon, cloves and ginger in medium saucepan. Bring to a boil over medium-high heat; reduce heat and simmer 2 minutes. Strain syrup and pour over remaining orange sections. Refrigerate 1 hour. To serve, spoon orange sections into bowls; top with syrup. Makes 4 servings

Nutrients per Serving:

Calories	105	(1% of calories from fat)			
Total Fat	<1 g	Dietary Fiber	3 g	Thiamin	<1 mg
Saturated Fat	<1 g	Protein	1 g	Riboflavin	<1 mg
Cholesterol	0 mg	Calcium	65 mg	Niacin	<1 mg
Sodium	4 mg	Iron	1 mg	Vitamin A	27 RE
Carbohydrate	27 g	Folate	42 μg	Vitamin C	77 mg

Dietary Exchanges: 1½ Fruit

INDEX

RECIPE INDEX